DAVID GOWER

A Man Out of Time

Rob Steen

VICTOR GOLLANCZ

LONDON

To Peach: here's to Summer

First published in Great Britain 1995
by Victor Gollancz
An imprint of the Cassell Group
Wellington House, 125 Strand, London WC2R 0BB

Unless otherwise stated, all photographs are reproduced
courtesy of Patrick Eagar.

A catalogue record for this book is
available from the British Library.

ISBN 085493 250 X

Typeset by Rowland Phototypesetting Ltd,
Bury St Edmunds, Suffolk
Printed in Great Britain by
Mackays of Chatham plc

Contents

Acknowledgements

I would like to express my gratitude to the following generous persons, without whom I would still believe the image, or else never have got this far in correcting it:

Jon Agnew, Tim Ayling, Adrian Aymes, Terry Barringer, David Bennett, Mike Brearley, Rory Bremner, Nigel Briers, Chris 'WG' Campling, Chris Cowdrey, Colin Croft, Jon Culley, June Davis, Paul Downton, Barry Dudleston, Patrick Duff, Alan Dyer, Ralph and Shirley Dymond (Hi Mum), Colin Fairservice, Alan and Jane Feldman (Hi Sis), Elizabeth Fouracre, Professor Michael Freeman, David Frith, Mike Gatting, Graham 'Weejie' Goldwater, Alexandra Gower, John Gower, Michael Gower, Thorunn Gower, Helen Griffiths, Michael Holding, Jon Holmes, Ray Illingworth, Jim Irvin, Kevan James, Martin Johnson, Allan Lamb, Alan Lee, A. E. Lorriman, Chris 'Matchmaker' Lightbown, Dennis Lillee, Brian Mason, Dr Philip Mawhood, James Maxwell, Kiershen McKenzie, Graham Morris, John Morris, Jim 'Matt' Munro, Mark Nicholas, Michael Norman, Jeremy 'God' Novick, Steve 'Goodfella' Pinder, Harold Pinter, Nick 'Brad' Pitt, Paul Pollock, Mark Ray, David Reid, Huw 'Jennings' Richards, Fred Rumsey, Jean Start, John 'Halliwell' Steen (Hi Dad), Simon Strong, Greg 'Motherwell' Struthers, Les Taylor, Ivo Tennant, Stephen Thorpe, Roger Tolchard, Mike Turner, Richard 'Jurgen' Weekes, James Whitaker, Derek Whittome, Dr Jack Wilde, Bob Willis, Pete 'Haarsenal' Wilson, Andy 'The Bucket' Woodend.

Thanks also to Stephen Green at the MCC Library, the *Sunday Times* library, EMI Records, all at the *Leicester Mercury* and Leicestershire CCC, and all the readers of *Wisden Cricket Monthly* who kindly participated in the somewhat one-sided debate, 'David Gower – Waster or Wasted?'

To the myriad writers and observers who have pointed me in the right direction, notably Ivo Tennant, Frances Edmonds, Alan Lee and Vic Marks; please excuse the liberal plundering.

Cuddly toys to Pete Watts and Paul E. Dyson (the cheque would have bounced anyway); Turner Prize to Patrick Eagar (where would a book about the most artistic of modern sportsmen be without the visual evidence?); Oscars to Richard Wigmore (Best Director) and John Pawsey (Best Supporting Actor).

Kisses to Laura and Woody, for remembering that the bearded monstrosity they have caught fleeting glimpses of these past months is closely related to their father. And to Anne, without whom I would have gone way past potty.

And, finally, to David 'Lubo' Gower, for having the lousiest nickname in history, and the divinest way of playing sport.

Foreword

In the interests of balance, I invited Micky Stewart to justify his share of the responsibility for denying us the chance to watch David Gower bat. Twice, maybe three times. I did not feel any compulsion to trouble Graham Gooch. For one thing, he is forever changing his mind. He has also had the honesty to admit he may have erred, albeit only once the damage was irreversible. I have no other alibis for my failure to see their point of view. Which I guess makes me every bit as inflexible.

There is one major drawback in trying to write an account of David Gower's first thirty-eight years; half of Brazil's rainforests have already been slaughtered in order for him to tell the tale himself. To my certain knowledge, five books have been published under his name; there may have been more. And, just in case one required further intimidation, *David Gower – The Autobiography* happens to be the funniest, most accurate sporting autobiography I have read. Happily, it left several faultlines. Such as how the outside world saw him. Since its publication, moreover, he has been forced to come in before his time was up. As a result, the ensuing pages cover an entire career.

As a cricketer Gower charmed and infuriated. The vast majority of us were content to live with both qualities, knowing that the good far outweighed the bad. To their editors' eternal discredit, less principled opinion formers, in their envy and their insecurity, preferred to incite hate. Happily, they were beating their heads against a wall that would have done Hadrian proud.

Much the same could be said of that other English cricketing colossus of the Loadsamoney Age, Ian Botham. If, in his pomp, Botham flitted between God and Satan, Gower lay somewhere in between, content to stir less intense, more reflective emotions. Both men, sadly, had the misfortune to play out their careers during a period of unforgettable ups and ten times as many downs. Thanks in the main to their efforts, the game was never boring, but frequently exhilarating and sometimes even beautiful. Better to have a Steven Berkoff – any Steven Berkoff – than a *Mousetrap*.

While writing this book I had Woody Allen on the brain even more than usual. Doing the rounds prior to the British release of Allen's *Bullets*

Over Broadway, a couple of quotes caught my eye. 'Well, I didn't feel I should be repentant for anything,' he told the *Time Out* film critic, 'it was the outside world that should be repentant to me. I was falsely accused of something and that accusation was fed and stimulated, shamelessly, by the press. To this day there are people who think Mia and I were married, and that I had some kind of affair with my daughter.' In the *Observer*, Andrew Billen prompted a touch of self-contradiction from Woody: 'People asked me about *Manhattan*, about the seeds of this story of falling in love with a younger girl. [He had recently had an affair with a seventeen-year-old.] There were no seeds because in my entire life I dated a million women, and almost always basically my age.' As with Woody, so with Gower. More than most contemporary icons, we have tried to analyse their character through their art. And, in both cases, that art is a good deal more representative than either pretends. But it does not tell the whole story.

Much as this book revolves around one man, it has been impossible to avoid recounting how the national team he adorned went from rust to bust. If you cannot stomach another trawl through some decidedly tattered back pages, further reading could be hazardous. If you can, and you get that far, you will notice that the later chapters are somewhat light on cricket. What choice does one have when one's hero takes a fall for reasons entirely unconnected to the chief motivation in putting forefingers to keyboard? Nor, presumably, to you buying this particular plundering of alphabet, dictionary and Thesaurus. Besides, why dwell on the bad when the good is so good?

'If, *on occasions*, this diary *might appear* totally, utterly and irretrievably biased in [his] favour, it is because this diary *is* totally, utterly and irretrievably biased in [his] favour.' Frances Edmonds was responsible for that frank confession. I trust I have stopped short of total, utter and irretrievable, but I know how she feels. David Gower is indeed, as Colin Bateman put it, a national treasure. By scorning inhibition, he has accomplished one thing above all else, something few Englishmen manage, and even fewer attempt: through his art and his character he has transcended the class system. And his, assuredly, is a tale with more than a touch of class. In every possible respect.

Rob Steen, Alexandra Palace, June 1995

1   Bad Timing

'Yes, but it's a jolly swizzle,' Jennings declared. 'I wasn't trying to be funny. I daren't open my mouth now, in case he thinks I'm being insolent; and that'll lead to another row, so that's a swizzle multiplied by a swizzle – it's a double swizzle.'

'No, it's a swizzle squared – not a double swizz,' Darbishire pointed out.

Jennings' Little Hut, Anthony Buckeridge

Do We Not Like That! On Friday 24 February 1995, the *Daily Telegraph* published an intriguing questionnaire under the teasing headline, 'If you had it your way . . .' A gaggle of public figures had been asked to nominate Things That Ought To Be Done Away With and Things That Should Be Brought Back. Popular candidates for extinction were Prozac, shell suits and clingfilm, while trolley buses, fresh air, letter writing, homemade marmalade and realistic train timetables ranked high among the would-be restorations. Typical *Telegraph*, yet fascinating for all that.

Thora Hird would do away with talk show guests talking simultaneously and bring back the corner shop. John Humphreys, scourge of Right and wrong, would outlaw Sunday trading and reintroduce the stocks for owners of indiscreet dogs. Maureen Lipman would ban TV programmes that rely on the public as the main attraction, and revive student demos. Michael Dobbs, author and joint deputy chairman of the Story Party, would hang those dastardly chappies who attack one at road junctions and have the gall to offer to clean one's windscreen; in exchange, he would reinvent the prehistoric – 'a winning England cricket team'. The erstwhile Story Party chairman, Jeffrey Archer, would mothball the one-day biff-and-swish matches, exhume the Batsman Who Walks and dust off the ration books ('for those who are overweight'). Ian 'Lord Peter Wimsey' Carmichael would get shot of 'war paint on cricketers' while Patrick Moore couldn't decide whether there was a more pressing need for 'policemen who hunt burglars rather than bully motorists' or for the new Doug Wright. Three respondents pleaded for human comebacks. Clare Latimer, the caterer who briefly sprang to prominence as the PM's wrongly alleged bit-on-the-side, went for Russ Conway; Douglas Adams, the noted inter-galactic hitcher, opted for John Lennon. Jilly Cooper, doyenne of the polo-breeches-and-sex-romp classes, chose David Gower.

The publication of the poll was timely. The last week of February 1995 was a disheartening one for English idealists. It was the week that began with the *Sunday Times* publishing some ludicrous claims that Michael Foot worked for the KGB, and went steadily downhill from there. A nation feared for one of its most gifted sons when damning reviews spurred Stephen Fry to go AWOL from his latest West End production. Arsenal sacked George Graham for his involvement in a £425,000 'bung' scandal; the Football Association suspended Eric Cantona for aiming a kung-fu kick at an abusive Crystal Palace 'supporter'. It was also the week that ended with the American boxer Gerald McClellan on the critical list in a London hospital. It seemed a pertinent moment to yearn for an entertainer who inspired hope rather than cynicism.

Spool back a month, to Rupertswood, Victoria, Australia. Toppers and canes jostle with bustles and bonnets as 'England' take on 'Australia' in a 40-over bunfight somewhat grandiloquently billed as 'The Ashes Commemorative Match'. The Lambs and Gattings and Pococks versus the Borders and Marshes and Thommos, all fresh off a steam train from Melbourne boasting restored carriages and other olde-world fineries. There is no particular anniversary to celebrate. But 113 years have passed since the first 'Ashes' Test match. Rupertswood is purported to be the home of the urn, so who needs excuses? The brains behind this corny colonial celebration belong to the members of the Birthplace of the Ashes Society, formed in 1992 with the express aim of promoting Sir William Clarke's country mansion as the site of Lady Clarke's presentation of a burnt bail to Ivo Bligh, over less widely documented claims. To press home their point, the organizers have spent nigh-on £35,000 transforming a school playing field into a more than presentable arena, complete with temporary stands and spanking-new pitch. The protagonists are drawn from the present and near-past: Stewart, Lewis, Small, Reeve, Allott and Marks for the Poms, Yallop, Jones, Sheahan, Lawson, Dodemaide and Stackpole for the Cobbers. The fare, as a result, still carries undertones of competitiveness. Batsmen are forcibly retired as soon as they reach fifty but nobody has any intention of being got out by legitimate means, the upshot 625 runs and two wickets. Even then, the takers are Stackpole and Lamb, combined Test return sixteen victims at sixty-four. Bowlers serve and batsmen gorge. To see the captain of the Poms slurping champers at the crease was to see David Ivon Gower in excelsis.

The golden poodle-cut of yore is now a silvery crinkle-cut, the blue-grey eyes a tad paler, the middle a trifle thicker, the refreshment a tad more potent than the juice on offer during the drinks breaks of his pomp.

In essence, though, nothing has changed. David Gower would have made an admirable successor to good Queen Vic. Reserved, sometimes to the point of aloofness, wary of letting the guard down, yet, beneath that protective veneer, chummy, witty and generous of spirit, intrinsically lazy yet bent on grabbing life by the balls and giving it a good shake. An all-round good egg, as one friend put it. An ideal monarch for an age when Englishmen preferred their heroes to remain heroes, when there was no television or radio or tabloids to inflate errors into crimes, or to console us in our own inadequacy by exaggerating the failings of those whom we envy. Bertie Wooster used to say it was only the fact that he couldn't actually think of anything that prevented him from saying something pretty stinging; by contrast David Gower has always given the impression that he thinks the stinging thoughts but is too sensitive to the feelings of his fellows to air them. As he exchanged pleasantries at Rupertswood with a mutton-chopped top hat 'n' cane and a chirpy bustle 'n' bonnet, gloves tucked in back pocket, flute tilted to lips, it was hard to conceive of an apter canvas for sport's last artist.

To watch David Gower at the crease was to behold one of the wonders of the twentieth century. Up there with Ali's shuffle, Best's shimmy and Blanco's ghostly apparitions, right alongside *Citizen Kane*, *Soft Time*, *Astral Weeks*, *Penny Lane*, *The Great Gatsby* and just about anything by e.e. cummings. As the most picturesque of sports – all those shapes and curves and flowing movements, the varying textures, the play of light and shade – cricket has thrown up more than its fair share of enduring images. The liquid strokes of Woolley and Graveney and Azharuddin. Holding purring to the stumps, a shotgun with a velvet silencer. Bedi resplendent in orange patka, tossing and twirling and teasing, a Nureyev with love handles. Knott the ravenous sparrow, leaping and swooping and plunging. Bland the white panther, Lloyd the black, each prowling the covers, scenting, tracking, preying. None, though, can match the natural, lissom elegance of David Gower.

At Rupertswood, some two and a half years after his final Test appearance, the distinguishing features were all present and correct. You would never have guessed that he had barely picked up a bat in the interim. At the moment of address, all is uncannily still. The back inclines about fifteen degrees, the head easy yet erect. As the bowler begins his approach the bat taps lightly: once, twice, thrice. The grip is loose, the forearms supple. Stay tuned, stayed tuned. Down comes the ball. A soft-shoe shuffle, a flex of the wrists. Length judged, direction ascertained, the blade, a brush soaked in primary colours, draws up and then sweeps down in a languid arc. It meets the enemy at the moment of greatest peril, at the height of its bounce; then scatters it to the farthest reaches with a bare flick. Timing, all timing. 'The finest timer of a cricket ball I have ever seen,' Ray Illingworth had exulted to me a few weeks earlier. The stroke's finish has a modest flourish: bat behind the left shoulder, bashfulness behind the ensuing smile. In a couple of days' time, that same sincere yet fragile expression would be beaming back to English hearths in the wee small hours, sweetening the latest sombre bulletin. Out on the field, David Gower's English cap record would be equalled (and subsequently passed) by a man four years his senior, a man who had already supplanted him as his country's highest scorer in Tests, an achievement rendered considerably easier by the part he played in depriving the record-holder of further opportunity.

It is possible, of course, to lose perspective when discussing sport. The same can be said of music and art, of literature and cinema. In the greater scheme of things they mean little, matter less, except as escape routes. They reflect society as it is while offering the vision of an alternative world, a world where everything is as it should be. When a major tunnel on that escape route is sealed, anger and frustration can obscure balanced judgement. Why else were so many reasonable folk brought to boiling point by the treatment meted out to David Gower? Why else did a few hundred influential blokes in bacon-and-egg ties get so hot under their collars that they attempted to see off the blackguards responsible and portray their crimes as symptomatic of the nation's declining moral fibre?

These were extreme reactions, admittedly, but then we demand a lot of sport nowadays. Perhaps too much. By its very codes and conventions, sport seeks to create its own utopia. A utopia where cheats do not prosper, where the best man wins and the game is the thing. Professionalism may have undermined these foundations, come close to destroying them, yet the basic values persist. Why else would the editor of the *Sun* happily devote eight pages to explaining why Eric Cantona's impression of Bruce Lee should be a hanging offence? But, having founded this parallel universe, sport is expected to set an example at all times. And woe betide those who let the side down.

Where musicians, painters, writers and film directors have the advantage is that their creations have an unlimited shelf-life. Their gifts can be appreciated by generation after generation. I cried the day John Lennon died because he enriched my formative years, and helped shape my view of the world; yet my young daughter will be able to derive every bit as much pleasure from what he left behind. Sport, conversely, is about the now. Video has been a boon, but replaying highlights is a bit like reading an extract from *Catcher in the Rye*. We can re-read books, or listen repeatedly to the same songs, in order to recapture mood and sensation, to jog a few memory cells. Without the uncertainty that distinguishes it from other art forms, sport, the art of competition, is incomplete.

All the more reason, then, to despair when we are deprived of the joy of seeing a game's foremost exponents strut their stuff. W. G. Grace was an active part of the English cultural fabric for forty-three years, Wilfred Rhodes for thirty-two, Wally Hammond for thirty-one, Jack Hobbs for twenty-nine. We even got thirty-three years out of Fred Titmus. David Gower was at our disposal for less than eighteen years, two or three under par for the contemporary English cricketer. Two or three years might not sound much, but in this context it is a great deal. Two would have been enough: a chance to savour the final chords. Above all, to express thanks. It's a short ride, and we want to be on board for the duration. David, it seems fair to say, was kicked off the Big Dipper before he had had his money's worth, or we ours.

This sense of being shortchanged, needless to add, would have been less acute had the Fringe held more allure, any allure. But to deny David Gower the intercontinental stage was to deprive his cricket of oxygen. Once he realized that the curtain would never rise again, a part of him died. Once it dawned on me that there would be no more chords and no goodbyes, a part of me died too. The last strain of innocence, perhaps. I suspect I was not alone. What exacerbated the feeling of loss was the fact that he was pushed off that pedestal. 'What a dreadful way to go,' he wrote in *Wisden Cricket Monthly* in July 1994. 'It seems that decorum and romance are the luxuries of either the chosen few or the amateur, with retirement nowadays likely to be blighted with concerns other than a chance to bid farewell honourably.' The subject of this outpouring was, in fact, Allan Border, whose own Test career had recently been forcibly terminated just as he was about to withdraw into the wings. Nothing, though, could disguise the sentiments discernible between the lines: not so much self-pity as an empathy for another victim of Tallpoppyitis. The final push in his case, omission from the 1993–94 Caribbean tour party, which in turn prompted his retirement two months later, merely followed a succession of hefty shoves.

Shortly after the ruinous Ashes tour of 1990–91, Chris Cowdrey, David's closest cricketing friend, took Graham Gooch aside and asked him whether his chum had cooked his goose with that waft to backward square in the last over before lunch in Adelaide. 'No, not at all,' came the reply. 'Everybody thinks that but absolutely not. He had a bad session, I talked to him about it, he was as good as gold. "Sorry, mate," he said, "don't know what I was doing." End of story.' Cowdrey pressed. So what was it? 'Wee-eell,' mused Gooch, shaking his head. 'He's a bad influence

... a bad influence.' In which case we can deduce that, having rendered himself a sitting target by being different, he was finally gunned down by a Tiger Moth. Another time, another place, and it might have been considered an honourable way to go, but there was no honour in Carrara. John Morris, whose international aspirations seemingly went up in flames on the same flight, scorns any suggestion that his co-pilot led him astray: 'Bad influence? Far from it. David Gower was the only senior player I had contact with on the whole tour.'

Granted, Gower did reappear fleetingly against Pakistan eighteen months later. This, though, can be interpreted as part-sop, part-PR exercise. Pressed into service at Old Trafford to aid an ailing side, he serenely gathered the 34 runs he required to become his country's highest Test run-scorer, then crossed into White Rose territory to ensure a series-levelling victory with an innings as cool and nerveless as any Headingley can ever have witnessed. A few weeks later, nonetheless, he was excluded from the winter party to tour India and Sri Lanka, lands where his experience and sure-footed mastery of spin would have been invaluable. Thus did the same series claim the other of the two most inspiring English sporting entertainers of modern times: Ian Botham had played his last Test at Lord's in June. Age was the official reason given in David's case, or, at least, the one the verbally maladroit new team manager, Keith Fletcher, was instructed to give to the press. Did Ted Dexter and his pals really expect anyone to buy this? Mike Gatting was only two months younger than Gower. The skipper, Gooch, was in his fortieth year! The history of English team selection, in all sports, is littered with cock-ups: Hunt over Greaves at Wembley; Astle for Osgood in Guadalajara; Andrew instead of Barnes at the Arms Park – sweat for flair in every case. Yet only the Cartwright-for-D'Oliveira furore of 1968 has ever outstripped the sense of outrage generated that September morn. There are not many causes that can unite Lord Gilmour, Tim Rice, Harold Pinter and Donald Trelford.

In their haste to keep a man in his place, the men who run English cricket have become experts at bringing the game into disrepute. The best seamer available has to turn on Teletext to find out that he needs to make alternative winter plans. A captain is taken at his word and sacked in the same breath. And David Gower himself is prevented from discovering that he was not the preferred appointee, in the full knowledge that the truth would leak out sooner or later. The selectors surely outdid themselves when they chose this particular squad. The previous Friday, on the eve of the NatWest Trophy final, Ted Dexter and Micky Stewart bumped into David at the Cricket Writers' dinner in the Lord's Banqueting Rooms, yet elected not to advise him of the decision they and their colleagues had arrived at earlier in the day. There was no effort to spare him needless worry or potential embarrassment. Peter Hayter, the amiable and well-connected *Mail on Sunday* correspondent, hazarded a highly educated guess two days later. When he in turn bumped into David at a testimonial match that afternoon, he declined to name his source but insisted he had his ear to the horse's mouth. The following morning, twenty minutes before the nation was formally informed, Gooch rang David on his car phone en route to Derby, and attempted to defend the indefensible. He and his partners, he explained, were concerned lest he destabilize the spirit of the side. You know, the usual shortcomings: not worshipping at the altar of physical fitness; not acknowledging the grave seriousness of it all; not looking miserable.

David was hurt, and rightly so. He was also livid. 'The toys went everywhere,' recalls his Hampshire captain, Mark Nicholas. The rejection was bad enough. What he found hardest to forgive (and, indeed, still does) was the mode of communication; just a crackling line and a slap in the chops. And this from Graham Gooch, a supposed friend whose Test career he had once saved from premature oblivion. Stubbornness, it is true, had not been an ally. He could have moderated his ways, if only for the sake of appearances. He could have bent a little more. But when you can't – or won't – see why you upset people, or, worse, convince yourself that their objections are unreasonable, there seems little point in compromise. Besides, one suspects it would have made scant difference. He was going down. On that Monday morning, Gooch delivered the rabbit punch followed by the kick in the crotch.

Yet there were other victims. Those who clung to the notion of sport as somehow superior to everyday life felt every bit as cheated. The corporate cloners had beaten the magician. Shortly after Gower announced he was quitting, Gooch admitted that he might have acted hastily. Gower's red mist gave way to a crimson fog. After the *Guardian*'s 'Centipede' had included Diego Maradona among a host of rule-benders in his list of the twentieth century's foremost spoilsports, one reader, Warwick Hillman, felt obliged to chip in his ha'pennyworth: 'Centipede's spoilsports could more accurately be described as cheats. For cricket enthusiasts, the worst recent spoilsports have to be Gooch and Stewart *père* . . . the awful pair spoiled a great sport for millions of us for no perceptible good reason.'

Did Gooch inform the selectors that he would only lead that sub-continental trek on the understanding that David saw in the new year in Hampshire? Might there be any connection between David's exclusion from the 1989–90 Caribbean party and the fact that its leader had been chosen to captain the previous winter's trip to India, only to be usurped by Gower after his own pocketing of the kruggerrand had caused the venture to be cancelled? Was David really a more disruptive influence than Botham, who, unlike him, was considered worthy of a place in England's 1992 World Cup squad? For all the antipathy between Gower and Micky Stewart, it is doubtful whether the execution could have been carried out without the support of the captain.

That said, for all the Machiavellian machinations – using county form as a pre-requisite for selection, leaving Fletcher to do the explaining on his first day in the job, shifting the goalposts when the runs did flow in the county game – it is hard to believe Gooch's ambition was so naked as to elbow a rival aside so he could supersede him in Wisden. Gooch, too, is an essentially decent man, albeit not as loyal a servant of his country as he is held to be by those who have allowed the stirring displays of his twilight to Tippex out his pursuit of the rand. More feasibly, his arrogance is such that he believes his way – the five-miles-before-breakfast, early-nights-with-a-mug-of-Horlicks-and-a-spoonful-of-grim-dedication way – is the only way. Here, moreover, he was utterly at one with Stewart.

Two months before that fateful cellular phone call, David had given a vivid demonstration of why he deserved a more flexible approach. Gordon Greenidge had his butcher's cut, Greg Chappell his easeful on-drive, Viv Richards that disdainful force through midwicket, yet, in my experience at least, nothing touched the Gower cover drive. And, fittingly, it was that signature stroke that enabled its author to supplant Geoffrey Boycott as his country's most prolific Test batsman. In contrast to his fellow musketeer Botham, we rarely recall David's pyrotechnics in context; method, manner and effect were always the same, blurred forever in splendid isolation, a plane apart. We cling to the slivers, the shards, the snapshots. Where we forget most players' opening nights, we cherish David's very first line, that impish pirouette-and-pull off Liaquat Ali (has any bowler earned wider fame as a direct consequence of a rank-awful long hop?). Some treasure the atypical flat-batted six off Bob Holland during that sumptuous double-hundred at Edgbaston in 1985, his annus mirabilis. Others relish the easeful pat to mid-on that took him to three figures at Lord's in the next home Ashes series, quite the most erudite two fingers ever shoved in the face of the English sporting press.

Aquib Javed would soon stake another claim to fame by becoming the first player suspended from an international match for misconduct, but to be party to this piece of history was surely a source of pride. A couple of hours before Aquib himself would be warned for intimidating that most bullyable of number elevens, Devon Malcolm, long before the security bullies invaded the field in pursuit of an aggrieved Pakistan follower brandishing a rolled-up newspaper, here was succour. Indeed, if ever justice was seen to be done it was done on 6 July 1992. With one creamy swing of the bat, the crown of English cricket passed from dullard to dazzler.

Comparisons of sportspeople from different eras are notoriously hard to make, let alone justify. Derek Lodge, the statistician, once declaimed at a Cricket Society dinner that Harold Larwood wasn't that quick. 'Clearly,' retorted the late Tom Pearce somewhat pointedly, 'Mr Lodge never faced Larwood.' To settle such disputes, cricket uses statistics, a wonky barometer that takes no account of context. For the sake of the anoraks, however, let us employ them to assess David's achievements, if only because the prosecution has so often wielded them against him.

Among the select band of batsmen to have scored eighteen or more Test centuries, only Bradman, Hutton and Hammond boasted a higher ratio of 150-plus scores than David's 44.4%. Just about every other time he gathered in a hundred, in other words, he went at least halfway to a second. Indeed, no other batsman ever rose more grandly to the occasion, or met the challenge with greater relish. Granted, a first-class average outside Tests of 38.45 pales beside the opposition, so it was easiest for him to improve. Nevertheless, the 15.1% advance at five-day level is more than twice that of any rival member of the 8000-run Club (both the other English members, Boycott and Gooch, suffered substantial drops). Among Englishmen who have exceeded 2000 runs against Australia, Sutcliffe, Barrington and John Edrich are the only others with an average higher than they managed in the remainder of their international careers. No contemporary batsman, furthermore, averages more against Australia.

Consistency, all who know David are agreed, is a hallmark of the man. Consistent in attitude, in temperament, in behaviour. Less widely appreciated is his remarkable consistency as a player, which is substantiated by Paul Dyson's painstaking research in the appendix to this volume. Let's start with the effect captaincy had on his productivity. Whereas the extra responsibility spurred Gooch, Atherton, May and Gatting to boost their averages by at least 30%, and, conversely, hindered Hutton (down 6.85%) and Cowdrey (down 17.46%), David remained largely impervious: in the ranks he averaged 44.51, with stripes 43.60. In terms of his average at home and overseas, the difference (3.24 more runs per innings abroad) is less than it is for any member of the 8000 Club bar Richards (0.72), Boycott (1.43) and Gavaskar (1.95). In terms of production before and after the age of 30, David (down 5.55 runs per innings) ranks fifth behind Border (who actually improved by 0.39), Miandad, Sobers and Gavaskar, with only Cowdrey (3.71) bettering him among Englishmen with 6000 or more Test runs. David averaged 6.17 runs more per first innings than second, a minor droop; Hammond (15.76), Barrington (21.29) and Hutton (22.36) all suffered significantly greater declines. Border apart, no other member of the 8000 Club aggregated more than 2000 runs in three separate berths of the order (the irony here is that while David scored more runs at No. 4 than anywhere else, his average was over 10 points higher at three and five, which suggests that, more often than not, he came in out of position). Along with Barrington, Hammond and Hendren, he is one of four Englishmen to top-score for his country in four successive innings; and twice, against Pakistan in 1983–84 and against Australia in 1990–91, he headed the contributions four times in five innings. Finally, and perhaps most revealingly of all, he accounted for more runs than any colleague in 32 of his 117 Tests, a ratio surpassed for England only by Hobbs, Hutton and Barrington.

Why, then, is he perceived as an under-achiever? Why did he infuriate as much as enchant? Was it because his gifts suggested he was capable of so much more, or was it because our demands are unrealistic? I'll plump for the latter. If those demands had been realistic, why did his supporters' nerves jangle every time he walked to the wicket? Why did we fret so when he took guard, faced that first ball, aimed that first drive? Because, while we yearned for him to succeed, we knew full well that the laws of probability rendered disappointment likely. We knew full well that, for every leg-glance clipped felicitously to the fine-leg fence, the timing and placing had to be absolutely perfect. We knew full well that his most productive strokes were also his undoing, that the gifts were also flaws.

The very concept of under-achievement is highly nebulous. Who sets the standards? Is it really possible to be an *over*-achiever? After all, if you do achieve something remarkable, the capacity to do so must have been there in the first place. David Gower may have fallen short of the peak of statistical attainment for which many (wrongly) felt he had the capacity, yet he achieved something far more profound, something that has eluded 99.99% of the people who ever bowled or kicked or passed a ball: he made statistics redundant.

Why not be thankful for what we did receive? Why let self-created exasperation obstruct rational judgment? My own inclination is to suspect that by-product of the consumer society, greed. In terms of pure aesthetics and entertainment value, surely sport's primary function, far better one of David's lyrical thirties than any of Boycott's monochrome centuries. How much easier it must be to merely exist at the crease, to eschew risk, to choose attrition over adventure, to be subordinate. While Botham mounted a mighty, violent insurrection, Gower essayed a subtle one. Given the weight of the forces massed against him ('stop flashing outside off-stump', 'stop flicking down the legside', 'move your feet', 'don't look so happy') the most remarkable aspect of Gower's career is that his revolt was so glorious so often.

Hence the need, in some quarters, to bring him down. The trouble with David Gower was that he was Mr Clean. There was no barmaid in the closet, no drug binges, no punch-ups and no ball-tampering. The hacks and the paparazzi, and the selectors, had their work cut out. They had to get him for something, anything. Taking a day off; optional nets; sailing the seas while the country sinks; trying to raise spirits by buzzing a ground in a biplane; and most grievous of all, not looking sufficiently suicidal in defeat. 'It's just not right, y'know,' as Len Hutton once said of Tom Graveney, 'this game is serious an' it all cooms too easy for him.' How easy it is to imagine Messrs Gooch and Stewart seconding that emotion.

To be fair, Gooch and Stewart are merely products of their time, and David the torch-bearer for another. One has only to hear his commentaries on radio and TV to know that. Where others delight in the scathing one-liner, here is an even-handedness only Richie Benaud can match. There is also a (mostly) judicious brain, a kind tongue and an unerring sense of perspective. Where most regard themselves as jury first and witnesses second, here is objectivity.

Unfortunately, such qualities count for little in the comparatively new world of sport-as-profit-and-loss-account, where national teams serve as standard-bearers for a nation's esteem, and where Bill Shankly's dictum about football being much more important than life and death is carved on tablets of stone. As a player, David was a free spirit; the laws of this new world dictate that the free-spirited be caged, sooner rather than later. As with Botham, it was the refusal to compromise that made him and, ultimately, broke him. Like Botham, too, he became a convenient scapegoat for collective failure. Unlike Botham, he carried on enchanting to the last. Unlike Gooch, or Gatting, he was denied the opportunity to bow out on his terms, a point he made publicly on the air in Perth, albeit in those characteristically wry, insouciant tones that reassure you he has put such trifles behind him. Thorunn Gower takes the stand on her husband's behalf:

I got annoyed when he was so laid back about Gooch and Stewart. That was an appalling way to behave. All those stupid excuses made them look like idiots. Unbelievably childish for a top-level sport. He's much more relaxed these days, especially since Alexandra was born, but I wish he'd carried on. It would have been nice for him to have gone on for a year or two more and finished it properly.

Would that have been possible in another time? Chris Cowdrey thinks so.

Definitely. David did have an amateurish streak. That was the problem. That was Gooch's point: 'We're in the late eighties/early nineties now: this boy's from the sixties or seventies. We've grown out of all this fun stuff, all this, ah well, we lost, so what. The public want to see us win these days. They want to see us grit our teeth and fight it out.' David fought against the West Indies as hard as anyone but it never looked like he was fighting. Didn't get hit, did he?

Mike Turner, David's closest associate at Leicestershire for fifteen years, is not so sure: 'If David had played as an amateur in the days of the amateur, he wouldn't have played any different. I can't believe he would have been any less "professional".'

For David himself, the rewards have clearly compensated for the opportunity costs of being a high-profile English sportsman in the intolerant eighties and nineties.

'*Was* there a more tolerant era?' he wonders. By the same token, he recoils at the demands placed on himself and his contemporaries.

The times when people said I was the most talented batsman in the world were the most satisfying ones. I'd like to be the best in the world in something, but if I don't get there it doesn't matter. So what? As opposed to some people these days who say, well, you've got to want to be the best in the world and if you don't get there it's going to hurt. That applies to all sports. We're very demanding about what we expect of our best, unless you've got the Bruno syndrome. It's either the Lennox Lewis syndrome or the Frank Bruno syndrome. Lennox Lewis was vilified for making a mistake. That's our problem. In a way I've enjoyed living in this era. The romantic way to look at it is to say, well, another era might have been the way to do it. But they didn't play as much cricket. It suited me, this era. I've grown up in it, enjoyed it. In practical terms I've timed it pretty well.

By the same token, I'd love to have played when the media held less influence. There are times when I think I could have fitted in better then. When I was walking off after making a century against India at The Oval in 1990, Dilip Vengsarkar said to me, 'You don't fit into this team.' 'Oh,' I replied, 'might as well, could be worse.' From that point of view I would like to have gone back a generation, or two. I enjoyed playing with Both, Lamby and others, but I'm sure I would have enjoyed being part of the Compton–Edrich era. Great fun. But the satisfaction comes from succeeding against the challenges. I wouldn't have derived any satisfaction from getting a stack of runs against, say, India in 1952. I've played against Lillee, Roberts, Holding, Marshall, Garner, Bedi, Qadir: some very good players. The innings I look back on personally are in those sort of circumstances. Forget the dour professional, every-day-counts bit. The modern-day romantic says, 'let's pick a day, let's go and play Roberts, Holding and Garner at Sabina Park'. Ah good, done that one. That's the crux.

I'll stick with my original thesis. An *Observer* profile published in 1984 caught the spirit better than most:

Gower might have been more at home in the 1920s or 1930s, cracking a dashing 100 for the MCC, the darling of the crowds, before speeding away in a Bugatti and cravat for a night on the town. The spirit is essentially amateur, but, to his credit, he has buckled down to modern times.

What price the sporting maverick in this age of the frightened professional? One only has to think of the casualties, of Frank Worthington, of Stan Bowles, of Stuart Barnes, to realize what a feat it was for David Gower to endure as long as he did. What price is paid by those who disdain the concept of sport as war, and worse, excel at it? What price is paid by those who have tasted real loss and can thus stomach unfavourable scorelines as they would a pinprick? Philosophies like that belong in a slower, less unforgiving era, an era when things were kept in proportion, when there were enough wars around to make substitutes not only needless but meaningless. An era, above all, when an Englishman was something to be. David Gower: a man out of time, but never out of place.

2   Taking Guard

'Real officer class. Languid self-possession. Confront him with a firing squad and he'd decline the blindfold.'
Pat Pocock, 1989

Frangas non flectes: You can break us but you cannot bend us. The Gower family motto is a masterpiece of understated defiance. It is also, of course, a philosophy entirely in keeping with the family's most renowned member. Not that the Gowers have ever been short on achievers. The family tree includes an admiral, a judge, an honorary consul, and an outstanding servant of the Colonial Service instrumental in the foundation of Tanzania. Towering above them all was David's great-grandfather, Samuel John Gower, a banker and trader who became British Consul for Austria, Tuscany and Modena, who made and lost countless fortunes, and helped found the state of California. No Gower gambled more, or bent less.

Samuel Gower's father had left the family estate in Glandovan for Leghorn in the late eighteenth century, and his sons remained in Italy for the remainder of his days. David could have been Italian, and then where would we have been? Or he might have been Kenyan: Grandfather Ivon was a judge there. His origins, nonetheless, lay in an England long forgotten. Documentation at the University of Wales traces the Gowers back to the early fourteenth century: a Richard Gower lived in Warwickshire while Edward Longshanks was hammering the Scots, fragging the French and doing horrible things to the Welsh. Chaucer had a chum by the name of John Gower, a fellow poet. This Gower wrote French ballads in his youth, progressed to Latin elegiacs for *Voz clamantis* (a salute to Wat Tyler), earned fame for *Confessio amantis*, and eventually went blind.

Richard Gower's descendants moved to Glandovan in the seventeenth century when William Gower married Jane Steadman, heiress to the estate that would remain in Gower hands until it was sold in 1953. Abel, William's grandson, sired no fewer than seventeen offspring; James, the seventh son, was David's great-great-great-great-grandfather. James's eldest brother was Sir Erasmus Gower, or, rather, Admiral Gower, Governor and Commander-in-Chief of Newfoundland in the early nineteenth century, while Abel Gower's second son, another Abel, was a successful banker and trader. Among the stack of estates the younger Abel bought in West Wales was Castle Malgwn, purchased in 1833 and inherited by a nephew named, same again, Abel, one of the original Abel's innumerable grandchildren. This particular branch of the thickly populated tree resided at the castle until it was sold in 1948.

James Gower, who lived from 1756 to 1809, followed Erasmus into the services, joining the Royal Marines, but the gambling instincts resurfaced in his son, George, who worked in Italy as a banker and trader. It was George who begat great-grandfather Samuel Gower.

Why Samuel left his land and material goods to his brothers is uncertain, but it is possible that they might have demanded some recompense for baling him out while he was playing the markets. The brothers remained in Italy but Samuel's widow returned to England with her sons, living in Sutton in what David's first cousin, Michael, the family historian, attests was 'a very modest manner'. Samuel's son Ivon progressed from the Colonial Service in Tanganyika to a judgeship in Kenya.

David's decision to embrace a sporting life had roots both strong and deep. And we're not just talking about the Admiral being buried at Hambledon. Whenever Ivon was on leave, he invariably got in a game or two for Sussex seconds. And, despite suffering from poor eyesight, David's father, Richard Hallam Gower, was more than proficient at virtually every sport he turned his hand to. A Cambridge hockey Blue, he would have donned whites at Lord's had he not put his studies first. Richard's eldest brother, Captain John Gower, was the Navy hurdles champion in 1938 and 1939, played hockey for the Navy and Hampshire, and wound up as the RN's director of PT and Sports. Derek, Ivon's middle son, who perished in action on D-Day, played squash for Kent and golf off a two-handicap. The boys' mother, Ursula, was more than adept with a tennis racket but her sister Phyllis was the real talent, playing hockey for England directly after the Great War. Neither was sporting prowess lacking at Castle Malgwn. In her heyday, Evelyn Gower, one of David's second cousins, was the finest woman golfer in Norfolk; for a number of years, her sister Lily was Lady Croquet Champion of Great Britain, as they put it back then. Indeed, their father had a championship lawn laid below the castle walls in addition to the one where the family swung their mallets. Neither is David the only sporty Gower of his generation. John Gower's son Michael, a First Class sailing instructor, is also a notable oarsman who rowed for Pembroke College, competed at Henley and won regattas at York and Norwich. Michael's brother Richard is a ski instructor at Aviemore who pole-vaulted for Young Scotland and won a number of events as a junior international rider.

Yet, so far as cricket goes, David's maternal family was arguably the greater catalyst. Sylvia, David's mother, played the game at prep and public school, though asthma would subsequently impair her athletic endeavours. Her father, Percival Clement Ford, was a fine all-round games player and a keen huntin' and shootin' sort who taught all of his girls the arts of cricket and made the odd county second XI appearance. Sylvia's elder sister, Elizabeth Fouracre, remembers their mother Jessie being as 'devastating' with a croquet mallet as she was delicate and dextrous at the piano (her love of music was duly handed down from daughter to grandson). Elizabeth herself was a school first-team regular at tennis, cricket and lacrosse. 'A mighty hitter', according to Michael Gower, such was her natural timing and strength her sixes in prep matches frequently cleared the ground. On one fabled occasion she drilled a shot over the road beyond and into a neighbouring garden.

Accomplished a sportsman as David's father was, he was a better administrator, rising high in the Colonial Service on the back of his sterling work in Tanganyika. In 1961, Julius Nyerere requested Richard Gower's assistance in formulating and implementing an infrastructure when Tanzania became the first East African nation to gain independence and hence admission to the Commonwealth. Posted there in 1940, Richard spent many years in the region around Ukutu, the 'small Chiefdom', as he put it, which was vividly portrayed by Speke and Burton during their mid-nineteenth century travels to the shores of Lake Tanganyika.

'Dick was neither emotional nor prudish,' recollects John Gower, 'but what I would call a very sensible Colonial Office chap. Excellent with the natives, spoke the language, did everything well.' Patrick Duff, David's godfather, had 'immense respect for Richard's brain, imagination and personality'. The two men met in 1952 while they were neighbouring District Commissioners. Duff's strongest physical memory is of a man 'with thick glasses, and as blind as a bat without them'. The relationship developed when he became Richard's second-in-command in the Morogoro District between 1955 and 1957, the year David was born.

Duff had been transferred to Morogoro in order to help 'restore confidence and rebuild the traditional administration after a minor rebellion'. This had been the upshot, he claims, of 'agriculturally imperfect laws against soil erosion – good in theory but inept socially and politically and so easy for the rising young local politicians to exploit'. After a period of mutual assessment, Richard assigned Duff to run his own section of Morogoro, a task he carried out 'with no more than periodic, courtesy reference'. This, to Duff, 'was the measure of his maturity and judgement, to know when he could forget a chunk of the problems and get on with his own thing'. Like father, like son. Richard's own thing was creating and nurturing a statutory town council, which he nursed to local independence.

Promotion to Permanent Secretary saw Richard Gower relocate to Dar es Salaam in 1959, and when, after forty-two years, the British finally renounced their mandate to administer Tanganyika, he was asked to stay on for two more years to help President Nyerere effect a smooth transition to independence. Duff remembers that 'He would have done that superbly, having no colour-consciousness'. Very like father, very like son.

Richard's articles for *Tanganyika Notes and Records* say much about the man. In 1948, he had bared his teeth, examining in detail two views of Masailand as seen through the eyes of the Scots geographer Joseph Thomson ('The Velvet Glove') and the German anthropologist Dr Karl Peters ('The Mailed Fist . . . a soldier first and last'). The Masai were (and remain) nomadic cattle herders whose elders and ritual leaders dominated a profoundly patriarchal society: white attitudes diverged greatly. Stanley (of Stanley and Livingstone fame) recommended requisitioning a force of a thousand men – as a bare minimum – to quell the natives, whereas Thomson chose friendship. Richard explained his conversion with a deliciously ironic touch:

> He refers to 'the terrible Masai' – 'the dreaded Masai country' – 'a tribe whose very name carried fear into the hearts of all who knew it' . . . After these awe-inspiring preliminaries, Thomson seems to have been agreeably surprised when he eventually came into actual contact with the Masai in the flesh. When he finally set eyes upon the dreaded warriors Thomson 'could not but involuntarily exclaim, "what splendid fellows"'.

This delicate, sardonic edge would find more than a few echoes in David's own approach to writing and commentating.

While Patrick Duff ended up with a CMG, Richard had to settle for an OBE. 'Dick might have got a CMG,' believes John Gower, who notes that he and his brother 'seem to have spent a good deal of our lives in Africa'. John himself was born in Nairobi in 1912, and only returned to England at the age of four owing to a bout of dysentery. Africa nurtured the other side of the family as well. Sylvia was born in Mombasa in 1919 and spent her first four years in Kenya, mostly in Nairobi, where her father, Percival Ford, was employed as chief mechanical engineer to the Uganda Railway. Elizabeth Fouracre remembers her younger sister as 'a *very* pretty child with blond curly hair and green eyes'; at least we know where David got his looks from. While their parents remained in Nairobi,

Elizabeth and Sylvia – there were sixteen months between them – were sent to prep school in Sussex and thence to public school at Wycombe Abbey. Shortly before the war, their mother returned to England and rented a house in Tonbridge while her husband headed for India and ultimately spent his last years in Brazil. Mother and daughters subsequently moved to Goudhurst when Jessie remarried Tom Bowring, a member of the prominent family insurance firm which for many years lent its name to the annual prize in the Varsity rugby match. After passing her matriculation and proceeding to London University, Sylvia, to her family's utter ignorance, joined MI5.

She had two spells in MI5's London office either side of a wartime evacuation to Oxford. Neither mother nor sister ever had the foggiest, as Elizabeth emphasizes, 'until my husband, who was in the army, came on the scene. "Oh," he said one day, "you must be in MI5." Sylvia was furious. Before she contracted asthma in Tanganyika – our father also had it, so it may have been hereditary – she was very lively, and quite strong-minded. As a young woman she always had her head stuck in a book. She was very determined, and we were all brought up to keep a secret.' As with her future husband, however, the pull of Africa was powerful. Not that that was the only thing they had in common. Their mothers had struck up a fast friendship in Nairobi; indeed, as the respective nannies joined forces for weeks on end, Richard and Sylvia spent much of their early childhood together. When the families lost contact, fate took a hand via a chance meeting on Tunbridge Wells station twenty years after the Fords and the Gowers left Nairobi. 'Sylvia and I were catching the train to London with mother,' remembers Elizabeth, 'when suddenly, while we were walking up the stairs, mother said: "Goodness, isn't that Mrs Gower?" After that the families renewed their friendship and Richard met up with Sylvia again.'

Richard duly proposed while on leave and married Sylvia in Goudhurst on 6 November 1954 (David was christened at the same church). The wedding photos show a slim, studious-looking groom with elegant fingers and swept-back hair arm-in-arm with a serene-looking bride in pearls and white gloves. They returned to Tanganyika, which is where David suspects he was conceived. He was born on April Fool's Day, 1957. Sylvia had gone back to Kent ahead of Richard, who followed her in time for the birth. Mother was thirty-eight, father forty.

Elizabeth Fouracre is convinced that, despite the onset of asthma, her sister thoroughly enjoyed life in Tanganyika. David's earliest memories are of a bungalow by the beach just outside Dar es Salaam. After that came a house adjoining the golf course, erected on stilts, as David put it, 'partly to lessen the prospect of finding some of the less edifying wildlife at the bottom of your bed'. He can recall 'the occasional passing snake which the garden boy would obligingly hammer to death with a rake', and still cherishes his photographic evidence of boy, rake and ex-snake. Quite why he never had a brother or sister is unknown, although Sylvia's advanced age and increasingly fragile health probably obviated the need for any debate. Still, at least David did not lack for companionship. The servants dwelled with their families in huts at the rear of the property; David was a regular visitor, playing with their children and accepting mug after mug of hot sweet tea. The master-servant, white-black divide was not so much bridged as buried.

The Gowers' social world revolved around the Gymkhana Club, where Richard hit just about every ball that moved: rugby, fives, golf, tennis, hockey and, of course, cricket. Not bad for a bloke in horn-rims. This instinctive hand-eye co-ordination was his bequest to his son. He was also the first to thrust a cricket bat into David's hands. Sylvia, all the same, was the source of the sinisterity. Dealing cards, David insists, is the only other activity he does left-handed on a consistent basis. Initially, he took up a southpaw stance, much to Richard's dismay. When father tried to persuade son to turn around and face the 'proper' way, mother intervened, insisting instinct hold sway.

The Gowers returned to England when David was six. Before leaving Tanzania, they went on safari in the northern game parks, a trip that did much to foster David's lifelong fascination for wildlife, not to mention his aspirations to be a game warden. At times of stress it was an environment he would often turn to as a panacea, a sanctuary. It would serve as a reminder of an alternative existence, a world without petty rules, a world where the only things that count, that really count, are bravery and loyalty, nature and instinct. A world, moreover, where he can be an anonymous member of the gallery, looking on in respect and awe at a simple society. At the end of the calamitous summer of 1989, after he had lost the national captaincy, lost his Test place, given up the Leicestershire leadership and effectively decided to end the two most important relationships in his life, he retreated into the bush, spending a week at Londolozi, a game farm in the shadow of the Kruger National Park. His chosen weapon, happily, was a Pentax. The bungalow he washed and slept in was part of a compound stretching down to a river where some of the wilder animals roamed. Armed with Land Rover and tracker, he spent the days snapping away at elephant and rhino and all manner of wonderous jungle cats. 'Best of all,' he would reflect, 'I revelled in the solitude and escapism of this magical world.'

Although Richard and Sylvia returned to Kent, and subsequently dispatched David to school in Hawkhurst and Canterbury, they eventually settled in Loughborough during the summer of 1964 when Richard was appointed Registrar of the Training College (later Loughborough College of Education). Twenty-one Holywell Drive was a modest semi, not that this surprised John Gower in the slightest. Richard was not the type to be bothered with outward shows of wealth: 'Dick was well off by any standards, never lacked for money. He didn't live in a particularly attractive house but that was part of his character. He didn't want a mansion: he saved for a rainy day. He was sensible with money. He did his wife and David proud. Sylvia didn't have to work.' At this time John remembers his six-year-old nephew 'astounding' the family with his 'aptitude for hitting balls out of the ground'. So far as he could tell, father and son were 'very close': 'They had a bond. When Dick died he [David] probably felt this was bloody unfair.'

David attended Quorn primary school before moving on to Marlborough House, and thence to his father's alma mater. 'Boarding school,' says John Gower, 'was very much what the Gowers did.' As far as his aunt was concerned, David clearly missed the family bosom but, typically, refused to externalize such deep feelings. For all the emotional solitude, it certainly taught him the value of self-reliance. 'Basically,' he was content to note in his autobiography, 'it was a very happy and carefree childhood.' Even though their time together was largely confined to school holidays, father and son found much to share, primarily cricket. Richard not only erected a net in the back garden but ensured David was permitted to take full advantage of the college's facilities (the Loughborough connection would not be forgotten: twenty-one years after his father retired, David returned to what was by now Loughborough University to receive an honorary degree). Not that the sporting education stopped there. The local attractions were sufficiently diverse to facilitate a balanced diet: Richard and David would flit between Nottingham Forest, Leicester City, Loughborough Town and Leicester Tigers. There was no favouritism, no blinkered loyalty to a single team. The result never would be the be-all and end-all.

Whether this could make up for being an only child is another matter; siblings help prepare each other for the intricacies of adult relationships. But an only child, or so runs a counter-argument, never has to compete, which, admittedly, can be both benefit and hindrance. So, does David regard being an only child as a benefit or a hindrance?

God knows. I've nothing to compare it to. It benefited me in certain ways and not in others. As a child I thought at times it would be nice to have a sibling; my siblings were friends from school, which isn't the same. You hang on to some but the way it turns out I've always tended to go forward, as with my career. I've kept in touch with very few. With a brother or sister you have a different tie. In emotional terms, I don't know. I'm gregarious, yes. I like company. If I'd had a brother or sister to compete against I don't know what difference it would have made to my attitudes to sport or to life. It's one of those imponderables.

Here comes another: had Richard Gower chosen the second day of the 1965 Nottingham Test against South Africa as his eight-year-old son's initiation to the longest of all games, might David have ended up a languid right-hander *à la* Colin Cowdrey? That day, exulted *Wisden*, Cowdrey 'showed himself a true artist', making 105 in a shade over three hours while ten colleagues could muster only 124 between them. Instead, the opening day was nominated, and the batsmanship on view occupied an even higher plane. Richard's penchant for willow and leather had not gone unnoticed by his colleagues at Loughborough. Jean Start, then secretary to the Principal, Dr Hardie, remembers him sending a suspicious note requesting permission to attend his grandmother's funeral: 'The Principal didn't see anything unusual about this but I remarked: "Do you think Dick is burying his grandmother at Trent Bridge?" This was a Thursday, the opening day of the Test match. Dick was highly amused when I put the same question to him!' Richard's decision to play hookey was a wise one, the impact instant and profound. On an overcast morning custom-made for Tom Cartwright's brand of wobble, South Africa were 16 for two when their broad-shouldered, straight-backed young No. 4 walked in; shortly after lunch they withered to 80 for five. Having moved sedately to 34 in the hour or so before the interval, the lad re-emerged with guns ablaze. In the next seventy minutes, he made 91 runs with some of the most glorious back-foot drives imaginable; his captain, Peter van der Merwe, contributed 11.

E. W. Swanton, never over-lavish with superlatives, began his report for the *Daily Telegraph* thus: 'An innings was played here today by Graeme Pollock which in point of style and power, of ease and beauty of execution, is fit to rank with anything in the annals of the game.' David gasped too, though he was not always sure why:

I saw bits of the innings – I didn't understand everything, but he didn't let me down. I saw him in Port Elizabeth in 1974 when I was on a public schools tour, and he got a hundred then too. And I batted with him at Jesmond one day and he got another hundred. Three out of three. I rate him as high as any you could mention. There's a certain fate in that, a certain destiny I suppose.

For all the palpable ramifications of this paternally arranged date with destiny, the maternal influence seems to have been equally important. Mention the word 'Gower' to most folk and the words 'laid' and 'back' are never far behind. Quite why this should be taken as criticism is beyond me: among other things, it denotes a flexibility, a capacity for perspective. Unfortunately, there are rather more voices to whom 'laid-back' is most accurately translated as 'indifferent'. Simon Barnes captured the innate contradiction: 'A laid-back winner is a hero: a laid-back loser has been slacking on the job.' John Gower regards his sister-in-law as the main, if unwitting, sculptor of David's most renowned character trait. Although her sister strongly refutes such a theory, Sylvia, contends John, was the inspiration for that perennial air of insouciance: 'Sylvia was pretty laid-back, and once my brother's influence faded that communicated itself more.'

Anyone capable of coming home from work every day without letting slip a morsel of office gossip, let alone keeping the identity of that work under wraps, has to be awfully good at putting on an act. David can vaguely remember his mother telling him that she had been employed by MI5, but professes complete ignorance as to the nature of the job. He might have made a half-decent Bond himself, so what price mum as Moneypenny? The whole point of being laid-back is to create the *illusion* of indifference. Contrary to received wisdom, David cared deeply about his profession. Seldom can a sportsman's body language have been subject to so much scrutiny, or such manifest misinterpretation. 'David has the wrong body language,' Clive Lloyd contended upon hearing of David's reappointment as England captain. 'I just wish he appeared to everybody as he really is – a tough cricketer, keen and a very good thinker. Gower doesn't miss much.' David readily admits it was merely part of the veneer:

> I spent years trying to make the point that, basically, you don't achieve what I've achieved without caring about it, and that whatever you could see on the surface was a screen to what was underneath. Because I didn't always throw a bat at the umpire as I was walking past him, you've got to guess what's going on. I've done damage to dressing-rooms but there's no point in getting photographic evidence of broken doors to show the lads – 'right, here's my new image'. You've got to say: trust me. The fact that I achieved something means I try. I'm fairly sensitive but I've learnt that there's a certain futility trying to overcome people's perceptions.

Lodged firmly in the memory – Old Trafford, 1988, the final morning of the rain-blighted fourth Test against the West Indies. England, resuming 189 behind on 60 for three with Gower and Allan Lamb still entrenched, had only to hang on for a couple of hours before rain returned to the rescue. Given all the hours that had already been lost, they scarcely deserved to survive, but since when was that a professional consideration? Malcolm Marshall bent his back but David began in a manner that brought to mind the title of an album by one of his favourite bands, Supertramp: *Crisis, What Crisis?* A smirk flashed across those languid features. What was that he had once said about facing the Barber of Barbados? 'The last thing you want to do when you're playing the West Indies is to encourage Malcolm Marshall in the idea you're not particularly enjoying it.' Nothing was going to persuade him to yield the psychological initiative. But after reaching 34, more than twice the next highest score in the innings – and, indeed, the highest for England in this whole non-contest – he was caught at slip off Marshall, essaying something Richie would have hailed as the height of ingenuity had the delivery bounced a fraction less. No other sport (with the possible exception of baseball) has a smaller margin for error: many is the kingdom lost for the want of an extra coat of varnish, or a millimetre of wood. The match's end came after barely an hour's further play. Within two minutes the heavens had opened.

My own circumstances complicated matters. Over the first four days I had looked after the 'nannies' (nanny goats – quotes); now I was entrusted with my first Test report for a national newspaper – *Today*. All around me in the press box, the mood was sarcastic. Grown men felt let down, angry, just as a ten-year-old might after seeing his team lose the FA Cup final in injury time. Over a period of thirteen months, our 'representatives' had played fourteen Tests without so much as a sniff of victory. As if that were not enough, 'our' captain had brought the entire nation into disrepute by having a stand-up row with a Pakistani umpire. At times like these, the committed fan can overrule the dispassionate journalist. Whereas I am sure that other, more experienced colleagues managed to keep a lid on their frustrations, I found complete fairness elusive. The following morning, Graham Otway, the official *Today* correspondent, rang around dawn's crack: 'Thought I'd let you know I've just had a call from Gower.' David, apparently, was furious. I was flabbergasted. All I'd done was to repeat for the zillionth time what every other cricket writer in Christendom and beyond had been banging on about for a decade: reckless driving, lack of foot movement, mental aberration – all the usual guff. Besides, who was I? A struggling freelance grateful for a byline in the country's least popular tabloid. Yet David was hurt. He had explained to Otway precisely what he had been trying to do, that the delivery had bounced a tad more than expected, defeating the attempted steer through the cordon. Suitably chastened, I resolved to take greater care in future.

Aside from its value as a defence mechanism, to be laid-back in the early seventies was to be hip. Everyone wanted to belong to the No Sweat brigade. And here was David Gower, the man who made Cary Grant look like Woody Allen in the middle of an anxiety attack. Being laid-back also makes it easier to adopt the intellectual high ground: men of few words earn respect because it is assumed those they do utter have that much more thought behind them. The flipness of tone and the Pythonesque sense of humour, one part subversion to three parts cool repartee, embellish the effect, reinforcing the defences, the relaxed delivery making repartee sound off-the-cuff, disguising the effort.

One of Woody Allen's most inventive creations was Leonard Zelig, a human chameleon who so craved acceptance and affection he developed the power to turn himself into a clone of anyone he met. David has a bit of that in him too. 'He was developing two accents in those days,' his mother once said, referring to his early days at Grace Road. 'One for me, proper English. And one for his friends.'

She was not alone in noticing the change. James Maxwell, nephew of the Reverend David Sheppard and a close friend at prep school, cottoned on when they bumped into each other during the 1976 MCC v. Champion County match. 'David was playing for Leicestershire and it was my first day as an MCC member. I met him as I was coming down the pavilion stairs and we agreed to meet for a drink after play. That was when I noticed he had a broad Leicester accent; the last time I'd seen him he had been a King's College schoolboy with a plum in his mouth, like me. He'd become one of the boys. I think it was quite a good thing to do: we've all done it. He didn't want to wear public school on his sleeve.' Given the prevailing climate, who can blame him?

David found himself trying to persuade people that 'a certain shyness comes along with all of this': it was such a struggle he scarcely bothers any more. A whole slew of misconceptions surround this most intriguing of English heroes: three, emphasizes David's estimable former 'ghost', Alan Lee, 'are perennial in their misguided dogma': ambivalence towards job, extroversion, 'no-worries' temperament. What cannot be denied is the underlying raft of contradiction that defies pat psychoanalysis. Insecurity – lack of a sibling, a certain rootlessness, the constant turnover of friends – made David want to fit in. Yet, at the same time, he had no intention of being lumped in with the herd. While Botham, say, is the in-your-face showman, more Bernard Manning than Bernard Cribbins, David has always been more complex. 'Superficially tranquil and compartmentalized,' as Lee put it, 'yet periodically stormy and turbulent.'

Too self-conscious to be outrageous, David settled for more subtle extravagances. How many people in the public eye would take out an ad in *The Times* announcing the *end* of his engagement? How many cricketers keep a record of the time it takes them to whip through the *Telegraph* crossword? How many sixth-formers declared the following interests on their university application form in 1974, the year of *Sladest*, 'Devil Gate Drive' and *Tales from Topographic Oceans*: 'Ludwig van B, Tchaikovsky and co, but also Baroque (Vivaldi, Bach, Albinoni, Scarlatti) and some lesser-known and performed composers such as Smetana, Friedemann, Ivanovici, Monti (pretty cosmopolitan bunch!)'. For all the outward – and inner – modesty, it didn't take his agent, Jon Holmes, long to detect this showy undercurrent: 'You had all the silly banter, still do: "How are you, David?" "Oh, I'm wonderful." Rory Bremner does this impression of him. David can't say "I drank a glass of champagne"; he'll say "I partook of some bubbles". He doesn't say "the cat is on the mat"; he'll say "the feline is recumbent". He twists everything.'

James Maxwell, who joined Marlborough House on the same day in September 1965, recalls David as 'academically top of school, very bright and very undemonstrative'. His handwriting was 'beautiful, absolutely stunning – he took a lot of care'. The new boys' first cricket practice proved a salutary experience:

> We were both invited, and although it probably never registered with me at the time, because I was David Sheppard's nephew I was given a bat and the master said he'd bowl to me. I'd never faced a hard ball before: I think it hit me on the head or something. I could hardly hold the bat! Everyone's face fell: I'd failed to live up to expectations. Then this very quiet, extremely shy, withdrawn boy picked up a bat, stood the wrong way round (as we saw it) and played very cultured shots. My uncle said he'd never seen as good a cricketer as that of that age. He became the talk of the prep school circuit in that part of England.

At the time, says Maxwell, David was a 'passionate' follower of those cynical if gifted Leeds United sides presided over by Don 'Readies' Revie. It was hardly a case of neighbourhood loyalty. That said, it does seem obvious where the appeal lay: Eddie Gray, Johnny Giles and Allan Clarke, men who made the difficult look simple, men whose fancy footwork made it all too easy to resist the stench of overt professionalism.

David and James Maxwell became firm friends during their last year at Marlborough House, spending weekends in the halls playing 'Test' cricket with a tennis racket or going toe-to-toe on the Subbuteo pitch.

> I was small and aggressive and voluble; David started very quiet. He was head of school, and, I think, captain of everything. Pretty all-round amazing chap. But he was never conceited, never thrust his talents at

people. Very benign, very equable. He led by example: he wasn't a driver of people. He was also extremely, er, influenceable. In his mind, I don't think he has ever fitted. I'm not saying he's a chameleon: I don't think he knows where he fits.

His parents visited school very rarely. I remember his father being tall and looking rather ill, very pale. You'd never have known he was this tremendous all-round sportsman. He seemed a quiet man, very likeable. It seemed a happy home: they were a typical English middle-class professional couple – worthy, honest, straightforward. David never talked about them, whereas I banged on about my uncle ad infinitum. I went to stay with them in Loughborough, the summer after we left Marlborough House I think. They lived in a reasonably modest house, with a nice garden; we played soccer the entire time I was there. He and his father seemed very close. You got the impression they'd played a lot of sport together from the year dot, that David had had a ball kicked or thrown at him from the start.

Even then, Maxwell feels, it was possible to detect the seeds of ambition: 'No one is hungrier than a public schoolboy – you're taken to the table and you're given the food, then suddenly it's all taken away from you. David would have noticed the cars that pulled up at school, the other boys' parents' houses. Ambition can be formed by that.'

Derek Whittome, the cricket master David nods to as 'a big influence', had no doubt about the gifts, nor the tendency to keep a distance:

I taught him from ten to thirteen: he was a brilliant cricketer even then. His dad was enthusiastic and had clearly imparted the basics but he had this natural gift for timing. You couldn't get him out. He was good at rugby too, and hockey, and without having to try. It all came so easy to him. It was difficult to rouse him, but then he never had to exert himself. Had he had things harder he might have exerted himself more. He was an above-average student, and very laid-back. Popular in a funny sort of way. He was hero-worshipped but he didn't project himself. He was admired from afar. He wasn't someone who endeared himself to you because of his personality. He was always himself. He was not a very good captain, partly because he was so gifted that he could not enthuse others, partly because he was too inward-looking.

3   Like a Shark Through Water

If you never trust anyone, then you're free to like everyone.
Quentin Crisp

Richard Gower remained at Loughborough College until a combination of Hodgkin's disease and motor-neurone disease compelled his retirement in September 1972. The wasting process was well underway: though his mind remained sharp, the body gave up the following April. He was fifty-five. Mercifully, David was not exposed to his father's disintegration on a daily basis: boarding school has its compensations.

Did David think he would have been as wilful had his father not been so cruelly cut down? The implicit allegation is examined calmly for a second or two. For a brief instant, the inquisitee appears to stifle an indignant response, then responds in that measured, eminently reasonable fashion that so annoys the sound-bite ferrets. Martin Johnson, one of the few journalists David has allowed himself to get close to, once told me that he would scan back through the sheaves of notes taken during an interview 'and realize that he hadn't actually said anything'.

Am I that wilful? Wilful has connotations of total absence of discipline: a good word to get a reaction. Depends. If you like a guy then he's got a mind that operates; if you don't then he's wilful. [Wilful] implies uncontrollable. Ask Brearley. Ask Illy. They'd say, 'of course not'. I'm also very aware that you can't worry about everything you say or do, so you have to trust your instincts, allow yourself some rein to enjoy what's around you before you become suffocated by the whole system. To be described as wilful would be wrong; to be described as totally law-abiding would be wrong. I've never been a hotel-thrashing pop star, but then I've never been a model citizen. It's a question of degree.

The implication, it should be said, is far from unequivocal. It might go some way towards explaining why, of all his regular England colleagues bar Boycott, David took the longest to marry and embrace fatherhood. Jon Holmes's vaunted management stable includes a few more men who reflect his own outlook – Mike Atherton, Gary Lineker and Will Carling,

33

all sensible chaps with fun in their hearts, proportion in their heads and iron in their souls; to Holmes, wilful is an apt word in this particular client's case, not to mention that of another. 'David *is* wilful. Strengths are always great weaknesses. Look at Mike [Atherton]. He's very stubborn. "I know you're right," he'll say, "but I'm still not going to do it." Same with David.'

Let's put it another way. Was there a part of David that held fast to the family motto, refusing to bend, refusing to be lured by the double-edged sword of compromise?

> Yeah. I can hide behind that or defend myself with it, depends how you look at it. There were a lot of times where I said, well, there's more to life than cricket, perhaps slightly naively. It's very easy to be young and blasé about it. I hate to keep coming back to him but Graham [Gooch] is quite a good example. He's actually identified it and worked on it. It's linked in with whatever else you want to do, or can do. My tendency would be to think, what else could I do? Could I actually be a downhill skier, join the Veterans' tennis circuit? If I'd thought about that a long time ago, maybe, but they're not very realistic now. They're still dreams. It was never a case of setting up a company that's going to be worth £50m in five years' time because I don't have the ability to do that. I don't really have the desire. I'd sooner win the pools, or the lottery. Say no more.

To John Gower, David seemed 'fairly stoical' when his father passed away. As a trustee of the will, John helped Sylvia 'tidy up the estate' and took a 'fatherly interest' in David: 'He was not a boy to throw his arms around me. I was no substitute. He was unemotional.'

Not that the King's School encouraged emotion. No boys' school does, least of all one of the few remaining educational institutions outside Eton where wing-collars are still *de rigueur*. Attending King's also meant being surrounded, nay deluged, by history. Enter through Mint Yard Gate (1860), then proceed past Parkers Gate (1561), past Chillenden Chambers (1390) and Cellarers Wall (1100-and-something), and you are within a few paces of Canterbury Cathedral. The school itself dates back to the sixth century, to St Augustine himself. Among its most illustrious Old Boys stand William Harvey, Christopher Marlowe and, more recently, that rarest of species, the English astronaut Colin Fowle. Carol Reed and Michael Powell, the eyes and minds behind some of the most memorable films ever directed by Englishmen, were in the same year together.

Some highly commendable results in the common entrance exams prompted King's to offer a scholarship – and hence reduced fees – on a 'take it or leave it' basis: family finances, as he put it, 'were not quite up to taking the gamble'. As an entrance scholar, a member of the elite, David not only had to stay on until he was eighteen, he also had to wear a gown: the toffs' answer to the branding iron. This status also elevated him to the so-called express stream, which meant taking GCEs a year early. Further pressure came in the shape of his father's exploits within those very same walls. Richard had been head of school, clever bod, captain of just about everything. From the age of thirteen, expectation yapped at his heels like some hyperactive Jack Russell.

Small wonder David came to regard King's as the Home Counties' answer to Colditz, and he was only too ready to clamber over the walls after dark to down a pint in the town. Or, better still, mosey off to the movies with a girl from a sister school. If rules were generally obeyed and nostrils mostly kept clean, japes were far from unknown, all the more so when David struck up a friendship with both the head's son, Andrew Newell, and Stephen White-Thompson, the Dean of Canterbury's son. Allies of this ilk made it somewhat simpler to acquire a key to the postern gate. David was fortunate to evade detection when a master discovered the rogue key in his possession: luckily, it had been cut badly, and needed a firm wiggle to turn the relevant lock; the mortar-boarded inspector gave up too soon. On other occasions he was caught bang to rights. Taste for ale nurtured by visiting captains from MCC and Stragglers of Asia, he and a classmate cycled one evening to The Beverley, a local hostelry around the corner from the cricket field, only to be apprehended in mid-quaff by a couple of masters. Life for the next fortnight was not amusing – 'confined to barracks, report cards, jankers, that sort of thing'. So much for a second Gower becoming king of King's.

David did scale the less than dizzy heights of house monitor but even then he fell a little short of setting the desired example. Convinced he was exempt from the 6 p.m. roll-call at the end of a free day, he boarded the train from Canterbury East to Ashford, then bought two tickets for the latest James Bond flick, the second for a girl he had met at one of the periodic school dances. Lad and lass had shared a couple of drinks and a couple of hours in the stalls before the search party eventually spotted the damsel in Ashford High Street. Although David eluded the search party's clutches and caught the train back to Canterbury, the effects of the drink and the lateness of the hour conspired to make him sleep all the way to Ramsgate, forcing him to hitch a lift back to school.

'I think I saw a note from the head saying he didn't appreciate his sense of humour,' recalls David Reid, David's housemaster in his final year. One of eleven boarding houses (two day houses were introduced when King's went co-ed in 1990), Linacre House was rebuilt in 1953 on the site of a canonical residence dating back to the eighteenth century.

Not that this hallowed status had prevented it from becoming a veritable House of Fun. One erstwhile occupant was Admiral Nelson's clerical brother, who once invited Lady Hamilton into the House and encouraged her to dance on a table. 'David was very much at the social centre of the House,' Reid asserts. As ever, David stood apart, even on the coiffure front. One shudders to think what Vidal would have done to the hairdresser responsible for the Drenched Poodle Perm.

Reid also took David for history, his best subject.

He demonstrated his intelligence with his O-level results and his As, although the latter were a bit variable. He got a C in French and a D in Economics and Politics but he also got an A1 for history, so he was clearly a contender for Oxford. I found him extremely intelligent, extremely pleasant, delightful, charming, and a bit casual. He probably didn't push himself after his father died. Yes, he did have some disciplinary problems, though not so much through bad behaviour as boredom, and certainly no worse than many others at that time. What difficulties there were probably stemmed from the traumatization. He wrote me a letter after he left and what he wrote showed how sensitive and shrewd he was about life at school. He's very good about keeping in touch, always replies to my letters, always willing to see you after play had finished. When he came to lay the foundation stone for the new sports hall we had a long chat. 'This is very embarrassing,' I told him, 'but I've got two young boys who'd be thrilled if you could send them a photo.' About three weeks later it came through the post: 'To Rupert and Benedict, with love from David Gower'. Before he went to Australia for the last time I wrote to him and asked him to send the boys a postcard. Nothing happened, then, on Christmas Eve, in plopped a postcard with a couple of kangaroos and a 'Sydney Cricket Ground' postmark – 'To Rupert and Benedict . . .'.

It is instructive at this juncture to record a graphologist's analysis of David's handwriting. According to David Bennett (who was not apprised of the author's identity), the artistic loops and easeful strokes, in a letter written to Reid two years after Richard Gower's death, denote a sharp mind, amiability, self-reliance and confidence. For all the evidence of emotional self-sufficiency, Bennett noted, he is 'deeply affected by past events' and also needs the occasional 'pat on the back'. Judgments tend to be sympathetic and carefully, if briefly, worded, although silence is often deployed as a guard against conflict. Being taken for granted can be a cause of impatience or even anger, yet the desire to chart his own course can make him indifferent to criticism.

Clarinet lessons were taken in good heart (if with no real passion), but the most mellifluous notes sprang from willow. Not that the teachers claimed any responsibility. The first XI coach when David joined King's was Colin Fairservice, now the last surviving link to those great Kent sides of the thirties, to Woolley and Ames, to Chapman, Freeman and Hubble. Here, at least, the comparisons with Woolley have substance.

At King's we used to have this indoor cricket shed, coconut matting on a hard surface, no room to run up. When new boys arrived I would invite them in before the start of the season for a little trial. You only have to see a boy of that age pick up a bat, wave it about a bit and play one or two shots, to be able to get a sense of timing, of co-ordination. David came along, and the first time I saw him I could hardly believe it. He had the elegance, the grace, the timing, the casual approach. The more I watched, the more amazed I became. I went back to the common room for tea and told some of my colleagues I'd just seen the nearest thing I'd ever seen to Frank Woolley.

For twenty-odd years, I had happily gone along with the notion of Woolley as the last word in elegant batsmanship. Who was I to argue? But the few frames of film I have subsequently seen of him have struck me as intensely disappointing. The strokes seem stiff, heavy, the legendary fluency hard to discern. To my eyes, at least, present beat past by a furlong or two. Fairservice can understand why: 'We nicknamed [Woolley] "Storky". Sometimes, when he'd finished a stroke, it looked as if he had these flamingo legs, very ungainly. He was lacking in grace in his later years; he may have been more like David when he was younger.'

During those early years at King's, Fairservice insists, David's thirst for nets was nigh-on unshakeable.

He spent a terrific amount of time during the Easter term in the shed with me. He was a great enthusiast, and that sprang from his father. Only met him once, poor man. But the thing that David had, only nature could teach him, that sense of timing: you can't coach that. And he was able to pick up the flight of the ball so early. In my fifty years of working with youngsters he was outstanding. I recommended him to Hubert Doggart when he was running the England Under-15 team: David went up to Old Trafford, did well, and I had a nice letter of appreciation back from Doggart, saying what a good player this boy was, and so on. If he wasn't going to make the grade, no one was.

A year later, David was summoned to Rugby School to play for the Public Schools against the English Schools Cricket Association: Gower and Cowdrey versus Gatting. It was a foul day; Richard Gower stayed in his car with the heater blazing. When David struck a six, the stroke was acclaimed by a tooting horn. It was the only time Richard Gower ever saw his son in representative action.

Fairservice contented himself with tweaking rather than adjusting.

This guy's got so much natural ability, I thought, he's going to find out for himself. He was still a hot-headed youth when I had him: flashing outside off-stump, going like a train, making 30 or 40 then getting himself out. He was a bit laid-back, literally and figuratively. Never leant forward. He always had trouble just outside leg-stump. But for heaven's sake, I said to him, beware taking advice. When you start making a few runs in county cricket you're going to have Tom, Dick and Harry coming up to you to give you all sorts of advice. For heaven's sake, I said, let it go in one ear and out the other, unless you know the chap giving you this advice has sound reasons for doing so, as Ray Illingworth had.

Fairservice makes no bones about his efforts to instil certain attitudes, attitudes he acknowledges were probably already ingrained:

I made sure he realised it was a game, that you played it for enjoyment, for fun. But at fifteen he'd already told his house master he was going to be captain of England. My job was to try and persuade him to have a sense of proportion, that his parents were paying quite high fees and that he was there first and foremost for academic reasons, and shouldn't let anyone down. I told him I hoped that, until he left university, he would treat it as a pastime. He took it with a little bit of a grin, didn't commit himself. He was such a charmer. He had a sense of fun, a sense of mischief. He was the one pulling the legs. That flying business was typical. What harm is there in a prank like that? Cricket is a gamble. Look at Milburn, losing his eye. Could happen to anyone.

Though David also demonstrated a considerable aptitude for rugby, the interest waned once Fairservice was no longer in charge: he didn't really hit it off with the new rugby master. That this was decidedly unusual is confirmed by Fairservice's successor as senior cricket master. Alan Dyer tended the stumps for Oxford at Lord's in 1965 and 1966 (when his opposite number was Deryck Murray) then declined to play in his final year because he didn't feel he had the right to reclaim his appointed place having spent the rest of the season studying.

David captained the firsts under me in his final year: he was a very likeable person, and he got on well with people. He was very keen on the game, not too hung up about winning or losing. Cricket obviously meant a lot to him: he watched it, read about it, was happy to take advice. He took fielding practice seriously and enjoyed it; he took the net sessions seriously, generated a sense of enthusiasm in those around him. Early in the season, when the wickets were slow, he'd still go for his strokes. My great memory is of the time and the timing. The ball used to come through quickly when the pitches grew harder, and some of the club sides used to bring some quick bowlers, and they'd really steam in. But David just stood up and stroked them.

Dyer's stack of musty scorebooks reveals that the 1974 season (his third in the first XI) saw David turn cameos into something approaching method acting. In 1972 he had made 292 runs at 22.46 (highest score 44), the year after 530 at 35.33 (with a best of 89). This time, as *Wisden* notes, he made 638 runs at 53.17, making his first hundred for the school – 105 against Stragglers of Asia – and finishing term with 148 against the Old Boys. Writing in *Wisden*, Rex Alston even went so far as to proclaim him 'a useful bowler', a conclusion seemingly culled from an inspection of the averages: thirteen wickets at 19.61. So far as Dyer can remember, the mode was off-spin, a craft David carefully concealed on the professional circuit (Kapil Dev was his solitary Test scalp). Against KCS Wimbledon the previous summer, nonetheless, he had emerged with the not inconsiderable figures of 16–10–8–6, including the hat-trick.

In many respects, the mid 1970s can be seen as the public schools' last stand, in cricketing terms at least. Among the Standen-McDougals and Hamilton-Dalrymples lurked a rash of able young cricketers. While David was going out with a succession of bangs, Paul Downton was excelling behind the stumps for Sevenoaks, and the pair were duly named in the party of public schoolboys bound for South Africa under the 'Crocodiles' banner (the political climate was sensitive, so no official representative team could be dispatched there, naturally). Accompanying them were a couple of other local likely lads, Tonbridge's latest Cowdrey, Chris, and his schoolmate Nick Kemp, a fast-bowling all-rounder who went on to play for Kent and Middlesex. Also on the scene that summer were Tim Curtis (Worcester RGS), Derek Pringle (Felsted), Mark Nicholas (Bradfield), Tony Pigott (Harrow) and Robin Boyd-Moss (Bedford). The Class of '74 numbered no fewer than six future Test players – it might well have been seven had ill-health not cut down Boyd-Moss – in addition to four future county captains.

David had, and gave, many reasons for not joining any of the 'rebel' tours to the Cape: fear of offending West Indian business connections, concern over sponsorships and endorsements, an inherent (if publicly unspoken) respect for the black majority, and, most credibly of all, a disdain for cheap imitation. He wanted to dine at the top table, to eat with the best. Money was never the sole motivation. Yet neither in public nor private did he betray any political reasoning. It seems safe to assume, therefore, that, as the Crocodiles wended their way through Cape Town, Bloemfontein, Port Elizabeth, East London, Johannesburg and, yes, Soweto, the wide-eyed seventeen-year-old had no misgivings. Nor did Nick Kemp:

> We were all very young, old enough to remember the D'Oliveira situation but probably not to fully understand the situation in South Africa at that time. We stayed mostly with local families who had three or four servants rushing round. I don't remember it ever being an issue. I know I didn't really think much about it other than what a wonderful country it was, what very nice people. I can't remember David saying anything. I'm not sure we all understood the significance of Soweto, though we knew it was important. We went to the football stadium to play their first multi-racial side – Barry Stead, the old Notts fast bowler, looked after them – and about 25,000 people came. Terrifying. David Walsh, the master in charge of cricket at Tonbridge who organized the tour with his Wellington counterpart, David Mordaunt, said it was an important day for cricket, and I remember wondering why. David's politics are right of centre but he has always seemed pretty ambivalent about the whole thing. If anything, he's an apolitical animal.

Kemp took to David right off the bat.

> I would always consider him a friend, a chum, an all-round bloody good egg, and he struck me as a good lad as soon as we met. Very approachable, someone I found very easy to relate to. A difficult person to get close to, a very private individual – I don't think anyone knows him apart from Thorunn and Vicki, and Vicki maybe not as well as she thinks she did – but at the same time a lovely, charismatic, super bloke. The noisier ones, the more outgoing ones among us worked that out fairly quickly. He liked to drink, even though we weren't allowed to. I can remember waking up in one house and coming down in the morning – there must have been eight of us staying there – and being given a beer for breakfast. He was a typical schoolboy batsman used to playing on bloody good wickets: if it was in his half he'd whack it in the air. Nothing terribly complicated. Winning and losing was irrelevant to David, but when it mattered there was no hint of giving a quarter.

What would develop into David's closest cricketing friendship, conversely, had hardly got off to the most auspicious of starts. 'The previous winter,' recalls Chris Cowdrey:

Tonbridge were playing King's at rugby and I kicked the ball over the head of their fullback. David and I were running for the line and we dived almost simultaneously, but he was ahead of me, much quicker than me, and he dived on the ball. I got there second and dived on it again, got up, raised my arm – and it was given. I think we won 6–0. He didn't forgive me quickly.

The anger, typically, did not last, as Cowdrey happily indicates:

You can throw sixteen people into a room who don't know each other and groups of twos and threes emerge for no reason. Paul Downton was another one. The bond wasn't cricket: as David put it, we shared a sense of lunacy. We found it very easy to take the piss out of each other. He was an extraordinary character, a genius at seventeen. His was a totally natural ability. He learned to play much straighter, particularly in defence, but I don't believe he ever worked hard on his game. He may disagree. But I think his was a mental game: he knew what he was doing all the time. He didn't need to go into a net and do it a hundred times. On that tour people would turn up and say, 'hey, we heard about this guy who made 70 yesterday, thought we'd come down and see what he was like'. He'd play beautifully then get a good-length ball on off-stump and carve to cover and you'd think, what a shame. And there we were, twenty years later, still saying, 'what a shame'. He played some shots no one else would even contemplate playing yet seemed very vulnerable. I thought he was too much of an individual to go on and play cricket for a living. A fantastic player, I thought, but does he really want to do this for a career? You could see him making loads of terrible mistakes. He never changed, never. Maybe it's stubbornness.

Given all these Kentish influences, why did David ultimately sign for Leicestershire instead of his native county? A partial answer comes from the written reply Mike Turner, the Leicestershire secretary/manager, received from Kent following his request for permission to register David, a request tendered comfortably more in hope than expectation. How could they have failed to spot him, he reasoned: 'I never dreamed they'd say yes.' The letter, dated 10 September 1974, runs, in full: 'Dear Mike, Thank you for your letter re. David Gower. I must confess I have not heard of him, so go ahead with our blessing. Kind regards. Yours sincerely, p.p. L. E. G. Ames, Manager.'

Ignorance, in this case, was far from bliss. True, it was Les Ames's fiftieth and final summer at Canterbury, so perhaps he can be excused the odd oversight, but there were surely other eyes and ears. Behind such apparent neglect, it should be said, lies a one-man conspiracy of silence. Whereas Alan Dyer had only just been appointed to run the first XI at King's – he admits to being 'terribly green' and claims to have had 'no contacts with the people who ran Kent schools cricket' – his predecessor had been in an ideal position to send some nudges and winks in the right direction. However, Colin Fairservice had grown increasingly cheesed off at the way his former employers treated their young, in particular his last great hope prior to David, Charles Rowe. In his last two summers at King's a couple of years previously, the Hong Kong-born Rowe had totted up more than 1000 runs while simultaneously picking up 103 wickets at less than 12 apiece in a dazzling variety of styles, including both leg-breaks and left-arm slows. He captained the Public Schools against the West Indies Young Cricketers: everything, it seemed, was his for the asking. In his first season, 1974, he finished third in the Kent batting averages and took three wickets for 137. Fairservice was furious: 'With me, Charles bowled leg-breaks. What did they do? Made him bowl flat off-spinners to keep the runs down. Criminal, criminal.' Rowe won his county cap but seldom thereafter gave a hint of what had gone before. By 1982 he was surplus to requirements; two years with Glamorgan and that was that. So disenchanted was Fairservice with the way Rowe was treated he resolved not to 'risk' consigning David to a similar fate.

Nick Kemp could see the point. When he and Chris Cowdrey made their debuts for Kent against the 1975 Australians, then Kent manager Colin Page walked over during one of the endless rain breaks and offered a few words of encouragement. 'He came up to us and said, "You don't deserve to be playing,"' Kemp relates. 'I suspect Chris wouldn't remember because he has a very different outlook, whereas it was in my nature to remember it. When I look back on how Kent cricket was run at the time I think how awful it was. It was appalling that they didn't pick David up, incredible.'

By the time Turner received Ames's letter, David had already made a few sit up at Grace Road. During the school holidays he had been turning out for Loughborough Town, and, as a consequence, came to the notice of Arthur Elliott, the club president and one of Leicestershire's co-opted county representatives, as such aides were then termed. On Elliott's say-so – 'He asked me if I'd seen this blond-haired boy, this left-hander' – Turner arranged a try-out for the second XI against their Worcestershire counterparts at Lutterworth. Mick Norman, his captain that day, remembers him playing 'a gem of an innings'. The pitch, Norman avers, 'was not terribly good', not that this deterred David in the slightest. Nor, for that matter, did any of the other hurdles that confront a schoolboy on his first day among the pros. 'He was a very personable young man,' recalls Norman, 'with a shock of fair hair and a nice, pleasant grin on one side of his face.'

He seemed very shy and laid-back; didn't say much. The young pros all had their usual mannerisms, attracting attention to themselves by being loud and not particularly welcoming to this young chap. Young pros are very suspicious, and I remember noticing this unnatural frivolity and having to remark upon it.

David fielded very well, chased everything. When we batted there was very little foot movement, and I remember some very strange mannerisms. While he was waiting for the ball to be delivered there was absolutely no movement at all; it was almost uncanny. Every player I've ever played with pats the crease, makes an involuntary movement of the feet, pulls his cap, does *something*. But here was a youth who was absolutely frozen until the ball was delivered. I remember wondering at the time how he would cope with the quick bowlers, but I didn't have long to find out. Worcestershire didn't have much in that department but anything short was dispatched in front of square, which is usually the sign of a fair player. Anything pitched up to him was crashed through the covers with that beautiful timing and elegance; anything short outside off-stump he gave himself a bit of room and gave it the full treatment. I also remember the way he picked his bat up. It seemed to have no weight in it whatsoever. He picked it up in typically uninhibited style, very high, played all the shots with this great sweep of the bat. Not for him the bat held waiting in the air. It was all old-fashioned technique.

Soon afterwards, Mike Turner recalls, an excited Norman urged him to give the boy the once-over. 'You've got to see this boy,' he insisted. Cue further outings for the Under-25s and second XI. Fresh vistas were beginning to open up.

Yet if David Gower was finding his way as a cricketer, he was rapidly losing it in academic terms. Understandably, his father's death had left 'a big gap', big enough to lead to some erratic conduct. At first, no one noticed much. David Reid was preparing to take his A-level history class to Normandy for the Easter vac when he heard about his prize student's loss.

The trip was scheduled to begin a few days later, so I telephoned Sylvia to express my condolences and ask about David. 'Please take him,' she said. 'He's been so upset this will help take him out of himself.' I like to think it helped, although he appeared quite normal. I kept an eye open but he seemed fine. But after that he found it difficult to settle in academic terms. He was halfway through his A-level course and up to that time he'd been sailing along. His A-level results were disappointing. He was at an in-between stage. If he'd got three As, he'd have strolled into Oxford; if he'd got three Es he'd have had to knuckle down and sit them again. Perhaps that unsettled him too. His mother was a regular visitor; she was a very nice lady and we communicated quite extensively. Somehow I felt David had this feeling that there were expectations. He didn't seem the type who felt pressure, academically or on the sports field, so if he did it must have been very subconscious.

David was fully aware of his father's determination for him to pursue an academic career. He freely admits he might never have become a professional cricketer had it not been for his death. It is hard to dispel the suspicion that the loss freed him from the straight and narrow.

The surest evidence of this came when David set off for his interview at St Edmund Hall. During the entrance exam he had decided to answer a question on King Arthur, whose career he had never studied. The risk paid off, and the fact that he was prepared to take it says much about this freer state of mind. On the other hand, UCL had already made him an unconditional offer to study law; maybe he wasn't that bothered. So far as everybody at King's was concerned he had also applied to do a law degree at St Edmund Hall; instead, flushed with the success of this gambit, he decided at the last to switch to his favourite subject, history, on the journey between Canterbury and Oxford – 'I panicked slightly'. When Richelieu and his chums cropped up during the course of the interview, and Merlin and Lancelot did not even rate a mention, David knew he was sunk. 'I didn't even go for a back-up interview. I'd started playing for Leicestershire Twos and I'd been smitten by the world.'

In mitigation, it must be said that his choice of college had been an untimely one. St Edmund Hall, it is true, had an enviable reputation as a sporting stronghold: of its nineteen cricketing Blues to that point, six had captained at Lord's and two – M. J. K. Smith and the South African, D. B. Pithey – had played Test cricket. Another recent graduate was Bob Hiller, one of the most reliable of all English goal-kickers. A decade earlier, David would doubtless have swanned in. The admissions policy, however, was changing, as it would elsewhere over the succeeding years. Sport, it was held, bit too deeply into study time; before long it would rank somewhere between a vice and a downright sin.

At the behest of mother and masters, David agreed to take two more A-levels in a bid to improve his grades and thus have another stab at Oxford. It was hereabouts that enthusiasm took a nosedive, the lure of even more essays and even more exams becoming ever more resistible as a viable option began to shape up. It was Bill Ashdown, Colin Fairservice's former Kent teammate and now a coach at Grace Road, who first suggested to Mike Turner that David was the reincarnation of Woolley. Terry Spencer and Maurice Hallam, the two recently retired stalwarts running the second XI, had also been smitten: cue an offer to join the playing staff for the 1975 season. David would have been content with £20 a week; Turner offered him £25 – 'He thought I was the most generous man in the world.' On 5 February 1975 Martin Johnson dictated David's name to the *Leicester Mercury* copytakers for the first time: 'The seconds will also be strengthened by the addition of David Gower, a left-handed batsman who hails from Loughborough. Gower impressed in trial games for the seconds and the Young Amateurs last season, and will be joining the club in April.' So it was that, on his eighteenth birthday, the first day upon which he could legally demand the right to leave school, David formally bade farewell to King's and trotted along to pre-season nets. Four weeks later he sent an explanatory letter to David Reid:

I have delayed writing, partly I suppose because getting down to these things has not been my strong point recently, but also because I wanted to be able to say that my experiences in the past month had borne out my decision to leave. In this I think it was the right decision especially as regards my own independence and moulding of character.

However much one escapes the restrictions at King's, I think it's still true that one leads a comparatively sheltered life there and I think that the greater independence this summer will afford me to overcome this, I suppose not too great, problem in my case, and leave me all the more ready to slip into university life.

By the way, I read that book you gave me and discovered how little local knowledge I had picked up about Canterbury during my 4½-year holiday there! Finally, can I just wish you all the best for the coming (sorry – already started) term – just hope we can at least keep the cricket cup in the house!

UCL would do, for now. The mind was still capable of doing what the heart didn't much fancy. Besides, he had no desire to upset his mother. Motions were gone through. Come September, he dutifully clocked on at Gower Street and embarked on a law degree. That sense of duty can also be interpreted as the reason why, contrary to every other account I have read of his scholastic career, including his own, David *did* take his first-year exams.

It is easy to understand why omission has been permitted to harden into accepted fact. After all, the innings that brought him to public attention – 89 not out against Roberts, Daniel and Julian when Clive Lloyd's mighty phalanx came to Grace Road the following June – was precisely eight more than the sum of those exam scores: 81 out of 400, i.e. 20.25 per cent. Any last-minute second thoughts would have been futile: he would not have been invited back. One of his professors, Michael Freeman, a Middlesex member, was hugely tickled: 'The late Professor Thomas, who took David for Roman law, and I wanted to send him a telegram when his results came through a couple of days later: "Congratulations on your 89 not out against the West Indies – that's eight more than you made for us."'

Professor Freeman was the man entrusted with teaching David the intricacies of our judicial system. Unlike so many people one interviews while researching a book of this sort, he is honest enough to confess that he may have formed certain impressions 'retrospectively'.

He came across as a bit of a playboy, looked like a rake from the twenties. He came into class with a lolloping walk, a bit like the one he came in to bat with, shrugging his shoulders, as if to say, 'this'll be a laugh for the next hour or so'. The library was regarded a bit like the nets. I don't know about lectures, but he always came to my classes, and his essays would have been perfectly competent, but they'd have been done on the hoof, I suspect. He would probably come to classes having done little work and waited for others to talk, and then ideas would come out. It was a bit like the beautiful cover drive he would execute without any practice. He has a lot of intellectual ability.

Needless to say, Professor Freeman was disappointed, albeit not wholly surprised, by how that ability was put to use. In one of his four exams David scored 7 per cent; in the professor's own subject he managed 17 per cent. His highest mark came in the least relevant subject of all: Roman law.

He wasn't a poor student. He passed most of his 'mocks' in January, and the ones he failed he didn't miss by very much, so I suspect he gave up in the spring. If he'd wanted to, he could have passed those exams with ease. It became quite clear as the year went on that he wasn't really bothering. If he had, I would have expected him to get an Upper 2nd. He was someone with a flair for language, and a wit, an ability to think on his feet. I can see him having done quite well at the bar.

One day in February or March Professor Freeman approached David in the student bar and attempted to distribute some unsolicited advice ('I was trying to be very avuncular, very paternalistic'). Come September, Freeman warned, his highest first-class score might still be 39; Leicestershire might decide to release him. Even if he did make the county grade, what was he going to do when he was thirty-five? Might it not be a good idea to get the degree and qualify as a solicitor? After all, there were any number of firms that would be only too delighted to have a high-profile cricketer on the books and grant time off during the summer. 'David turned round to me and said: "By the time I am twenty-three, I will be captain of England."' At this point, the avuncular tone turned mildly sarcastic. Whether this story is apocryphal is hard to tell, just as it is difficult to know whether David really did tell his housemaster at King's he would achieve the same goal.

On 13 July 1975, one of those long-gone (if hardly lamented) Sundays when BBC2 would devote an entire afternoon to cricket at its most bastardized, James Maxwell watched his friend make his senior debut for the Running Foxes. Surrey beat Leicestershire by 27 runs at Grace Road: D. I. Gower (opening in place of the injured John Steele) c. Skinner b. Intikhab 11. 'I wrote to him straightaway: "Well done, great to see you on TV, are you going to keep this going?" "Dear Max," he wrote back, "thanks for your letter. Yes, I think I might give cricket a go. Seems more fun than working". The broad tenor was, I'll do it for a laugh. That filled me with absolute horror. I was probably more ambitious for him than he was for himself.' And so say all of us. 'But remember,' advises Rory Bremner, 'he is an Aries.'

4 Summer Wheeze

Spread your wings, come on, fly awhile.
Ballerina, Van Morrison

'They have no tradition to inherit, no heroes to emulate. They are regarded as subordinates, an inferior race with a secondary role; nothing much is expected of them and therefore not much is forthcoming.' If Guy Willatt, the former Derbyshire player and chairman, was characterizing his erstwhile county when he uttered those words in 1970, he might just as easily have been referring to their east Midlands rivals, Leicestershire. Only just, mind. Having hitherto had no use for a trophy cabinet throughout their previous nine decades, Leicestershire made up for lost time with a vengeance, claiming six prizes between 1972 and 1985. From 1971 to 1984, their lowest championship placing was ninth. On nine occasions during that period they finished in the top five of the Sunday League. They also reached four 55-over finals, winning three. David's timing, as ever, was impeccable.

If anyone can be said to have come remotely close to being David's surrogate father, that man is Fred Rumsey, the amply girthed, genial chatterbox from Stepney who founded the Cricketers' Association while wending his way from Somerset and England left-arm quick, via Derbyshire PRO, to Lord's Taverner and popular travel agent. David even called him 'Dad', though not, perhaps, with any great seriousness. Rumsey is twenty-one years his senior, yet the pair hit it off famously when they met at a cricket dinner in Stamford ("75 or '76,' recalls 'Dad', 'I can't remember exactly'). They had much in common, attests Rumsey – 'style of living, approach to cricket, love of wine, saw both sides, a bit laid-back'. Unwittingly, Rumsey believes, 'I slipped into the father-figure role'. There were no bonds or ties, he insists: 'I was just happy to be there'. He was there in 1980 when David fleetingly contemplated jacking it all in after being dropped by England for the first time, hauling in his old friend Greg Chappell to restart the ignition. He was there thirteen years later, 'discussing the future' and kipping at Gower Manor for a couple of nights while his surrogate son was deliberating retirement. Some might consider Mike Turner to have equal claims on surrogate dad rights, partly because he pre-dated Rumsey and sought to influence David's educational decisions, partly because they worked so closely for fifteen years. Turner himself does not make such claims. This shrewd, personable and persuasive man already fulfilled essentially the same function at Grace Road.

As club secretary and, from 1969, in the then unheard-of capacity of cricket manager, which entitled him to 'full executive authority', Turner gradually achieved an overhaul of the county circuit's least prepossessing premises. A new players' pavilion was opened by the Lord Bishop of Leicester in 1965; the club's Centenary Appeal in 1978 helped fund the building of a new dining room, sponsors' suites, an indoor school, terrace seating around the ground, and a new office wing. The bulk of the financing, however, was attributable to Turner's business acumen: the Betting and Gaming Act had just brought the scratchcard lottery into vogue, and he soon logged their potential, generating the best part of a million pounds. His sagacity on the playing front was equally valuable. Turner it was who signed the ageing but still combative Tony Lock in 1965, and, four years later (thinking his Test career was over) the similarly evergreen Ray Illingworth. These two supplied the steel and expertise, transforming subordinates into competitors.

Besides taking to him from the outset, Turner also felt a degree of empathy with David. His parents, too, had urged him to take a university degree; he, too, had rebelled.

Sylvia was very keen for David to go to university, which I fully understood and appreciated. I'd spent a couple of years with Leicestershire before entering the army education corps and it seemed natural that I should go on to Loughborough to do a PE teaching diploma. But when my national service ended I was in love with cricket. In many ways I could see the same happening to David, that he'd get a taste for cricket and not want to study, so I was also keen he should go to UCL. I felt I had some extra responsibility because his father was gone and his mother pleaded with me to try and persuade him. In his first book he referred to me as being a headmaster-like figure, which I wasn't too thrilled about at the time, but now I can understand it – sort of. Having said that, he was obviously an exceptional talent, and I thought he had a great chance of a long international career, so I introduced him to Jon Holmes because I felt he should have someone to advise him from the point of view of financial management as well as from a business point of view. In those days, Jon worked for the county's brokers and for some reason I had an affinity with him.

David initially regarded Turner as 'very much like another schoolmaster' and came to think of him as 'my protection in many ways, and an adviser'.

What really struck a chord with Turner was David's approach, both to people and game.

> He frustrated me enormously at times, especially when he was captain. On the other hand, he was always charming, always courteous, always polite. And he played the game exactly the same way. He played it as I believed it should be played. It is naive, perhaps, but I still believe people should walk. I still believe cricket should mean fair play, and, to me, David demonstrated that. As a generalization I'd have thought he was an extremely popular bloke, not only in his own dressing room but on the circuit, simply because he never had any nastiness in him. People have said to me over the years, 'God, I don't know how you can stand Gower being so laid-back'; on the other hand, no one ever said to me, 'what a terrible fellow he is'. Nearly everyone likes him.

The grass wickets at Leicester Polytechnic were sodden when the John Player League champions reconvened for pre-season training on David's eighteenth birthday. There were some notable absentees: Chris Balderstone was still helping Carlisle United in their forlorn struggle against relegation from Division One; Roger Tolchard was in South Africa with D. H. Robins's mob; Graham McKenzie was coaching in what was still known as Ceylon. The remnants of the first-team squad adjourned to the gym before spending the afternoon in the Grace Road nets. Barry Dudleston was completely taken aback:

> There were a lot of triallists there and I didn't know David from Adam. I was in the next net when he took his turn and we were aware that he was getting bowled every third ball but the other two were disappearing to all parts of the field, with amazing timing. We even stopped to watch every now and again. There were a lot of others who didn't get bowled out, who wore bat, pad and bollocks, but who didn't have the talent. But this lad, whose feet didn't move, who waved his bat like a wand, and when he did make contact it was havoc. You just knew this was something special.

Martin Johnson, then the local cricket correspondent, caught his first glimpse of the new boy during the traditional pre-season soccer game in the top car park.

> He was quite shy really, and still is, I think, until he gets to know people. He wasn't as bubbly a character then as he is now, not as outgoing. I think it took him a while to find his feet. Being overawed

is too strong a word. I think he probably respected the people that were there, people like Illy, Davison, Higgs. He always gave the impression, early doors anyway, of being a good listener, but I think he was having a mental reverie. Apparently, whenever they had a team talk, Gower just lay down and went fast asleep.

In time, Johnson and Gower would become friends, an uncommon state of affairs between journalist and star; ultimately they collaborated on David's autobiography. On reading it, there is a sense of subject and ghost fusing as one. For all their manifest differences, the fact that they shared a similarly Gobi-esque sense of humour proved a sturdy foundation for a durable relationship.

When the squad assembled for the annual photo call, Nick Cook, a left-arm spinner from Leicester, was taken aback by his fellow freshman's tenuous relationship with clocks and watches. 'It was a big day for us first-year fledglings, or at least I thought so, because despite waiting for David for well over thirty minutes the photo-call went ahead with one D. I. Gower absent.' Much as timekeeping was an apparent mystery to David, no less so were the workings of the combustion engine. 'One day David arrived at Grace Road with two black eyes: most of us assumed he'd been in a fight,' recalls Cook. 'Only later did the truth come out. His car, a Triumph Spitfire if I remember rightly, was overheating. On lifting the bonnet up David saw all the steam coming from the radiator. Without any thought, he unscrewed the radiator cap, only to be scalded.'

Cook also retains fond memories of some hairy – and alcohol-fuelled – extra-curricular activities when Leicestershire played Cambridge University at the start of the 1983 season, shortly after David had returned from the most profitable of his five Australian tours. 'David, myself and a couple of other teammates allied ourselves with two students to go punting. Vessels were purloined from King's College in the small hours; the River Cam was in full spate. We weren't very good at punting, so Gower thought he'd try a different technique – only to disappear into the cold, dark, fast-flowing river. He emerged seconds later, looking like a drowned rat, and at the speed of a trident missile.' Needless to say, David went on to make 72 a few hours later. The following day's papers were full of purple epistles to the style and elegance: little did the readers know that he might as well have batted blindfold. Little, moreover, did Chris Balderstone suspect that his opening partner's refusal of off-side singles had an ulterior motive. 'We told him he had to get his first 10 runs on the leg side,' recalls James Whitaker. 'He hit his first two balls into the covers and each time Baldy set off for the other end then ran back. Same thing third ball. He took ages to work it out. The boys were pissing themselves.'

David's first real friend at Grace Road was Mick Norman, scorer of 17,441 runs and twenty-four centuries in twenty-three seasons for Leicestershire and his native Northants but now only available when school holidays freed him from his teaching duties at Bilton Grange, the 'feeder' prep for Rugby School.

> After that innings for the seconds against Worcestershire the previous season I talked to David's mother, which is probably part of the reason why he warmed to me. We chatted about his future as a cricketer, what he was going to do when he finished his studies. She seemed quite pleased but very cautious. I remember going to Grace Road the next morning full of enthusiasm, and telling Mike Turner I was extremely impressed with this boy David Gower. He only got 30 or 40, but the style, the making of it, was incredible. Mike wasn't convinced. He may not admit it now but I do because I left his office steaming. He said he was a player who looked as if he had potential but would have to change an awful lot. Weak defence was his criticism, and no footwork. I told him David was a one-off and, footwork or no, he was going to make a big splash.

Leicestershire, of course, were about to make a sizeable one of their own. The summer of 1975 was notable for a number of breakthroughs. Britain voted to join the Common Market; the West signed a human rights pact with the Soviet bloc, and, by way of emphasizing the new detente, astronaut Tom Stafford and cosmonaut Alexei Leonov shook hands 140 miles above the Atlantic. At Grace Road, home to the third most popular sporting attraction in Leicester, history of an only mildly less pleasing order was made. The reconstruction programme embarked on under Lock, and hastened under Illingworth, had reached fruition. Geary and Berry, Walsh and Astill, Watson and Marner: so many stout servants had fallen short. But now, glory be, the championship was claimed for the first time. Unencumbered by Test calls, Leicestershire did not suffer their first defeat until July, and that a one-wicket loss at The Oval (Illingworth's emotions must have been a trifle mixed: first hat-trick in a twenty-year career and still beaten!). They did not sustain another. And the triumphs didn't stop there. Ian Chappell's Ugly Australians were beaten, the Benson & Hedges Cup lifted for the second time in four seasons, and the Warwick Pool Under-25 tournament was won by the second XI, who also finished runners-up in their championship. The Running Foxes had finally got somewhere.

In a pecking order of Great County Dynasties of my lifetime the

Running Foxes of 1972–77 rank just ahead of the Neale-Botham-Dilley-Hick Worcestershire XI of the late 1980s though well behind the Middlesex XIs of Brearley and Gatting, the Essex XIs of Fletcher and the Yorkshire XIs of Close. Not even the captain's nearest and dearest would describe Illingworth's charges as a particularly inspiring combination. Diligent, hard-boiled and resourceful, yes, but more an effective collective than a fusion of the bold and the gifted. And an imported collective at that: ten players appeared in at least sixteen of Leicestershire's twenty championship fixtures that season, not one born within the county boundaries. What dynamism there was came courtesy of the tough, rambunctious Rhodesian, Brian Davison, an ex-soldier whose 1498 first-class runs at 53.50 included a career-best 189 against the Australians on a day when the next highest home contribution was the skipper's 34. At the heart of this coming-of-age lay a mature side, so mature, in fact, that, by 1981, more than half the regulars had retired.

Even more crucially, here was a side as adaptable as one of those multi-purpose kitchen implements K-Tel were flogging on the back of their pop compilation albums. Illingworth (963 runs and 48 wickets), Balderstone (1213 runs and 41 wickets), Steele (1198 runs and 33 wickets) and Birkenshaw (580 runs and 40 wickets) all welded effective batting to persistent, niggly spin. Although the slow boys, refreshingly, accounted for more than half the wickets, those venerable new-ballers 'Garth' McKenzie and Ken Higgs also did their bit, while Norman McVicker, an enthusiastic, jocular first-change, averaged 34 with the bat to supplement his 46 victims at 25. Yet no one typified the prevailing spirit better than Chris Balderstone, who, a year later, would become the last Englishman to boast a CV containing both First Division football experience and a Test cricket cap. On the second evening of the title-clinching fixture at Chesterfield, the lanky Balderstone, having helped his county glean the six bonus points required, whizzed off down the motorway to help Doncaster Rovers hold Brentford to a one-all draw – an unprecedented double. The following morning he returned to extend his overnight 51 into a match-winning 116 not out, then took three for 28 to finish the job. By rights, 15 September 1975 should have been the inaugural St Jack-of-all-Tradesmen's Day.

As twelfth man, David was at one remove: foot in the door but not yet part of the furniture. Come that final, cherished evening, he happily assumed the role of chief champagne pourer. Unsurprisingly for a boy whose life had revolved around tuck shops and homework six months earlier, his own contributions had been negligible. With first-team openings understandably rare following an initial stint as twelfth man against Worcestershire in early June, he was confined almost exclusively to second-team duties, finishing second to Martin Schepens in the run lists with 620 at a shade under 35; his highest score came against Glamorgan – bowled by a full toss for 98. The colleague with whom he most readily identified, predictably, was Davison:

Davo was a freer spirit, more fun, very good at separating the onfield from the off. He was also very competitive, and a very tough guy: when you've spent a few years in an anti-terrorist squad cricket must seem like a doddle. He wasn't one to let pressures or form affect him. If you were out of form and wanted to curl up and die, he'd have no sympathy. 'What,' he'd say, 'you're having a bad time at *cricket*!'

There were two further 90s for the second XI that season; so much for David's claim that, up to 1976, he had never been dismissed so close to three figures: another instance, perchance, of that capacity for erasing regrets. He also co-authored the three-figure opening stand with Nigel Briers that smoothed the county's path to the Under-25 final, drawing some favourable murmurings from Jim Laker. Terry Spencer touted him as 'one of the hottest young properties in the country', an opinion shared by Mick Norman, who became all the more convinced during a second XI championship fixture against Middlesex.

David really looked the part that day. I'd arrived at Grace Road ready to play against Hampshire in the B&H semi-finals when Illy tapped me on the shoulder and told me I was twelfth man. That didn't displease me too much because I wouldn't have to go out and face Andy Roberts but I'd be collecting the cash if we won. A few minutes later, another tap on the shoulder – the seconds are one short and Terry Spencer has just telephoned to say he wants me. When I got to Lutter-worth we were about 17 for four and Spencer was waving his arms furiously to get me to get my pads on. At the same time, I noticed out of the corner of my eye a rather large black chap limbering up with his foot on the sightscreen. Crikey, I thought, he takes a long run. It turned out to be Wayne Daniel, to whom Middlesex were giving a trial. Golly, he was quick. Yet while everybody else was ducking and weaving – I made a few, mostly off the edge and through the slips – David had oodles of time to play. The wicket was not the best, either, but he played with great panache, great confidence, the confidence of youth, impetuosity if you like: he proved he was a player. Barlow, Gatting and Emburey were also in that Middlesex side, and we were soundly thrashed, but David came up smelling of roses.

Less than a month later, Gower was on his way back to Loughborough after a profitable jaunt to The Hague, where he had been presented with a bat upon being named as 'Batsman of the Week' while representing England North in a somewhat innovative event: a European Under-19 tournament (it only took him a fortnight to mislay the prize). When he phoned his mother from Leicester station to request a lift home she suggested he had better take a taxi to Grace Road, pronto; John Steele had reported injured and Mike Turner had been ringing all morning. That afternoon he took his senior bow in the Sunday tilt with Surrey, and started as he meant to go on: 'Gower played one or two pleasant shots,' reported the *Leicester Mercury*, 'before falling to a careless stroke.' Thus were the first seeds of reputation sown. No less typical was David's imaginative approach to the role of drinks waiter. Lurking discreetly among the orange squashes he ferried out during one game was a G&T.

The serious business began two and a half weeks later at Blackpool. Here, again, was a career in microcosm. Coming in on the second day of the championship match against Lancashire at 111 for five, David proceeded to break his duck with a snick between first and second slip, which he repeated for his next scoring stroke. Still, sketchy starts persisted throughout his career, and portended little. 'It may be pure superstition,' he mused a few years later, 'but if I have gone in and hit the first couple for fours, I have usually felt uneasy . . . the days when I have hit the ball cleanly from the start and gone on to a big score have been rare indeed.' The fluency grew, and he had made 32 out of a 45-run stand with wicket-keeper Roger Tolchard when he was caught at mid-on off Ken Shuttleworth, the former England fast bowler who was soon to have his own peg at Grace Road. 'Gower likes the atmosphere of playing in front of a crowd,' noted the *Leicester Mercury* correspondent, with characteristic perspicacity. That Gower would initially prove far more prolific on Sundays than weekdays was scarcely coincidental.

The starlet's first cameo, however, was insufficient to prevent a prompt return to the chorus line, if only because Illingworth's exasperation over a couple of wicketkeeping cock-ups off his bowling led him to choose two stumpers for the next game.

But David could scarcely have wished for a finer tutor in the art of commitment than Illingworth, nor a more diametrically opposite pole. Among the ranks of professional Yorkshiremen – Close, Boycott, Trueman – cricket is every bit as much of a lifeforce for 'Illy' as it is for his more obsessive fellows. He's just that bit better than them at putting himself in perspective. A blurter rather than a communicator, likeable yet tactless, he has always reminded me of an enlightened despot. Things get done, good things get done, but his way or not at all. 'The severest criticism of Ray Illingworth,' Mike Brearley once proffered, 'is that he did not sufficiently discourage the element of selfishness which is part of most professional cricketers.' Close saw him along much the same lines: 'The trouble with Illy is that he always wants his own way.' He certainly got his way in March 1995, ousting Keith Fletcher and nailing down the 'supremo' role he probably should have had ten years earlier. Then, at his first press conference in the new post, Illingworth announced his aim was to 'get what cricketers we have to play consistently to their ability'; at Leicestershire, he did that with knobs on.

'Our semi-affectionate nickname for him was "Dial-a-moan" because of the inevitability of repercussions from his tongue when things went wrong,' David reflected shortly after Pudsey's finest export returned to his Yorkshire in 1979 (since he was one of the few dressing-room occupants he could turn to for help with his daily crossword, Illingworth called David 'Brain'; when he wasn't calling him a show pony, that is . . .). On the other hand, David did not take long to detect that softer, well-concealed subtle side, the side that prompted Illingworth, in his capacity as chairman of selectors, to prefer spending time with his family to having to sit through an entire series of debates over a well-concealed urn. 'If I was out cheaply, through having played a bad shot, he might sometimes have a go at me,' David reflected in 1979:

> But whereas some captains would unhesitatingly come down like a ton of bricks, Raymond would more often give me a few moments alone, then just come to me quietly and say something like: 'What are you?' It was enough to make the point. We both knew what it was.

The mutual respect would endure long past Illingworth's departure from a position of direct influence. As captain of England, David would consult Illingworth from time to time, as well one might one of the two most astute postwar England captains. 'I took a lot from Ray. He was very good for me and to me. He instilled the basic attitudes, turning the public schoolboy into a professional cricketer.'

Illingworth's tempered wrist-slapping, however, set an unfortunate precedent. A decade later, David would confess to Rory Bremner's wife Suzy that he wished he had had more 'bollockings'; throughout his career, the silences, or near-silences, that invariably greeted him upon his return to the dressing room after a dismissal did little to stir him into making amends. In many ways, he found the pussyfooting counter-productive. The point was, the aura of 'languid self-possession' that Pat Pocock would subsequently refer to left colleagues unsure how to approach him.

There were further modest championship outings at Northampton and, with a certain sense of irony, Tunbridge Wells. Even then, the return to his birthplace only came about thanks to the magnanimity of another ex-England captain. The match, a critical one, was already in progress when Brian Davison returned to Leicester upon hearing of the death of his father-in-law. However, Mike Denness, ever the gentleman, gave his permission for David to step up from twelfth man. The ending was part-storybook, part-anticlimax. True, the visitors squeezed home by eighteen runs, thanks in the main to an unbeaten ninth-wicket stand between the Supermacs, McVicker and McKenzie. By the same token, David's own contributions of 1 and 11 scarcely suggested to Kent that they were destined to pay for their neglect.

Between times, David had been drafted in for the Gillette Cup quarter-final against Gloucestershire, only to be bowled by Mike Procter for 2 as Leicestershire made a valiant if ultimately futile assault on the visitors' towering 314. The 40-over biff-and-swish did yield hints of David's quality; at this stage, the length of the contests ideally suited his attention span; besides, it was pretty much what he had been accustomed to for the past ten years. There was an unbeaten 57 at No. 6 against Essex (for whom an England discard named Gooch scored 38) and 54 going in first against Gloucestershire. *Wisden* duly singled him out as 'an exciting prospect', an emotion doubtless endorsed by the country's car dealers. By now, David had acquired the family Ford Anglia, a vehicle that had somehow survived the journey from East Africa to Loughborough fifteen years previously; it failed to last three months in the new owner's hands. On the way home one night, David rolled it into a ditch at Narborough; mercifully, both car and hedge were more grievously hurt than driver. Next up was a Mini of similar vintage: within a week, the engine had exploded. Happily, the era of the sponsored car was dawning.

Mick Norman was keenly aware that David had an inherent disadvantage, and did his best to help him overcome it. 'Public schoolboys are not always welcomed with open arms in county cricket, at least they weren't in those days. They were always considered a threat, though not to me because I was about to retire. But he was thoroughly likeable, and made himself popular with everybody. I always encouraged him.' Barry Dudleston endorses such a view:

David was a breath of fresh air. I left Leicester in 1980 and in all that time nobody had ever had a bad word to say about him. To a degree he was a more private person than people thought. You'd look around at the end of the day and he'd vanished: nobody would know where he'd gone. He wouldn't be in the bar every night, reminiscing about the game, in everyone's pockets for four hours after play was over. He had those two compartments to his life. Very nicely, without you even realizing it, he never actually let you get close to him. Whether that was because of, or in spite of, his father dying, I don't know. At the same time, there was this flip sense of humour. In one of his early games we were playing at Lord's and staying at the Clarendon Court and he came down to breakfast in jeans and a t-shirt. And Illy – talk about a generation gap – gave him a bollocking. There was plenty of mutual respect there already but he frustrated Illy.

Illingworth himself picks up the story:

David was lazy in the extreme when he started. I gave him some rollockings on dress, on dashing into the dressing room at the last minute. At Trent Bridge soon after that Clarendon Court episode he came in with a black shoe on one foot and a brown one on the other. He'd obviously just dashed out of bed, curtains half-drawn. To be fair, he took the rollocking well and we came down to Taunton and – sharp intake of breath as he walks into breakfast in his dinner suit ('dinner jacket, dress shirt, bow tie and smart strides', David would subsequently itemise, 'my sense of the ridiculous'). 'Is this all right, captain?' he said. 'Yes,' I said, 'have you just bloody walked in?'

David claims there was a pause of about ten seconds while Illingworth unscrambled his eggs and calculated precisely the right rejoinder; Barry Dudleston remembers it as 'one of the few times Illy was lost for words'. Illingworth felt tolerance was needed, as well as discipline:

I accommodated David when he was seventeen: he was the finest timer of a cricket ball I'd ever seen. I never tried telling him to stop playing his shots. We sent him in early on Sundays to give him a chance to play them. If you had to make a criticism it would be that things have always come too easily for him. He's been pretty lucky financially as well. The money started to go up when he came into Test cricket; his mum died and left him two hundred-odd thousand: he never had any financial problems, from twenty onwards, anyway. He didn't have worries the way most players do, not that this created any ill-feeling. He was very easygoing, possibly a bit too easygoing. He never did anything to annoy you but . . . it's the modern generation, I suppose.

The old moaner was also quick to detect a technical weakness:

David had no real idea how to play the turning ball at all: the amazing thing was how much he improved in twelve months. Unbelievable. We used to keep one wicket that would always allow some turn, and Birkenshaw, myself, Steele and Balderstone all bowled to him a lot over that period. In my final season with Leicestershire, Jack and I bowled to him in the Lord's nets and never once got him out. His development was one of the most exciting experiences in my whole career.

By way of reciprocation, David made it clear that Illingworth's greatest legacy to him was what he taught him about facing the twirly boys and fiddly men; specifically, 'the need to be decisive'.

'If I were to pick a fault,' continues Illingworth:

it would be that he never worked quite as hard on playing seam bowling when the ball was moving around. We had some marvellous batting wickets, a good, hard track with very little grass on it, so the ball did come on a bit. To see him play on those pitches was something else. You'd always come out on the balcony to watch him play, even as a seventeen-year-old. He took some world-class quick bowlers apart on those wickets. He probably felt he didn't need to do a lot more.

Illingworth recalls the ever quipful Birkenshaw being especially voluble when it came to doling out reminders about the need to concentrate. 'I can remember David playing a rather casual shot in a championship match and Jack getting up and shouting at him from the balcony, "Gower . . . !" It was a sort of growled shout which was nevertheless audible all over the field with the implication of its tone quite unmistakable. David looked up. He understood.' At first, Illingworth also remonstrated with the youngster for his mental lapses: 'Because we got him when he was very young and hammered him for a year I think it made him capable of playing big innings. The raw material was always there.' Before long, the scolding gave way to the nudge. 'Do I have to say anything?' the captain would ask the errant youth, and leave it at that. As early as 1979, David admitted that his approach was too ingrained for modification: 'I know I am an instinctive batsman and that will never change. Once I have played myself in, I play strokes naturally. My sort of player is always giving the bowlers a chance.'

On the eve of the 1976 campaign David collected £25 and the Livingston Cup as the county's most improved uncapped player. 'Unless some unforeseen lapse in form occurs,' wrote Martin Johnson, 'Gower surely has a big future in the game . . . but how sensible he is to have resisted the temptation to go full-time before scaling the last rung of the educational ladder'. Within a couple of months, temptation had prevailed. On 9 June, David left Gower Street for the last time and motored to Worcester for a Benson & Hedges Cup quarter-final. He contributed 35 to a promising Leicestershire total of 268 for five, but not even Illingworth's canny field placings could curb Ormrod, D'Oliveira and Imran Khan as they drove the hosts to victory with two balls to spare.

'The great worry for sportspeople,' says David now, 'is that you try something, suck it and see, then find out after five years that it's not happening, so you've wasted five years. If it goes well, you carry on. I didn't go into cricket with any real concepts, but pretty soon it became one. I played well enough quickly enough.' One innings against Clive Lloyd's rampaging West Indian tourists was more than sufficient to vindicate David's decision to forgo security. Fortified by a scotch from Hazel, the life and soul of The Cricketers pub adjoining the press box end at Grace Road (Roberts and Daniel were on the bill: so much for that mythical nervelessness), he resorted to 'the duck-hook' more than a few times during an unconquered 89 full of courage, and no little vivacity. But for Illingworth's declaration, Nigel Briers is convinced he would have reached three figures: 'He was magnificent, took them all on. He was quick with his feet, exciting. There was a certain beauty about it.'

With due sense of occasion, however, the maiden century was reserved for Lord's. That was the day David felt the loss of his father most acutely, which may help explain why Professors Freeman and Thomas believe he snubbed them at the close. In what *Wisden* saluted as 'the only quality batting of the match', David cast aside the memory of a first-innings blob in a vibrant stand with Davison. Uncowed by the uneven bounce that had enabled Mike Gatting, of all people, to pick up three wickets for nine runs in his opening six overs in the first innings, the third-wicket pair shared an unbroken alliance of 236 after Mike Selvey had reduced Leicestershire to 8 for two second time round; Middlesex's two innings raised just 213 runs as the eventual champions went down to their heaviest defeat of the season. Little did the gallery suspect that David had returned to his hotel room around dawn that morning, or that he had slept through lunch despite being in the nineties, or that 'the repeated stabs between overs from the business end of Brian Davison's bat' were merely a means of keeping him awake.

'Dave was paralytic,' avows Roger Tolchard. 'It was amazing he got through the Long Room and on to the bloody pitch! He never made contact for half an hour. Then, all of a sudden, he started playing and never looked back. But that's the game.' Martin Johnson claims he was 'spark out' during lunch:

> He had to be kicked and shovelled back out. He played and missed two balls before he got his hundred; he looked completely out of it. There was a bit of everything in that innings. Probably his entire career. The half-asleep shot, probably a drop in the gully at some stage, some delightful shots, then he'd drop off for ten minutes. The only time he ever really defended was if he was in trouble, and at times like that he took a deep breath and concentrated very hard on the bowling for a very short period of time.

The experience also had a familiar ring for Michael Freeman. The law professor's own county were heading for the abattoir yet here he was, revelling in the slaughter, and none too guiltily at that: 'I had the same philosophy as the boy at Lord's who said, "Please God, let Barry Richards make a hundred and Hampshire 120."' Any sportsman who can turn the opposition's supporters into gleeful turncoats has to be cherished.

Although the Drenched Poodle Perm made its inaugural appearance in *Wisden* the following spring, David's other five championship outings that summer brought meagre returns. It cannot have helped to be opening one match and then demoted to No. 8 the next, not least since his natural berth was in the middle order. Indeed, there would probably have been even fewer opportunities had Dudleston not suffered four finger breaks. His highest score post-Lord's was 33, fashioned at the top of the order in the final fixture at Taunton, where a rumbustious 88 from the sturdy young Somerset No. 4 played no small part in consigning the outgoing champions to defeat. Thus was David introduced to a one-man arsenal by the name of I. T. Botham.

David's county input was also restricted by the Young England tour of the Caribbean in late July and August, a memorable venture for many reasons but primarily of a romantic nature. Tolchard recalls him dating 'a thirtysomething divorcee' when he first joined Leicestershire, and David had moved on to a 'steadyish' girlfriend in London when he met a glamorous lass from Reading named Vicki Stewart in a Grenada bar. She was in town visiting her father, an agricultural adviser: 'David was making a thorough nuisance of himself with me, but I didn't fancy him at all. He just wasn't my type and I wasn't in the least interested in cricket.' At first, David had to take a back seat to Chris Cowdrey. Indeed, so keen was Vicki to impress the captain, she stowed away in a cargo boat bound for Trinidad, scene of the next 'Test'. 'Vicki was sort of my girlfriend,' recalls Cowdrey. 'I used to see quite a lot of her in Reading when we got back. We used to have a joke that our relationship – mine and Vicki's that is – fell through when I found David's England tie on her bedroom door. There was an element of truth there – I did lose my tie on tour – but there was no question of him stealing her off me.'

Another graduate from the Crocodiles tour, Nick Kemp, makes no bones about having turned a brighter shade of green: 'I've got some wonderful photos of Vicki on that Caribbean tour: I was intensely jealous. She was sixteen, with auburn coloured hair, all the bumps in the right places, pretty face, white teeth – absolutely stunning.' One way or another, remembers Kemp, there was no shortage of fun once all the six-foot-eight local quicks had clocked off. 'We had quite a wild time. Hubert Doggart and Les Lenham, the management team, kept a pretty close rein on us, but when we were allowed out on our own we gave it a rip. We were a bunch of nineteen-year-olds on a jamboree. David wasn't the life and soul; he was one of those people who was right in there, but not carrying centre stage.'

With half a dozen future Test players on board, the trip was a resounding triumph from a playing perspective, all six games being won despite a rash of injuries. David finished third in the tour averages to Gatting and Cowdrey with 441 runs at 33.92, the most vital knock coming in the four-day 'Test', when his 49 was the second-highest innings in a low-scoring match. 'Barbados was the first time I saw the genius,' remembers Cowdrey. 'He had a bit of a problem, left some kit at the hotel, a bat, maybe a pad, so he went back to retrieve it and, as a consequence, arrived late. Typical Gower: he walked straight in and just took command. Four after four after four. He'd made 45 out of an opening stand of 50 when he was bounced out, caught on the boundary. What a shame, we thought, but it was incredible. I don't think he knew any other way to play.'

Did that way signify a certain vanity, a dash of self-admiration? 'An element maybe,' David concedes. He prefers to call it instinct.

Everything you do in the space of point four of a second *has* to be largely instinctive. In other words, when you go out to play you're relying totally on instinct . . . well, 80 per cent. The 20 per cent is the day you realize you can't play that way and the conditions mean you have to adapt your style, but that's also part of your instinct. I remember, very early on, going out to bat against Norbert Philip at Grace Road. He got a couple of quick wickets and was bowling quite sharp, and it probably did need someone to hang in there for another half-hour while he got tired. I went in there blazing. That's my best method of countering this. I played a couple of huge shots then nicked it. It was an adrenalin situation. You come back fighting. Experience counters it in a different way. Part of it, though, was not really wanting to compromise.

Cowdrey found the comparison between Gower and Gatting an intriguing one. 'David didn't have a big tour but Gatting had a great one: first at the ground for practice each day, practise all day, good fielder, bowled a bit. You could see he was going to play for England. Gower you thought, well, this guy's fantastic, he's unbelievable, but is he ever going to get the runs Gatt gets? Gower was the best player on that tour but you'd have backed Gatting to make it.'

Malcolm Marshall, one of two opponents David would bump into at Test level (Everton Mattis was the other), had made a swift impression on the tourists when they took on Barbados Youth, skulling Bill Athey with a first-ball bouncer. First impressions proved indelible:

> From the moment I first saw Gower I realized that here was a player of exceptional talent. Gatting did not look happy unless he could lunge forward at every ball, Athey was the most technically correct, but when it came to class, flair and the ability to improvise, Gower was simply streets ahead. I should imagine Hartley Alleyne must have seemed pretty quick to the English boys but twice he strayed a little in length and line and Gower belied his frail looks by punishing him with searing boundaries. I turned to a crestfallen Hartley – and I take no credit for my remarks – and told him: 'This boy will play for England.'

On his return in early September, David kick-started a successful Sunday chase at The Oval, collecting 48 in 37 minutes with seven fours, whereupon the humdrum beckoned in the guise of a winter assignment at the local Bostik traffic office, as 'deputy clerk in charge of teas'. Label-printing, van-driving and tin-stacking were not quite as taxing as his employers would have wished: 'I thought my incentive for doing things fast would be to put my feet up and have a longer break. Instead, I was regularly given a rollocking for lazing about.'

October brought a reminder of the one profession where they paid you to laze: a silver and onyx trophy – plus £250 – as Leicestershire's most promising player of 1976; two months later he signed on the dotted line and turned full-time cricketer. To Martin Johnson, this was something of a misnomer: 'He always gave the impression he was playing the old-fashioned amateur, that it was a bit of a hobby. Even in those days you got that feeling.' At the time, nevertheless, Johnson's reports betrayed more than a sneaking admiration. 'To say that David Gower bats,' he informed his readers the following May, 'is rather like Nureyev saying he does the hokey-cokey.'

Not that this change of status presaged a change of approach. 'I've thrown my lot in with cricket now, and have no regrets about doing so,' he assured the *Leicester Mercury*. 'But while I'm not afraid to work hard, I'll never let this game get on top of me. If I got ten ducks in a row I wouldn't get into a state about it. When I leave this game I want to do it under my own steam, not with the assistance of half a dozen blokes in white coats.' Little did he realize how close he would come to doing just that.

At the start of his first full county season David moved into the spare room in Roger Tolchard's Leicester apartment. But bar the fact that both were former public schoolboys – Tolchard's alma mater was Malvern – there was little initial common ground between the flatmates. There were ten years between them, for one thing, not to mention a profound difference in attitude. For Van Morrison fans, if David was *No Teacher, No Guru, No Method*, 'Tolly' was *Hardnose the Highway*. It is difficult, nay impossible, to picture David taking a 40-over game seriously enough to be given out obstructing the field, as his landlord was at Lord's in 1972. Off the last ball of an innings. With a century to his name.

All the same, Tolchard likes to think some of his dedication rubbed off. Indeed, the relationship prospered to such an extent he would ask David to be his best man.

> Despite the age difference we got on fine. Dave was a nice young lad, very pleasant, honest, straightforward. His batting reflected his personality. He was totally modest about whatever he did. Even in the early days, you would never have known whether he'd made a duck or a century. There was a front there, mind, and you never did get inside him. He was a typical teenager: late sleeper, clothes everywhere, washing-up piled in the sink. He probably cooked more than me. He talked a bit about his problems with spin but I could never talk cricket for long; I usually end up arguing with people because I don't agree a lot of the time with how others see things. I used my feet as a defensive technique, to kick the ball away, and David also learned to play with his pads; it messes bowlers up. He never gave the impression he wanted to make money; life just went on. I knew his mum quite well and I think I probably suggested to her that he moved in with me when it became clear he wanted to leave home. Because of her age she was more a grandmother than a mother.

Vicki was a frequent visitor to the bachelor pad. 'Back then, I never felt totally comfortable with her,' Tolchard says of the woman who is now godmother to one of his children. 'You had to like her but I was probably pleased for David when they didn't marry. It just didn't seem quite right, but of course there was no way of telling him that. She was there when he needed her; he never saw it any other way. Marriage never crossed his mind, just as it never did mine until I was thirty-five.'

In social terms, Martin Johnson recalls the twenty-year-old David as 'a bit of a bravura stopout artist'. When he wasn't entertaining or galli-vanting, he could be found propped up in bed, stereo blasting out the tempered technocrat-rock of Supertramp or Genesis, or, at more con-templative moments, a touch of Vaughan Williams or Ludwig Van. Sometimes he would leaf through a *Wizard of Id* cartoon book or *Punch* (in preference to the 'less subtle satirism' of *Private Eye*), at others immerse himself in a Wilbur Smith or le Carré. Eating has always been more pleasure than necessity – John Gower recalls his nephew taking 'an age' perusing the menu when he took him out for dinner during his student days – but even at this juncture the experience was incomplete without a bottle of Pouilly Fuissé. Beer was consumed 'in moderation'; having acquired a taste for it in the Caribbean, rum soon became the preferred alternative. When the Leicestershire players were invited to a cheese and wine party at Lord Crawshaw's residence in aid of Tolchard's benefit, David's growing passion for port was assisted by a successful bid for a bottle of Croft '45.

Vino was uppermost on the booze list, however. Some regarded David's penchant for fine wines as his way of showing off his sophistication. Others saw it as a social lubricant. He would say that his palate demanded it. At the last count he had over fifty cases of claret and port stored in temperature-controlled cabinets. 'He found wine early doors,' remembers Johnson, 'but it took him a long time to go up through the bottles. He used to be a £2.99 man. I did about twelve summers with Leicestershire and there were only two blokes who, if I met them in the bar after the close, I did not feel the need to say "bad luck" or "bloody well played" just to get the conversation going. James Whitaker was one and Gower was the other. Gower would never look for a word of praise or be half on the defensive. He had no interest at all in what I'd written.'

David did have an interest in Dutch landscape paintings and antique furniture, and took photography seriously enough to replace his trusty instamatic with an expensive Pentax once his graduation to the international arena had made such extravagances possible. 'I enjoy catching people off-guard,' he explained in his first book, *With Time To Spare*, written with Alan Lee and published in 1980 in association with David Gower Promotions. 'I will happily sit for long periods waiting for the right moment. I want to do it well, not just have a batch of meaningless snaps.' If a thing was worth doing, went the rationale, it was worth doing bloody well.

Martin Johnson was less convinced:

When he found out that he could actually make a fairly decent living without too much work, I think his natural character flipped in. I've always been of the opinion that you can't really change people's characters; you can change the player. I think in cricket, more than any other sport, you can almost tell a bloke's character within half an hour of watching him on the field. And Gower was absolutely in that category. If an easy option was there kicking around, he'd seize on it and say, 'y'know, old Bloggs thinks the answer to a string of low scores is to switch off'; whereas eight people out of ten would say, 'we've got to get down to some hard work'.

And still more contradictions – or was it simply a desire for the best of all possible worlds? In *With Time To Spare*, Alan Lee characterized his co-author as 'a country boy by birth and upbringing, but a city lover periodically, by nature'. David confirmed this apparent conflict: 'I am not the rural sort who could exist solely in quiet countryside. I seem to have a personality which craves the best of both worlds.' Much as he was prone to seek out the pastoral atmosphere of Rutland Water or Charnwood Forest, standing in the middle of Leicester Square, 'just studying people and the way they behave', also had its attractions.

This aptitude for the multi-dimensional was reflected in David's fielding. From his vantage point as principal target, Tolchard was ideally placed to assess David's capabilities, capabilities all too easily forgotten in the wake of the shoulder problems that drastically impaired his effectiveness throughout the second half of his career. When he and Derek Randall were in harness – the one gliding, the other scampering, both attacking, daring, conning – the run-out was malice aforethought rather than an accident waiting to happen. The best outfielders normally hunt alone; few international sides can ever have boasted two such prehensile presences simultaneously.

David credits Ray Illingworth as a prime influence: 'He would hold sessions in which he crucified us for being casual, and took us back to what he called "the ABCs of cricket". They included using two hands to pick up the ball whenever possible – at school, it had seemed "flash" to only use one hand, and I carried that attitude on to Leicester, where Illy rapidly drummed it out of me.' Tolchard was awestruck: 'He was brilliant, quick as light. He could field at slip or gully and catch anything, or come up close because he was as brave as anything, or be a panther in the outfield. He never looked quick because he just glided.'

With the selectors, for once, resisting the mono-dimensional allure of statistics, David was chosen to play for the MCC against Middlesex at the start of the 1977 season (how many other batsmen have earned such an honour after a dozen first-class appearances?). Coming in at No. 5, a role more appropriate to his mindset than that of opener, though still not ideal, he was run out for 25, a good score on a seamer-friendly pitch that allowed only Botham to reach 50. Soon afterwards came an even more valuable brush with reality. Opening against Surrey at The Oval, a stream of crisp and creamy cover drives against the new ball earned an introduction to the sharpest end of Robin Jackman's rasping tongue. Was this dilettante really interested in playing the game properly, queried the Shoreditch Sparrow, or words to that effect. The bowler's oldest ruse worked a treat: palpably unsettled, David quickly fell leg-before. 'It's the sort of thing a batsman eventually comes to terms with,' he subsequently reflected, 'and occasionally learns to enjoy, but it was all rather new to me at the time and I didn't quite know how to keep my concentration in the face of it. In a nutshell, I was beginning to learn that county cricket was a job as opposed to a recreation.'

Luton in August rammed home the point. Against Northants in a John Player game reduced to ten overs a side, he went to hook Alan Hodgson but succeeded only in top-edging the ball into the bridge of his nose and under his left eye. Though he retired hurt with a couple of fast-developing shiners, and was whisked off to hospital for a couple of stitches, he was back in the fray six days later. As fate would have it, Northants were the opposition once more, and Hodgson was primed. Nerves were soothed by an on-drive for four, and although Bedi undid him without much further ado, Illingworth's benefit match the following afternoon saw David restored to the rudest of health with an unbeaten 135, the season's highest individual one-day score to date. Resilience, quite clearly, was one of his stronger suits.

That Leicestershire regained the 40-over crown that summer was due in no small part to David's 622 runs at 56.56. Installed as opener in place of the off-form John Steele, all his substantial knocks, revealingly, came on Leicestershire soil, where he amassed 491 runs at 122.75, exceeding 75 in five of his eight sojourns at the crease. The bond with the Grace Road regulars was strong from the outset; it needed to be. In fifteen summers, he would manage just eight championship hundreds there. Such early extravaganzas constituted insurance for the years of implenitude.

Illingworth still sounds breathless when he recounts the day David waded into Mike Procter. In the first over of the Sunday match against Gloucestershire, David despatched the redoubtable Durbanite for three fours before pulling in the reins: 'I kept telling myself that I mustn't give it away'. He didn't, either; at one stage he faced nineteen balls without scoring. Then there was his first Man of the Match award. The previous summer, Hertfordshire had become the first minor county to reach the quarter-finals of the Gillette Cup; this time the colts fell at the first hurdle as David stroked an unbeaten 117 in two hours. On the basis of deeds such as these, he was awarded his county cap.

Gower and Tolchard shared many a spirited limited-overs partnership, liaisons the impish Devonian still treasures.

I loved batting with him. He was magic on Sundays because he had the ability to get the ball away. I'd be playing tip-and-run and he'd be easing it into the outfield, all on the deck in the arc between extra cover and gully. Not ideal at Test level, admittedly, but highly effective on Sundays. He scored so many runs in that arc, in all forms of cricket.

He looked to run as well, which suited me fine. My priority was not so much to fire him up as encourage him. 'C'mon, Dave,' I would keep saying, 'don't let *him* get you out.' And when he did get out, I'd always defend him. I would always say, 'unlucky – doing a bit today, isn't it?', hoping he would cotton on to the fact that when it was doing a bit he would be that more careful.

If David would have preferred both encouragement and criticism, in some respects he got it. 'There was never any sympathy with Illy,' alleges Tolchard:

Everything was always expected. There were never any well-dones. I used to give him an earful about that. I also used to have a go at him for not caring. During the championship season, we were seven down against Warwickshire at tea on the last day, with more than 100 to get, and I noticed Illy had his bag packed and was heading for the car. I was 50-odd not out. 'You off, Illy?' I said. 'Thanks.' In the end, I made a hundred and we won by one wicket. Illy's strength was his logical thinking, his down-to-earth character. He didn't play hunches; if it was turning he'd bowl the spinners until the opposition were bowled out, which could be a bit frustrating at times.

Yet for all David's exploits over the shorter course, consistency at first-class level remained elusive. His solitary championship hundred of 1977 was a majestic, matchwinning 144 not out against Hampshire at Grace Road; in his other twenty-eight championship innings, by contrast, he could manage only 445 runs, spinners proving his undoing nearly half the time. It was, perhaps, with this inconsistency in mind that he was omitted from the England party bound for New Zealand and Pakistan, even though Packer 'defections' had ruled out Bob Woolmer, the circuit's most accomplished opener cum first-drop. Gatting packed instead, as did Paul Downton. While Illingworth denied a claim by the chairman of selectors, Alec Bedser, that he had advised him not to pick David on the grounds that he wasn't ready, he did admit asking one of the other selectors, J. T. Murray, not to plunge him in against Australia earlier that summer. 'I wanted to let him develop and learn with Leicestershire,' Illingworth reasoned in his *Leicester Mercury* column. 'I have never been approached officially since then ... I've been pressing for Gower to be included in the tour party for some weeks. The fact is, I've never ever spoken to Bedser about the matter. It looks as if he's just making a feeble excuse for not picking him.' At least the Lord's Taverners, who voted David their most promising player of 1977, were able to detect a touch of class when it was staring them in the face.

Tolchard totally refutes any inference that David's lack of productivity in the championship was indicative of a burgeoning scorn for the county game:

It always amazed me that people thought he was getting out on purpose, that he didn't care. That was so unfair. I can't believe he ever went into a county game without wanting to get some runs. He had the ability to cream balls the rest of us were happy to keep out, good length balls that everyone else had to block. It was unbelievable to hear Boycott saying he should have blocked the ball more. Given an ability like David's he should have been encouraged to play more shots. You might lose games playing the Boycott way, but you don't win them.

As fate would have it, David savoured his winter rather more than Gatting did his (by the time the fledgling Falstaff was granted his second England tour, David had reached 1000 Test runs more rapidly than any Englishman before or since). First up was a month in the Far East with one of Derrick Robins's customary star-studded outfits, during the course of which its youngest member collected centuries in Hong Kong and Malaysia followed by a top score of 59 in his side's only innings against a powerful Sri Lanka Board President's XI. David and Chris Cowdrey 'behaved pretty poorly' and grew close. David had gone on another of the philanthropic Mr Robins's sorties the previous winter, this time to Canada, where the visitors encountered problems aplenty in Edmonton from those opposed to Robins's apparent efforts to undermine the anti-apartheid movement by maintaining sporting links with South Africa. David had little sympathy for the demonstrators' motive, as he saw it, reasoning, somewhat cynically, that they 'picked on us as their practice targets for the Commonwealth Games two years later'. Robins had long since left the Midlands to settle in South Africa, and was widely regarded as a pawn of apartheid; David found him 'genial but moody', and defended him to the hilt.

On the face of it, he was justified in doing so. It was Robins, after all, who had taken the first multi-racial side to the Republic in 1973–74, and Robins who had persuaded the home board to field its very first multi-racial XI. 'They [the Edmonton demonstrators] were overlooking the fact,' David argued, 'that by organizing teams to undertake multi-racial cricket tours out there, he had made considerable efforts to break down apartheid policies.' However, the fact remains that Robins's love of cricket blinded him to the salient point that the very existence of such tours as his undermined the widely agreed policy of sporting isolation, the policy that would ultimately do so much to help bring down one of the twentieth century's least palatable regimes.

David spent the rest of the winter of 1977 in a land riven by controversy of a rather less significant hue. When the Somerset captain, Brian Rose, was selected for the England tour, the Perth club, Claremont-Cottesloe, cast around for a late replacement and invited David on the recommendation of former teammate and Cottesloean, Graham McKenzie. There was scant evidence of arm-twisting. Weekdays were whiled away on a beach obligingly cooled by the afternoon sea breeze (the 'Fremantle Doctor'); two or three evenings were given over to coaching, and weekends to a grade competition denuded by the Packer rebellion. The battle between tradition and future was now being waged on David's doorstep. Not that that was going to stop him soaking up his rays. 'I loved the sun, loved the fact that it shone all the time,' he reflected on air during the fifth Test at the WACA in 1995. 'I coached a seven-year-old who became a gym instructor. Did a good job, didn't I?' He also met Nicholas Duncan, who subsequently started up an Australian branch of SAVE, a New York-based charity raising funds for Africa, particularly for the preservation of the black rhino.

The faster pitches in Western Australia forced David to revamp his technique against pace, beginning an evolution from an almost exclusively front-foot style to one that saw just about everything essayed off the back foot. He felt 'safer and more balanced' there. Wittingly or not, he was emulating one of his heroes, Gary Sobers. Nick Kemp is reminded of a conversation he once had with the maestro after a round of golf in Barbados.

We were talking about his 254 for the Rest of the World against Australia in 1971–72. 'What's the secret?' I asked him. 'I noticed that you hardly moved your feet in that innings.' Well, he said, the art of batting is not stepping forward or back; you wait until the last possible minute to hit the ball. If you say you're going to play forward you're not going to be in the right position if the ball isn't totally there. You play everything off the back foot.

If it's good enough for the great Garfield himself, who are we to argue?

5   Songs in the Key of Youth

'Everybody wants to be Cary Grant. Even I want to be Cary Grant.'
Cary Grant

Twenty-six-point-nine-four. *Twenty*-six-point-nine-four. Has any batsman ever been hailed as a world-beater with such a paltry first-class
average? Has any player ever been picked for his country on such flimsy
statistical evidence? Fifty-four completed innings, 1455 runs, five fifties
and two centuries: that, on the surface, was David Gower's less than
unanswerable case for inclusion in the England XI for the first Test
against Pakistan at Edgbaston in 1978. For the first time, the two finest
English cricketers of the impending Thatcher era were united under one
flag. Ian Botham was the one who scored the century, his first in a home
Test, but who remembers that?

Thousands, on the other hand, remember precisely where they were
and what they were doing the moment David scored his first runs for
England (who says television undermines the national fabric and debases
culture?).

The capacity to turn a mundane context into an indelible memory is
a gift confined to few sporting moments – to either the truly inspirational
or the truly awful. Other candidates include the moment Some People
Came On The Pitch Because They Thought It Was All Over; the
moment Bob Willis harpooned Ray Bright at Headingley; the moment
the Hand of God gave the world's greatest juggler of leather spheres a
needless leg-up; the moment Trevor McDonald led off News at Ten
with those shots of Eric Cantona extracting revenge on the yob who
insulted his mother. True, the ball that made Liaquat Ali Khan the best-
paid after-dinner speaker in the history of Habib Bank may have been
truly awful for the bowler at that precise moment, but I'm sure he got
over it.

David Gower was the last of the Modern English Jazz Quartet to land a
gig at the Talk of the Town. Gooch was first capped in 1975, Botham
in 1977, Gatting in January 1978. The state of the nation, moreover,

seemed as unhealthy on the greensward as it was poorly elsewhere. Only one English sporting team fulfilled its function over those final depressing two years of the last Labour government: the flannelled collective. Between successive Ashes slaughters came comfortable wins over Pakistan and New Zealand; Willis chilled, Botham thrilled, Gower twirled; Brearley was Patton with a PhD. 'Brearley goes down as one of the great captains,' emphasizes Bob Willis, 'but he happened to have Botham at his best, me at my best, Old at his best, Lever at his best and Hendrick at his best. Mike Atherton would dream of having *one* of those at their best.'

Somewhat conveniently, the opposition was about as bracing as a weak cup of Darjeeling. The best had embraced Packer's brash new world: Chappell, Lillee and Marsh; Lloyd, Richards and Roberts; Majid, Zaheer and Asif. England had lost Greig, Knott, Underwood and Woolmer from the side that retrieved the Ashes in 1977; bar Alvin Kallicharran, the West Indies selectors had to come up with an entirely new XI (and, in contrast to their English counterparts, their shortlist was *really* short). Neither the advent of the Modern English Jazz Quartet, nor the skills of an outstanding bandleader, could camouflage the decline in technique spurred by the introduction of a *third* one-day tourney in 1972. Neither could either bridge the gulf in desire prompted by Packer. In much of the Commonwealth, where career choices were more limited, where future possibility counted far more than a painful, acquiescent past, it was money that lit the torch. The rise of the non-white nations and the belated establishment of cricket as a remunerative profession are inextricably linked.

While the soulless concrete bowl that is Edgbaston will forever, perversely, be synonymous with the first flowering of Gower, the blooming actually began nearly a month earlier, during the MCC–Pakistan match at Lord's. In fact, it is seldom remembered that Liaquat won the pair's first duel, bowling Gower for 16 when Wasim Bari's Packerized party – no Imran, no Zaheer, no Mushtaq, Majid or Asif – came to Grace Road at the end of April. Having gone in at No. 5 both against the tourists and in Leicestershire's opening championship fixture, here, significantly, David batted at No. 4, behind the England captain, Brearley, and two other uncapped aspirants, John Hopkins of Glamorgan and John Whitehouse of Warwickshire, the Cricket Writers' Club's Young Cricketer of the Year back in 1971. With no formal trial scheduled, the selectors had taken the opportunity to run the rule over a number of likely lads in advance of the Prudential Trophy one-day series. At No. 5 was Gatting, at No. 6 Larkins: five ambitious young men chasing one place. With the ball jagging every which way off the pitch, those hardened swingers

Sarfraz Nawaz and Chris Old had a whale of a time; the upshot was one half-century in thirty-five attempts. While Whitehouse and Hopkins aggregated 17 runs in four innings, and Larkins made 16 and 0 not out, David revealed his mettle by scoring more runs than his four rivals put together. His 71 in the second dig was hailed by the chairman of selectors as an effort 'oozing class'. He was the only batsman in the match to disdain the shackles of nervy introspection. To be himself.

Self backed, instinct trusted, it was pretty much plain sailing from there on. A call-up for the first 55-over international at Old Trafford resulted in an auspicious but by no means earth-shattering contribution to a total of 217 for seven, that seemingly innocuous wobbler Mudassar Nazar beginning an unlikely hold over David by nobbling him mid-stride for 33 (the scorer of the most sluggish century in Test history would claim his wicket four times in five-day play, the same as Hadlee would manage, and more than Thomson, Roberts, Walsh, Wasim or Qadir: David always did have a penchant for walloping the best balls and getting spanked by the unworthy). There were no such short measures at The Oval. Entering at 60 for two, he relied primarily on hooks and drives to reach 53 out of 78 off sixty-eight balls, and then, in a furious flurry, add 41 with Old off the final five overs. Unafraid to take the aerial route, he was dropped at long-on off the left-arm spinner, Naeem, but that was the only blemish on an otherwise pristine knock. The standing ovation that greeted his eventual unconquered 114 was intoxicating.

For some unfathomable reason, I felt obliged to work that day–in exchange, that is, for various promises from Hamley's colleagues that I could bunk off once the Tests began – and a quick scan of the following morning's rave notices confirmed that I had indeed missed something out of the ordinary. In the *Telegraph*, Michael Melford wrote that David's hundred 'must have fulfilled the highest hopes of those who have been waiting eagerly for his elevation to this company'. 'Everything . . . paled into insignificance after the glory of Gower,' exulted Pat Gibson in the *Daily Express*. 'Greatness? Perfection? Genius?' wondered Peter Laker in the *Daily Mirror*. 'Well, maybe not yet. But such are the enormous natural gifts of the tall, fair, twenty-one-year-old Leicestershire left-hander that the world seems to be at his feet.' In the *Daily Mail*, Alex Bannister highlighted 'an uninhibited approach to back up his stroke range and gifts of timing – and what better timing than to start his international career at £1000 a Test'. In *Wisden Cricket Monthly*, editor David Frith waxed lyrical: 'The power of his shots seems related to effect rather than cause. These were moments long awaited: a face fresh to the public at large, a touch of class, and an impressive absence of emotion to go with it; there was talk of Woolley and Pollock . . .'

The experts were scarcely less effusive. 'Some people are born to play Test cricket – on this evidence, David Gower is one of the lucky few,' asserted Bob Willis, a man unaccustomed to doling out compliments. Wasim Bari was no less adamant that David should play in the first Test: 'The only question about him is whether he is any good against spin.' The hosannahs had been led by no less a luminary than Hutton. 'David Gower is the best young batsman I have seen since Colin Cowdrey,' Sir Len had declaimed on the eve of the season. 'He impresses me more every time I see him and I can assure everybody that there is nothing wrong with his outlook and temperament.'

A warning of a rather more telling nature came from Barry Richards, whose autobiography, published that month, submitted painful evidence both of apartheid's foremost sporting casualty and the perils of the professional game in England: 'Seven days a week of cricket would dampen, both physically and mentally, the eagerness of most lovers of the game . . . The ritual has left me totally numb . . . when I walk off a county ground for the last time it will be with an enormous sense of relief.'

Unlike Richards, fortunately, David now had an alternative outlet to alleviate the numbness. The opening night did not disappoint. After Pakistan had been turfed out for 164 on the second morning – Old seven for 50, including four wickets in five balls – he came in at a time of relative serenity: last man Brearley, run out 38, 101 for two. As if the poor chap's plate wasn't piled high enough, Sarfraz's strained ribs had pared back Bari's seam department to an opening batsman (Mudassar) and a twenty-three-year-old left-armer winning his fifth and penultimate cap. A banker of medium build and shaggy flared hair that would not have looked out of place being mussed by Nell Gwynn, Liaquat had made his Test debut at nineteen, against the West Indies three years previously, taking one for 90 in nineteen overs. He it was who had put the kybosh on Old's second hat-trick ball, but now apologies were tendered. His first offering to David was an invitation to treat, pure and simple. Cafeteria bowling, as the pros call it. Pitched two-thirds of the way down, it sat up, chest-high, petering away down the legside, begging for a birching. Instead, David swivelled 90 degrees and eased it through midwicket, a father gently cuffing an errant son. His first thought was, 'What have I done now?', swiftly followed by self-affirmation: 'It was an extravagant, impulsive way to get off the mark, but it was not just a rush of blood to the head. It was a short, bad delivery – and that is the same whether it's your first or five-hundredth ball.' Alan Lee, for one, suspects that David would have preferred it had people not drawn 'quite so many conclusions'.

When David was missed at mid-on on 15, mistiming a drive on a sluggish track that prevented consistently accurate timing, it seemed all too apt that the miscreant should have been Liaquat. In all there followed nine fours, mostly collected off his legs and through the covers. With a sublime flick through midwicket off the artful slow left-armer, Iqbal Qasim, he became the youngest Englishman since the war to reach 50 in a Test. Colin Fairservice characterized his pupil's style as 'stroking with power'; another apparent contradiction yet none the less accurate for that. Despite giving Radley 100 minutes' start, David overhauled his partner when he reached 58, and then promptly succumbed to the matchstalk man himself, Sikander Bakht, mistiming a daring clip that was intended to clear Javed Miandad at square leg but succeeded only in gently looping to him. A few moments earlier, a half-chance had brought Radley down the wicket for a word to the wise: 'Make them pay for it this time.' They fell on ears deaf to compromise.

During the ensuing week, David received thirty fan letters; in one, a Leicester girl christened him and Tolchard 'Starsky and Hutch'. Suddenly, everybody wanted to know everything about the Drenched Poodle Perm. It was not the easiest of transitions. His attitude towards autograph hunters, for instance, hinted at a certain lofty contempt born partly of impatience, but primarily due to a sense of propriety and a desire for privacy. He refused to sign at hotels – 'it is no different from being badgered outside my front door' – and took exception to being hassled after a bad day. He also resented those who sent pictures of other players with the request that he obtain their signatures and send them back with his own, finding it neither 'subtle or flattering'. The real bugbear was revealed in *With Time To Spare*: 'It gives me quite a kick to see a look of happiness on a kid's face when I have signed his book. But it just gives me a pain when I see mean, sour faces thrusting cigarette packets or grubby scraps of paper at me and virtually demanding that I sign "for my son/cousin/brother/friend etc".'

David made it abundantly clear that he was cognizant of the attendant pressures. 'Miracles are expected of me,' he pointed out with due prescience. But being around so many experienced players at Grace Road had eased the jitters, as had Willis's insistence that he had 'plenty of time' at his disposal in which to score 'plenty of runs'. He conceded he had had a tendency to be 'too casual by far'. He gave his weight as 12 stone and his height as 'five foot eleven and threequarters and a bit'. According to Scyld Berry, writing in the *Observer*, 'his concentration wavers whenever a pretty young thing passes the window'. All the same, he dismayed a good few suitors by revealing that Vicki was 'steadier than most' in girlfriend terms. Mind you, he did leave the door ajar: 'She is the No. 1 choice if it comes to the crunch, but my only plan about marriage is to avoid it – certainly for a long while, anyway.' He attributed his success to timing and temperament: 'The only thing is, the easygoing nature sometimes goes too far and becomes casual. And then you have to really watch out.'

Only something really ugly could possibly dim the afterglow at Edgbaston – and did. At 12.10 p.m. on the fourth day, Bob Willis, having been warned in the first innings for excessive deployment of the bouncer, went round the wicket to the obdurate and plucky nightwatchman, Qasim, unleashed another and saw it rip through the target's hands, smashing him in the mouth. Qasim was led away, bleeding profusely. The TCCB 'bitterly regretted' the matter; the not entirely scrupulous Brearley defended it by asserting that every batsman took a risk, that nightwatchmen should expect to be treated as would a specialist, and that, in any case, distinguishing between intentional bumpers and balls that rear off a length was no simple matter. A convenient if not convincing alibi. For the next Test, the captains were encouraged to exchange lists of non-recognized batsmen, for all that was worth. In ensuing years, English bleating about similarly ruthless West Indian tactics would ring rather hollow.

The reverberations were still being felt while David and the recalled Gooch were adding 101 in 97 minutes at Lord's, whereupon Botham embarked on the first half of the most productive match-return yet recorded by a Test all-rounder: 108 (bowled Liaquat, incidentally) then, in Pakistan's second innings, eight for 34. David was bowled for 56, his cocky attempt at a paddle outsmarted by Qasim's quicker ball. He then proceeded to Leeds, where he top-scored with 39 in the only English innings of a sodden, soggy contest. (Had it not been for those meddlesome elements, England would probably have become the first side in history to win six Tests in a summer.)

Another fifty in the second one-day international against New Zealand set the table for the first four-course meal: a maiden Test century at The Oval. On the eve of the match, Jon Holmes invited David for a pep-flavoured meal on the King's Road.

Why don't you get big scores, I asked, why only 50s and 60s? And he explained, rationally. They were very good reasons. Right, I said, 'I think we've got to aim, not for 100, but 150'. After the meal, I dropped him off at the Charing Cross Hotel and the cabbie said to me, 'who's that then?'. I said it was David Gower. 'Never 'eard of 'im,' said the cabbie. The next day he got a hundred and I thought, well, he'll have heard of him now. If David focuses his mind he can do things. When he was first dropped by England, in 1980, we went out for a meal while Leicestershire were playing Derbyshire at Burton. I told him he had to grind it out. We talked about motivation and all that: the next day he went out and got a hundred again. I remember driving back from Yorkshire that evening and hearing the scores on the radio. I was so delighted I drove off the road. He really wanted it.

As David emerged from the Oval pavilion that Friday afternoon, the need for caution seemed paramount. On a low, slow pitch, Richard Hadlee's eighteen-year-old new-ball partner, Brendon Bracewell, had launched his brief Test career in style, sending back Brearley and Gooch for a combined return of two runs. Once again, though, Gower and Radley, the affecting and the effective, repaired the damage with something approaching a strut. David's was not a flawless innings, far from it. Chances were floored at mid-on when he was on 44 and 52. And Hadlee, equally helpfully, bowled just eight overs before withdrawing with a back strain. During the course of a three-and-a-half-hour stint dominated by assured, sensible strokeplay aimed classically through the V, David nevertheless demonstrated a hitherto unsuspected aptitude for concentration. The manner of his demise said even more: when Botham called for a single, he declined then set off anyway as his partner galloped away, knowing full well he hadn't a hope in Hades. A No. 4 with 111 to his name sacrificing himself to spare a No. 6? Unheard of.

At Trent Bridge, where Pollock and Sobers had so entranced him as a lad, David made 46. Then his 71 in the first innings at Lord's was decisive in blunting the threat posed by a souped-up Hadlee as he and Radley added 109 in the last 110 minutes of the second day. A clean sweep of the series was sealed when, after Hadlee had blown aside Boycott and Radley cheaply, the Golden Wonder came in to pull Collinge for six and share a matchwinning stand of 70 with Gooch. With 438 runs in the two series at an average of 54.75, and only one score of less than 39 in eight visits to the crease, his graduation to the highest rung of the profession had been more skip than jump. Between times came a captain's century against the hapless tourists for Young England, taking the lion's share of a 157-run stand with Gatting after Hadlee had reduced the youths to 83 for four. For the second consecutive season, having been served up Botham twelve months earlier, the Cricket Writers' Club had the simplest of tasks in nominating their Young Cricketer of the Year.

Willis welcomed Gower's crispness:

He slotted into the side very well, showed a lot of confidence in his own ability. His temperament always shone through. He played and missed outside off-stump a lot, but then so did John Edrich.

Left-handers do. It's infuriating when they get out, but good judges from other countries, the top Australians and the top West Indians, really rated him. They could never understand how he was ever out of the side. I was always criticized for being a Boycott-Amiss-Edrich fan: I never rated these flair players too much because they got out too often. On the 1970–71 Ashes tour, if we won the toss, the first three in the order were Boycott, Luckhurst and Edrich, and you knew you wouldn't be fielding that day. Now, you win the toss and bat and No. 10 is putting his thigh pad on. I liked a batsman who batted as long as possible – to give me enough recovery time – rather than a miss one, nick one, purl one: blimey, he's got 60. I like a nice mixture in the side: five blockers and one flair player.

David's habit of sitting with his back to the play did not surprise Willis: 'Amiss, Greig, Knott, Fletcher . . . none of them wanted to watch. Some of them didn't even watch when they were next in. They felt it was taking up adrenalin, that even listening to the crowd was putting pressure on them.'

Like Gower, Bob Willis is a man apart, a man whose chief occupation nowadays, organizing lunches for the amply heeled at the Café Royal, seems rather at odds with the image that made him the unlikeliest England captain of modern times: the Van Morrison/Bob Dylan fixation, the provocative, anti-establishment stance, the tendency to enter an impenetrable, trance-like state whenever he was bowling. Over the ensuing years, he would grow closer to David than most cricketers did, sharing his affinity for quality wine and taking his part forcefully during the Stewart –Gooch crisis. Indeed, Chris Cowdrey contends that Willis was some-what of a father-figure. Willis deems the notion fanciful.

I hope I've given him some support in his rougher moments, but I don't think I was a father-figure. It's fair criticism to say that he didn't really think things out always, and he has much too short a fuse for his own good, but that was part of his genius: he behaved instinctively, batted instinctively. You have to take the foibles. David was different to [other mavericks], mind, because – if you'll forgive the cliché – he was much more of an establishment figure. He never stepped out of line, discipline-wise, for years and years. Holmes got a hold of him fairly early and told him that that was the way you behave to the people who are paying the bills. All Holmes's clients are pretty squeaky-clean.

Jon Holmes is the ex-public schoolboy who gave up insurance broking – 'independent financial adviser, that's what you call us now' – when he read Mark McCormack's biography of Arnold Palmer. In many respects he can be considered the head honcho of the nearest English equivalent to McCormack's muscular IMG empire, an empire that owes its global pre-eminence to the canny ex-golfer who first explored the possibilities of marketing and managing sporting heroes in the megabucks era. As Jon Holmes explains it:

I was doing a job I was not terribly keen on, I loved sport, and being an agent wasn't hard work. Plus, not many people were doing it. It was the land of the instant expert. Mike [Turner] had seen how I did it with Shilton and thought, this guy probably knows what he's doing. I don't think I tried anything particularly clever. Marketing sportsmen is using the media, which you can do in a number of ways. My view is that you can't fool all of the people all of the time. Therefore, the press and media have the power to make or break, and, much as [the media] behave appallingly at times, we can't beat you, so we have to play along with it. And if you're going to have wars, have wars with individuals. Fight a guerrilla war, not a pitched battle.

So Holmes encouraged David to talk freely to the press; as a consequence, his term as an untouchable was more protracted than most.

I encouraged him, on the whole, to be honest: if you make a cock-up, put your hands up because that way you won't be chased forever. It's not a question of saying, oh, you must become a champagne-drinking, upmarket product who's got this laid-back image, because he's like that. So all you do is simplify it a bit and try to avoid people having a go. All I ever do is suggest. I encourage clients to meet people. I always say, if you're a prominent sportsman, you can ring the chairman of ICI and there's a chance he might phone you back: five years after you've finished – no hope. If you get invited on TV, go and do it, but don't bite off more than you can chew. They're learning PR skills that will stand them in good stead.

As Willis infers, it is almost as if Holmes set out to start his own boys' own club: Gower, Lineker, Carling, three stars unsullied by scandal; Atherton has had his ups and downs but he belongs too; in broad terms, so does Shilton. Holmes makes no attempt to conceal the roots of this coincidence.

They're all goodie-goodies, aren't they? Well, Shilts was on the pitch at least. Because I think the game is the important thing. I always say, if you do the business on the pitch, then the business off it has got half a chance. If you're not, frankly, we're struggling. Anybody involved in sport, writers included, start off as romantics. Sport is daft; it's not real, and we're all very lucky because it's not part of the real world. I remember Hugh McIlvanney saying that whether or not this was a proper job for a man of his age, he could console himself with the thought that it is easier to find a kind of truth in sport than politics or economics. That's probably right. We're all frustrated players.

By the end of the summer of 1978, David had secured a modelling contract with a grooming and promotions agency in Leicester recently taken over by the wife of the England soccer full-back, David Nish. The transition to young smoothie delighted Holmes:

David was a scruffy sod when I met him and he remained scruffy for some time despite numerous bollockings from me. I sent him home from a golf club once for not looking the part. He was very intelligent, very keen on the game, a bit indecisive, but very young, in a world that was completely alien. He didn't have a particularly close relationship with his parents, didn't have a particularly close relationship with anyone. I liked the streak of rebelliousness. That unconventionality appealed to me, together with his capacity to think and to want to be original in terms of what you do and where you're going. The higher the stakes, the better he got on; I liked that too.

Botham, insists Holmes, was not viewed as a rival for the sponsor's dollar. 'Botham was the best-loved cricketer in England by those who knew nothing about him, and by people who actually knew more about the game I think David was. No one else could have been the subject of an MCC rebellion. To the man in the street, Botham was a bigger character; to those within cricket, David represented something special. Different market, different world.'

Holmes feels that a lack of parental warmth – or, to be fair, what he *perceived* as a lack of parental warmth – had a lot to do with the erection of that omnipresent invisible barrier.

He's a brilliant communicator one on five, or one on ten, but he's not very good one-to-one. We used to drive down the motorway together, and it took until Milton Keynes for me to say, well, what about so-and-so, and only then would he come out with it. He's always bottled feelings up very well. Because he was taught to, because that's where he came from. When the Indians came to Leicester in 1979, he got out and smashed the stumps down. I saw him two days later, walking down the street in Leicester near my office, and he asked me what I thought about it. I said I thought it was quite good. 'What do you mean?' he said. Well, I said, it was the first time I knew you bloody cared. Listen, I said, all this business about going out and being, oh yah ... I have a feeling it's a bit of bravado. He strutted. It was a defence mechanism. Didn't want to show people what was inside. He isn't like that anything like so much now, and I think a lot of the credit goes to Thorunn and having a child.

So how did Holmes penetrate that outward imperviousness? 'I could open up to him. I've got a different style, deliberately. I was public school and university educated, but I don't expect people to realize that immediately':

That's a bit different to his way of thinking but he could see where I was coming from. We had similar backgrounds. People found him difficult to manage because they were frightened; they didn't know whether he liked them or not, didn't know whether they could open up. I don't think he was difficult to manage. Talk straight and he's fine. We've always had a reasonable relationship. I enjoy his sense of humour and the way he is. I treat him more like a mate, as I do with Carling and the others. Gower's said to me on several occasions, 'you wouldn't last five minutes with Botham because you give so much abuse and take the piss that Botham would punch you, or there'd be a tremendous fight'. That's possibly true. It's a case of acknowledging they're special but treating them as if they were normal, yet never forgetting they're special. He needed reassurance. I wouldn't say, come on, you're a great player, though. I'd say, here, you can do that. He's got a temper, but thumping the table is as far as he would go. He does get seriously upset but it doesn't last long. I've never had a real row with him. He wouldn't do that too much to me because I would just find it too funny.

Mike Turner believes Holmes convinced David to 'work' on his image, up to a point. 'There are distinct marketing advantages if you have the right image, and while David was naturally very courteous, I'm quite sure Jon also impressed on him that there was enormous value in maintaining the style and image that David conveyed.'

Leicestershire derived a substantial economic advantage from the reflected glory as subscription and turnstile receipts went up. Yet they failed to accrue much obvious benefit outside banking hours. In 1978, David continued to open to telling effect on Sundays, scoring 362 runs at nearly 52 (ironically, an inferior run-rate prevented the champions from retaining their crown) whereas he failed to reach 50 in the B&H, where run-rate again cost Leicestershire dear, this time at the group stage. Intriguingly enough, he would average less than 30 in 55-over play over the course of his career, making this easily his worst event; an eloquent comment on its superfluity.

To their credit, his colleagues accepted that this went with the territory. Indeed, Nigel Briers recalls the anger with which he and the rest of the dressing room greeted the criticism David received for allegedly surrendering his wicket without a fight. They also knew, as Tolchard put it, 'that he'd win you half a dozen games a season'. Barry Dudleston took the realistic view: 'It must be very difficult to come back from a Test match and be able to concentrate to quite the same degree. I know very few who are not like that. You just have to accept that if you have a Test player in your side, whether he's got his mind 100 per cent on that game is always going to be debatable. That's not necessarily criticism.'

Taking his cue from John Snow, Willis can be considered the precedent-setter: in 1980 and 1981, he took forty wickets at more than 30 apiece in twenty championship appearances for Warwickshire.

> David is a steely character but the problem was he couldn't motivate himself for county cricket. Neither could I for long periods of time. But look at Atherton's contribution to Lancashire in 1994. We're fast getting to the situation where England players aren't going to play county cricket, and the process started back then. One of our problems is that we kow-tow to the oh-he-keeps-getting-runs-in-county-cricket school, the Mike-Gatting's-averaging-68 school. What was Bill Lawry's description of county cricket? Second grade district level or something. He's not far from the truth.

Oblivious to such extraneous factors, a number of members began to convey their displeasure to Mike Turner:

> They'd say, 'well, of course he only plays for England'. It was different when Illy was playing for England. I was very close to Raymond; we're a similar age, and I know the stresses and strains he endured at that time. He was remarkable in that he could switch off at the end of a Test match and come back and play in front of an empty crowd and still have his mind on the job. David was a different ball game. I can imagine that, after a Test, having been on that high, the coming down really was a coming down. His great asset was that he didn't really outwardly change in his manner and his attitude and approach, whether he was up or down. To me, this is part of his charm.

Australia beckoned for both members of the Tolchard household. Selection may have come as 'a great relief' to David – he thinks he found out via a news bulletin during the John Dunn Show – but there was never much doubt that a maiden Ashes voyage would follow his auspicious foray on the high seas. No fear of flying here, not even in the most literal sense. John Lever's detestation of plane rides was 'noisily obvious' – the chirpy Essex left-armer would clutch the arms of his seat as if anxious it might blow away, and chat even more incessantly than usual – while other members of the party grew 'unnaturally quiet' as take-off neared. Not that David noticed much thereafter: for him, 24-hour flights provided a good excuse for an extended kip.

The second year of Kerry Packer's circus meant that, for the first time in Ashes history, there was competition for the public dollar. David had 'no hard-and-fast thoughts – unlike some of the established England players'. The fact that so many colleagues were 'strongly anti' did not stop him from espying the benefits. 'For me the best point about Packer,' he noted in the diary he co-wrote with Bob Taylor and Pat Murphy, *Anyone for Cricket*, 'is that he has woken up the administrators and made them pay us something nearer our true worth. That was indirectly due to Packer, though it doesn't mean I approve of World Series Cricket. By taking established players away from Test cricket, WSC has given people like me a chance to get into it – but I accept that this is a selfish way of looking at it.'

Liberal use of the bouncer was the only area of the game that could compete with Packer for headline space, and David's disdain for a helmet came to an end before the first Test. At that stage, his tactics against the short-pitched ball were far from clearly defined. During net practice prior to the opening fixture, Willis served up an assortment of bouncers: 'I hit one, nick one, and duck a couple more. I'm trying to discipline myself to play on bouncy wickets, to organize the brain to leave the bouncers alone.' It took a reflexive glove to prevent Geoff Boycott from suffering a serious facial injury at the hands of a teenaged Carl Rackemann; the opener would patronizingly recall his assailant as 'Carl Whatsisname'. A couple of days before the first Test, Fitzwilliam's finest, in consort with Tolchard, arranged a visit from a helmet salesman. David, together with Taylor, Miller, Old and Botham, snapped one up for £15: 'If it helps my confidence, what have I got to lose?'

Cranial protection had been slow to take off on the county scene since Brearley modelled his ghastly reinforced scrum cap in 1976. In 1978, however, the Packer pack returned with tales of skull-cracking, turning the full-blown helmet into an increasingly in-demand accessory. Dennis Amiss had even designed his own, a natty little number that would not have looked out of place on the set of Rollerball. Aesthetic considerations aside, the helmet was an inevitable, pragmatic and, above all, desirable development. Commentators who would never have to face Roberts or Lillee or Thomson bemoaned it on two counts: that it encouraged bouncers and, somewhat less grievously, that it made it hard to recognize incoming batsmen. The safety of the protagonists is what counts, especially in a sport whose officials are reluctant to apply the law, either in spirit or letter. Was not Thommo himself adamant that it was only luck that stood between his 1974–75 victims and the casualty unit, or perhaps the morgue?

Since he was so rarely hit while batting, it could be argued that David had less need for a helmet than most, given the eyesight and timing he had at his command. The bottom line is that helmets have fulfilled a critical function, as David duly discovered in Adelaide during his maiden first-class game on the tour. Unhinged by the latest Aussie tearaway, an asthmatic insurance salesman by the name of Rodney Hogg, a helmetless Radley staggered back on to his stumps after being struck on the head. David was next in: 'It is no use pretending that I was not apprehensive about it. I took guard over a patch of blood, fresh on the green of the pitch. I had watched Hoggy bowl against Western Australia when I was in Perth a year earlier, but now he looked quicker, certainly more aggressive in his approach.' Boycott remembered David giving the opposition bowlers 'apoplexy'; in his own estimation, he played and missed 'about four times', then ducked into a short one, taking a whack behind the shoulder. 'It could have been a lot worse,' he reasoned. Radley, whose injury robbed him of a Test place he would never regain, will assuredly testify to that.

Recovering his poise, David emerged from a numbing defeat with credit, making 73 and 50. Soon, however, the runs dried up: 'Several more batsmen had been hit on the head and Bob Willis had "pinned" two against Queensland. I was anxious, I confess. I wore a helmet in the first Test and psychologically felt more assured.' Later in the tour, in an up-country fixture at Newcastle, Tolchard fractured his right cheekbone while batting and took no further part in the tour. Incidents of this nature became the norm as time passed: but for helmets, they would have been even more frequent, and even more bloody.

'Chat' Taylor, a nimble, bubbly wicketkeeper sixteen years David's senior, echoed the sceptical when he suggested that his co-diarist had to prove that his confident showing against Pakistan and New Zealand had not been 'a flash in the pan'. That made two closely scrutinized players in the one room: Derek Randall's erratic displays since his unforgettable 174 in the 1977 Centenary Test had prompted accusations of brittleness. In common with just about everyone else in the party, David regarded him as 'an amazing character', though some found his eccentricities harder to bear. As a fielding combination they were irrepressible. 'There was some friendly competition there,' David recalls:

Randall was better in the covers but there wasn't really a pecking order. I remember watching him at Grace Road during my first year: he fielded brilliantly. The ground he covered! I think he ran out Dudleston: it was never a contest. Depending on whether a right- or left-hander was in, one of us would man the covers, the other mid-wicket or just behind square. We tended to cover a side each so you could move around, get different views, which keeps you fresher. I liked to be very close at cover, to cut down the angle, stop them getting one or four. That was a challenge.

In personnel terms, the chasm between David's first and last tours Down Under could hardly have been wider. 'It was the happiest tour party I've been with,' enthused Bob Taylor. 'Our management was first-rate (they didn't accept every social invite, for example, this helping to cut down on the ear-bashing) and everyone seemed to blend well on and off the field.' Botham's laddism was mostly well received, and David fell hook, line and sinker for his rampant self-belief. Indeed, the Somerset swashbuckler was the one contemporary ever to inspire awe, a mixed blessing as it transpired. In return, Botham admired David for being 'honest and straightforward'. Unlike his captain, David had a fondness for Phil Edmonds's arrogance, respecting his brain and wit. Willis, the afro-haired vice-captain, also found favour. 'An interesting contrast to Brears,' David noted at the time. 'He'd wield the big stick if necessary, although he maintained a sense of humour. A very confident character, straightforward, with a good cricket instinct. He gave me some sound advice if I ever skipper a side: "If you think of something, just do it, don't hang around wondering if the time is right."' The other star turn was Ken Barrington, assistant manager and author of such timeless aphorisms as Smog Or Gas Board and Two-Man's Land. David's impressions were sadly prescient: 'In the dressing room he was like a player, worrying his guts out.'

Off the field, David could be spotted on the squash court with Tolchard and Gooch – another maiden voyager – or shooting pool with anyone who was handy. If the tour allowance was sufficient for the purposes of carousing – 'David was always one of the lads,' recalls Tolchard, 'always out drinking with them' – it seldom matched David's palate. That said, he did once break the rota of steak and pizza by splashing out on a bit of pheasant. His entries in *Anyone for Cricket* are littered with comments such as 'inexpensive' and 'not bad for two and a half dollars', reflecting that characteristic eagerness to keep the purse strings pulled tight. The name of the downmarket restaurant he frequented in Adelaide earned him his most durable nickname: Lubo. When he came on as twelfth man at Newcastle in the aftermath of Tolchard's unfortunate injury, he spent much of the time scanning the crowd 'for crumpet'. The groupies were cheap, if not always cheerful. Late one night at the Melbourne Hilton, 'three very boring and gruesome young ladies' paid an impromptu visit to Room 1008 and were 'ejected' after a lengthy debate. 'Just because we're 12,000 miles from home,' he mused, 'doesn't mean there's any need to lower one's standards.'

Running dangerously low on runs and confidence prior to the opening Test, David was called before Brearley and manager Doug Insole in the captain's hotel room. The confab lasted about twenty minutes, during which Brearley sought to discover 'if my attitude was right, if I was thinking enough about my game'. It was suggested that he curb his habit of 'getting forty or fifty and then getting out playing a rash shot'. Brearley reflected on the contrasts in light and bounce between English and Australian pitches, 'but we didn't come to any positive resolutions'. The aim, David realized, was not to rollock but to encourage – 'something we all need at some stage'.

It was Willis's conviction that neither Gower nor Randall were applying themselves – 'They've got to be spoken to,' he advised his captain over dinner. That spurred Brearley into action. He had had a few words with 'Arkle' in Melbourne a few days earlier, and concern over his room-mate had been heightened during the game against Victoria. After David had been caught and bowled by Julian Wiener, a Test opener in the making but an extremely occasional offie, he quipped to all and sundry: 'You can't let a bloke like Wiener bowl at you, can you?'

Not that Brearley had any intention of muscling in for a spot of wing-clipping:

I had no wish to suppress his instinctual flair; and I appreciate that he is bound to play and miss more than others as he plays so many cover drives. We must have talked for half an hour; I was impressed. He had given thought to the problems. As he said, the biggest change from English pitches was likely to be the higher bounce – though we have seen little of that so far. He wondered how much he would have to change his technique to balls just outside the off-stump. 'I score a lot of my runs to third man and square on the off-side; so I don't want to cut out too much,' he said. He was also aware of his habit of leaning too far towards the off-side, which tended to make him play across balls on the leg stump, and hit them in the air. Doug Insole and I pointed out the need to think in terms of long innings, and for him not to be too ambitious with his square shots until he had felt the pace of the pitch. He added that he had enjoyed batting with Boycott, but had been a little disconcerted by Geoff's saying, more than once, between overs, 'If only I could hit the ball like you.' He thought it an odd attitude from so senior a player, and a man who had scored 100 first-class centuries.

Brearley appreciated the tranquillity but later confessed he would prefer to 'see other feelings come through more obviously . . . excitement, fear, anger'. In those pale eyes, Brearley detected 'innocence and decadence'. To David, the principal benefit of the chinwag was the evidence it furnished of his captain's 'thoroughness'. He also admired Brearley's cool repose, his self-assurance, and his self-deprecating humour. 'Mike will rarely say much to us before we take the field,' he said a year later:

other than a few comments during the final fifteen minutes, just to harden our concentration for the day ahead. He sets fields precisely, and looks after bowlers to the extent of consulting them constantly about everything from field placings to methods of bowling at a particular batsman. To me, he is visibly monitoring things from over to over and always has a plan, but he will invariably check to make sure that his bowlers are capable of carrying it out . . . Mike seeks the opinions of other players more freely than Raymond [Illingworth]. Whereas Illy would always listen to anyone who had a view, Mike actually goes out of his way to consult, always bringing in the bowler, the wicketkeeper and some of the other senior players.

David was fortunate enough to attend regular field seminars from two of the captains' captains: he took more from Brearley than Illingworth because there was more of him in Brearley than Illingworth. Brearley, too, was prone to bury – or not even acknowledge – emotion and disappointment; as a result, he, too, was liable to explode under the strain of suppressed feeling. Twenty-seven years on, Tolchard still blanches at the stand-up row his captain had with Edmonds in Perth after the latter, not unexpectedly, had neglected to take his twelfth man duties with the degree of vigour and seriousness required. As a consequence, Edmonds did not play a Test all tour. Although he had arrived as the spinner in possession, the gifted if contrary (not forgetting unashamedly provocative) Zambian, the one member of the party who occupied the same intellectual planet as Brearley, constituted a threat; indeed, his differences with his county captain would cost him the Middlesex leadership in addition to at least twenty Test caps. 'Brearley's the hardest man I've ever played with,' insists Tolchard:

He was clever enough to know how to be nasty and cruel. He had a right go at Edmonds: one of the nastiest scenes I've ever seen in a dressing room. Phil didn't want to wait on people hand and foot so Brears tore him off a strip. 'You selfish bastard' and so on. You don't have to do that in front of people. Illy's just a down-to-earth Yorkshireman who just got on with playing but was never nasty. Brears saw everything, knew everything, hated losing, loved winning. Never missed a trick. You felt that pressure with him all the time as an opponent. I didn't mind it; I loved playing against him because it made me more stubborn. I wouldn't bow to the pressure.

This seems an appropriate moment to pause and address the Brearley versus Illingworth debate, a study in diametric opposites. Richie Benaud rates this pair, along with Ian Chappell and Keith Miller, as the finest captains he has known: few would contest the right of the first three to occupy such exalted ground. With the two English nominees, appearances, as ever, were deceptive. Brearley was the more ruthless as well as the more tempestuous; for all that, however, David deemed his former county captain to be the sterner and more forceful of the two; Illingworth though, also had the lighter heart. Brearley talked of captains receiving 'repeated intimations of our own fallibility'; was forever victimized by the greatest ball ever bowled, or the donkeyest drop. As national captains, neither accomplished much against the best: apart from that marvellous series against the Rest of the World in 1970, when England were far gamer than the 1–4 result implied, Illingworth never had to contend with Richards, Procter or the Pollocks; Brearley never had to lead a garrison against a Caribbean battering-ram.

By and large, Brearley's opposition can be regarded as the weaker, yet his resources were considerably slimmer. The message remains abundantly clear: between 1967 and 1972, a period during which Illingworth presided over his country's longest-ever unbeaten run, England were the most consistent force in Test cricket; Brearley caught the fag end of the good old days. Norma Desmond insisted it was not that she was no longer big but that the movies had got smaller; did we get smaller or did the rest of the world just get bigger?

As players and men, Brearley and Illingworth had little in common. Illingworth was the crafty dictator who did everything by the book and pulled his weight; Brearley was the master communicator and strategist whose slip catching was more valuable than his batting. While the Cambridge don oversaw two of the most astonishing comebacks in Test history in the space of a fortnight, Illy coaxed victory from the fire in no fewer than three final Tests. In addition to his 122 wickets for England, he also scored two centuries, which was two more than Brearley. The latter, furthermore, contributed no more than a solitary half-century to each of the three Ashes triumphs that place him shoulder-to-shoulder with Border, Bradman and Darling among Anglo-Australian leaders of the twentieth century. Without Botham – whose twenty-six Tests under him included fifteen five-wicket hauls, seven centuries and forty-one catches – the man the Aussies dubbed The Ayatollah might never have amounted to much more than Hampstead's sportiest psychologist. By the same token, it could also be argued that Brearley's degree in people was precisely what brought the best out of his ace.

Gower is reluctant to betray any preference:

It would have been interesting to have been a direct contemporary, to put my experience alongside theirs, to see how I would have felt about their decisions. They both gave off a sense of paternalism which you can play on as a youth and get rid of as you go on. If anything, Brears was too clever for me. I didn't know whether to compete or what. I can't remember whether it was on that first Australian tour or my second, but at a team dinner on the eve of a Test, after I'd been a bit raucous, chirping away, Brears said: 'It struck me that you get noisier as you get nervous.' In fact, it's the other way round: none of us are infallible. It would be nice to say Raymond was good with mechanics and Brears with people, but it's not that simple. Brears is trained to understand people; Raymond learned. Without studying it in the way Brears did, he had the ability to get through to people. He talked a lot more about himself, whereas Brears would look at you. In that sense he was a degree above. But regaining the Ashes in 1970–71 was a major captaincy achievement. Brears never quite did that. I wouldn't want to choose between them. Why bother?

What stayed with David was the aftermath of Brearley's dismissal during the Adelaide Test: 'Mike, who had been short of runs anyway, was adjudged caught behind off a delivery which, we all thought, had only brushed his shirtsleeve. He arrived back in the dressing room and, for two memorable minutes, the air was blue. His personal frustrations must have built up throughout the trip – none of us knew until later that he had once considered leaving himself out of the fourth Test – and, like everyone else, he had a breaking point.' Then there was the Achilles heel – Botham. 'Mike loves having Ian Botham in the side,' David observed at the time, 'because he always wants to go on bowling. The only time a problem arises is when "Guy" is clearly not bowling well, yet still wants to carry on!' It was a problem that would defeat David all too regularly, and at considerable cost.

Boycott confirmed that Brearley, Willis and Insole were not alone in expressing concern over David's form before the Brisbane Test. 'But then

David is a touch player,' he reasoned, 'one who reacts to the big occasion. He can shrug off a run of poor form just because the situation appeals to him.' That the situation appealed can be ascertained by David's output over a series dominated by fast bowlers, poor pitches and abrupt batting collapses, a series featuring six centuries (four of them Australian) in six Tests, a series decided by the most painstaking innings of Derek Randall's life and a seventh-wicket stand between Geoff Miller and Bob Taylor. Amid this rubble, David stood out as the only batsman on either side to average over 40, and the only one to exceed 400 runs.

England's eventual 5–1 romp was illusory in the wider context. Of the Australian XI Graham Yallop led into action at the Gabba, only Kim Hughes remained from the side that had taken part in the previous Ashes encounter at The Oval sixteen months earlier. Over the course of the rubber, Yallop, Hogg, Geoff Dymock and Allan Border would cement their reputations, the last three going on to play in the opening Test of the following winter's three-Test series, which Australia would win by a comprehensive 3–0 margin (fulfilling the fears Brearley doubtless harboured when he objected to the urn being at stake). In 1978–79, however, inexperience was almost as decisive as the intellectual gulf between the respective captains.

England never really relinquished the initiative handed them by Gower's dexterity in the field. Seeing from his springboard in the covers that openers Graeme Wood and Gary Cosier were bent on dropping the ball in front of them and charging for that nerve-soothing first single, he moved closer in anticipation as Willis bowled the innings' fourth ball, swooped on the run and threw underarm to hit direct and whistle out the hulking Cosier by a nose. When it came to clamping on the helmet – a comparatively elegant number, naturally – he felt comforted, reassured. Which was certainly more than you could say of his teammates when Botham and he convened in the middle on the second afternoon.

The fourth and fifth wickets had fallen with the total on 120, four runs on, the atmosphere, as Boycott recalled, 'electric . . . extraordinary'. As Hogg and Alan Hurst rumbled in, Boycott marvelled, they were 'lifted by the crowd whose mood had changed from frustration to aggression, [and] faced by two batsmen whose only idea of defence was to attack'. The pair posted the fifty stand at nearly a run a minute; while England were taking tea at 176 for five, a supporter brandishing a Union Jack was subjected to a hail of beer cans. The new ball was taken soon after the resumption, but the young guns paid no heed. 'Hogg steamed in and Gower and Botham carried on regardless,' wrote Boycott: the harrumphing probably carried all the way back to Fitzwilliam. 'Gower elegant through the covers for four and three, Botham four through the slips,

11 off the first new-ball over!' It couldn't last, of course. Botham, to his thinly disguised incredulity, was adjudged caught behind as he aimed to deposit Hogg into the Woolloongabba Creek; David followed four runs later when a firm-footed drive off Hurst flew in the same direction. By then, however, they had added 95 in 100 minutes, grabbing back the whip hand. On the fifth day, with England, chasing 169, on 74 for three, the Becurled One duly helped unruffle feathers with an unbeaten 48 that secured a seven-wicket victory, England's first at the Gabba since 1936–37.

England's inaugural Test win at the WACA followed a fortnight later, and it was there that David Gower came into his own. Put in by Yallop, England lost Gooch and Randall to Hogg for 1 and 0 respectively, and when Dymock had Brearley caught behind for 17 shortly after lunch, David entered at a distinctly precarious 41 for three. Over the next 248 minutes, of the 158 he and Boycott added for the fourth wicket, David made 102, giving his partner two and a half hours' start and passing him at 32. By the close, England were 190 for three, David 102 not out with nine fours, Boycott 63 not out with no boundaries.

Bill O'Reilly's characteristically trenchant report in the Sydney *Sun-Herald* certainly made intriguing reading:

There might be some people, difficult though it might be to find them, who would say that the dour English opener did a great job for his country . . . I am not one of that peculiar brand of enthusiast. Boycott batted badly. He grooved himself into a disciplined course of batting that was negative in every respect. The effect he had on the magnificent methods of David Gower cannot be described in lesser terms than calamitous. In Gower, England has a new breed of batsman designed to change the whole face of English Test batting. He stands high over his bat, moves gracefully to the ball and hits it with a flow or rhythm to all points of the field. Early in his innings he was hit on his helmet by a bouncer [from Hogg] into which he ducked evasively. He faced up to the next ball, went inside it and forced it hard wide of mid-on. That was sufficient to show me that he possessed a temperament which is bound to take him to the greatest heights. Had Gower been lucky enough to have been partnered by a batsman capable of seeing that he got his fair share of the bowling instead of his having to watch Boycott fiddling about in deadly fashion he would have had at least 150 runs to his name.

Not untypically, David's diary concentrated far more on the ups than the downs. The first hour was 'fairly torrid' as Hogg hurled down a succession of supersonic off-cutters. Three-quarters of Hogg's missiles were kicking chest-high. 'All of a sudden,' the bowler later cursed, 'you look around and see he's got 20; you think to yourself, "where the hell did he get those runs?".' David's teammates were often at a similar loss. He was grateful for the way Boycott 'urged me on with sound common-sense', and drew reassurance from him. At tea, Hogg had a quiet word in his shell-like about his persistent refusal to make contact with his worthiest balls: 'You're a fucking impostor, Gower.'

Getting his mitts on a new cherry before the close, Hogg beat Gower three times running: on each occasion David withdrew the blade in time. 'Delightfully uncomplicated' was Brearley's considered verdict. 'In the next over he hit Hogg for two fours square on the off-side – one off the back foot, the other off the front foot – a mark of his class.' A straight drive off Hurst did the trick three minutes before the close. Sylvia Gower was tracked down to her 96-year-old mother's bedside in Tunbridge Wells. It was a toss-up as to whether she was more unhappy about the technical faults that were restricting radio and TV coverage, or the manner of her son's exit: 'David got himself out with a sloppy shot, not at all like him.' She recalled how David had been given Bradman's *The Art of Cricket* as a boy, and gone straight out into the garden to practise a particular stroke, first with a stick, then with a hockey stick.

Brearley called for moderation the next morning, and David hung in with cool resolution for the first half-hour, scoreless if not strokeless. He could hardly be faulted when Hogg went round the wicket and whizzed down one that pitched off and somehow hit off: 'It was too fast for me to adjust. Fair enough . . .' That evening, David failed to get changed in time to catch *Midnight Express* with some of the younger members of the party and ended in the bar celebrating 'suitably' with Chris Tavaré and one or two other county confrères who were wintering in the area. 'Bump into Bernie Thomas in the lift, can't find the words,' he scribbled in his diary. 'Wonder if he'll tell the manager about me having a few?'

Ask Bob Willis to cite his favourite example of Gowerian majesty and he plumps for this particular jewel: 'Just the audacity, playing with that assurance.' Tolchard still curses the fact that he missed it: 'I'd always wanted to play Royal Perth [golf course] and I had to choose that day, didn't I! I'll never forgive myself for that. I never wanted to miss another day's cricket after that. The pitch was like lightning; even the nets were. I had more balls bowled to me in the nets there that I didn't see than anywhere else in the world.' Sadly, David was unable to console his landlord with an action replay. While Hogg was putting England through the mincer in the next Test at Melbourne, David did manage to top-score in both innings (29 and 49), even if he was out to the last ball before lunch on the first day. Honesty, it must be said, may have been his undoing: when a delivery from Hurst gloved him, noted Boycott, 'Gower took an involuntary step forward to walk and that may have cost him his wicket; the umpire took a long time to give him out, there was obviously the suspicion of doubt in his mind, and Gower's reaction may have tilted the scales.' David concluded the rubber with a breezy 65 when the protagonists returned to Sydney, marking the beginning of a mutually beneficial friendship; the earlier Test at the SCG, the decisive chapter of the series, had been something of a false start, and certainly not a pleasant introduction. Plagued by a raging temperature, an extremely dicky throat and the odd facial eruption – he'd caught Willis's virus – David laboured in the searing heat for the best part of two hours to make 34 in the second innings, an effort as vital as it was painful (even Botham could manage only 6 in 90 minutes). No one was quite sure whether Brearley's broadside on the first evening or Randall's marathon 150 was the bigger catalyst; either way, David slept through some raucous celebrations after England had overturned a 142-run deficit to win by 93.

He made amends when the Ashes were retained in Adelaide, leaping gleefully into Botham's arms after diving to catch the dangerous Hughes on the final day: 'At the time I was very keyed up, thinking to myself, "This is just the time to rub it in – if anything comes to me in the air, I'm going to dive for it." I was so delighted when that actually happened but I was embarrassed later when I saw my reactions on TV. It's not my usual style and I didn't want people like "Annoyed, Neasden" writing to the captain, "Dear Mr Brearley, would you please restrain your team from kissing and hugging?" I made amends shortly afterwards when I dived to catch Carlson, remembered to curb my enthusiasm and just lobbed the ball back to Chat.' Boycott considered the hugging to be 'somewhat effeminate' but Brearley had little patience for the killjoys:

> I had more letters criticizing us for the exuberance of our celebrations than for any other aspect of our cricket. My view is that the Englishman has, in the last 20 years, become less stiff-lipped, less embarrassed by displays of emotion; we are more intimate as people, more open and informal than a generation ago. On the whole, I approve of the change, and the obviously shared pleasure and enthusiasm at each other's success was a factor in our overall success.

The one other protracted display of Gowerian majesty was reserved for the one-day international at the MCG, a match England lost yet one where his imperious century flowed at a run a ball. The best came last: facing the final delivery of the innings, he swept from 97 to 101 with a peerlessly placed drive off Trevor Laughlin that lasered its way between deep cover and deep extra. *Wisden* called the innings 'magical'.

Rumours were rife that he and Botham were being courted by Packer, but, in David's case at least, the grapevine was ill-informed. In purely economic terms, he was doing rather nicely: beside his tour fee of £5500 (an 80 per cent improvement on that guaranteed the previous winter's tourists), he returned to Leicester in February with his £1500 share from the players' pool of promotional income and prizemoney. Educated guesstimates placed his income at £20,000; on the way over, he and Mike Hendrick had discussed turning themselves into limited companies. In a bizarre homecoming at Heathrow, the tourists were greeted by Captain Sensible of the Damned at the head of a pack of punks, placards at the ready: 'Boycott for President' demanded one, 'Brearley Must Go' another – Sir Geoffrey, asserted the good Captain, 'is the hero of punks across the country'. Pity neither hero nor villain had landed with the party. Nor, for that matter, had David; after dutifully sharing out the hundred bottles of champagne supplied by the Victoria Sporting Club to the first century maker of the series, he had trotted off to Singapore for a fortnight. In his absence, Alec Bedser, the chairman of selectors, tipped him as a possible successor to Brearley and criticized the tendency of the counties to appoint senior players as captains, broadly hinting that he would have preferred Leicestershire to have made David vice-captain to Illingworth's heir, Ken Higgs; Brearley hailed David as 'a minor genius who may one day become a major genius'.

In mid-July, thirteen months after his five-day debut and in his thirteenth Test, the minor genius confounded superstition by returning to Edgbaston and reaching 1000 runs for his country in record time. On a flat track against a superannuated Indian spin attack, there was no earthly need for a helmet. Shirt unbuttoned to breastplate, curls a go-go, it was as if Adonis had escaped Olympus for the day. He spun languidly to pull the left-arm seamer, Ghavri, drilled Vankat's off-spin through mid-off and over midwicket, and late-cut the same bowler with the delicate certainty of a seamstress threading a needle. A pause to drink in the musings of *Wisden*. There, with no little piquancy, alongside an article mourning the passing of Woolley, was David's entry as one of the Five Cricketers of the Year: the first Leicestershire player to be so honoured for forty-six Aprils and the fourth overall. 'He typified a new, precocious breed of strokeplayers, imperious and exciting, who added colour and glamour to an otherwise bedraggled English summer.'

A good-length googly from Chandrasekhar is transformed into a full toss by a jaunty two-step, then diverted through midwicket by gentle persuasion. 'A certain amount of contempt in that,' comments Richie Benaud as Ghavri is caressed through point. By the time 200 approaches, Venkat, the Indian captain, has long since settled for a field better suited to the sixtieth over of a Gillette tie, and the landmark is duly reached with a controlled squirt through an untended cordon. A thumb is raised, the face enveloped in a rueful, almost embarrassed expression. 'Something new,' the lugubrious Jim Laker informs BBC viewers in a tone bordering on pleasure. 'Something fresh.' In the summer of 1979, every Englishman wanted to be David Gower.

6   Elegant Chaos

So when you look at me
You better look hard and look twice
Is that me, baby?
Or just a brilliant disguise?
Brilliant Disguise, Bruce Springsteen

'There is but one crime,' pronounced Cyril Connolly in *Enemies of Promise*: 'to escape from our talent, to abort the growth which, ripening and maturing, must be the justification for the demands we make on society.' While England's first female Prime Minister was committing all manner of heinous crimes in her first term of office, David Gower seemed intent on aborting growth. The first three-and-a-half years of Thatcherism saw him furl his wings and enter a sympathetic nosedive; perhaps he accepted that the treatment of the miners and the unemployed rendered the flaunting of riches an act of callous disregard.

More likely it was the combination of a flawed technique – the same flawed technique Tom Graveney would pinpoint a decade later when David sought his advice – and his innate stubbornness. Excepting the 1980–81 Wisden Trophy rubber, between the third Test against India in 1979 and the start of the third contest of the 1982–83 Ashes series, a total of twenty-eight Tests (of which England won seven and lost eight), he mustered only 1533 runs in fifty innings, at an average of 33.33. Not once, moreover, did he reach three figures. If he could not escape his talent, he certainly did his best to mislay it.

The first specks of perspiration on the golden brow had been spotted at the start of the 1979 season. Presumably finding it difficult to rewind after Australia, David worked hard in the Grace Road nets with Birkenshaw 'to try and get the feel of hitting the ball fluently again', yet that boozy punt up the River Cam bore all the tell-tale signs of a starlet still tootling around on cloud nine. With only 56 runs behind him in five championship innings, he had a run-out with the seconds against Worcestershire prior to the World Cup but that didn't do the trick: in the few overs of play possible, he was caught behind for 18. His four efforts

Tom Bowring, Sheila Newholt, Sylvia and Dick Gower plus newly christened David. Goudhurst, 1957. *(Elizabeth Fouracre)*

Dick takes time off from reorganizing Tanganyika to bowl to David at the Kinondoni (government flats). Note the striker's unfamiliar stance. Dar es Salaam, 1961. *(Philip Mawhood)*

Ray Illingworth, appointed supremo five years too late to prolong David's career, presents him with his Leicestershire cap a few days after the latter had top-edged a hook into his right eye. Grace Road, 1977.
(Leicester Mercury)

No, not *that* shot but another in that maiden Test innings against Pakistan, this time off Sikander Bakht. Edgbaston, 1978.

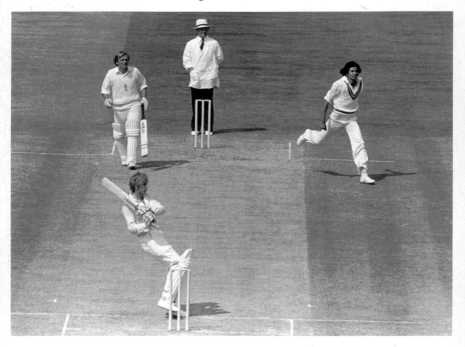

David pulls imperiously during his unbeaten 200
against India. Edgbaston, 1979.

Second only to Randall among contemporary English fielders until beset by shoulder problems, Gower, untypically, floors Andy Roberts, whose blows earned the West Indies a two-wicket victory. Trent Bridge, 1980.

David carves through the covers in the days when West Indian wicketkeepers had reason to stand up. Barbados, 1981.

Rodney Marsh gazes in awe as David crashes a delivery through point en route to being named International Cricketer of the Year. Brisbane, 1982.

David informs the umpires that an owl would be hard pressed to bat in this light. Brisbane, 1982.

Disbelief suspended after falling prey to a dubious decision on his first tour as England captain. Vengsarkar, Gavaskar and even the bowler, Sivaramakrishnan, look suitably sheepish. Delhi, 1984.

Thomson is dispatched through the covers during David's highest innings against the oldest foe. His 732 runs remain a record for an England captain in an Ashes series. Edgbaston, 1985.

David poses during the Test that marked his crowning glory; a couple of days later, the Ashes were regained. The Oval, 1985.

Overleaf: David grins and bears it as he addresses the gentlemen (and otherwise) of the Fourth Estate, during the tour to end all tours. Port of Spain, 1986.

in the World Cup then raised 50 runs all told. Frustration bubbled over when, less than a week before the first Test, he made 4 and 11 against the Indian tourists. In the first innings he was caught down the legside off Ghavri and, in an highly uncharacteristic move, promptly made a fine mess of his stumps.

'I had not been playing well and the team were struggling,' he explained:

> So I saw my innings as having two aims. With the first Test approaching, it was a chance for me to have a look at the Indian bowlers, and I wanted to play well to get the team out of trouble. The wicket was not good – there had been uneven bounce all season – so I was thinking about the short balls and the varying heights. But I was bobbing on without too many worries until I got myself out. It was a ball to have a swish at, but not a ball to get you out. I knew I was out. But I felt suddenly and fiercely annoyed with myself, and just for a few seconds I had the urge to hit something. The stumps were closest. More a half-hearted swipe than a real slog, but as soon as I made contact, three thoughts came into my mind. I knew it was not right, I knew it was an unusual spark of emotion . . . but primarily, I knew it had cheered me up.

David made off for the pavilion, smiling. Mike Turner gave him a bit of a wigging but 'Tolly' and the rest found the explosion of emotion most amusing; Jon Holmes couldn't decide whether he was amused or relieved. Yet even at Edgbaston David would feel troubled. He had come armed with new gloves, new pads, even a new bat, but timing, at first, remained elusive. By his own admission, he might easily have perished to any one of the first three balls he received, though this was at least partly attributable to the fact that, having been taken by surprise when the fall of Gooch at the end of a lengthy third-wicket stand with Boycott found him re-tuning the TV in the dressing room, he had barely adjusted to the piercing sunlight. Indeed, he got off the mark with an exasperated mishit that lobbed fractionally clear of mid-on.

There were some flickerings against Middlesex at Grace Road, an aberration that did not remotely surprise Mike Brearley. 'David probably tried that bit harder against us,' he surmises, 'because there was a bit of needle. There were more people he wanted to score runs against, to prove a point against, bowlers like Edmonds, Emburey and Daniel. It was more like a Test match.' On this particular occasion he grafted his way to 98 before John Emburey induced a catch in the outfield – had the shot gone for four Leicestershire would have won the match and rewarded new skipper Higgs by finishing fourth in the championship, despite just four victories in twenty-one games. The Lord's Test a few days later saw him smite Bedi for six on his way to a silky 82 out of 114, off 95 balls. But the greasy pole beckoned, and he slid with alacrity; his remaining eight first-class innings of the season yielded three ducks and only 131 runs (including an unbeaten 84 against Northants).

Then while Botham was flaying all and sundry at Headingley, David recorded his first five-day duck, leg-before to Kapil Dev, a bowler whose guile would exert something of an Indian sign over Gower: only Geoff Lawson (fourteen dismissals) would exceed the ten dismissals Kapil Dev ultimately totted up against him.

The inevitable press criticism was taken with comparative coolness, according to Martin Johnson:

> He wasn't bad at taking criticism, I don't think. He doesn't like it very much, and he doesn't care much for it in the journalistic field either, but, to an extent, none of us do, do we, really? He didn't react too badly: I think he thought nearly all of it was misinterpretation, that if people were really on the ball they wouldn't believe what was written. And, you know, 'what do they know about playing cricket on a miserable Tuesday in Derby'. I don't think the criticism ever bothered him; it was always counter-balanced by the great public affection.

In subsequent years, the *Leicester Mercury* would allow Johnson 'this sort of running criticism page – and it was largely Gower-inspired. He (Gower) would occasionally come up and say, "I suppose you're going to give me a grilling." One Saturday at Old Trafford, just before play, when no one had got a run – Gower hadn't, Briers hadn't, nobody had – I was given a copy of the Sunday team. "I see Balderstone is absent again," I said to him. Balderstone was easily Leicestershire's best one-day batsman but he had been pitched out on grounds of old age. Gower, who was captain by then, said to me: "I have a feeling you're really going to let me have it this time, aren't you?" And I said, "I'm going to effing slaughter you; I'm going to absolutely effing slaughter you." "Yeah," he said, "I won't buy the paper, then." And with that he sauntered off.'

At the height of this, his first experience of professional turbulence, the very worst thing David felt he could do was 'to lie awake every night brooding about it . . . It's just a question of trying to play normally, trying to do the right things, and being confident that things will eventually come right.' A hastily arranged tour of Australia – a rash gesture of goodwill to the home board following the demise of World Series Cricket and the outbreak of peace with Packer – did little to bolster that confidence. It was abundantly clear that returning Down Under so soon had blunted David's edge. After all, Australian tours are quadrennial events, not annual bunfights.

Not that that lessened the tension. Nobody cared that, for the first time in a century, the holders had resolved not to put the blessed Ashes urn up for grabs, nor that the West Indies shared the spotlight. Then there were the additional burdens imposed by the plethora of limited-overs internationals, a legacy of World Series Cricket, as were the floodlit day-night matches. Here was the forerunner of the present-day tour: eating and packing, buses and planes, cricket by day, cricket by night. David found it extremely difficult adjusting the body clock to the schedule necessitated by late starts and later finishes: he still found himself waking 'at the normal time' and thus being left 'pretty tired and unwell'.

And, bearing scant relation to Yallop's second-stringers as it did, the quality of the opposition did little to lighten the heart. Lillee, Marsh and the Chappells were all back, and bent on extracting a few pounds of flesh for the humiliations of 1977 and 1978–79. David felt as if he 'had never been away ... apart from the four or five new faces, the routine was much the same and I don't believe I was alone in finding it more difficult to motivate myself.' He acknowledged that this might also have been 'something to do with my concentration not being as long as it should be'. He even went so far as to openly confess that there were times 'when I hardly knew where I was or what I was supposed to be doing'.

There was plenty of supporting evidence. In the opening first-class fixture against Queensland, he did manage a second-innings half-century on a pitch Boycott insisted was a 'green-top' (well, Brett Schuller, a quickish if not quite world-beating left-armer, did nab Sir Geoffrey in both innings for 11 and 20). All the same, Boycott knew something was up after Schuller had dismissed Gower for 2 first time up. Boycott recalls,

> Nets were available later in the day but I didn't go; I felt a friendly game of tennis would do me more good at that particular stage. But I noticed one familiar player in the nets next to the courts – David Gower, quietly working at his game, determined to polish his perform-ance after an early disappointment. Boycott playing tennis and Gower practising in the nets? Seems somebody got their images crossed somewhere.

Not for the first time, nor, for that matter, the last, assiduousness in the nets achieved next to nothing. After another iffy fifty against Tasmania came scores of 44, 17 and 7 in the first three one-dayers, preceding 17 and 23 in the first Test. In the second innings he came in at 26 for 2, saw two chances fluffed then flipped Dymock to midwicket. Boycott deemed the latter an 'infuriating' way to go, especially since he had ventured down the pitch the previous over to give his partner a gee-up. 'You do know that we are trying to save the match, not trying to win it,' he had reminded David. 'I did not say it cuttingly for I had no intention of telling him how to bat, and no thought of asking him to play like me. But we had already lost two wickets quickly and he was playing with the expansiveness of a millionaire.'

At this stage in David's development, however, the concept of knuckling down to grind out a draw, of being content to spoil, was utterly alien. Although Brearley, in particular, was a constant source of companionship and encouragement during this period, an upturn was not immediately forthcoming. David was in a quandary: he knew he 'had to do something to get out of the rut'; he also knew he would 'destroy myself completely' by concentrating 'unnaturally hard' on making alterations, on 'doing things right'. Returns of 3 and 13 in the rematch with Queensland were succeeded on the opening day of the Sydney Test by the ignominy of being bowled for 3, not by Lillee or Dymock or even Pascoe, but by Greg Chappell. Delivered on a pitch whose dampness left it bordering on an old-fashioned gluepot, the ball *was* a good 'un, pitching leg and hitting off; David, reported Christopher Martin-Jenkins, forgivingly, 'aimed across the line in that loose-wristed way which looks so silky when he hits and so careless when he misses'. Then the one-day international on Boxing Day brought matters to a head: 'As soon as I walked to the wicket I knew that I didn't feel right. In a way, I might just as well have turned round and walked straight back to the dressing room. I kept losing track of my feet. I didn't know where my hands were, or where the bat was going.'

Already demoted from four to six in the order, Derek Underwood's intrusion as nightwatchman (a highly successful intrusion at that) left David entering at number seven in the second dig at the SCG; at that juncture, England were a net 83 for five, and subsequently an effective 152 for seven when Chappell disposed of Randall and Botham in the space of four overs. Sparring and sparkling by turn, David had led his usual schizoid existence; if there was seldom any sense of permanence, he persisted gamely through the nicks and flicks. Bob Taylor shored up an end during an eighth-wicket stand of 37, but when Graham Dilley went seven runs later, David was on 82, England just 196 to the good and Willis the last man. In Perth, unpromisingly, Willis had been the No. 11 who had had the gall to strand Boycott on 99.

Thoughts of victory all but extinguished, David abruptly cast caution to at least five winds. In successive overs, Lillee was hooked and square-cut to the fence, Chappell delicately late cut. He was two short of his century (out of 142) when Lillee, inevitably, had Willis taken in the slips. David bore the blame, insisting that he had 'erred anyway' by taking a single off the second ball of the over. 'Geoffrey wasn't a very happy bunny in Perth, he couldn't believe it,' Willis recalls, 'whereas David was very philosophical. I had no confidence that I would survive Lillee, who was bowling leg-breaks at 90 miles an hour, but I didn't fancy getting out to any of the others.' Brearley was delighted at the turnaround, though he modestly – and probably correctly – consigned his own influence to the realms of coincidence. A couple of days before the match, he had asked David to dine with him and a group of friends 'who had nothing to do with cricket'. He felt David was 'a bit jaded', that he was enduring one of those low, depressed spells wherein 'even successful innings seemed flat and worthless afterwards' and that 'some stimulating company might help him to put things in perspective'. Ask Brearley which Gower innings springs most readily to mind and he cites this one without hesitation: 'It was quite a difficult pitch even by that advanced stage. The ball was moving around; he must have played and missed thirty times – a typical Gower innings. I always thought people overlooked the fact that strengths are wrapped in weaknesses.' In the end, Greg Chappell ushered his country to a six-wicket win with the contest's second unconquered 98.

For David, offerings of 3, 12, 10 and 27 in the remaining four one-dayers removed much of the gilt from Sydney, whereupon the third and final Test saw Lillee dispatch him cheaply in each innings at the MCG. Restored to No. 4 in the order, he had yet to get off the mark on the opening afternoon when he was involved in the run out that ran down Gooch on 99; as if hypnotized (needlessly) by remorse, he soon played slightly across one that darted back a shade off the seam and pinned him in front. Far more culpable was the forlorn pull that cost him his off-bail on the fourth afternoon, in the last over before tea. He sat alone in the dressing room for the next hour, head in hands.

Dennis Lillee wasn't fooled. He had glimpsed more than enough to know that he had met a worthy adversary:

I'd seen David a bit on TV the previous winter but I never form an opinion until I've played against someone. We knew he was very aggressive, and there was no doubt we saw him as a man you'd rather see walking the other way to the pavilion. He was so lackadaisical yet he seemed to have so much time, like all the great batsmen. He always seemed to be playing with entertainment in mind rather than self-preservation or averages, and that was often to the detriment of the team because he would get himself out. On his day you would wonder where to bowl next, then all of a sudden, he would get himself out. You often had the feeling that, no matter where you bowled, he's

101

going to plaster you then mistime a drive, or drag one on. Yet if he'd decided to become ultra-cautious he might not have made so many runs. A beautiful player – that flick to leg, the cut shots. In the one-dayers probably more than anywhere else, he could change the whole game. He was a lot like Doug Walters, who I rate very highly. Doug's technique against the moving ball was also dubious at times; he was also a hard-wicket player.

Lillee also warmed to David once stumps were drawn: 'You're not going to meet a nicer guy. He became one of my great friends in the game, terrific to have a beer with, a really terrific person. As with so many of those who seem, outwardly, to exude confidence, he didn't strike me as being so confident inwardly.'

In losing all three Tests, England had cause to rue the regression of Willis (three wickets in 98 overs), the remission of Hendrick, whose injured shoulder prevented him from bowling a ball, and the omission of Edmonds, discarded in a howler almost certainly attributable to the captain's hostility. The county elders were scornful. 'Men like Barrington, Graveney, Cowdrey and May wouldn't have thrown their wickets away like our lot last winter,' opined Gloucestershire's trusty seamer, Brian Brain, in his forthright diary, *Another Day, Another Match*:

> They're getting paid exceedingly well for not playing professionally. David Gower, in particular, makes my blood boil. I can name thirty other English players who wouldn't have sold their wickets as cheaply as Gower in the winter. He should be left in county cricket for a season to learn his trade. It would break my heart to miss out on all that money by dropping out of the England scene, so perhaps Gower will eventually realize cricket's not always about champagne, it's a bread-and-butter game.

Boycott's hundredth hundred three years earlier had prompted a fan to send him a cut-glass goblet inscribed with the novel theory, 'Genius is infinite patience'; clairvoyance was hardly required to forecast that the world's Most Infinitely Boring Batsman would be just as dismissive as Brain:

> I suspect he thought it would all be rather too easy, another inevitable piece in a rich pattern. Cricket doesn't automatically work that way. He showed no discipline or application in any of his batting, playing like a man who had scored 30 before he had faced half a dozen deliveries. There were very few matches outside the internationals in which to find form so his problem gradually got worse rather than better, and David doesn't help himself by that characteristically flip attitude.

It looks as though he doesn't care and that certainly can't help his cause. He seemed incapable of putting together a steady, sensible innings – it was shots all the way, disappointment all the way, and he never seemed to learn.

Whatever Boycott's feelings at that time, David did find him useful to talk to – when, that is, the latter was in 'a listening mood'.

In light of subsequent events, David's contemporary observations of Gooch and Boycott make revealing reading. Knowing the latter's propensity for negotiating singles with a Cyclopian lack of deference to a partner's better judgement, David took the wise precaution of calling every ball whenever the oddest couple were in harness. However, more than any other batting partner, Boycott made David concentrate: 'I believe his presence gives me a subconscious feeling of security. He has often said to me, "I wish I could bat like you" and I have never yet decided whether he is being sarcastic or serious.' The respect for Gooch was more personal than technical: 'Zap is one of my particular friends in the side, and I am as happy in his company as with anyone. He is living proof that cricket, even at the highest level, can and should be enjoyed, and he has the ability to see the funny side of things on the field and break up what might have been becoming a dull day.' Things change.

Aside from the suspicion that repetition had un-whetted the appetite, David also volunteered an explanation for what he now describes as 'easily' the worst of his five Australian tours. 'I would love a break,' he admitted, and with good reason. Throw in the Golden Jubilee Test in Bombay (lbw to Kapil Dev – who else? – for 16) and he had played in all of England's twenty Tests and twenty-two one-day internationals between June 1978 and February 1980: only Botham could match such resilience. Bombay saw the latter perform the most formidable all-round turn in the history of five-day play – 114 and thirteen for 106 – but his output, too, was about to recede. Mind you, this had rather more to do with the demands on mind than those on body: appointing Botham captain in succession to Brearley was tantamount to the producer of Mastermind appointing Harry Enfield to replace Magnus Magnusson.

David freely admits that the first Test of the 1980 Wisden Trophy series rammed home the perils of facing men hurling leather-clad projectiles in your general direction some way in excess of the speed limit. 'Andy Roberts was comfortably the fastest bowler I had ever faced,' he acknowledged, 'and suddenly the physical risk became more apparent.' In the past, David would look to seize the initiative against the quicks, hooking or cutting, ducking only as a last resort. If anything, the helmet increased the recklessness. As Roberts, Holding, Garner and Croft bore down, a certain tentativeness crept in, albeit only temporarily. He was not alone.

Not that the drive to Nottingham had found him in the pink. Blue, maybe. A reserved 57 during the tourists' two-day win at Grace Road augured well, but, for what it was worth, 35 not out was his best effort in seven championship knocks, including three ducks in four innings (including a pair administered by his county nemesis, Northants' unassuming if Right Honourable Tim Lamb). A rare gesture of intent in the Benson & Hedges Cup, the superfluous competition he usually treated with silent contempt, saw an unbeaten century secure victory over Derbyshire, albeit too late to earn a place in the last eight. Further match-winning Sunday efforts against Sussex and Derbyshire brought a bit more respite.

The first Test yielded only 20 and 1. In this captivating, low-scoring contest, his most grievous error was to spill a daunting swirler from Roberts with three wickets standing and 13 to get. 'Ironically, I'd had three catches like that in recent weeks,' the miscreant recalls ruefully, 'into the skies, over the shoulder, twenty-yard run – and caught the lot. I knew if I got there I'd catch it . . .' Getting hands to the ball was something of a feat in itself, and certainly not one that any of the other nineteen ungloved participants could have accomplished without undue difficulty. But, nevertheless, the selectors did unto him what he had done unto Roberts.

This Test featured a shameless attempt to invest home advantage with something more than merely geographical meaning; a good old-fashioned seamer's haven had been prepared with the express intention of negating the tourists' pace phalanx – precisely the sort of pitch David detested. Had he held the catch instead of sparing Roberts to administer the deciding blows, England might easily have been the ones to emerge victorious from what turned out to be the only conclusive match of the rubber, a rubber in which the Caribbean hurricane was subsequently blown off course by lousy weather and plucky home batting on a succession of turgid surfaces. For all the tapering-off of his own input with bat and ball, Botham might thus have gone to the Caribbean more fireproof than ever, returned with an acceptable defeat, and clung on to the captaincy for a couple more Tests. Which would have meant no Headingley '81 . . . It is hard to decide whether Botham, Brearley or the entire nation owes David a greater debt.

Some would argue, of course, that that perceived blunder simply furnished the selectors with a convenient excuse to slap the prodigal down. Chris Tavaré, with 13 and 4 on debut, had contributed even less, yet he survived. No one had proffered David any advice, though this was almost certainly because he never sought it. A legacy, perhaps, of Colin Fair-service and Mick Norman's profound suspicion of apparently well-meaning advisers and their motives? Or were they intimidated by his icy outward serenity? David prefers to cite it as proof of one of his own shortcomings: 'I'm not very good at asking advice. It is a failing at times.'

Yet should any of this really have provided sufficient grounds to axe Gower? Three Tests earlier, after all, David had bested the best bowler in the game. Willis firmly believes that David's 98 in Sydney should have served as sufficient insurance:

> I don't think there would often have been a case for dropping David. If someone is averaging 40 in Test cricket I would want him to fail ten innings running. Obviously there were times when David didn't help himself, wasn't always seen to be doing the right thing, but that's what individuals are about. You are always going to have enough players in a side who are going to toe the party line, do the right thing all the time, but we're not very good in this country at blending genius into teamwork.

Jon Holmes concurs to an extent, contending that 'there was a large element' of trying to keep the young pup in his place. 'Jealousy was a very powerful motivation. You're dealing with big egos, and I think that ultimately may have led to him leaving cricket when he did. That's all I'm prepared to say.' Holmes is also prepared to say that David's unfortu-nate knack of giving the impression of being above sweat and toil served him ill. 'David doesn't believe that trying is cheating, but that showing that you're trying is a bit off. There are those who don't like that sort of attitude.' It seems reasonable to conclude that Alec Bedser and his fellow selectors were among 'those' in question. 'They felt they were running the school first XI and certain people were getting above them-selves. "A spell in the colts wouldn't do any harm" – that sort of thing.'

On reflection, David refuses to find fault with anything beyond his own form. At the time, he presented his thoughts diary-fashion in *Wisden Cricket Monthly*, sensibly eschewing the self-righteous tub-thump of the spurned hero in favour of a spot of self-affirmation:

> June 15: the second Test side is announced – without me. Life goes on. All I feel now is that I have to keep playing as ever and concentrate on scoring runs. If that sounds simple and obvious, it is. Certainly, I feel that to try to do anything as radical as attempt to change technique would be inane. If I simply apply myself to batting as I know how, and back my innate ability, things must come right. As they say, there is 'time to spare'.

There were deceptive signs of rejuvenation at Burton-on-Trent. Stirred by his agent's promptings the previous evening, David entered at 7 for two and duly made exactly 100, his first championship hundred for three seasons. Unfortunately, this presaged neither sudden good fortune, nor an improvement in mood. In a Sunday game at Ebbw Vale, Birkenshaw stood in the nets hurling balls at him from a few yards' range, the aim to 'tighten my technique against the seamers'.

This unusual attention to technique had its roots in what David perceived as a tendency to fall leg-before or caught behind when trapped in what Ken Barrington referred to as 'two-man's land' – neither fully forward nor fully back; he had enlisted Birkenshaw's assistance to work on 'getting me more forward'. At Lord's, he scratched out six runs in half an hour yet drew Brearley's congratulations for the excellence of his judgment of which balls to leave. He was always going to thrive on hitting balls on the up, at least partly because this generated 'a lot more satisfaction'. While the foul weather repeatedly scotched any possibility of gathering a momentum after Burton, he was galvanized by the goodwill and support he discovered around the circuit: 'I'm encouraged by spectators sticking by me, and players, in various teams, telling me they are convinced I have the talent to get back.' It was 'nice', he said, to get a letter from the chairman of selectors after he had been omitted at Lord's, 'in which he intimated I had an international future – if I sort myself out regarding runs and confidence' (the letter is still tucked away in a box somewhere).

Beneath that stiff upper lip, however, lay a reservoir of self-doubt. 'David got *very* depressed when he was dropped,' recollects Fred Rumsey:

> There was talk about giving up, though only talk. Holmes was concerned and asked me to give the situation some thought. I felt he needed to talk to someone else: he knew what I'd say. David is very knowledgeable about the game – wait till he gets expounding – but, like me when I was playing, he didn't like talking about it much while he was off-duty. I thought it might help to find someone he respected.

That someone was Greg Chappell, an interesting choice, given his position as captain of Australia. The reasons were not based exclusively on Chappell's standing as the era's most complete batsman, nor on his recent insistence that it was impossible to intimidate a good player. Rumsey's final year at Somerset had been Chappell's first:

> Greg used to take our nappies down to the laundry. My wife and I were both close to him, and we kept in touch. So I phoned him and said: 'The favour I am about to ask of you may not be good for you

or Australian cricket in the future, but I'd be delighted if you'd speak to David. Somehow, he's losing it, something to do with confidence.' And, out of loyalty to me, Greg agreed. The Aussies were playing at Trent Bridge in the last week of August so Holmes, David, Greg and I arranged to go to an Italian restaurant there. Up to that point I hadn't realized the depth to which Greg considered the game. One particular theory he expounded was the most sensible thing I've ever heard about batting. He was always very solid early on, and the reason for that, he told David, was because he played with the inside half of the bat. Doing that meant he played very close to his pad, and so didn't leave a gate, and also that he played very straight. The ball that gets you caught behind is the one that moves fractionally, and whereas most people would get an edge, the way he played meant that he'd hit it quite thickly with the outside half of the bat. He also told David how he played exclusively to mid-on and mid-off until he reached the thirties, and then looked to blossom, which explains why he got out so often in the thirties and forties: that was the point at which he started to attack.

Holmes also listened intently, and vividly remembers the most useful tip of all:

The essence of what Greg said was, don't listen to what anyone says about your style, because you can make runs and you've proved it. Give yourself short time-targets: still be in after half an hour, still be in after an hour. Because if you stay in you'll score runs; you're incapable of scoring slowly. I thought that was very good of Greg, a brilliant bit of thinking, and very effective. I used to send David cards when he went on tour, and they always said two things: one, don't go to South Africa; two, concentrate.

David remembers being gratified by Chappell's interest: 'Holmesy was probably over-sympathetic for a bit but Chappell said one or two interesting things. The gist was: "You're a good player, and you could be a very good player. We've all had our problems, you have to rise above them." In a way I repaid him, or Australia, by talking to Justin Langer during the 1994–95 Ashes tour.'

Chappell had reinforced David's misgivings over the value of compromise but, to be fair, self-assurance had already begun to filter back, if not with total conviction. At Taunton a week prior to that evening in Nottingham, the pumpkin looked ready to turn back into a coach. 'A beautiful innings,' wrote Alan Gibson in the *Times* as he sought the right words to describe Gower's 94 on the opening day: in David's case, the simplest words always were enough. When the beauty was in its infancy, a Somerset devotee turned to Gibson and said: 'D'you know, I'd like to see him make 50.' When the landmark was reached, Gibson suggested he could resume his parochialism. 'No,' came the assertive answer, 'I'd like to see him make a hundred.' Gibson was 'on the point of asking him whether he would settle for 150, and I am sure he would have said yes' when David was caught at slip. 'Brightness,' wrote Gibson, 'fell from the air.'

There was more beast than beauty in the two-hour 84 against Northants at Grace Road. At Southampton in Leicestershire's final championship fixture, David provided the struts and beams for a two-day victory with 138 in three and three-quarter hours, on a pitch that defied anyone else to reach 75. His last dozen first-class innings of term reaped the comparative riches of 525 runs, enabling him to total 929 first-class runs for Leicestershire, outstripping his previous best by nearly 400. For the first time, he would even contrive to average more for county than country, though a ratio of 33.17 to 25.25 was scarcely significant. More revealing was the corporate profit-and-loss column. In four of their last six championship outings, the Running Foxes, hitherto winless under Davison, their third captain in as many seasons, took the spoils: three of those successes, moreover, were largely down to the man who was reputedly their least reliable cog, who, quipped Ray Illingworth somewhat acidly, 'bats for England and fields for Leicestershire'.

By now, happily, David had reclaimed his rightful place in the national XI. He made 45 in two hours and 35 in 95 minutes to leave his stamp on the rain-stained Centenary Test at Lord's. In starkest contrast to its predecessor at the MCG, this match was an event whose brooding, care-worn mean-spiritedness – Gower, Dennis Lillee and the ebullient Kim Hughes apart – rendered it damper than the dampest squib. David's third-wicket stands of 96 and 81 with Boycott did much to ensure the draw when many felt Botham should have sounded the charge as Tony Greig had done in the 1977 celebration. However, it was the memory of David's levity against the otherwise rampant Lillee that lingered. The eminence grise of pace had made short work of Gooch and Athey at the start of England's first innings to leave David padding in at 41 for two. He clipped his second prune to the midwicket rope, then collected three consecutive fours via two hooks and a drive. 'For a while,' he would reflect, 'I felt as though nothing could go wrong.'

So much so, in fact, that when an inside edge off Lillee sent Rod Marsh the wrong way and struck a lurking helmet, he became the first batsman in Test history to be awarded a five without the ball crossing the boundary. But Lillee had the final say, bowling him neck-and-crop. Along with Hughes's impish two-reeler, those bravura opening frames provided compensation of sorts for the umpires' pedantic refusal to start play until 3.45 on the Saturday, if not for the unseemly altercation between one of their number and a sozzled pink-ginner on the pavilion steps. A letter to *Wisden Cricket Monthly* typified the chorus of disapproval: 'With apologies to the *Sporting Times*: In Affectionate Remembrance of ENGLISH CRICKET which died at Lord's on 2nd September, 1980. The body will be re-cremated and sent to the home of bureaucracy, officialdom and the tactics of defensive, unadventurous cricket.'

On the eve of the match, David had asserted that his enforced break had given him 'a chance to relax and play without so much pressure', and suggested that those watching would witness 'a lighter mental approach'. In his *Daily Star* column he also conceded that the press criticism 'may have contributed to a loss of form'. Overall, he found the occasion a 'slightly disappointing' experience from a personal as well as a collective perspective: 'I made a start in both innings, played fairly well, then got out when, as they say, on the verge of greater things. I can imagine all my mentors and my fans tearing their wigs to shreds.' Nevertheless, the debate over his candidacy for the Caribbean was brief.

He proceeded to begin the main agenda of the winter in the Caribbean with, quite literally, a tour de force, collecting 187 in under eight hours against a more than useful Young West Indies attack numbering Marshall, Daniel and Harper. In acclaiming it as 'a great booster', Brian Rose reckoned there were four or five chances, though 'excited' spectators insisted there were six or seven: 'If this was the type of Gower the selectors had been searching for over the previous two years, they found him among the storage tanks of Point-à-Pierre.' Not that this surprised Paul Downton, the thoughtful, amiable wicketkeeper whom David had befriended when they toured the Caribbean with Young England in 1976. 'David had a habit of scoring runs in the first game of a tour. He set out his stall to do so and usually achieved it, because then everything, he reasoned, would come easily.'

Torrential rain in St Vincent proceeded to ravage the next segment of the itinerary. Downton roomed with David for a spell, and detected few changes from their schooldays:

He was a good 30s to 70s man on that Young England tour and never really changed. Because he was a struggler himself, Brearley thought the ease with which he batted was quite marvellous. But you always felt he got himself out. That didn't make him frustrating to play with at that stage, but it got slightly so in the middle and latter stages of his career. You always felt he could give you more. When I met him on the Crocodiles tour in '74, we became good friends, so in many ways we grew up together. He was clearly very bright, but I can't remember any in-depth conversations apart from talking about life after cricket. The fact that he didn't sign for Kent hadn't been that hard to understand. I don't think he saw himself as a Kent person: the only real association was boarding school. He was quite stand-offish when I first knew him, slightly awkward, and there was this slightly offbeat, Pythonesque sense of humour: the jokes were a bit forced and didn't always come off. Although he was becoming more confident in '81, he was not a natural extrovert. Whenever Middlesex played Leicestershire – and he wasn't on Test duty – we would dine together after stumps. It struck you that he knew superstars – Gary Lineker, Tim Rice, Robin Askwith, Willie Thorne – but didn't have a group of mates.

On that Young England tour, Cow [Cowdrey] was a good mate of mine already and he was the natural, as a leader as well as with the girls: he was the one with the charm and the charisma. Whereas David struggled for a while with the girls – he became better looking and more confident as he became more successful and the days of the Brillo pad hair passed – which is why he pursued Vicki. He thought nothing of driving from Leicester to Reading and back of an evening to see her. They were a slightly strange pair, and they fought a lot. Not surprisingly, she got caught up in the whole thing of being David Gower's girlfriend, which made her slightly dismissive of other people. If one was to be horribly cynical, you would say that, as his success rose, she became more attached. But he was frightened to cast adrift. He became lonely in the mid-eighties, especially after his mother's death, but then he always did strike me as quite lonely.

'I understand where Paul's coming from,' empathizes Fred Rumsey:

In becoming a star individual, you do live on your own island; you do get a bit lonely. There was that loner factor about David, and there were times when he would get lonely. He found the missing link he was looking for when he met Thorunn. You can always tell when he's happy, but he doesn't need friends around him all the time: he just likes to know they're there. Very few people understand his intensity. Being laid-back was a manufactured thing: he's just more reticent than most, particularly back then, because he has a problem with being open.

Downton was not in the least bit surprised to find that life under Botham bore scant resemblance to life under Brearley. 'The spirit of the

110

party was quite good, but even though we had a very professional core of players – Willey, Gooch, Emburey, Boycott – it was a bit chaotic under Botham. He surrounded himself with his drinking mates, Graham Stevenson and one or two others, and we didn't really see much of him.' Ennui spread like wildfire as the rains lashed down in St Vincent. 'Time has still passed slowly,' David wrote in his *Wisden Cricket Monthly* diary, having noted the dual attractions of three-card brag and James Clavell's interminable *Shogun*. In a snapshot that kindled memories of Tony Hancock's immortal 'Sunday Afternoon at Home' – 'Is that the time? I thought it was at least Tuesday' – he informed his readers that Willis 'has been heard frequently to follow an unmomentous few words of conversation with a muttered, "another three-and-a-half seconds gone".'

Then there was the cricket. After some uniformly sound bowling in the first one-day international at Arnos Vale had whisked out Clive Lloyd and company for 127 on a pitch as smooth as the Elephant Man's forehead, David put on 65 with his captain to lift England from 15 for four, only to be outsmarted by Alvin Kallicharran, of all people. Chest-on and arms flailing, Colin Croft revved up again and the last six wickets fell for 45, leaving Botham's men two runs short. The first England tour to feature Botham, Gooch, Gatting and Gower was plunged into even deeper despond as, in turn, the first Test was lost by an innings, the second one-dayer by a street, and the third Test by a country mile.

Between times, the real world intruded. Robin Jackman's South African affiliations triggered unrest in Guyana and, ultimately, the abandonment of the second Test. For a few days, an early return flight was in the offing, a prospect that figured fairly high on the communal wish-list. While David Bairstow 'gleefully anticipated' a pint of hand-pumped Tetley's and Gooch dwelt on the possibility of seeing his beloved West Ham sooner than he thought, Frank Keating asked David what he thought of the affair: 'I dunno,' came the reply, 'I s'pose it's all a bit of a joke.' It was, in effect, the D'Oliveira saga in reverse, even if the *Daily Mail* did venture that 'wretched Guyana . . . comes very near the top of the list of countries least qualified to take a stand on human rights'. Amid the ensuing welter of histrionic tirades from those who did not believe the sports boycott to be either a valid or a viable weapon against apartheid – and a few who did – a *Guardian* leader proved more perceptive than most: 'To have governments picking and choosing among properly selected visiting players, declaring that some have passed some arbitrary pollution point while others have stopped just short of it, is an intolerable process.' In the *Daily Express*, Pat Gibson looked ahead with acuity: 'The tragic irony of the Robin Jackman affair is that Guyana has given English cricket an offensive shove towards the welcoming arms of South Africa.'

To cap it all, on the second evening of the third Test in Barbados, 'The Colonel', Ken Barrington, suffered a fatal heart attack. When Botham imparted the news to his side, every man was 'devastated'. David saw Barrington as 'an ally . . . a rock-like father-figure'. Barrington's death, he lamented in *Wisden Cricket Monthly*:

> was the saddest thing that could have happened, and the immediate effect on us can be judged by Robin Jackman's bowling of the first over that Sunday morning, when he cannot remember actually seeing the batsman. We all still miss 'The Colonel', as much for his good humour as for the encouragement he would foster on us all, especially his protégé batsmen such as myself.

Among the myriad ifs, buts and maybes that have plagued English cricket since that tragic night in Bridgetown, one stands out. 'The Colonel' was a man with Queen and Country steaming out of his ears, a man regarded with fondness and respect by the coming generation: might he have stopped the rot? On his own, of course not. As part of a complementary management set-up? Quite possibly. 'A lot of the problems I encountered in future years might not have arisen,' reasoned Botham more than a decade later; along with Brian Close and Brearley, Barrington was one of the few people close to the captain 'with the guts to stand up and say: "Don't be such an idiot."' By the same token, it must be said that it was his very dedication to the cause that cost Barrington his life: any doctor worth his salt would have instructed him to cut back his involvement. All that can be said with certainty is that the void he left, as coach-cum-raiser of spirits, remains vacant.

David responded to Barrington's death with some of the most bloody-minded batting of his career. While the first two Tests had promised more than they delivered, there had been no question about his form on tour. Early on the third morning in Trinidad, Croft truncated a diligent three-and-a-half-hour knock by trapping him leg-before for 48 with one of his trademark leg-cutters. In the second innings, David and Boycott forged a third-wicket alliance of 61 to halt the hordes for nigh-on two hours; once more, though, David failed to pick up the baton the following morning, glancing Roberts down the legside. In Bridgetown, Croft had him taken at slip for 17 as England limped to 122; second time round, he and Gooch sped England from 2 for two to 122 for two with a percussive counter-attack; then, with the edge of the woods in sight, Lloyd resorted to Viv Richards, who restored order by coaxing David to play on to a straight off-break. David held his hands up: 'As soon as Viv came on I told myself, "You mustn't get out to him." For more than two and a half hours we had survived the fast bowlers and it is very difficult not to let yourself relax a little when you see a slow bowler come on. The stroke was a bad one, a black mark.' Gooch noted that his partner 'was desperately upset, feeling that he had let everybody down'.

Antigua's inaugural Test nonetheless found David feeling sufficiently chipper to consider jettisoning the helmet. When Croft proceeded to score a bullseye on the protected bonce, David was relieved to have had third thoughts. It was Croft who gnawed away at England's first innings with six wickets, the sightscreen proving too low to cover his tangential approach, with the result that Emburey and Stevenson were both bowled by balls they failed to pick up. Time consumed rather than runs scored – 32 and 22, for the record – was the more important contribution here, although the best batting pitch of the rubber and the loss of the fourth day had almost as much to do with England's survival as did doughty centuries from Boycott and Peter Willey. 'David played with more maturity than he had shown before,' enthused Gooch, 'cutting out much of his bat-waving outside the off stump.' Croft remembers being suitably impressed: 'As a left-hander he was doubly difficult to get out. He coped better than most with what we threw at him.'

But Paul Downton interpreted the scene rather differently:

David was really pissed off in the second innings because he had to go in and block it out for two hours. 'What's the point in this?' he said. You could see the frustration he felt at having to shackle himself . . . he was someone who was certainly very conscious of style: sometimes it was more important to him how he scored runs than actually making them. That became a problem in later years, and became part of his downfall, I think.

Clive Lloyd also remained unconvinced: 'David has looked good making his thirties and forties, but England should be thinking of getting him into the sixties and seventies and really building an innings.'

Finally, David obliged, regaling Sabina Park with the innings he cherishes above any other. In the first innings, Croft bowled him for 22, behind his legs to boot: embarrassment unconfined, resolve stiffened. Marshall's strained rib muscle and the loss of three hours' play to drizzle on the fourth afternoon conspired to aid England after they had gone in again 157 behind, but a welcome showering of luck was not the only thing that saved them from a 3–0 series defeat. As David sat down in his hotel room, preparing his notes on the first three days for a TCCB tour book, he became:

increasingly conscious that I had not really done justice to myself. I got up the following morning determined not to return to the dressing room when my chance came without at least a century against my name. Perhaps it was a selfish attitude. But people throughout the ages have written that the makers of large centuries have all had a streak of selfishness about them.

On the rest day, Lloyd accentuated English fears when he announced that the pitch was beginning to behave mischievously. For all Botham's subsequent bombast, the scoreboard was soon reading 10 for two, yet David walked in feeling 'better than I had done on any previous occasion on the tour'. Marshall was soon deposited through the covers, 'right off the middle of the bat: everything was right about the stroke'. He felt 'at home, untroubled'. Then Croft gloved Boycott with a snorter: 32 for three. Then David's six over third man off Holding implied a frantic state of mind, though not to those who knew the shot to have been wholly intentional. Against bowling of this nature, he reasoned, the uppercut was as profitable a shot as any. Lloyd immediately summoned Richards and, with his second ball, the non-deviating offie bluffed him again with a short, wide 'four-ball' that David took his eyes off while mulling over which perimeter board to hammer: this time, though, Lloyd floored the slip offering and, in the 55 minutes to lunch, he and Willey flogged and flayed 59 before the heavens spilled their contents. The pair endured when play finally resumed, adding another 43 in the 70 minutes possible. Although the next morning found noses sniffing grindstone, Richards did for Willey with his 'come-on' ball when the partnership had raised 136. Roland Butcher exited at the same score: suddenly, England were 168 for five and teetering. An off-form, becalmed Botham hung around while 47 were added for the sixth wicket and, after four and a quarter hours, a four off Larry Gomes swept David to his fourth Test century, his first for thirteen Tests and for almost two years. 'Come on,' he continued to exhort himself, 'come on.' Holding then had Botham snared in the gully: the score effectively 58 for six with the best part of four hours to go and the new cherry freshly deflowered.

Enter Downton: Holding purred in and pounded away but the door was about to be bolted. 'In the first innings we'd been blown away by the new ball on the second morning, and I'd got a duck, so I wasn't particularly confident,' winces Downton:

At full-strength, [the West Indies'] pace attack was as good as they've ever had: in '84, Eldine Baptiste was the weak link, in '88, it was Patrick Patterson, but they had Marshall in the wings for most of that series. There was a feeling Botham was going to have a dart and get out just before the new ball, and that was precisely what happened. Because of Barrington's death, it was important for us to battle it out, to show

114

guts, but David didn't really change the way he played: he was just in control, in command. He played brilliantly for a twenty-three-year-old. I felt he was actually quite enjoying it. We'd chat at the end of each over, have a laugh about something and give each other encouragement. When we got to tea, there was only a short session left so we knew we were in with a shout.

The shout had evolved into a sure thing by the time Larry Gomes trundled in to bowl the final over: the seventh-wicket pair were still in residence and David had matched Gooch's 'magnificent' first-day 153: 'I toyed seriously with sticking on the same total. I even mentioned it to Downton . . . but when Gomes bowled me a particularly loose delivery, I couldn't resist.'

Michael Holding not only relished the battle, he savoured the skill of his vanquisher. Although the Jamaican Jaguar was one of the few cricketers to reject the rand for explicitly political reasons, he and David were united in other areas, principally image and appeal. Aside from the odd isolated explosion – Christchurch 1980; Old Trafford 1976 – Holding was also a model of decorum. Yet if David's laid-back persona was at least partly a facade, Mikey's reflected the reality; David, in comparison to Holding, seemed positively highly strung.

'Gower's adventurous style,' Holding believes:

made him the type of batsman you thought you could get out. Given his day, though, he could embarrass you. I much preferred bowling at players like him and Greg Chappell. It was always a good challenge, an enjoyable contest, and at Sabina he played a supreme innings. He was probably one of only two players who would have graced West Indian cricket – with Botham. His foibles would have been accepted in the Caribbean in return for the pleasure given.

From his pew high in the stands, Fred Rumsey couldn't stop beaming.

David possessed something denied to all but the very greatest batsmen, and I'm talking about Bradman, Compton, Sobers and Pollock here: the ability to hit at the point of the ball, as it makes contact with the bat, not through the line as the manuals say. He watched the ball right on to the bat. His timing allowed it. That's why he could hit the ball at the top of its bounce. That's why he could play with a cross-bat. People criticized him because he was always getting caught flashing outside off-stump, but Compton had the same criticism levelled against his sweep.

David savours the memory of this innings as he does few others:

I was proud of that, even though Malcolm broke down. That cut off Holding for six – instinct at its best. I remember David Murray, the keeper, coming down the wicket at the end of the over – or maybe after that same ball – and saying, 'Shot, man.' I talked to myself more than I normally did. It was a case of finding an extra reason to add something to your basic performance, whether it's disappointment, frustration, the need to prove something to yourself, or to others. It's largely selfish, doing it for yourself, to restore your own confidence, self-belief, self-satisfaction. I was very determined to make that innings count. It was my last chance. I felt as if, had I left without a score, the whole tour would almost have been wasted.

The salvage experts dined together that evening. Recalls Downton, 'He had a definite sense of satisfaction, of the big coming-of-age.' The entire tour, in fact, can be seen as David's coming-out party. A total of 376 runs in the series at 53.71 was impressive – even if he did average more in the island fixtures. An even better measure of his efforts can be gleaned from a breakdown of England's most productive partnerships: in all, there were just fifteen partnerships of 40-plus, of which David was party to nine, including two of the three to breach three figures. He attributed his enhanced discipline to the wet wickets he had been forced to negotiate the previous summer, compelling him to play 'a number of blocking-type innings with scoring a secondary consideration'. He also tipped his hat to Peter Shilton, who had popped over to the flat before Christmas to spell out 'the need for self-motivation, the necessity for getting away to a good start'. Not only had he proved himself a match for the most malevolent attack in the game, he had, on occasions, dominated it in a fashion few others – Gooch, Gavaskar and, briefly, Amarnath – could even contemplate.

One can only surmise, therefore, that a combination of relief and anti-climax lay at the heart of his comparative ineptitude when the opening bell sounded on another Ashes series two months later. 'It takes a long time to recover from a West Indies tour,' Downton reasons, 'not only because it is mentally exhausting but because it's the one tour that runs into our season. One minute you're playing in bright sunshine, in front of big crowds, with all the euphoria and noise, then suddenly, two days later, you're at Lord's, it's wet and cold, and the ball is seaming not bouncing.' To his credit, David gritted it out for five hours against Downton and Middlesex, making 108, but this was succeeded by scores of 47, 2 and 5 in the Prudential Trophy series, the prelude to a summer in which personal underachievement contrasted starkly with the now seemingly mythical exploits of one I. T. Botham. It seems pertinent to point out that the pair shared few partnerships of any substance. As the People's Champion plundered his pocketful of miracles that summer, is it possible that David was a little cowed?

The irony here was that David saved his best for the shires. Though the most adequate word to describe Leicestershire in 1981 was middling – a B&H semi-final here, a NatWest quarter-final there, eighth in the championship after waiting until mid-July for their first win – David contrived to enjoy his most bounteous county campaign yet. There were no fewer than four championship hundreds: only in his final summer at Hampshire would he emulate this. In notching 1000 championship runs for the first time – at a creditable 56.05 – a couple of scores were settled. At Tunbridge Wells he made 115 when no one else could pass 56; when Northants set their neighbours 261 in a shade over three hours, it was his two-and-a-half-hour hundred that turned impending stalemate into heady victory. In ten Test innings, however, he eked out just 250 runs, reaching the twenties seven times but only once venturing further. On six occasions he was in for at least an hour. Indeed, the only ground where he failed to make at least one visit last that long was Headingley: others were due a share of the spotlight, notably his ex-captain. Before the sixth Test at The Oval, the temporarily reinstated Brearley rang David to advise him that Paul Parker would play in his place. Although his county form might persuade some otherwise, these, surely, were the signs of a man who had conquered Everest but had nothing left for Ben Nevis.

Downton attributes some of the blame to the conditions, tailor-made as they were for the hitherto unheralded Terry Alderman, whose 42 scalps supplanted the Australian Ashes series record set by Rodney Hogg in 1978–79.

It was a wet summer, the ball was moving around and David never looked at ease. He preferred the bowlers to be a bit quicker than Alderman, preferred the ball coming on to the bat. It would be unfair to say that he was never a battler – he battled brilliantly in Antigua in '86 when the pitch was up and down – but he hardly ever looked good battling. He was never a very good slow-wicket player because he'd always play the same way. He made 20 quicker and easier than anybody, but whereas you'd think most batsmen, when they get that far, were set, he was never set. You always felt there was a chance he could get out at any time. That would have caused some dressing-room resentment, but I can't remember anything ever being said, probably because people had so much respect for him. Even Will [Willey] admired him, and they were complete opposites.

All the same, the opposition also numbered one D. K. Lillee, complete with trendy headband: a Lillee who had gained more in guile than he had lost in zip. Four times he sent David on his way; Lord's, typically, was the only place where the latter flourished for long. On a tricky surface, England, already one-down in the rubber after losing on a stinker at Trent Bridge, were lurching at a net 21 for two on the fourth afternoon when he joined the man who made him concentrate harder than any other partner, Boycott, winning his 100th cap and hell-bent on occupation till kingdom come. Lillee was carved and cut by the new arrival, Ray Bright was pulled for six; the pair added 123 in 193 minutes before Lillee finally unglued Boycott for 60. By now, a draw was odds-on, yet Lillee was even more relieved to eject David with a lifter that stopped a shade and kissed the shoulder of the bat with his quarry eleven runs shy of a maiden Ashes hundred on home soil. 'He was masterly that day, had the attack by the throat. I can remember great forties of his but he rarely exploded against us in my time. We often felt he was ready to, but it was usually a case of bowling tightly enough and waiting.'

If David's first trip to the Indian subcontinent turned out to be more satisfying than his third tilt with the Aussies in two and a half years, five scores between 64 and 89 in seven Tests scarcely represented repletion. Inspiration, tellingly, was in short supply. While Sri Lanka's inaugural Test was one for the scrapbook – not least because it proved that English cricket has not always grudged oxygen to those in greatest need – the less said about the Indian leg the better. While David was patrolling the boundary in Bombay during the first Test, a missile sped for his head: the next few hours were spent divesting his hair of fragments of banana. He was vastly more impressed by what the country had to offer than by the subsequent sham that passed for public entertainment. Unlike so many colleagues, he refused to gripe the usual gripes about rotten itinerary, insufficient booze and foul food: 'Some of the lads were fed up at times but I find it's only hard work if you let it be.' Unlike many, he was keen to take a glimpse beyond the boundary.

There was the Taj Mahal and the elephant rides, and those white tigers at Delhi Zoo. Nagpur was markedly less alluring; Nagpur means 'Snake Town', and if no wriggly slitherers were encountered in the flesh, there were 'frequent interviews, some quite intimate, with a fellow called Rodney the Rat'. David vowed never to return but did so a month later ('not one of the airport officials believed we wanted to get off') en route to the Kanha wildlife reserve. There, accompanied by Mr and Mrs Gooch, he spent a memorable forty minutes enraptured by the sight of a ring of elephants encircling a tigress.

Appropriate as the hunt was, attempts to track down an endangered bison known as the gaur – pronounced 'gower' – proved futile. So did several of David's bids for a run: in all, one of the fleetest-footed men in the game sustained six run-outs. The four before Christmas, he revealed in *Wisden Cricket Monthly*, 'concerned me greatly in my new year's resolutions'. The final ignominy came at the end of the day's proceedings against North Zone at Jammu. David was trying his best to disguise his impatience with pushy autograph hounds. While scribbling away for one stargazer, he strove to explain who he was by spelling out his name: 'G . . . O . . . W . . .'. Evidently reassured, the stargazer unwittingly fired back the ultimate put-down: 'Tavaré!'

What humour there was on the pitch was also accidental: the Indian board would have been better off staging a single-wicket competition between Boris Spassky and Bobby Fischer.

The opening – and, as it transpired, decisive – Test in Bombay saw David run out for the second time in fifty Test innings before reverting to a more familiar pattern by falling leg-before to Kapil Dev. England's performance, asserted the *Daily Telegraph* correspondent, Mike Carey, 'was so inadequate that one couldn't help thinking that they had been influenced, perhaps subconsciously, by thoughts that everything was against them'. Unfortunately, the us-and-them sentiments persisted, uniting the party yet simultaneously sapping their capacity for positive thought. Willis had 'never known a group to get on so well together', a considerable feather in the captain's hat. The obverse side of the coin was Keith Fletcher's inability – or reluctance – to dispel the mood of paranoia, a shortcoming that would eventually cost him his stripes. His opposite number, Sunil Gavaskar, put more effort into slowing the game down than acquiring runs, yet, for some reason, Fletcher, a popular choice as Brearley's successor, permitted himself to be dragged into a war of attrition he was only ever going to lose. If India bowled 12 overs an hour, England replied with 11. The remaining five Tests were drawn, amid a mood of utter torpor: in three of them, the final day arrived before two innings had been completed. The nadir came in Calcutta, where an estimated world record attendance of 400,000 witnessed a scoring rate that seldom rose above two an over.

A week after what *Wisden* would describe as David's 'mature' 89 in Colombo, the highest individual contribution to Sri Lanka's first Test match, five fellow tourists consented to exchange their souls for a mess of potage. The announcement of the names of the so-called 'dirty dozen' who had elected to take the rand and run did wonders for the angst quotient. Fletcher resisted the blandishments to keep the job he craved and was rewarded with the sack. When he learned of his fate via the clipped tones of the new chairman of selectors, Peter May, and proceeded to drive down the country lanes of deepest Essex in a remorseful daze, he must have reassured himself that one shafting a lifetime was enough for any decent, law-abiding chap . . .

Only three defections were of any real consequence: Emburey (the Colombo matchwinner), Gooch and Willey. Risking national – not to mention paternal – opprobrium on top of a three-year Test ban, believed Gooch, constituted an acceptable price for ridding oneself of such purposeless cricket, especially when the alternative offered far more readies, and hence security. His bosom pal Emburey simply didn't see why he shouldn't play where he wanted and for whom he wanted. Willey had every reason to think that he would only ever be picked by his country when courage was the priority, and, correspondingly, was as blunt as his reputation demanded: 'I've got nothing on my conscience. I'm just here to play cricket.' Comments of that nature provoked heated exchanges in the Commons. 'We do not have the power to prevent our sportsmen and women visiting South Africa, or anywhere else,' declaimed Margaret Thatcher, flexing the royal 'we' with customary deftness. 'If we did we would no longer be a free country.' Many commentators quite rightly homed in on the hypocrisy of outlawing cricketers while British trade with South Africa was running at £1756m a year, but it was those anonymous *Guardian* leader writers who once more struck the biggest blow for considered analysis and reasoned judgment: 'Sporting boycotts have become the shopsoiled currency of international diplomacy . . . Some sportsmen are not very adept at political complexities. That is one small excuse . . . but it is just about the only excuse available.' The *Sun*, meanwhile, had a brainstorm: 'They have, of course, every right to accept the gold of the state that practises the evil gospel called apartheid. But in doing so, they cannot be said to be principled defenders of freedom.'

David had spent much of the past twelve months to-ing and fro-ing. He had been an intrigued party from the initial stirrings in the Caribbean ('clandestine meetings with shadowy figures emerging from hotel rooms – most people kept their options open, waiting to see what money was being offered'). Jon Holmes advised him he would be 'risking too much from the commercial angle'; yet playing in South Africa held a strong appeal, money aside. He had been present at the conception of 'Operation Chessmatch' ('Do you know how Karpov and Spassky are getting on?'). In India, as owner of one of the two most marketable talents in English cricket, and therefore a crucial bargaining tool, he had been in on all of Chief Recruiting Officer Boycott's hotel-room hugger-muggering. At the crucial meeting in Bombay after the first Test, he informed Gooch that he could count him out. Gooch always believed he was 'unsympathetic to South Africa'.

As mentioned earlier, David has, at various times, given many reasons for his decision not to join the rebels, all of them credible if not necessarily worthy, and none of them expressly political. The plain truth is that he was fast evolving into the almost purely apolitical animal he is today. When the *Observer* canvassed a cross-section of public figures about their voting intentions prior to the 1987 General Election – David, significantly, was the only sportsman polled – he supplied a few gentle hints:

In common with many sportsmen when tackled on politics, I would normally aspire to the odd vague comment and assume an air of relative indifference. In general, I tend to feel that most of what one hears on TV and reads in the press comes under the category of random hot air, with the 'RHA Factor' increasing markedly during elections. In the end nothing that Messrs Kinnock, Steel or Owen say is likely to deter me from wishing the Conservatives a successful return to power. However sensible and reasonable Mr Kinnock might appear now and again, most of Labour's high profile support is enough to inspire thoughts of emigration, and I would be quite happy to see the Alliance come second. So, if I can shake off my natural lassitude, any cross I can manage on polling day will be against a Tory name.

Even though this particular issue strayed far beyond the confines of this parlour game we call party politics, Fred Rumsey believes that a political sensibility did enter the equation.

I flew in to Delhi on 23 December, for two days, because my travel company operated there and David was helping out, arranging tickets. When we went out for dinner, he said: 'You'll be pleased to know I've decided not to go.' And his reasons coincided exactly with what I'd have said. At the time I was involved with the West Indies through my travel company, and there's no way I would have jeopardized that. Besides, it's very easy to lose your sense of ethical responsibility. I disliked apartheid but I could see the problems. I'd spent a year coaching there myself, writing too: Donald Woods was my editor. I felt that tours of that nature were only going to intensify the situation. The way through was the way it ended up. David's reasons weren't just personal or selfish. He cared a tremendous amount about the fact that English cricket shouldn't suffer. Whatever Boycott says, he never committed himself to going; he was quite deliberate about that.

As the summer of 1982 struggled to release itself from spring's remorseless grip, David had other matters on his mind. There was the Leicestershire vice-captaincy he had assumed in March; Mike Turner had got the nod from Lord's: 'They had their eyes on David as a possible future captain, and unless he captained us he was a non-starter.' Then there was the not inconsiderable side issue of having to remind himself that there was more to Test cricket than churning out pretty fifties.

Then there was the large modern house in Ratcliffe Road he now shared with Vicki – despite the 'customary problem of fidelity which single young cricketers tend not to find that easy to stick to'. Discreet as he strove to be, 'the occasional slip-up was unavoidable'. There had been an 'inevitable erosion of trust' but the relationship was sturdy enough to survive the odd blarney, as Rumsey confirms: 'Around that time, Vicki and David were very much in love.' Increasingly, Vicki was handling secretarial duties as well as keeping the house in order, and evidently was more than happy doing so. In Richard Harris's 1979 play, *Outside Edge*, still going strong in regional rep, Miriam is never quite certain whether she prefers Rog to have a good innings or a bad one: 'If it's a good one, he relives it in bed, shot by shot, and if it's a bad one, he actually replays the shots until he gets it right. He can make a really good innings last all winter.' For all the recent undulations and ululations, Vicki knew there was something she could always rely on for consolation: David was no Rog.

7   Leading from the Middle

'Why do so many players *want* to be captain?'
Derek Underwood

Some are born to lead, most to follow, while a precious, splendiferous few have no choice but to boogie to their own beat. Judged by the highest standards, David Gower was to captaincy what Jim Callaghan was to prime ministry: adequate at best, invisible at worst. Yet what right did we have to expect anything else of someone whose appreciable cerebral powers were tempered by indolence? Geniuses find their craft too much of a doddle to inspire lesser mortals. Inspire them, that is, by direction as opposed to deed. Instinct cannot be explained, much less instilled. Perhaps lacking sufficient confidence in his own judgement, David the captain espoused an admirably enlightened collectivism, a philosophy that paved the way for his deepest cricketing regret, namely the insertion of Australia at Leeds in 1989. Seldom did he impose authority, or rally the troops, preferring the loose rein. He accorded them the respect due fellow workers, but that pre-supposed them to be equals, which they palpably were not (that said, had they been less unequal, he might have stood a chance). Some lead from the front, others with a prod from the rear. David led from the middle. There are those who believe he should never had led at all.

The critics queued up, darts poised. 'He is too laid-back, perhaps too self-centred,' Clive Lloyd, the most successful of all Test captains, charged in 1988. 'Gower lacks the authority to impose his will when senior players are questioning his tactics. And he cannot whip his men into renewed effort when their spirits are flagging. That was only too evident when England were in the West Indies in 1986. They just gave up. They thought: "Our opponents are better than we are and if we lose it's no big deal." No real captain would have allowed his team to surrender meekly like that. Gower did.' Bob Willis, who went to the Caribbean in 1986 as assistant manager, endorses Lloyd's overview: 'To say he was too self-centred to lift a beaten side is reasonable criticism. David was a very good self-motivator, but I don't think he could motivate others.'

Captains perceived as having squandered opportunity's initial knock are seldom granted a second: David was, and tripped even more heavily. In his diary of the 1989 Ashes tour, Geoff Lawson cited the fifth Test as 'the only easy Test I've played'. England, he asserted with due incredulity, 'just caved in . . . their total lack of spirit was unbelievable'. For all that the two were friends, Lawson did not stint in assigning a hefty proportion of the blame to David's captaincy:

> He seems to have had one plan out on the field and when that hasn't worked he's been stuck for alternatives. That is the main difference between him and AB [Allan Border]. AB did not really want the job in the first place and struggled to come to terms with it for a while. But he is a smart bloke who when he sets himself to do something works at it until he's improved enough to satisfy himself. AB has learned to be a good captain; Gower does not appear to be too interested in learning. I know that his captaincy is not highly regarded by his teammates.

Harsh words, perhaps, especially since so many of his teammates in 1989 were distracted by 'rand-y' thoughts, yet there was much to fuel them. The nub of it is that David would have been a good deal better off without the distraction of captaincy.

He is entitled to disagree, of course. Yet, even as he expounds his philosophy, taking extreme care to suppress any semblance of a whinge, it is difficult not to detect a pang of regret. Besides, it was just a job.

> The basic principle [as captain] is to try and create an atmosphere that allows people to relax enough to perform at their best, and you adapt when they don't. I had players coming to me at various times and say they liked how it worked, while others would whinge because you were treating someone differently. You can go and spend half an hour with every man in the side every day and leave yourself an hour and a half for sleep. Or you can deal with people as they come to you, tackle problems as you spot them, the assumption being that you will miss a lot of the problems because people will go somewhere else. That's why you rely on a management team. Players realize captaincy is hard, that you can only deal with so much. Clive [Lloyd] had the knack of getting people under his wing, which is a very good trick. Take Dujon. Dooj was pretty impressed with Clive. Early on in his Test career, Clive said to him, basically, 'hey man, let's have a few beers and go out for dinner', just to introduce him to the way things work. Unfortunately, the changes we made in '84 and '89, you need a lot of dinners.

That's where it's hard. You can put more time in, but only at the cost of something else.

Does occupying a different wavelength to most of one's peers not constitute a handicap?

I don't know. I have a certain cosmopolitan outlook. I can get on with, and talk to, all manner of different people. My nose doesn't go up there by a long, long way. I wasn't a dictatorial captain: I always had this vision of an open house. If there is a point to be made it is that wasn't what was naturally allowed to happen. Take Gatt, for instance. He was a good vice-captain in India, and a good captain: people would go to him and he would come to me. Same in the Windies. You have to retain the mixture, the right blend of authority; you can't be down there in the same trench twenty-four hours a day.

For all that it was a cleverly crafted illusion, did that wonky grin, that 'I'm above all this' smirk, not impart the wrong vibes?

Perhaps, but that's up to how people want to interpret it. That applies to players as well as observers. Part of the impression of being able to rise above it, to keep it in perspective, was perfectly natural, sometimes it was consciously done. We might have been having twenty bells of shit being knocked out of us – it's never quite as simple as it looks. Against the West Indies it was a case of showing them I wasn't about to commit suicide. My head went down against them, a lot more off the field than on it, but you have to retain some veneer of control, a front. We can either commit suicide or go on playing, and the best alternative is to carry on playing. You've somehow got to carry on being cheerful and think of a solution. And if we don't we're still going to get hammered, so we're not that much worse off. People misconstrue it when you're under pressure because they think you should be wearing black. But if you wear black immediately, you're no better off. You're worse off. If you smile about it you're still in the crap but you're still smiling. The worst thing is if you get accused of not caring. It's not a question of not caring; it's a question of somehow trying to work out how to deal with it.

In this respect, honesty can be regarded as David's worst policy. All too typical, and admirably so, were the closing words of an interview he did with the *Times* in 1989, appearing as it did on the morning of the second Texaco Trophy match against Australia, under the highly un-original headline 'Laid-back and laissez-faire'. England had won the first game: never again would they emerge triumphant under Gower's leadership. 'You've obviously got to take it [professional cricket] seriously enough to work on it,' he mused, 'and you do care – but you've got to say to some degree: "OK, fine, it's a game of cricket, I didn't have a great day, I'm human, I'll do it tomorrow." You've got to be able to relax . . .' Perhaps it was the identity of the interviewer, one Catherine Bennett, a feature writer far removed from the hack pack. The candour, however, was foolhardy. 'I seem to have got away with it,' he replied when Ms Bennett suggested that he seemed a reluctant force for cricket's moral rearmament. 'By and large I've managed to survive with a relatively clean image, but who knows what lurks around the corner?' Even the accompanying photo was ill-advised: new captain, chest hairs exposed, eyes looking upward as if at some distant peak, standing under a shower. Landed once more with a role that demanded a goodly helping of bullshit, in defeat more than victory, David's front was never more than gossamer-thin.

Had he been born ten years earlier and concentrated on turning vibrant fifties into a few more big scores, it is conceivable that Chris Cowdrey might have occupied a status not that far below Brearley's. An enthusiastic, vigorous, at times inspirational helmsman at Kent – most notably in 1988 when he led an average squad to within a point of the championship – Cowdrey's limited attributes with bat and ball could have been accommodated more readily at Test level (well, more than once) had the available crews been more seaworthy. As chum and peer, Cowdrey is firmly of the view not only that David should have remained in the ranks, but also that a stubby finger poked into the chest of a bumptious Pakistani umpire cost England the services of her ablest skipper of the period.

> I think he [David] would have been better off going through his career without the burdens of captaincy. What Clive Lloyd said about his being too self-centred was harsh, but . . . I would compare Gooch to Gower. They like to captain how they play. Gower likes a relaxed atmosphere, doesn't believe in all the training, believes in enjoying it *and* giving 100 per cent out in the middle, which probably doesn't work. Gooch tried to captain with all-out concentration – running, nets. The one in the middle may be Gatting. Under him, everyone enjoys it but they practise as well. He had a nice blend of both, which made him the best available.

All Middlesex bias aside, Brearley concurs:

> I didn't think Gower should have been captain, and they should have appointed Gatting in 1989. I was a long way from Faisalabad but the

provocation did seem extreme. He shouldn't have wagged his finger at an umpire but he should have been advised to apologize immediately and get on with the game. They got embattled instead. He should have been fined and that should have been the end of it. You can't expect people to be little saints.'

Cowdrey makes the most pertinent point of all: 'Very few of the really great players, the real talents, make good captains. When have they ever? They should be left to get on with their own game.'

Guilty of ineffectual stewardship though David frequently was, he was scarcely short of alibis. For one thing, had he reigned during pre-tabloid days, he might have been spared the vindictive excesses of an envious media bent on justifying their jobs by turning sporting failure into treason. The very length of Tests and tours enables cricket to grip the national consciousness in a manner unparalleled in the entertainment world. The unceasing pressure brought on by nearly two decades of inferiority has thus conferred on the England captain the title of Pin-Cushion-in-Chief.

Leadership is a fraught job (does somebody really have to do it? Isn't that why we have committees?). In cricket more than any other sport, the captain receives credit and criticism in vastly disproportionate quantities. In the introduction to his *The Art of Captaincy*, Brearley quotes the French general who, upon being asked whether a famous triumph had not, in reality, been won by his second-in-command, pondered and replied: 'Maybe so. But one thing is certain: if the battle had been lost, *I* would have lost it.' When, in 1981, he was recalled to lead England at Leeds, impending scene of the least forgettable five days of his life, Brearley received a number of letters of support, one of which struck a powerful chord. 'Dear Brearley,' it began, unpromisingly. 'There is an old Italian proverb: if you want to know that a fish is bad look at its head.'

No team sport demands as much of its captain as cricket does. No team sport, come to think of it, demands so much from one person. Not only must a cricket captain bat, bowl and field, he must devote his mind to the three Ds: decide, dictate, deliver. Instead of concentrating exclusively on his own performance, he must tend to the needs of ten others. Much as Mike Atherton's psychiatrist might regard the experience as an invaluable rite of passage, the burden can set the stiffest of upper lips quivering, and unnerve the nerveless. 'Sales managers don't sell,' reasoned Brearley, 'foremen don't hump.' Being neither salesman nor humper but, rather, mere genius, David should never have been asked to lead a team – especially not a succession of inadequate ones.

Leaving aside that defence, for now, let us consider his own shortcomings. As with Sobers, his thaumaturgy should have disqualified him. Bradman and Viv Richards are the only bonafide geniuses to have prospered as leaders, yet their records mask deficiencies in tactical appraisal and man-management. David's captaincy prospects were hardly enhanced by shortage of concentration, nor by a dearth of overtly serious intent. If the mind was more than up to it intellectually, it fell way short in terms of rigour and application.

At the same time, only the crass would denounce him as a poor leader and leave it at that. On 2 September 1985, after all, he had stood proud and erect on the Oval balcony, smile as broad as Vauxhall Bridge, left hand clasped around the neck of a bottle of Bolly, right cradling a replica of the urn, arms raised at 10.10 as if conducting 'Land of Hope and Glory' on the last night of the Proms: it was hard to picture a happier captain or a jollier ship. And justly so. He had, after all, become only the fifth England skipper to regain the Ashes in front of his countrymen (after Grace, Carr, Hutton and Brearley), leading from the front with such force that his 732 runs enabled him to leapfrog Compton and, even more unthinkably, Hutton: no Englishman had made more runs in a home Ashes rubber; no English captain had made a more vividly personal contribution in any rubber against anyone. 'David is not only a great player,' enthused Richie Benaud, 'he's now a very good captain.' High praise indeed, coming as it did from one of the acknowledged maestros. Flattering, arguably, as his allotment of thirty-two Tests now seems, David did have other moments of head-boy headiness. In India, on his first tour, he had become the first visiting captain to win a series on the subcontinent after going behind, and the first England captain since Hutton thirty winters earlier to win any overseas series by overturning a deficit. Meagre opposition or no, neither feat was insignificant; nor were those match-saving hundreds at Faisalabad and Lahore in March 1984, his first two Test outings as de facto successor to the ailing Willis.

It would be erroneous, then, to infer that Gower's form deteriorated during his tenure. Of the seventeen men to captain their country on more than thirty occasions (Illingworth, Imran and Kapil were the only ones not to deploy the bat as their prime weapon), Lloyd, Richards, Simpson, May, Gavaskar, Border, Sobers, Javed and Greg Chappell all finished with a superior batting average, only Reid, Brearley, Pataudi and Gooch with an inferior one. Yet, by the same token, Gower's input barely blipped during either of his terms in office: the difference between his average as private and general was minimal: 44.51 to 43.60. Among England captains, only Hammond (who advanced from 58.23 to 59.25) wavered less.

The salient point is not what David did do, but what he might otherwise have done. At the time of his formal accession, at Birmingham in June 1984, he had collected 1522 runs in his previous fifteen Tests at an average of 60.88, with five centuries and eight fifties – comfortably the most impressive sequence of his career. 'One wonders to what depths England might have descended without the batting of David Gower,' wondered Dennis Lillee after he had carried off the International Cricketer of the Year award at the end of the 1982–83 Ashes series. The first innings of the rubber in Perth had seen him in his pomp. 'I always tell people that that 72 was the innings I played best in,' he states with due if understated pride. 'I just got in there, moved and hit. The feet moved like nothing before or since. They moved bloody well. Everything was clicking. I was sharp, pin-sharp all the time. Really good. I didn't turn it into a hundred because of a minor misjudgement: bit of a clip, just enough off the ground for Dyson to dive and get his fingers under it in front of square.'

The third Test in Adelaide duly yielded his first Test century in thirty-eight attempts with what Robin Marlar described as 'that air of superiority and condescension when he knows he is playing well'. Willis declared it 'one of his most responsible innings'. He also made three hundreds against New Zealand in the one-dayers, notably the 158 off 41 overs in Brisbane, wherein he elbowed aside Viv Richards to claim the highest individual score yet recorded in the World Series Cup: neither Allan Lamb nor Fred Rumsey ever saw him bat better. To the former it was 'further proof of his new maturity' as well as one of the finest one-day efforts it had ever been his privilege to witness. 'It seemed as though my bat only had a middle,' David recalled. 'At times like that you only wish you could bottle the formula.' In the World Cup that summer, he led all-comers with 384 at 76.80, completing a run of twenty one-day internationals in which he had amassed 1086 runs at 63.88. During his 130 against Sri Lanka, he deposited five sixes into the Taunton car park, 'without', in Peter Roebuck's words, 'ever appearing violent'. Those seven-hour efforts in Faisalabad and Lahore had prompted no less a judge than Zaheer Abbas to class him as 'the best player in the world'. Unencumbered by the burdens of leading others, who can say how many other 1985s there might have been?

There were other mitigating factors, of course. For one thing, David had to contend with the erratic thought processes of the selectors. Of all the multifarious juries responsible for awarding him his 117 caps – there were no fewer than fourteen voices and eight choruses between No. 22 and No. 117 – two stand out: the May-Sharpe-Titmus-Stewart quartet of 1988, and the following summer's Dexter-Gower-Stewart trio. Here were two groups of genuine improvisers, the majority of whom seemed intent on parading the abundant manpower at their disposal – if not quite the quality of choice – by picking thirty players in each summer (including those nominated for the aborted 1988–89 India tour); who, in the space of seven Tests, appointed no fewer than five captains. Only one name is common to both groups.

With all that in mind, thirty-two Tests in charge is scarcely evidence of a hopeless case. Only May (41) and Gooch (34) have been deemed worthy of more, though Brearley and Illingworth (31 apiece) would certainly have outstripped those totals had they been appointed five years earlier. At the height of the fallowest seasons in English history, however, David's intrinsic unsuitability for the post was as transparent as his record was opaque. Of those thirty-two Tests, just five were won, a ratio that enabled him to supersede Archie McLaren as Blighty's most blighted leader. No other English captain has sustained as many as eighteen defeats. No other Test captain, of any nationality, has ever finished on the wrong end of *two* 5–0 scorelines. Both humiliations were administered by the West Indies of Richards, Greenidge, Haynes, Gomes, Dujon, Holding, Garner and Marshall, 11 consecutive wins between Barbados on 4 April 1984 and Adelaide on 11 December 1984 amid an unbeaten run of twenty-seven games between the start of the second Test in Sydney on 2 January 1982 and the end of the fifth Test on the same ground three years later. In terms of complete series, conversely, David won two and lost three, gaining a victory and a defeat in his two Ashes confrontations. Somewhere between those hills and valleys lies the true character of his captaincy: midway between satisfactory and must-do-better. Moderate rather than mediocre. Had he applied himself more assiduously, he might have done better, but probably not much.

That he was draped with such an ill-fitting mantle as often as he was can be attributed to the poverty of the competition. When he returned home from Pakistan in the spring of 1984, Peter May warranted that there was 'still some way to go' before he could be assigned the captaincy on a full-time basis. Dennis Lillee, for one, heartily disagreed: 'There is no question that Gower . . . stands out as the man to lead England out of nowhere.' Options, though, were thin on the ground, as was borne out by the subsequent indecisiveness. Post-Greg Chappell, Australia have had three captains in a twelve-year spell that has seen them duff up the Poms and Kiwis with relentless regularity yet consistently falter against the West Indies and Pakistan; post-Brearley, England, who have persistently thrown spanners into the Caribbean works in the 1990s, have appointed ten captains: one every sixteen and a half months.

Whether England's fortunes would have been improved under a Brearley or an Illingworth, or even Gatting, is a moot point. In Gower's case, certainly, Bob Willis's theory about Test captains only being as good as their bowlers is hard to dispute. It may, however, need clarifying: modern Test captains are only as good as their *pace* bowlers. Granted, Shane Warne may one day disprove it by making a Brearley out of Mark Taylor, but, for now, I'll stick with my thesis. True, the partnership between the Middlesex twins, Edmonds and Emburey, was at its apex during Gower's first spell in charge; on the other hand, sadly, Willis's own retirement deprived England of her one world-class paceman, leaving a void that has never subsequently been filled. Gower had the misfortune to captain England during the age of helmet and forearm guard, an age, moreover, when the opposition carried much the heavier artillery. Among the leading bowlers over the past decade and a half, we have witnessed the pomp of the Magnificent Eight: Warne, Holding, Marshall, Ambrose, Imran, Waqar, Wasim and Richard Hadlee. Extend that to a Top Ten and you'd probably want to incorporate Walsh and McDermott. All but one pacemen. No Englishmen.

By the middle of the summer of 1984, not only had Willis, Old and Hendrick all played their last Tests, but Botham had passed his peak as a bowler. He still exhilarated the gallery like no other, yet all too infrequently. There would be some deafening roars against the old foe in 1985, when he dyed his hair blond and metamorphosed into Rambotham to bully his way to 31 scalps at the rate of one every eight overs. Sadly, though, the temporary acceleration in speed and hostility served only to disguise the decline of that magnetic outswinger. In his 73 Tests up to the end of the 1984 season, Botham took 312 wickets at 26.25, at 54.11 balls per strike, including twenty-four hauls of five wickets or more and four of ten; in his remaining twenty-eight Tests, he stole and suckered 71 wickets at 37.85, strike rate 69.49, with three five-fers. David found it difficult, Botham confessed, 'to get the ball out of my hand', whereas 'Brears would just say, "Get off. You're bowling like a prat."' To Brearley himself, David 'appeared to be bulldozed by Botham', as, he felt, had Willis. Brearley takes the matter a step further: 'I had Gower and Botham at their easiest. As they got older they became that bit more stubborn, that bit less respectful.' Loyalty has its downside. All the same, it must be stressed that most of the country also clung to the hope that Botham could rewind and replay the miracles of 1981.

Anyway, keeping Botham on a tighter leash would have been a betrayal of everything David stood for. So, does he regret giving Botham his head?

Not too much. There should have been a marginal difference of degree. In the same way as I looked at other captains to give me my head, why should I try and curb a talent that is no less than mine, and far broader than mine? Why would you want to do that? In 1985 he'd produced everything in spades. Why worry? 1984 was a real baptism of fire without much support: we had a weak side. By '85 we had a better one, so by '85–86 we should have had a reasonable side, but we didn't. Then we lost the plot completely.

At the memory of the least joyful tour undertaken by an English crew since Bligh set off for Tahiti, the defence begins to waver; a sense of helplessness threatens but fails to dent that inherent loyalty towards a soul brother.

I gave Ian his head and it worked the previous summer, so the next cricket you play, your natural assumption is that this has to be the way to go. If it ain't bust, don't fix it. It was bust by the time we worked it out. I think it got to the stage where, in the middle of that tour, I said to Ian, 'we nearly dropped you': end of speech. To drop him would have taken it one stage further. I'm not sure that a fall-out would have resulted, but . . .

Neither did it exactly help that Botham's support was weak. In England's 109 Tests between Willis's departure and the end of the 1994–95 Ashes series, no one succeeded in breaching the 150-wicket barrier. The two men of pace who might have changed all that, Norman Cowans and the similarly headstrong Neil Foster, were impaired, respectively, by insensitive handling and a rebellious body fatally undermined by overwork. Since Packer raised the stakes, it is no coincidence, surely, that these also happen to be the underlying factors in English cricket's persistent failure to make the most of its resources. Richie Benaud cited captaincy as one part skill to nine parts luck. However many times David demonstrated a modicum of aptitude in that capacity, Dame Fortune was absent. Something of a paradox for the man who believed he was 'on the side of the angels'.

Before he could be crowned King of England, or so it was stipulated, David had to occupy the throne at Grace Road, though Barry Dudleston, for one, believes Leicestershire should have tackled the matter in the way Lancashire subsequently did with Atherton: recognizing that a part-time captain is of little benefit to anyone. Roger Tolchard, in contrast, lent wholehearted support to David's appointment at Leicestershire, even though it cost him his livelihood:

David was vice-captain in my last year as captain, 1983: they wanted to push me out so he could step up. I always thought David was a captain in the making. He always thought about the game, always understood it as well as anyone. The question is, how much is captaincy getting the other lads going and how much is just operating on the field at a given time, choosing the right option? As a captain, David wasn't suited to a side that needs more than guidance, that needs stirring up, whether with the clenched fist or showing you care deeply. With a side like that you can't just go on letting things happen but, in a way, David did just let things happen. He's that sort of fellow. He is such a nice guy that he had to be a captain of a bloody good side. He'd have been a brilliant captain of a good side.

Mike Turner, conversely, admits to uneasiness over David's elevation in October 1983, which explains the appointment of the uncompromising Willey, newly signed from Northants, as his deputy. Turner had been instructed to trim £40,000 from the club's running costs: in addition to Tolchard, out went Davison and the two Caribbean pacemen, Ferris and Roberts. So, even when he was available, the new skipper would scarcely have an abundance of experience or talent on tap. 'When we appointed David captain,' Turner recollects, 'I was concerned, in my heart of hearts, about his lack of experience.'

And it didn't help him that we didn't have a very good side. We won the Benson & Hedges in 1985 but nothing more in the eighties. If he had had a good side, he would have been a better captain. How good a captain would Clive Lloyd have been if he hadn't had such good sides, at national and county level? I don't think David was an outstanding captain by any means, in a leadership or tactical sense, but I'm sure he had the support of the players. At the same time, I certainly didn't regard it as an easy dressing room, and that in itself might tell you something about David. On the other hand, there were some strong personalities – like Peter Willey, Jon Agnew – and different factions, which is why I hesitate to express criticism.

To me, the main criticism was that David didn't want the uniform approach himself, therefore the side didn't have a uniform approach. Things like punctuality are important to me; they weren't necessarily important to David. I know that's an insignificant point, but once a side is drifting, you've got to have discipline.

Hence the promotion of the formidable Willey to vice-captain. Ask Turner to nominate the best three captains during his three decades at Grace Road and he names Lock, Illingworth – and Willey: 'I'm sure if you asked one or two players during that period, they would say, "God, not Peter Willey". But the thing was that when he filled in for David for the 1987 season, and did a good job, the club was going through a transition ... The county needed someone who was really going to crack the whip and instil more discipline.'

In Jonathan Agnew's estimation, David the Leicestershire player was less of a problem than David the Leicestershire captain.

In playing terms, there was definitely an acceptance of the way he was. I'd much rather have someone like David coming back to his county without any airs or graces, without any cockiness. If he's just scored 200 in a Test, he'd never talk about it unless he was asked. I used to drive with him a lot to away games and you'd notice the volume of the cassette gradually creeping up as the journey wore on. If you wanted to talk about the day's play, you'd have to be the one to bring it up. Deep down, he would have been disappointed that he didn't score more runs for Leicestershire, although he often scored them on the big occasion. At the same time, there was a bit of jealousy towards him, especially when he was captain. If he came back to Leicester and didn't appear to be putting absolutely everything in, there'd be one or two who'd moan about the golden boy and falling asleep in the slips, or say 'look at that flash so-and-so'. But that's an easy thing to say. It's wrong to expect any England player to come back and win games single-handed. So maybe it's in the fellow's interests to look a bit more switched on than David was at times. Certainly, when he was captain, one or two felt he ambled through matches, and wasn't quite as in touch with what had happened while he was away as he should have been. He might have phoned Mike Turner, but I was never aware of any calls to see how we were getting on.

Les Taylor was the victim of David's most notorious piece of absent-mindedness:

You always had an idea if you were going to be dropped, and Aggers and I would use our own special signals to tell one another whether either of us had been told. On this occasion, we both conveyed the signal that we were in. Then, as we walked on to the field, somebody noticed that we had 12 players, so David turned around rather sheepishly and told me I was the one who had to go. That was bloody bad. I fired him a broadside, and probably went crazy for a couple of days, but that was it.

Agnew recalls another flash of temper, this time from David himself:

I remember him giving us an absolute roasting at Yeovil one year when things weren't going right. Eventually we'd taken a wicket, and he absolutely let rip. 'Professional cricket . . . disgrace . . . should be doing this, should be doing that, fielding's rubbish.' He was very forceful indeed. He has got quite a short fuse, and those sort of things only tended to happen when he snapped. You didn't know what his breaking point was, how far you could go, but you could see it coming. His patience did go at times on the '84–85 tour of India. Graeme Fowler just used to enjoy watching him and waiting for him to go. There was one explosion in Calcutta when there was a constant melee around him. He was yelling at these poor little Indian guys. I say poor, but they were a pain in the arse, thousands of them. Wanted autographs. He did one or two then the whole mob surged forward. Bang, that was it. But whenever that happened, he was smoothed over within about ten seconds. Totally. Then he's back to the way he was, no grudge or animosity. But when he goes it's quite an explosion.

Team talks were the speciality. 'It wouldn't be a rallying speech,' recalls Agnew,

he'd just sit down and lay out his thoughts, and they were very good actually. He's a good communicator. He never banged heads against the wall or gave it the 'C'mon lads', but he did make it pretty clear what he expected from us every season.

Downton found much the same at Test level: 'He was very good: very lucid, very fluent. He prepared what he was going to say and got the message over very well and very forcefully.'

As Agnew stresses, moreover, denying David his county stripes would have diminished his already skimpy enthusiasm for the county grind, with potentially fatal consequences.

I think he needed the captaincy, that was the trouble. County cricket just didn't turn him on. Peter Willey always used to say he captained by the clock. You know, I'd bowl for an hour and a quarter and then come off; at ten-past-one you knew a spinner was going to come on for an over. At the same time, in some ways having him as captain did us good. We could feel David Gower was our captain, which from a team point of view was quite important. It was something of an uplifting experience. And he wasn't a bad captain by any means. What I liked about him as opposed to others I played under was that he'd respect you for being an intelligent individual. As a bowler, I thought he was a dream: I could set the field I wanted, I could bowl to what plan I wanted, and only if it went wrong would he come up and say, 'come on, what's going on?' I'd say that I was trying to so-and-so and he'd say, 'well, it doesn't seem to be working, does it?' Well, I'd reply,

I'll give it one more over and try and get one more wicket; if not, you win. And he'd say, 'Right', although he was firm enough when it didn't work. I really enjoyed that, because I liked to feel that I was able to think for myself, which is, I hope, what made me a successful bowler. It's ironic really: it was for that same reason, for being an individual and being intelligent, that he was seen off at the end. Interesting. I think he expected to be treated, not with the same courtesy, but with the same understanding. I loved him for that, I really did.

It began with a whimper. Pakistan at Lord's, defeat by ten wickets. That said, the most far-reaching event of the 1982 season had occurred in mid-May, when David was appointed captain of the MCC side to play India, ahead of Keith Fletcher. Unusually, the England selectors were responsible for naming the XI, so speculation about David being road-tested for the latter's job was fierce. In Gooch's estimation it was 'an absurd idea ... I did not believe that the selectors could be seriously contemplating giving the number one job to one so woefully underprepared for it. What is more, I told "Fletch" so, and, although I think the snub had caused him some concern, he still at this stage felt that he was likely to keep the job.' Instead, at 4 p.m. on the last day of the match, Fletch was sitting in his garden when the announcement about the Test captaincy came through: it was neither him nor David, but Willis. Baffled, angry and hurt, Fletcher drove off into the wilds of Essex. In his first difficult phone call as chairman of selectors, Peter May had dropped the ball as soon as he picked it up: there was no explanation. In May's autobiography, revealingly, there is no mention of the reasoning behind the decision, still less of Fletcher.

Gooch was aghast. 'I wondered if he [Willis] had the personality for the job. I also thought it an unsuitable marriage with the stresses and remoteness of fast bowling. But, most of all, I wondered why on earth the change had been made at all.' With hindsight, it is not hard to see that Willis's knowledge, intensity and commitment made him the best fill-in available. But is it stretching the conspiracy theory too far to wonder whether the bitterness Gooch felt on Fletcher's behalf coloured his judgement of David?

A week prior to the opening instalment of the three-match Test series against Pakistan, David had survived a chance to gully on 4 to take apart the tourists' Imran-less attack, collecting twenty-nine boundaries in an unbeaten 176 off 219 balls that outstripped his previous highest score for Leicestershire. It also dispelled the pall that had settled over him during a sub-par rubber against India, which had been decided at Lord's when Botham won his personal thrust-and-parry with Kapil Dev (who did for

136

David, unsurprisingly): in five starts, England's new vice-captain failed to reach 50. Abdul Qadir had only six overs at Grace Road that day, but even when the stroppy little wizard had a lengthy twirl in the first Test at Edgbaston, David made a delightful 74 in England's 113-run win. A happy end to a match that began with David in doubt in the wake of an injury sustained while fielding against Essex. When Fletcher miscued a drive off John Steele, the silly bugger at silly point caught it full on the left side of his unprotected face. Reeling back from the force of the blow, David was led away to hospital with blood streaming everywhere, had four stitches inserted below his left eye, then reported for the Test with a badly bruised cheekbone. He had never considered wearing a helmet, he said, let alone fielding somewhere saner, this despite the fact that he had seen Botham break Gavaskar's leg in a similar incident at The Oval during the third Test against India. During the course of his fourth Test in charge, Willis, meanwhile, had done himself a nasty, ricking his neck trying to avoid being pinged by one of Imran's bumpers, and he cried off for Lord's. At which point it all went pear-shaped.

Jackman subbed for Willis, leaving the stand-in skip with four seamers (Botham, Pringle and Ian Greig being the others) and another who had been reborn as a flat offie (Hemmings); subtract Botham and the remaining trio entered battle with seven caps and 15 wickets between them. Murphy's Law reigned supreme. First David lost an important toss, then Mohsin Khan sculpted the first double-hundred in a Lord's Test since Donnelly in 1949, with a Gowerian flourish; Sarfraz and Qadir forced England to follow on; the first Sunday's play in a Lord's Test saw our old friend Mudassar nab Gower for a duck during a wicked spell of wobblers (3 wickets for no runs in six balls) that turned the screw with a mocking finality. There would have been even less fare for the Sabbath crowd had it not been for the second-slowest half-century in first-class history, by Tavaré (who else?). 'It is perhaps harsh to criticize Gower for his handling of such an unpromising attack in his first Test as captain,' sympathized Brearley, 'but he did, I think, fail to make the best use of it. The one man capable of bowling above military medium was Botham. The situation demanded that he be persuaded, cajoled or instructed to concentrate on attacking in short bursts.' There was no persuading, cajoling, or instructing, merely exasperation: Botham sent down 44 overs, taking three for 148.

It might have been a better idea for all concerned had one of David's dining companions on the Saturday evening at Bistro 57 in St John's Wood High Street, Robin Jackman, not ignored superstition by ordering duck and insisting the rest did likewise. They paid the price. First thing next morning, Jackman, 0 not out overnight with three runs required from the last-wicket pair to avert the follow-on, was pinned leg-before by Imran without addition. England went in again and David and Lamb deigned not to bother the scorers either. Not for another 119 Test innings – a world record – would Gower go so hungry.

The 'Bistro 57 Affair' remains Lamb's favourite Gower yarn, though there was plenty of competition in store. The pair embarked on a firm friendship that summer when the Lasher from Langebaanweg won his Test spurs after spending four years as a squire in the shires. 'He made me feel at home, made me feel relaxed,' remembers Lamb fondly:

> It was very difficult coming into the side with my background. 'God,' you thought, 'there's going to be a lot of players who will resent me'; no one actually said anything – you just felt it. David was brilliant in that sense. We had a long chat. He never let anything on, never showed his true feelings, and I got to know him better than most. He has a very short temper, snaps very easily: a stupid comment, someone bothering him in a restaurant. At the same time, he was friends with everyone in the dressing room, and very close to Willis. We liked the same sort of things – good food, good wine, enjoying ourselves. Both [Botham] too. We all had that idea that it was there to be enjoyed: play hard, on the field and off. David could take a challenge. We all liked a challenge.

Willis promptly returned for the concluding Test and David finished term in style, top-scoring with 74 in the first innings of a low-scoring decider at Leeds, which was settled by Fowler's debut 86. He also passed 1500 runs in a season for the first time, whereupon Australia brought more meaningful splendours. The following summer, Willis remained in charge despite his fateful insertion of Australia at Adelaide and his side's distant second place in the series. England fell in the semi-finals of the World Cup but David had a ball, and the plunder continued with two centuries against New Zealand. There were also four hundreds for Leicestershire, including a decisive unconquered 108 in the championship win over Glamorgan at Hinckley. In the second round of the NatWest Trophy, he swept to 138 against Gloucestershire at Grace Road only to be trumped by Zaheer's 158 as Leicestershire gained the unwanted honour of posting the highest 60-over total ever by a side batting first and losing. The final day of term was celebrated with a touch of the Mack Sennetts at Old Trafford as Gower and James Whitaker served up 189 runs in seventeen overs to speed Steve O'Shaughnessy past Percy Fender's 63-year-old mark for the fastest first-class century.

Gower led England for the second time against New South Wales on the 1982–83 Ashes venture; the only advice he remembers being offered was Jackman's suggestion that he shouldn't try to be Brearley, or Fletcher, or even Willis, merely himself. Although he incurred a baker's pair – 0 and 13 – a 26-run win compensated. His next match in the driver's seat, against Victoria, brought the only known instance of a pair of fat ladies – 88 and 88. A draw there gave way to victory over Tasmania, Gower combining with his old mucker Derek Randall for the unbroken stand of 99 that ensured England achieved a target of 264 in four hours. Before the Adelaide Test, however, he told Willis he was feeling disheartened. '[He] was concerned about some criticism he had heard over his contribution on the field as vice-captain,' the captain noted in his log. 'I reassured him that I was perfectly happy – he is more willing to offer opinions than at the start of the trip. I can also appreciate that it must sometimes be hard for him to attract my attention when I am marching thirty yards into the distance, head down and intent on my next ball.'

Not that that prevented Willis from casting doubts upon Gower's suitability for full-time promotion, even if the two were friends, and even if he did regard him as a deep thinker, albeit one decidedly reticent when it came to delivering judgement:

> I would not burden David with the captaincy at this stage of his career when he is just emerging as a world-class batsman. You have to take a lot of responsibility and make a lot of decisions for other people, and I don't think that would help David's Test-match batting. It is quite hard work being a superstar and the responsibility would not help ... I have had a lot of constructive suggestions from David – more as the tour has gone on and he has grown in confidence as a player and matured as a person. But I think when things are going well for someone personally it is far easier to offer suggestions and encouragement to others who are not doing so well.

Pakistan was a disaster – Willis and Botham departed the tour injured, and early, leaving a playing strength of only 13.

All this, furthermore, had come panting on the heels of an unremittingly disastrous trip to New Zealand, the first of the Ian Dury Tours – 'Sex an' Drugs an' Rock'n'Roll/Is all my brain and body need ... very good indeed'. David believed it all began on the very first night, when a case of 'mistaken identity' linked Botham, Lamb and Willis to some 'poorish' behaviour and late-night carousing at the Auckland Sheraton: 'Now you may find it hard to believe that a hotel bar in New Zealand can contain three characters bearing a passing resemblance to that trio, but I can assure you on that occasion there was.' Henceforth, the Great British Public were regaled with a new phenomenon: the Botham Snorts Bird Shock Horror. Neither did it help that the tour manager was

Alan Christopher Smith, the man whose epitaph will doubtless read: 'If I have to say anything, which I don't, my only comment would be "no comment", but don't quote me.' Confronted by attitudes of this nature, journalists have a tendency to track their prey with even greater zeal.

None of this would have mattered had things been proceeding smoothly on the field. Instead, having whipped the hosts 3–1 during the summer, England conceded a series to the Kiwis for the first time. In the second Test at Lancaster Park, England failed to include a specialist spinner for the third time in 596 Tests and for the third time suffered the consequences. On those previous occasions, at Melbourne in 1932–33 and Brisbane in 1954–55, they had been merely humiliated; this time they lasted until the third afternoon, following on against the Kiwis for the first time in fifty-nine meetings and ultimately falling short of three figures in both innings for the first time since Queen Victoria ruled half the world. Discount the rain and the whole farce had consumed less than two days. If one match forewarned us of the horrors to come, this was it. One England follower had been in the neighbourhood visiting a cousin, and dropped in on the debacle. Sylvia Gower's timing did not quite match her son's.

Things had come to such a pretty pass that even 'AC' caved in and issued a statement when, three days before the second Test, the drug allegations reached a new high, so to speak. When pestered for her views, Vicki Stewart offered a straightforward 'ridiculous' (Donald Carr, the TCCB chairman, would interview David on the matter upon his return, the upshot a clean bill of health for all concerned, for now . . .).

So, to Pakistan. 'Gower,' reported Matthew Engel, 'was obliged to lead out a demoralized rump of a team.' Having floundered against Hadlee, Cairns and Chatfield on the seamer-friendly pitches of New Zealand, David responded with two of his most dutiful innings. Fortified by a brace of fifties in Karachi, he saw Pakistan march to 449 for eight declared in Faisalabad then entered at 214 for three and led his side to 546 with his second highest Test score to date: 152 in 426 minutes with sixteen fours. 'It was hardly a thing of beauty: that was not possible on such a pitch,' acknowledged Engel. 'But it was an innings of responsible mastery, played by a princely cricketer about to enter his kingdom.'

He swept in through the front door in Lahore, by which time Graham Dilley had limped home: twelve green bottles. Taking up residence for the entire fourth day, David guided his side from 189 for five (effectively 87 for five) to 344 for nine with an unbeaten 173 in 423 minutes, cracking 49 of the 71 added from 14.4 overs on the final morning and setting Pakistan 243 in 59 overs, a necessarily inviting target. It must have been

140

the beard: 'It was a bit of a joke organized by the social committee. They said we all had to be clean-shaven on leaving New Zealand and grow something in Pakistan.' Clean-shaven, David averaged 20 on that tour; the subsequent growth accompanied an average of over 100. Victory loomed when the hosts collapsed from 173 without loss to 199 for six (Cowans five for 42 before being dropped, predictably, for the first Test of the summer). As David continued to steer the ship from slip, scenting dry land, all he needed was Hans Christian Andersen as twelfth man. 'Only diffidently did he bring his fielders in once Sarfraz put up the shutters,' bemoaned Scyld Berry. 'But that criticism is minor compared with the admirable effort which enabled England to make a great escape. Gower's team did not level the series, but they brought respectability back to English cricket.'

The accession, it must be said, gained mass approval. 'I thought Gower should have been captain two years ago,' opined John Edrich. 'It's a pity those two years have been wasted with him not getting the experience he will need this summer.' Writing in the *Daily Mail*, under the headline 'Captains who make us *all* winners', Shaun Usher compared David to Bryan Robson:

> Significantly, the steel showed [in Pakistan] when he rebuked Neil Foster, baby of the team, and veteran wicketkeeper Bob Taylor, the oldest member, for tantrums of dissent, frustration and operatic disbelief at umpires denying their appeals. Stung by a Pakistan umpire's plea to 'behave as Englishmen', Gower took swift, abrasive action. 'We have a proud record in England for our behaviour,' he insisted, 'and certain things just do not go on. There's no reason for it to happen now.' *Stirring stuff, proving that the new generation has faith in timeless standards, the vital role of sportsmanship in sport. A captain to whom all of us, not just the team, can respond.*

An *Observer* profile entitled 'The Young Lochinvar of Cricket' awarded its seal of approval while expressing sound reservations:

> While some may judge by the cherubic appearance that he is too soft or mild-mannered, he has developed a veneer of hardness, if only to deal with those hangers-on who want to tell him at length that he reminds them of Woolley. The accusation of mental laziness – quite aside from the fact that he did not make the most of his brain academically, and has been known, like many a cricketer, to doze off while fielding in front of three men and a dog – is a more serious one.

Not that David, or England, stood a chance against a West Indies side that had long since swapped the calypso for the Rastaman Vibration.

Here was the most unstoppable cricket force ever to invade these or anyone else's shores, and that includes Bradman's '48ers. From the victims' point of view, it was downhill all the way from that near-tragic moment at Edgbaston on the first morning of the series, when the local likely lad Andy Lloyd had his only Test innings truncated, and his eyesight permanently impaired. Haynes and Greenidge were the world's most prolific opening duo; Gomes, Richards and Lloyd comprised a middle-order for all seasons; Dujon possessed David's own feline ease at the crease and not a little of Knott's athleticism behind the stumps; Harper, quite possibly the finest all-round fielder the modern game has witnessed, caught flies in the slips; topping the bill was the Unholy Trinity, Holding, Garner and Marshall, who divvied up 68 wickets at 19.41 apiece, striking once every 7.2 overs during the course of a rubber that saw not one of England's ten innings pass 300. Lamb made three hundreds and Fowler one, but there were only seven other fifties among the other ninety-four home knocks. Gower made one of them, a 57 not out at Leeds; his other nine innings yielded just 57 more.

What few realized was that, behind the captain's own inert displays lay a grazed knuckle, one that, had it been suffered twenty years earlier, might well have cost him his life. David suffered it at Lord's during the MCC-champion county match, shortly before embarking on his first championship match in the saddle by making 70 against a useful Derbyshire seam attack. The cut became infected, the swelling extended to the lower part of the arm and he was admitted to a private hospital in Leicester, missing the last two days of the match and the whole of the next month, a period covering all four Benson & Hedges zonal ties. He made 102 upon his return at New Road but the legacy would remain. For the rest of the season, he would relate, the source of the original infection 'remained very stiff and sore'. To this day, he cannot flex the finger or bend it as easily as the corresponding finger on the other hand.

David's sole innings of substance in the Test series came at Headingley, where he made more than a third of his side's second innings total of 156. By now, all was confusion. In the first innings, Paul Terry, on his skipper's say-so, emerged at the fall of the ninth wicket, broken arm and all, in the interests of seeing Lamb to his century; mission accomplished off the last delivery of a Holding over, the batsmen began walking off, whereupon David waved them back. There was some logic in this: England, after all, only needed another 21 to avoid the follow-on. But Terry was hardly in a fit state to defend himself and he duly succumbed to the first offering Garner speared down at him. Perhaps it was the Headingley Factor. The captain's faith in miracles was certainly touching.

Richie Benaud and Clive Lloyd both offered succour, insisting that

David had ended the summer with honour and dignity intact. Paul Downton concurs:

> That was a big learning experience for David, a very difficult series, yet that flippancy seemed to keep him sane. He didn't take it personally, which is a good thing. I don't think any other captain available would have done things much different or much better. It's quite difficult to give a team talk when you're three or four down in a series. The expectation before every match was that we would have to play out of our skins to even match them. The personnel was constantly changing, and Peter May was particularly ineffective. I'll never forget the dinner before the Lord's Test, which was Chris Broad's debut. May went up to him and said, 'Peter May, Brian, welcome'. He'd seen his name as Brian Christopher Broad in *Playfair*! Then there was Botham. He was a bit of a divisive influence: he spent a lot of time in the West Indies' dressing room. I, for one, felt he was too much under Viv's sway. He wasn't a good loser or a good battler: he found it hard to believe he was doing anything wrong. Lamby had a great series and I did all right, but we were blown away. We weren't good enough to compete. David managed to rationalize it in his own mind – which I'm sure was the best thing to do – that not much different could have happened under anyone else.

The nearest England came to a draw was at Lord's, much as a nine-wicket loss might suggest otherwise. This was David's first real brush with 'those dreadful press chaps' (© P. B. H. May). His absence from the dressing room balcony was noted on the fourth evening when Lamb and Pringle opted to take the light. Had the fourth estate but known he was glued to Dan Maskell and Wimbledon. 'When you are playing the West Indies,' he reasoned, 'the new ball is due and it's dark, I don't consider that it is really my place to order a senior batsman to stay out there.' Not that Lamb would have taken much heed: 'If David had been on the balcony I doubt whether it would have made any difference. I was so sure that the decision I took was right I never once looked in the direction of the dressing room. David would have needed a megaphone to get my attention.'

Brearley, on the other hand, believed the critics were justified in their baying: 'The responsibility was the captain's, and he could not deflect the blame by pointing to the outcome.' Namely, chasing 343 in one day, a thunderous double-century from Gordon Greenidge off 214 balls and a gleeful nine-wicket romp, the fifth highest Test chase to date. England at least had the satisfaction of becoming the first side in seven Tests to compel a West Indies No. 3 to take guard in the second innings, albeit only just: the only wicket was Lamb's early running out of Haynes. Botham never played better against the West Indies, making 30 and 81 to chalk up 4000 Test runs, and outdoing Bailey and Trueman by taking eight for 103, the best figures to date by an English bowler against the West Indies on home soil. It was his final contribution, however, that had the most telling effect on the outcome: 20.1–2–117–0. Yet only an arch-pessimist would regard it as a match lost. A contest wherein England had held the edge was settled by a batting blitzkrieg seldom matched in Test annals for audacity. Granted, it would be over-generous to describe the bowling as accommodating, yet any side capable of even contemplating such a target, let alone skating home with more than eleven overs to spare, is surely an extraordinary one by any standards. A match stolen, not lost.

'Total crap' was David's considered verdict in his autobiography. *Daily Express* readers were afforded a more delicately worded insight:

> I tried to peg back the scoring rate [but] when you set a field on the off-side the last thing you want to see are fours disappearing in the opposite direction. International bowlers know when they are letting down the side and I don't believe you solve anything by storming over to them then and there. I saved it for the dressing room. When we got in for tea the dressing room door was shut, the balcony doors were shut and I spoke loud and clear. The printable version of what I said was: 'We haven't performed well for England this afternoon, we bowled badly and we fielded badly. Let's get it right whatever happens now, let's at least perform like a Test side.'

The summing-up was nothing if not candid: 'I think I must have experienced the whole range of emotions. Elation, satisfaction and disappointment; at times fearfulness . . . and eventually feelings of hopelessness and even anger.'

David may well have needed the captaincy to maintain motivation. His ego certainly craved it. As a foretaste of heartache, however, Lord's 1984 ought to have been sufficiently unsavoury to dissuade him from pursuing it further. Why *do* so many cricketers want to be captain?

8   Look Ma, Top of the Greasy Pole

'I'm sorry you lost but I'm feeling so much happier seeing David Gower smile.'
Pammie Gavaskar to her husband, Sunil, December 1984

On his maiden voyage as skipper of HMS England, David would dearly have wished to have had Botham aboard, but the People's Champion had decided it was high time he laid down sword and scabbard and rested those weary six-league boots. Sceptics would attribute the harmony of the crew to his absence; that the vessel ultimately survived all manner of buffetings had rather more to do with the example set by their resilient captain. Had he been hovering in the vicinity, Richard Gower would have been glowing with pride.

Well remunerated as the flag-wavers in India seemed to be – £9500 fee plus £200 for every previous tour – they would not be much better off in real terms than the Bodyline squad were. Larwood, Hammond and Sutcliffe each made £400 plus £175 in 'merit' money; Bowes, Tate and Mitchell totalled £475 a head. And don't forget, each of these luminaries would also have been pulling in a county wage five times that of a miner. A skilled worker in a major industrial centre could command up to £182 a year, a miner a shade over £100.

Chris Cowdrey vividly recalls David's pre-tour address at Lord's:

> Forty minutes, an hour, whatever it was, spot-on. It was, look lads, this is India for you. He told us what to expect. He went through everything from pitches turning square to buses that never turn up to planes that are delayed by six hours. 'You never know what you're going to get with the umpires,' he added, 'but no dissent.' The message was straight-forward: enjoy.

In the final week of October, a couple of days before the party was due to assemble at Heathrow, Cowdrey phoned David to say he could be a non-starter. It was a tricky one, no question. Loyalty to country versus loyalty to friend. Without David rooting for him in selection meetings, it seems improbable that Cowdrey would have been in the lineup in the first place; that summer, he had made 951 championship runs at 31.70 and taken 22 wickets at a touch more, with a best of three for 64. A troublesome groin, it is true, had slowed the swagger he had shown at the crease in 1983. In August, moreover, he had single-handedly sentenced the would-be champions to their first defeat for three months, smashing an unbeaten 125 in oppressively humid conditions at Colchester, lifting Kent from 47 for six to 201 all out in the only innings of the match to pass 50; neither of Essex's collective efforts realized 125. Bearing in mind that five one-dayers were scheduled in India, vital wickets in the NatWest semi-final against Warwickshire and a creative 58 against Middlesex in the final were also persuasive in the search for an all-rounder capable of filling in for Botham. The pelvic problem, however, had worsened: Cowdrey advised David that he would be unable to bowl for the first three weeks. 'Thank God for that,' came the snappy rejoinder. 'That was all he said,' marvels Cowdrey. 'I said, well, I probably won't be able to do very much. "Well," he replied, "how long's the tour?" I dunno, I said, three and a half months or so. "Well there you are," he said. Which was great. Another captain might have been scurrying round for a replacement.' The selectors never knew a dicky bird.

Asked by a radio interviewer how he would seek to moderate the players' supposed off-field conduct, David appeared to be suitably forewarned and forearmed: 'That won't really be down to me. That'll be down to how well newspaper editors control the imaginations of their reporters.' The customs of the host nation, admittedly, meant that David had fewer worries on that score, yet scarcely could he have feared a more gruelling initiation. 'England got more than they bargained for,' were John Thicknesse's nicely understated opening words in his tour report for *Wisden*. In New Delhi on Wednesday 31 October, a few hours after the tourists had landed, they were roused from their slumber by the news of Indira Gandhi's assassination. On 4 November, by which time the tourists had been forced to seek refuge in Colombo, riots swept the land as Hindu in turn sought vengeance against Sikh, bringing the death toll since the prime minister's death to an estimated 2500. Less than four weeks later, Percy Norris, the British High Commissioner, was shot dead en route to his Bombay office, the same Percy Norris who had entertained the tourists so royally twelve hours earlier.

In the case of both the Gandhi and the Norris slayings, David and his compatriots were billeted at a hotel barely a couple of miles away. In both instances, to his undying credit, Tony Brown, a tour manager described by Vic Marks as 'forthright, instinctive and prepared to act on the spur of the moment', consulted Lord's and the Foreign Office, then resolved to stay on and play on. Five hundred miles from Bombay, scene of the first Test, a poisonous gas leak from a storage tank at a Union Carbide pesticide plant in Bhopal killed, blinded or caused liver and kidney failure among some 200,000 inhabitants.

The itinerary had to be revamped, England's trip to the north being delayed in order to allow time for the Sikhs to cool down. Even then, the fifth and final Test in Kanpur was only staged with the compliance of 4000 police and troops. Before the tourists arrived there on the dawn flight from Delhi, their hotel was evacuated and searched. Wherever they went, armed guards would surely follow. Slim crowds were another disturbing feature. 'For the first time in three decades,' Mihir Bose reported in the *Sunday Times* during the Delhi Test, 'the crowds and even the commercial sponsors are fighting shy.' So shy, in fact, that the only gift received so far by the teenage leggie, Laxman Sivarama-krishnan, who picked up nineteen wickets in the first two Tests, was a box of Black Magic chocolates – and that came from his captain. But then bats and balls were no match for murderous fundamentalists and homicidal corporations.

A great deal rested on the captain's shoulders, and David was at his most unrufflable on the morning of Norris's execution. It was here, more than at any other time, that he called on the spirit of his father. The shooting occurred half a mile from the Wankhede Stadium, scene of the first Test twenty-four hours hence. The players had been due at the ground for practice at 12.30 a.m. At 11.30, captain and deputy went to each room in turn to remind the occupants that everything would proceed as planned. 'What sort of practice would that be, then, captain?' wondered Fowler. 'Target practice?' While Gatting's influence may have been stronger, Marks conveyed the general incredulity: 'Cricket seemed so insignificant.'

Tony Brown blew a fuse when the noises off reached a climax. If anyone felt that strongly, the manager suggested, they could collect their passports then and there, and pee off. Even though there were no takers, fear still consumed the collective soul. Mrs Norris dispatched a good-luck letter. Sunil Gavaskar, somewhat insensitively, expressed surprise that his counterpart's stated intention was to avoid defeat, contending that such inherent negativity spread throughout the side, thus bolstering Indian morale after a run of thirty Tests without a sniff of the spoils. At the press conference on the rest day, David let that starched upper lip do the talking. Not once did he allow himself to wheel out one of the more obvious alibis for one of his country's least inexcusable losses, of this or any other tour. The inescapable fact was that England had lost six Tests on the trot. The TCCB stirred itself into a frenzy of action: a working party under the auspices of the Leicestershire chairman, Charles Palmer

– its brief to examine causes and remedies. Perhaps the tourists were spurred by their sense of pique at this perceived slight.

David brought off a number of man-management coups, notably in the case of Mike Gatting, who finished the series with nearly 600 runs. If Cowdrey gave rather more in the field than he did with either bat or ball, David's other hand-picked selection was a more conspicuous triumph. 'It was especially pleasing from my point of view,' Gatting subsequently wrote, 'to have been able to repay David for having faith in me.' And what faith! Gatting's international career appeared to have been consigned to a grave at the Nursery End. Getting oneself out shouldering arms in the first innings of a Lord's Test may have been careless; doing likewise in the second was plain suicidal. David not only insisted on a recall – Gatting's skill against spin was more renowned than his technique against high pace – he also ensured the Middlesex captain went as his deputy. 'Apart from those first few Tests when Brears had been in charge,' remarked a duly beholden Gatting, 'it was the first time in the whole of my England career that I had ever felt someone genuinely wanted me in the team. Until then, I'd thought I was always tagging along, under sufferance, as a last resort.'

David also possessed the foresight (and humility) to ask Gatting where he preferred to bat, and duly relinquished his No. 3 berth to him. The mere asking of such a question, rejoiced Gatting, 'was like being given a sense of dignity'. Much as he readily confesses to a goodly degree of self-interest, Lamb suspected that proposing Gatting as vice-captain might prove self-defeating, and lost no time in telling David so: ' "Watch Gatt", I said to him. I knew he was pushing for the captaincy. Tactically, he was the better man. I always felt I could have done the lieutenant's job then because I got everybody going.'

David's second most conspicuous achievement in personnel terms was to get the best out of Phil Edmonds, the maverick who once informed me that his career had been blighted by an inability to tug forelock. Although his fourteen wickets in the series came dear, 41.71 apiece, he conceded barely two runs an over, and combined with Pocock to plug the opposition's biggest guns, Gavaskar, Amarnath and Vengsarkar; more crucial still were those deep incisions in the victories at Delhi and Madras. Since that day at Leeds a decade earlier when he bowled out the Aussies on debut, Edmonds had missed the best part of seventy caps – for reasons unrelated to injury or form. Of course he could be a hugely annoying bugger. Of course he could be an arrogant sonofabitch. Yet his keen intellect, expertise, and determination to bowl the perfect ball, *every* ball, were qualities his country could ill-afford to sacrifice on the grey altar of conformity. David, happily, was considered more or less an equal. 'He

[Gower] clearly commanded Edmonds's respect and support even if there was the odd disagreement over technicalities,' wrote Marks, 'and this was crucial to our success.' Edmonds provoked Brearley beyond endurance merely by challenging him; intellectually or otherwise, there was never even the vaguest hint that David deemed him a threat.

Another astute move was to play down the potency of Sivarama. David attributed his dozen wickets in Bombay to bad batting while publicly resisting what must have been a barely suppressible urge to blame the umpires. He told his charges not to fret. Norman Gifford, the assistant manager, predicted Sivarama would not see the series out. As it transpired, he was declared Man of the Series – a highly dubious adjudication – despite taking just five wickets for 443 in England's last six innings. In Calcutta, marvelled Marks, Gatting's assault was that of 'an irate school bully, whom Siva increasingly wants to avoid at all costs'. Thereafter, the Bombay ducker was awarded only three more caps, dredging up three victims at 109 runs a throw: he was finished at the top within a year, a week after turning twenty.

The silver lining in Bombay was Gatting's maiden five-day century – at his fifty-fourth attempt. Mike Selvey knew how much that meant to the Portly One, and thus to his colleagues. 'You won't find it in there yet, Gatt,' he cracked on air when his Middlesex teammate joined him in the commentary box and began flicking through *Wisden*. The millstone-shedding mood was catching. The next episode in Delhi yielded England's first Test success in thirteen starts and David's first in eleven stints while in possession of the accursed chalice – two more records. Not, mind, before the pessimistic mood in the dressing room at lunch on the final day had prompted the captain to blow what little there was of his top. By way of a double-barrelled pat on the back, he awarded himself and Robinson (whose 160 more than doubled any other individual effort in the contest) a match off. Our intrepid duo duly spent five days tiger-spotting in Rajasthan. While they were there, a London newspaper cartoon depicted a slender, curly blond holding a bottle of the bubbly stuff and peering at the label to work out how to open the blessed thing: the lampoon now holds a prominent place in the target's study. David always could laugh at himself.

India, suddenly, were in disarray; having slit his own throat with a gormless wa-hoo, the supposedly untouchable Kapil Dev was offered up as sacrificial lamb and dropped for the Calcutta Test. There, unhappily, the hosts swapped impetuosity for sloth: by rights, Eden Gardens should have been renamed Hades Field. In five days, only two innings were completed, and the spirit of 1981–82 was needlessly exhumed as India crawled to 437 in 203 overs, with Shastri's interminable 111 the deadliest killjoy. The prospect of a riot loomed when Gavaskar peeked out of the dressing room during a snailish stand between Manoj Prabakhar and Chetan Sharma: 'Gavaskar down, Gavaskar out,' chanted the section of the crowd nearest the players' quarters. Amid unconfirmed BBC reports that the local police commissioner had beseeched Gavaskar to declare in the interests of civil order, the innings was finally closed at lunch on day *four*. David had pointed up the pointlessness of it all by serving up three overs himself. When the torture ended, Edmonds put down his newspaper and crossed himself. When Gavaskar led his side on to the field, they were met by a hail of fruit. 'Dotty as they are about cricket,' reasoned John Woodcock in the *Times*, 'even the people of Calcutta realize that the game can have no meaning unless *some* effort is made to win.'

Cue joy unconfined in Madras, eleven wickets from Neil Foster ensuring that double-centuries from Gatting and Fowler – the first England pair to achieve such a feat in the same innings – were converted into the handsome victory they so richly deserved. At one stage, as Peter May 'gazed inscrutably ahead from his wicker chair' (*Wisden Cricket Monthly*), the scoreboard read 563 for two: even at The Oval in 1938, the best England could manage was 546 for two. David declared five overs into the fourth morning, whereupon Foster sent back Gavaskar with an out-swinger as India, trailing by 380, limped to 22 for three. When the final day dawned with six second-innings wickets required, David resisted the lure of the second new ball and opened up against Shastri and the new star, Mohammed Azharuddin, with his spinners, Edmonds and Pat Pocock, provoking an outbreak of harrumphing among the Test Match Special team, Trevor Bailey in particular. An overnight 246 for four, still 134 behind England's mammoth 652 for seven, had inched to 259 for four and thence 259 for six when Edmonds did for Shastri and the captain himself held Azharuddin at silly point off Pocock. When the recalled Kapil counter-attacked with the fury of a hero scorned, David called for the new ball and saw Cowans force a slip catch.

That the crowd saluted the winners with such gusto can be attributed at least in part to the enterprising approach fostered by the opposition captain. 'This was the performance of a high-spirited and blazingly determined England team,' wrote David Frith, 'oblivious to bad memories.' We know where they learned that trick. After the one-day series had been won, 4–1, the local press focused on the victors' 'professionalism'. Yet still the digs flew. A decade on, Frith can still feel the fury and shame he experienced on the press bus after the third day's play as the boys from the dailies got stuck into David for demoting himself in the order every time a wicket fell. 'Had it been the Australian press bus,' Frith raged at the time, 'the raucous strains of Waltzing Matilda would have boomed above the honking traffic all the way back to the hotel.' It seems there are some people who cannot be pleased *any* of the time.

David's reticence was excusable. His form, in truth, had not so much been mislaid as buried. His scores in the first three Tests had been 13, 2, 5 and 19. In Bombay, according to Marks, he had been 'completely at odds with himself in the middle. Usually when he fails, he still manages to look composed and his dismissal surprises us, yet here we expected him to get out at any time: even he seemed resigned to imminent failure. The prospect and the process of batting no longer seemed to excite him.' When he did finally go in at the Chepauk Stadium, at 604 for five, there was nothing much to gain and a fair bit more to lose: predictably, he was duly bowled for 18 – by Kapil Dev.

Cowdrey echoes one popular theory for the drought:

He had two or three terrible decisions early in the tour. I can just imagine the umps: 'give Gower, give Gower'. That lbw in Delhi came when Sivarama was bowling round the wicket: probably pitched middle, going down legside by two foot! Terrible. But there was no dissent. He'd told us not to show it, so he couldn't. He came back to the dressing room and sat down but he'd given his sweater to the umpire, so back dashed the chap to deliver it. 'Excuse me,' Gower called over in a firm but polite manner, and beckoned him over. 'Right,' he went on, 'do you understand anything about angles?' They talked for a few minutes and in the end the umpire backed away, saying, 'thank you very much, thank you very much'. At that moment he was as low as I had seen anybody. Completely distraught. 'We're going to lose again, I've been fired out: the crowd wanted to see me.' They used to chant 'Gover, Gover'. He was probably as low then as he'd ever been in his career to that point. He used to play this Cliff Richard record, 'Where Do We Go From Here'. Played it all the time.

Before the final Test David expressed concern over his eyesight yet he then proceeded to redeem himself. Entering at 222 for three on the fourth day, he saw Gopal Sharma, the debutant offie, pick up three wickets for four runs after lunch to leave England wobbling on 286 for six, still 68 shy of averting the follow-on. Directing his first ball through the covers, and aided chiefly by Edmonds in a stand worth 100 in forty overs, David did the necessary, making 78 off 202 balls in four and a half hours to preserve the ultimate spoils. In the second dig, by way of self-affirmation, he opened when Fowler went down with tummy trouble, and remained unbeaten until stumps were pulled thirty-six overs later. Swigging merrily on a bottle of beer, he was hoisted on Gatting's ample shoulders, a couple of hundredweight of gold bauble in his grasp – and then dropped the lid on his piggyback's head.

Cowdrey nonetheless remembers a subdued David spending much of the ensuing evening alone.

> He was completely lost for words after it was all over. He sat there in his room and had one or two drinks (he hardly drank all tour), on his own, playing 'Where Do We Go From Here'. Eventually one or two of us went up there and dragged him out. He does go into his shell a bit. He finds it very hard to see the high side or the low side. That night he retreated. Not looking back, moving forward all the time: it made life harder for him in some ways. He should have looked at the good side, been more approachable, because he is a personable bloke. When he went to Hampshire, Mark Nicholas used to ring me and say: 'I don't know what to do with him; I can't even speak to him'.

In this respect, commanding such a callow corps was a distinct plus. Only Gower, Lamb and Downton could be considered Test regulars: come summer, Edmonds, Gatting, Robinson and Richard Ellison would all play integral roles in the reclamation of the Ashes, though sadly not Fowler (for all that his tally of runs after twenty Tests exceeded by 100 that of Boycott and Edrich at the equivalent stage of their Test careers, by 150 that of Grace and Randall, and by 200 that of Gooch; the last-named, a candidate for Tyburn Gate three years earlier, would be welcomed back with loving arms). David's sides against India averaged fewer than twenty-two caps per head, making these the least experienced England tourists of the 1980s. May, Bedser, Sharpe and Smith (A. C.) could take a bow, although their hand was forced: Gooch, Emburey and Willey had still to serve the final winter of their bans.

The team was, for the most part, young, lively, enthusiastic and unspoilt. The social committee comprised Cowdrey, Fowler and Marks: Gatting was fined for being too chubby; Lamb for demanding that his curtains be drawn at night (a whirring brain rendered Edmonds, his roommate, a virtual insomniac, and Phillippe Henri liked seeing the sun rise as he pored over every nook and cranny of the *FT* index). Cowdrey was rechristened 'Prince' in deference to his habit of strolling over to the nets, constrained as he was from bowling by a perpetual groin strain, lustily whack a few balls, thank the bowlers for their trouble and return to the dressing room, as Marks put it in his best sardonic style, 'for light refreshments'. The Prince looks back with an unabashed grin: 'It was probably the sort of tour where Gower could look around him and say, "Yes, I could enjoy this."'

Paul Downton reinforces the view that the most telling factor on tour was the presence of so many of the captain's mates. 'David's own form was poor, which didn't help, but he kept going and everyone rallied round. There was a very good team spirit, extremely good. The blend was very good without Botham. It was a side of David's contemporaries. David was quite relaxed. With Cow and me and Allott and Lamby and Foxy there, he had a number of good mates, people who'd grown up together. Some might have seen it as cliquey, but what happened with Ghandi and Percy Norris brought everyone together. After Bombay, everyone who'd been to India before said we'd get the flattest wickets you'd ever seen for the rest of the series, and there was no way we'd get back. But we had a bonus at Delhi because the wicket was like a mosaic, which made us feel we had a chance. Maybe they overdid it trying to prepare a wicket for Sivarama, but Gatting finally getting that hundred, even in defeat, was a boost.'

With his customary perspicacity, John Woodcock focused on the excellence of the fielding – with the boundlessly energetic Cowdrey leading the way – as an indisputable indicator of team spirit. 'A harmonious tour,' concluded Marks, who would start the week-old *Telegraph* crosswords and leave David to complete them. 'There had been no ugly incidents and the players had ended as friends. This had stemmed from the healthy relationship between the two captains.' David's opposite number, Gavaskar, did not disagree:

> Once the captains have a fair respect for each other, I think the rest of the team follows. If a captain comes back to the dressing room and starts having a go at his opposite number, that obviously affects the attitude of his side. I got along with Keith Fletcher in 1981–82 but we couldn't really share a joke together, whereas with David right from the time we walked out to toss we used to pull each other's leg.'

It was far too easy, Gavaskar continued, 'to criticize a captain, especially with hindsight. He [David] looks to be an innately good human being and therefore bound to gain respect from his players. After the Delhi Test, Pammie [Gavaskar's wife] said to me: 'I'm sorry you lost but I'm feeling so much happier seeing David Gower smile.'

David's forte, it was universally agreed, were his team talks. Before the Delhi Test, he concentrated on minds rather than techniques, stressing the need for desire, for togetherness. 'He was quite impressive,' vouchsafed Marks, 'if a little self-conscious.' Reason and control were seen as two of the prime assets; Gatting, added Marks, was left to repeat the content in more 'belligerent' fashion. Gatting admired David's basic message: 'He wanted to be allowed to play the way he wanted to play, to express himself, and to encourage all the other players to do likewise.

153

And that's right. Trying to change people puts them under unnecessary pressure.' Do we really need any further clues as to why the maverick tendency – Edmonds, Fowler, Pocock and Cowans – all enjoyed their most productive tours under the Young Lochinvar?

Fowler recorded the sight of David adapting to the demands of being a touring captain with wry amusement: 'It is quite funny watching him. From being a person who disregarded discipline – he wasn't a rebel, he just ignored it – he has been put in a situation where he has to determine the framework.' Indeed, talk of compulsory nets prompted Fowler and his fellows to dub their skipper TC – Turn Coat. While the chairman of selectors' autobiography, instructively, contains not so much as a syllable about the captain whose side had so embarrassed him just a few months earlier, he was at least prepared to allude to the odd quality: 'Above all, England looked a happy side, much keener than many nowadays to discuss and analyse the day's play.'

Marks's tour diary went by the punsome title, *Marks Out of XI*, but between the covers there was much that went beyond the skittish. 'O moral Gower,' ran the first line in a nod to Chaucer, 'this book I direkte to thee.' David, this gentle, immensely affable West Country farmer's son observed, 'grew steadily in stature'. He was 'no less approachable than in the past'; there were 'no clashes of personality and no threats to his authority'. He was, however, 'fortunate to have a young, united side, who were always prepared to accept his decisions whether they seemed right or wrong'. A nagging question lingered: 'Will Gower have the strength to wrench the ball from Ian's hands in a Lord's Test against Australia . . . or will he shrug his shoulders?'

'David was fortunate in India,' reiterates Jonathan Agnew:

He had a lot of really brilliant tourists. It was a really happy tour. I joined it after the first two Tests: the team spirit was absolutely brilliant, fabulous, and obviously not just through David. There wasn't one whinge about being in India, and it was a long tour, the last five-Test tour there. And we had some quite testing times. Men with machine guns in our dressing room at Chandigarh. But whereas on the '92–93 tour you felt that the players hated every minute, this was totally different. And I guess David set the standard for that.

Had the tour ended in Kanpur, he could have expected the red carpet and a life peerage on his return. Instead, he and his weary confrères had to schlep to Australia for a one-day irrelevance under the hypeful banner, 'Benson & Hedges World Championship of Cricket'. Even that deeply blue and deeply patriotic organ, *The Australian*, characterized the affair as 'cricket indigestion'. Since the excuse was the 150th birthday of the state of Victoria, however, more than a few red-faced dignitaries from the Mother Country were to be heard tut-tutting as their boys lost all three games. Having shelled out £3m to stage the show, the hosts were scarcely best pleased when, rather than an Australia-West Indies final, or, better still, an Australia-England showdown, they got India and Pakistan. Gatting claims, understandably, that he and his comrades 'were very, very tired' and played 'some very tired cricket'. Injuries to Robinson and Cowdrey added to the burden, as did the day-night format, a mystery to most. Small wonder there had been universal thanks for the week off the players were permitted beforehand (David spent three days in Tasmania with his old mucker, Brian Davison). And small wonder Gatting likened the furlough to 'going on holiday ... however hard you tried to think about dragging yourself into the nets, it was just like being in paradise'.

'The whole thing fell apart when we got to Australia,' Agnew recalls with a discernible shudder:

> which I guess was the real downside of David captaining a side overseas. In some ways it was understandable. I'd missed the start, but the rest had been away since October and it was March by the time we left for home. The spirit completely disappeared when we got to Sydney. Everyone disappeared for a week to do their own thing. I remember walking around the hotel and not seeing anyone. We actually got beaten by a New South Wales second XI. The batting order was completely reversed and the whole thing was an utter shambles. Those who weren't playing were wandering around the beach and I remember coming off wearing my England sweater feeling absolutely ashamed, totally humiliated: we were hideous. Tony Brown was doing his nut. It was the lowest I'd ever felt as a cricketer.

That, though, is to dignify an occasion that meant little or nothing to the mentally drained. Better to set store by the gratitude of Fowler. In telling his captain how much he had enjoyed the tour, the chirpy opener cited one of the chief reasons as David's uncontrollable habit of treating him as a responsible human being.

David had clearly got half the hang of the job. In his first full series, he had failed to score many or win any. In his second, he had again failed to score many; this time, though, he had not only won twice but taken the rubber, setting fresh landmarks on the way. If the opposition seldom played to their potential, and lacked any obvious successors to even one of the remarkable Bedi-Chandra-Venkat-Prasanna spin quartet, to rebound as England did under such onerous circumstances, with such a callow side, was surely nothing to sniff at. Yet sniff they did. From the handy vantage point of his hearth, Jim Laker dismissed it as a fluke.

Luckily, May and his fellow selectors were more impressed, and, accordingly, stood by their man for the Texaco trophy, and the first two Tests. This apparent show of trust, however, is put into perspective by the fact that David's opposite number in the impending Ashes series, Allan Border, had been appointed the previous December with the reassurance that he would have enough room and time to grow into the job. Ravaged by retirements – no Lillee, no Marsh, not even the obligatory Chappell – and further depleted by South African defections (including Alderman, Rackemann and Hogg, an entire new-ball attack), Border's tourists represented as good an opportunity as any to take the next step. 'David Gower remains "laid-back". It's in his nature,' warranted David Frith when the captain was reappointed. 'But there is now a steely glint in those blue-grey eyes: any wonder, after what he's been through . . .'

The return of Botham was as unwelcome in some quarters as that of Gooch, Emburey and Willey was reviled in others. 'I hope Ian Botham does not play for England again,' M. A. Grantham wrote to *Wisden Cricket Monthly*. 'I have a young family – enough said?' Due indeference was the tone of the reply from M. R. Frost to this less than sly dig at Botham's alleged (and subsequently admitted) consumption of the wicked weed:

Let me assure Mr Grantham that not only does the occasional joint totally expunge any neutral cricketing ability one may possess, but it also has another side-effect, which will soon become apparent to the medical profession, viz – a feeling of sudden and uncontrollable hostility towards pompous sods. I would also counsel Mr Grantham to steer his children away from the poetry of Coleridge and most definitely the plays of Oscar Wilde. Yours in Technicolor . . .

Mr Grantham had his supporters, among them Don Mosey, the writer and radio commentator. A deep lover of the game (rather more as it was than what it had become), possessed of a devilish mind and a dry turn of phrase, Mosey was adamant that it was his gruff, decidedly non-Old School Tie tones which lay behind his enforced early retirement as BBC cricket correspondent. Easy as that is to imagine, his caustic demeanour also played its part in his downfall. His subsequent work, with pen especially, was shot through with bitterness, most notoriously a virulent biography of Ian Botham, with whom he had once purportedly been friends. Gower also copped it in the neck. Mosey was unimpressed with the England captain's dislike of criticism from the commentary box: 'Does the silly lad suggest that Jim Laker, Tom Graveney, Ted Dexter, Ray Illingworth, Trevor Bailey, Fred Trueman and Tony Lewis are not experts? Criticism is not new. It has not been dreamed up specially for this highly sensitive bunch of prima donnas who represent England in this era.'

Even David's one-time co-diarist, the mild-mannered Bob Taylor, inserted an oar, deriding the England tourists for 'sloppiness and bad behaviour'. Taylor's pronouncements, it should be said, were based on the Australian leg of the tour. The captain's reply was unequivocal: 'Our results in India disprove everything Bob says. What stood out more than anything was the team's discipline, approach and dedication.' In the aftermath of the glory, glory days of Empire, as ever, memories of failure seemed indelible.

Neither was there much change after the first Texaco bash at Old Trafford, for all that, as a match, it was an utter corker. Praise for Botham's highest score in seventy-three limited-overs internationals, 72, the highest of the contest, was drowned out by the gnashing of the SARS (Society for the Abolition of the Reverse Sweep). Brian Statham rightly named Botham Man of the Match. The People's Champion also bowled tightly, took a vital wicket and two catches – but that didn't stop the nit-pickers. In defeat, the emotions David provoked among the press corps were not even mixed: the captain's nemesis, Geoff Lawson, running through his extensive repertoire of cut, swing and variation of pace, bowled him for three. In the second match at Edgbaston, also lost, wicket-keeper Wayne Phillips sprang high to intercept a speeding edge and send him back scoreless. Thus continued a run that had seen him enter the one-dayers with a highest score of 57 from thirteen knocks. Dropping Border, whose unconquered 85 decided matters, was scarcely the most advisable means of redressing the balance. To some, prominently Illingworth and Laker, a resignation might soon be in order, if only to enable Gower to concentrate on what he did best.

As David himself would admit, the key to the ultimate flowering of Gower lay in a catch. When David Boon, 45 not out off 47 balls, drove Willey into the St John's Wood section of the stratosphere, the captain scampered back, hovered under the descending missile with studied deliberation, then clung on as he tumbled. 'When he went out to bat in the sixth over,' noted Frith, 'there was a purpose in his stride.' Sufficient purpose for a match winning (and Man of the Match winning) 102. Jeff Thomson was hooked for six; advancing to McDermott, the young flame-haired flame-thrower from Queensland, he caressed the ball away, crossbat and on the up. At the other end throughout stood the massive, impassive Gooch, the unlucky Fowler's replacement, whose own unbeaten 117 helped put together a third-wicket stand of 202, a record for any wicket in a one-day international staged in England. Time-capsule stuff. Two centuries in three days, too, for the Human Hangdog, but then nothing of any real consequence until the final Test. Perhaps the quality of the in-house competition was too daunting? A standing ovation greeted David at the end of this knock. 'It's at times like this that you realize who your friends are,' he said at the close. 'The support I've had from my colleagues has been invaluable. When things do not go your way in this class of cricket it is easy to feel sorry for yourself. But I had support from within the dressing room and I felt the support of the crowds – they were willing me to do well.' Those exhorting him to resign 'fired my determination more'.

The question on most lips was whether the burden had been suffocating the batsman. Shortly before the first Test, David was interviewed by the *Times*' Simon Barnes, who believed his subject had 'acquired his own personal cliché, and clichés are always double-edged': the laid-back victor is a hero, the laid-back loser a slacker. David rejected the popular rationale for his slump; the converse, he maintained, was true: 'My batting form has affected my performances as captain. When I stood in for Willis in Pakistan, the confidence I gained from batting helped me on the field as captain. If your personal contribution is a good one then your confidence is higher, you see things more clearly and you are more confident about the decisions you make. But poor form affects your decision-making.' What David did not reveal was that, on his return from Australia, a 'deeply concerned' Mike Turner had arranged a complete medical, suspecting that his lack of runs might be connected to the infection he suffered the previous summer. 'Few people realize the gravity of this illness,' stressed Turner when he finally made his concern public at the end of the summer. 'I was told by a leading specialist that had David suffered from the same condition a few years ago he might easily have died. Happily, after the examinations this year, he was found to be in general good health, although he needed to have a rest or a holiday because his fatigue threshold was very low.'

For David, as ever, the seeds of renaissance lay in the roots of instinct. The *Times*' Simon Barnes, in fact, memorably declaimed that David was not 'one of those players who likes to go slumming for their runs'. You could sense the mood of self-assertiveness on reading of his efforts to graft, how he had occupied the crease for lengthy periods 'without making a lot', that his 'natural game' was 'a little freer', and that he was fully aware he trod 'a very fine line' because of the reliance he placed on the complexities of timing. A decade on, the sentiments are no different:

The troughs always tended to end with something like that. As always, I'd tried to be good, I'd tried to work on technique, it's all failed, so now I'm going to just *play*. Look at the ball, hit it, hope for the best.

I came to Lord's with no runs and lots of pressure, hangings afoot, and just *slatted* it. Got away with it, got a hundred, a lucky hundred, and that changed the whole thing round. You're playing well, and then you build on it. Right, I've got my hundred now, I can relax a little bit.

On the eve of the Ashes series, he relaxed even more, reaching a century with a six off Jeff Thomson en route to 135 against the tourists at Grace Road, during the course of which he shared a county record second-wicket stand of 252 with Chris Balderstone. He could even sleep easy after the first Test at Headingley, a vibrant, run-soaked affair won by Gower's Shower with five wickets and less than an hour to spare (left to make 123 in three and a half hours, England, attested Matthew Engel, 'crawled over the finishing line like exhausted marathon runners'). The home XI included no fewer than five alterations from the one that had held off India in Kanpur four and a half months previously: Botham, Emburey, Gooch and Willey returned from their various exiles while the recovered Allott came in for Foster. Botham and Emburey purloined seven wickets apiece, and Robinson cut and carved his way to 175 off 271 balls. However, it was Botham's 60-run salute on the Saturday afternoon that ignited the fire. Not that David could afford any personal complacency, marking his return to first-drop, the traditional berth of the master batsman, by making 17 (caught behind off a front-foot push) and 5 (edged drive to second slip). The knives were not discarded, merely sheathed.

To Lord's next, and, despite the return of Foster for Cowans and the reunion of Edmonds and Emburey on their home patch, some sobering prognostications. Since 1961, England's record at HQ has spiralled from the humdrum (four wins, one defeat and eight draws between 1962 and 1971) via the horrid (three wins, two defeats and nine draws between 1972 and 1981) to the downright hopeless (two wins, ten defeats and six draws between Mohsin's match in 1982 and Wessels's match in 1994). What does this signify? That Old Father Time is a symbol of all that must be toppled to make way for the New World Order? That the pink-ginned plutocrats do something to Johnny Foreigner's dander? That ex-comprehensive and grammar schoolboys are intimidated by the complete disregard for egalitarianism displayed in this wonderfully preserved antique world? Whatever the cause, the curse showed little inclination to shift in 1985.

For David, mind, there was consolation in defeat. In the first innings, persisting at No. 3, he top-scored with 86 off 146 balls, his highest score in Tests since he formally succeeded Willis as captain, and enough to persuade his elders he was worthy of retention as skipper for the remainder of the series. Not that that stopped the tutting that pursued his dismissal: caught at slip driving, on the stroke of tea. He prompted a few more tuts on the Saturday evening, sending in two nightwatchmen with the upshot that Botham came in at 98 for six; Botham made 85 but, with proper support, how many more might he have made? Writing in the *Guardian*, Matthew Engel stated that David would have scored a few psychological brownie points by emerging himself in place of Botham and proposed that David lacked the 'extra mystical dimension of captaincy'; a reader from Ealing likened such criticism to 'condemning Moses for not being able to walk on water and resorting instead to the rather prosaic expedient of dividing the seas'.

Requiring 127 in nearly as many overs, and galvanized, as they had been in compiling 425 first time round, by Border (196 and 41 not out), Australia rose from a bed of nails at 65 for five to glean the remaining 62 while incurring only one further loss. One-all.

At Trent Bridge, David resolved to alter his luck with the toss – six losses on the trot – by flipping a ten-franc coin. The ruse was successful: Border may have been unsure which side was heads and which tails. Self-affirmation then rose even higher on the agenda. In conditions that reminded Matthew Engel of Skegness on a good day, Gower and Gooch proceeded to add 117 at four an over after Robinson had paced a dash to 50 in twelve overs. Gooch lost patience, cutting Lawson to gully, but David glided on, patently more relaxed by his reappointment as captain. 'How good it is to see David Gower moving that front foot,' Tom Graveney apprised viewers as he leaned forward to steer McDermott through the covers: 'A majestic shot.' A nudge behind square off O'Donnell finally brought him to his first Test hundred in twenty-four attempts, coming off 167 deliveries: the grin could scarcely have been cheesier if it had been carved out of stilton. Jennings Wins Again.

Adjourning on 107, he resumed on the Friday in even more aggressive fettle. When McDermott overpitched, a push to the cover boundary brought him to 150, excising Bob Wyatt's highest score by an England captain in Locksley Country. Sweeping past Graveney in the all-time England run list, he eventually succumbed for 166 (seventeen fours, 283 balls) when O'Donnell made one lift and leave him to furnish a catch for keeper Wayne Phillips, by now a one-man cordon. To Mike Carey in the *Telegraph*, it was an innings 'touching the rarefied heights of brilliance'. The crowd thought so too, standing to a man to render thanks. 'An absolute joy to watch,' declared Jim Laker, seemingly recovered from his allergy to all things Gower.

Saturday afternoon brought a more searching test of character. Greg

Ritchie was steering his side towards a first-innings lead after England had slithered from 416 for four to 456 all out on a stillborn pitch, when Botham had the chunky Queenslander top edge to third man and caught by the tumbling Edmonds, whereupon the celebrations were stifled by the sight of umpire Alan Whitehead's upraised right arm. No one had heard him call no-ball. Earlier in the over Botham had been convinced that he had earned the most obvious leg-before in recorded history. Now, as Ritchie joined him at the non-striker's end, he let fly with a flurry of words which, by his own admission, 'you wouldn't find in the Bible'. Vengeance writ large on every subsequent ball to Ritchie, Botham was then warned for running on the wicket, then intimidation. The cameras appeared to suggest he was spraying some more un-Biblical words in the general direction of umpire Whitehead, but Botham denied this. He asked his captain to intercede. 'It was a tinge explosive,' David later confessed. He strove to defuse the situation in the best way he knew: a quiet, assertive word. Botham admitted he had allowed himself 'to get carried away' and took the advice in good heart: 'David calmed things down, told me not to let what was going on affect my concentration and, for the moment, the steam evaporated.' Beetroot-red, Botham nodded his head vigorously, the cock of the walk accepting that he doesn't quite know it all. Never, not even under Brearley, had the People's Champion been made to look quite so meek.

Not for the first time, Manchester's highly idiosyncratic notions of summer prevented a definite conclusion to the fourth Test, a contest that otherwise went the hosts' way pretty much from gun to tape. David elected to field and saw Australia dispatched for 257 in the final over of the opening day when Edmonds bowled the belligerent Victorian all-rounder, Simon O'Donnell, with the first ball of a new spell. Neither was that the captain's only masterstroke. Botham reasoned that the best way to get shot of the menacing Phillips was to feed his favourite square cut. David concurred, and duly set a field that soon had Johnners and Co. choking on their choccie cake: a slip, two backward points, conventional point and a squarish cover. When David trotted over to complete a 7–2 offside field, Trueman apparently swallowed the entire contents of a pack of St Bruno. Phillips went for 36, suckered by Botham's 'magic long-hop' and caught behind – cutting.

Australia eventually went in again 225 behind after Gatting's maiden Test century on home soil had enabled David to close at 482 for nine, to which he himself had contributed a studious 47. On the final day, rain drove the players on and off as if they were ewes being herded in and out of their pens. To the American author, Donald Carroll, now domiciled in England, it is this capricious climate that renders his adopted home's invention of cricket all the more incredible, and its recent humiliations all the more explicable:

> As far as I know, the English are the only people ever to come up with the novel concept of an outdoor sporting contest in which the point is frequently for their own side to be actively engaged in actively playing not to win – ie playing for a draw. And just to make sure they don't accidentally win ... they added one ingenious element; or, rather, they added the elements. With perfectly straight faces, knowing that England had the worst weather in the world, they decreed that nasty weather could stop them playing for a win. I ask you.

During one pavilion-ward scurry, Botham, Border and Gower trooped off together, verily the Three Caballeros: Botham with sweater pulled theatrically over those peroxide locks, Border freeing a smirk through pursed lips, David giggling and fiddling with his opposite number's bat. Some, believe it or not, contended that this show of mutual affection illustrated a lamentable dearth of the requisite aggressive spirit expected of Ashes combatants. Botham would even watch the first day at The Oval from the matey comfort of the Australian dressing room! Another example of declining standards, what? When Richie Benaud brought the matter up, tongue at least partly in cheek, David was the personification of sweet reason: 'I don't think you can criticize people for getting on well.'

At this stage, David's biggest migraine was the profligacy of his opening attack; hence the inclusion at Edgbaston of Les Taylor ('the pitman turned pro' in the choice words of Neil Hallam), at the expense of his Grace Road partner, Jon Agnew (fourteen overs for 65 in the first innings at Old Trafford). The swing doors were in full flow: Agnew had replaced the injured Sidebottom at Old Trafford, the latter having stepped in for the injured Foster at Trent Bridge. The brief for the archly self-critical Taylor, one of the meanest of hombres in the 40-over game, was to make the Australian openers, Wood and Hilditch, graft a bit more. He encountered a dressing room with a superiority complex. The sense of impending, inevitable conquest was catching:

> I always remember walking in, looking around, and knowing we were going to win. 'I'm among the best twelve players in the country,' I told myself. We all felt that way, that they'd got the selection right. The place was so full of confidence. It also seemed very happy. There were so many characters, so many noisy buggers, especially Lamb and Botham. On the field there always seemed to be three or four people, not so much pulling the strings as offering information to David.

Goochie, Gatt, Botham (who always got his own way) – there were a lot of county captains there. If there was a fielding change, those four would discuss it. Botham had the vision for bowlers and batsmen, but the others didn't. I don't recall David saying anything of a personal nature before we went out, but what was he going to tell a county colleague? Botham took me under his wing, assuring me that I had been chosen on the basis of what I had done and that I should just go out and do what I always did. Suddenly, just before we went out, the buzz stopped. I buried my head in the paper while Goochie gave it the old up 'n' at 'em, really serious stuff. Meanwhile, Lamby would be giving these sly digs. We all knew we were going to do the job. I can't remember David saying too much, other than 'let's go, let's do the business', but then I wouldn't have caught too much because of my hearing problems. As a captain, I don't think you need to say a lot in those circumstances. He had the team he wanted.

The tide duly turned at Edgbaston, just as it had the previous summer. David flouted tradition – and forced Johnners and Co. to choke even harder on their choccie cake – by inserting Australia for the second Test running, a hitherto unprecedented act in an Ashes series, not to say unspeakable. Resuming at 335 for eight on the third morning following two days of rain disruption, the guests lost Lawson and Holland by the end of the opening over, David skating in from deepish extra to run out the former with an underarm daisycutter. Initiative seized, David joined Robinson at 38 for one fortified by that morning's announcement that he would lead England in the Caribbean, and immediately stroked Thomson to the point boundary. Upon pulling the same bowler square with a convincing swish, he examined the lower half of his weapon with a wry, quietly superior smile, apparently aggrieved that he hadn't middled it fully. 'There's an air of good humour around,' remarked Benaud as the erstwhile Terror Thommo deigned to see the funny side. 'That's one for the memory,' the same alumnus of the booth proclaimed as David launched into the cover drive that took him to three figures. Having given the equally unquenchable Robinson the best part of an hour's start, David had gone twenty runs past his partner by the time he wound up the day by sending an extra-cover drive humming to the fence. By then, the second-wicket stand had raised 317, the seventh 300-plus stand forged by an English pair in a Test; when Robinson at last played on to Lawson on the Monday morning, the alliance was worth 331, in Ashes terms second only to Hutton and Leyland's 382. 'Robinson and Gower's ability to get balls away for fours was uncanny,' goggled Border. 'It might have been just one of those days. I hadn't experienced one like it. Now we're having to try to save the match after batting for the first two-and-a-bit days. That's ridiculous.'

Before a meagre crowd and a lowering sky, a helmetless David reached his highest Test score with an extra-cover drive off McDermott – 202 off 285 balls. At the other end, Gatting offered a chummy slap on the shoulder and the corblimiest of beams. Oh, that *he* could make it look so exquisitely simple. Botham supplied the icing. First ball: Wham! Back over McDermott's head into the pavilion. Second ball: Pow! Through midwicket for four before the fielder could twitch. Fourth ball: Thwack! Same shot as the first, same bowler, fifteen rows further. Who could ask for a more irrefutable statement of English self-belief?

With just two days remaining, Benaud had assured readers of his syndicated column that Australia could only lose if they did something really asinine. When David declared late on the fourth afternoon, 260 on, Richie seemed certain to be proved right once again. Ellison had other ideas. Included alongside Taylor instead of Paul Allott, the expansively shouldered Kent swing bowler reduced Australia to 37 for five by stumps, including an absolute purler to bowl Border. Dense drizzle prevented a resumption until two-thirty the following afternoon, and Phillips and Ritchie appeared to have seen off the worst when the hard-hitting keeper went back to crash Edmonds square. The next thing anyone knew, David was standing at what is best described as stupid mid-off, holding the ball aloft and sporting a facial expression that looked more hopeful than expectant: 'Please, sir, I'm holding up my hand, but please don't pick on me because I don't I know the answer.' How could he? At the moment he took the rebound he was spun halfway round. With the other close fielders united in an appeal of rather greater conviction, David Shepherd, whose view had been obscured by the catcher, consulted his square-leg assistant, David Constant: Phillips was given the finger. The ball, apparently, had ballooned off the cowering Lamb's instep as he sought evasive action at silly point. Graveney regaled viewers with 1985's finest double-negative: 'I don't honestly think that there's any question that wasn't out.'

Border was livid: 'There was no way in the world that the umpires could tell that the batsman was out. He should have been given the benefit of the doubt.' Benefit of the doubt, lest we forget, is supposed to favour the batsman: how, indeed, could anyone be certain that the ball had not touched the ground before David intercepted? David himself cites Constant's prompt affirmation as the most telling aspect. One question remained: what in heaven's name was the captain doing in that position in the first place? You wouldn't catch Viv or Clive or Brears there. Egalitarianism ruled, OK.

An incandescent sun had the patriotic decency to greet the protagonists for the Oval Test. Upon being asked whether he would like 'a patriotic belter', David insisted there was no need: 'When you are one up with one to play you don't mind drawing, but I think we are good enough to win 3–1.' He also emphasized the benefits of a traditional five-man attack comprising two quicks, a seamer and two twirlers. It was an orthodoxy he always favoured, all the more so after the climax at Edgbaston: seeing Botham 'champing at the bit', he had summoned him in place of a well-grooved Edmonds and was instantly rewarded with the final wicket. 'I'm in the happy position now of having such a balanced attack that I don't have to overbowl Botham. Perhaps last year against the West Indies I gave him too much work to do, but now I can use him as a normal part of the attack and use him as a strike bowler. It's what he does best.'

That morning, the *Times* ran a profile of a champion on the verge of achieving every fifth-former's dream. David Miller, the author, highlighted 'gentle iconoclasm' and the manner in which he 'discreetly played down his background and speech . . . the everyman's voice of a Smiley'. Miller also focused on the chameleon tendencies: 'Able, intelligent, popular, there is flexibility in his nature, in seemingly wanting to be all things to all men, which leaves people unsure: gregarious yet private, personable yet emotionless, an ardent modern professional with the almost lazy aura of an old-fashioned amateur, a winner without the killer instinct.' Aura is the key word. Flexibility, by its very nature, prohibits categorization, confounds those who seek to define.

In any case, the events of the first day rather put the kybosh on the killer instinct theory. A draw would suffice, but David was intent on some dream topping: 'It was time to rub it in, to finish with a flourish.' Calling the toss correctly for the fourth time in succession, the fates were still firmly in his corner when he went in at 20 for one: on 2, he attempted to stun a rising delivery from McDermott and saw the ball lob clear of an airborne cordon off a remote corner of the willow. There were other early alarms, notably a four over slips and an inside edge off successive balls from Lawson, but for the next five and a quarter hours, he and Gooch added 351 at nearly 4.75 runs an over as all kinds of strokes whistled around the Kennington expanses. 'There were several symbolic moments,' warranted Matthew Engel:

After one Gower hook McDermott simply stood and stared hopelessly at the ground for ages. Later, the Fosters balloon, which looked the weediest of the various advertising stunts attempted by competing Australian lagers, broke loose from its moorings to become a hazard to aviation, and the fielders stared as if hoping to hitch a ride.

Gooch was the one wearing the white helmet but otherwise everything was as it should have been. David won the race to 50 (off 64 balls) but by the time the score had reached 170, the pair were neck-and-neck on 72. A one-handed drag-cum-sweep brought the captain to his century off 123 balls, the swiftest of the series and his fifth of the summer against the Baggy Green-Cappers; Gooch, needing 71 more deliveries, got there in the next over to complete his first hundred against Australia. When David stroked Lawson square, a flock of pigeons took up squatters' rights in mid-pitch, presumably to get a better view. Most batsmen would have indulged in a spot of macho shooing; not David, not now. Erect at the crease, bat frozen in the address mode, he waited patiently for the flying rats to leave of their own accord.

Gooch was the first to 150, whereupon David matched him with a contemptuous drive off the debutant, Dave Gilbert, but then fell for 157, slashing McDermott to gully. 'By then,' reported Engel, 'Gower had taken his total for the series to 732, the fourth highest by an Englishman. I think I can say with some certainty that it is the highest total by a batsman who was as dispirited and as close to the plug hole as Gower was only three months ago.' By then, too, Australia had lost all hope of clinging on to the urn. Thus ended the most satisfying day's cricket of David Gower's life.

Can we assume that the phoenix possessed a rather broader streak of competitiveness than had hitherto been suspected? 'Well, yes and no,' David hedges, before forgetting to make a case for the latter:

Yes, there has to be a sense of competitiveness to motivate yourself to do more than the basics. This is where competitiveness is good, because it gives you that little bit extra. Without that, you wouldn't do it. Whether it's playing sport, or writing, you're trying to raise your own standard. There's competition of a nature in virtually everything you do.

An eventual total of 464 meant that England had averaged 86.79 runs per wicket over their last four innings, whereupon an exuberant display in the field finished off a weary, beaten foe. And nobody excelled more than Botham, who shrugged off the discomfort of a twisted left knee to take a couple of slip catches that were not so much athletic as a snook cocked at Isaac Newton. When David held Hilditch in the covers he flung the ball back as if he were the first XI new boy at pains to contain his joy for fear of looking unmanly. The question of whether to enforce the follow-on prompted much debate: the dressing room couldn't agree. Nor could the gaggle of ex-England captains present – Hutton, Illingworth, Denness and Lewis. Clive Lloyd, who wasn't there, said he would have batted again. David chose enterprise and, fittingly, prospered in front of the first sold-out fourth-day crowd for a Test in England since the war. Ninety-six minutes may not sound like particularly good value but there were no requests for refunds. Ellison broke the heart of the middle-order before Les Taylor, the oldest man on the field, delivered the final thrust; disposing of Murray Bennett via a low return catch in his follow-through to seal victory by an innings and plenty. Not since 1956 had England gained two such comprehensive victories in successive Ashes Tests. As the crowd surged on, David shook the hand of each and every fielder, and placed a matey arm on Gooch's shoulder.

Taylor remembers 'a helluva celebration' when the players returned to the dressing room. 'David got four or five bottles of champagne and we shared them with the room attendant. Then everything went quiet for ten minutes because David shoved everyone out. He wanted to be on his own, to savour the moment. Ten minutes later the Aussies came down and it was bedlam again. Those moments last forever.'

Conjuring up sepia-tinted recollections of 1926 and 1953, the crowd massed in front of the pavilion, chanting where once they would have cast their trilbies to the heavens. 'Cricket's a funny old game,' was Peter West's original opening gambit, at which point David, cringing inside as well as out, teased the man from Auntie by turning away and making as if to leave the balcony. It had been a case, he breezily explained, of trying to 'play through the bad times and look to the good'. The West Indies, he quipped, must be 'quaking in their boots'. It was left to the vanquished Border to articulate what the romantics were musing (the same decidedly unromantic Border, incidentally, who would subsequently question whether his charges had 'forgotten the reason for playing Test cricket, the feeling of national pride'). 'Cricket,' so far as the Australian captain was concerned, 'was the winner.'

For cricket to be the winner, arguably, it is necessary for the bat to have its way. And, for all Ellison's swing, the controlled wiles of Edmonds and Emburey, the sheer bullishness of Botham's bowling and the legerdemain of his slipfielding, the master key was the speed with which England scored. At Headingley they had run up 533 at 4.26 an over; at Trent Bridge, 456 at 3.51; at Old Trafford, 482 at 3.41; at Edgbaston, 595 at 4.44; at The Oval, 464 at 3.92, including 376 for three in the opening three sessions, their highest in a single day's play against the old foe since 1938. Gower and Robinson's 331 flowed at a touch under a run a ball, and the 351 stand with Gooch at a shade over.

Test calls, of course, meant that Leicestershire never came within sniffing distance of such luxury. They gained just two championship victories, neither of which came in David's presence, for all that his centuries against Sussex and Glamorgan came close to breaking the habit; they eventually wound up sixteenth, the club's worst placing in eleven seasons. Due in no small part to three abandonments, they failed to win a Sunday game in their first half-dozen attempts, and lost to first-class opposition at the first time of asking in the NatWest. Nevertheless, on one of the few days they were at full-strength, they managed to capture the Benson & Hedges Cup. Fresh as their captain was from the splendours of Nottingham, David's first domestic Lord's final maintained the summer's momentum. It also saw him get much the better of his counterpart, Gooch of Essex. Chasing a modest 213 for eight, he mingled judiciousness with some luscious driving to decorate a third-wicket alliance of 83 in seventeen overs with Willey. Hands, feet and head seemingly in perfect conjunction, it was clear only something Herculean could stop him. And so it came to pass that, on 43, his highest score of the 55-over campaign, he drove sweetly over cover point only for Alan Lilley to soar for a stupendous one-handed catch. Willey's unbeaten 86, allied to his dismissal of Gooch for 57 (after David had had the presence of mind to hand his miserly offie the new ball), ensured both the Gold Award and a five-wicket win with three overs to spare. For the first time in the post-Illy era, Grace Road had something to shout about.

David received a reminder of mortality when only twenty-five people turned up at the Friends' Meeting House in Leicester to see him donate more than twenty lots to an auction of cricketing memorabilia in aid of Ethiopia, including seven pairs of flannels and several pairs of size 9½ sports shoes; the poor turnout was attributed to the lateness of David's addition to the catalogue. Somewhat more par for the course was the response to his donation to a raffle run by Gregory's, a favourite restaurant of his and Vicki's in Stoneygate, all of the proceeds of which went towards the purchase of a bone-marrow transplant unit at Leicester Royal Infirmary: a pair of old Y-fronts fetched £93. In November, while David was doing some promotional work in Barbados for a Stoke-on-Trent-based hotelwear company, came the ultimate accolade: an invitation to join Liz and Phil aboard HMS *Britannia*.

Ah, the Summer of '85, the last summer of blissful cricketing memory, a powerful antidote to the ghosts of Heysel and Bradford. On the panelled wall to the left of my desk, hangs Patrick Eagar's rousing monochrome shot of Botham thundering McDermott back over his head at Edgbaston, peroxide mane permed in time, left foot pointing daintily in the direction of mid-off. Here is the blacksmith incarnate, forearms and biceps bulging with uncowable force; cricket as it was intended. The vision boasts even greater clarity when I replay the highlights of David Gower's happy hours. I slide *The Ashes Regained* into the VCR, to inspire thoughts of what might come, and remind myself of what did. Remind myself, moreover, why I care so much for an activity whose disciples squabble over whether Hobbs made 197 first-class hundreds or 198, why I am still so entranced by a game run by men in thrall to their own past.

To David, in cricketing terms, the Summer of '85 represented his turn at being Edmund Hillary. Or Roger Bannister. Or, better still, Roy of the Rovers. At the time he declared that he had never enjoyed a summer so much; not that you would know it to read the updated, paperback version of *Gower The Autobiography*. Among its 246 pages, summer 1985 rates just two. Loath as he is to trumpet himself, there is almost certainly another reason. Maybe time, and pain, has flattened the goosebumps. Ask him about it and he will tell you how much he cherishes the memory of the crack, yet he seems unwilling to allow himself to bask – an endearing as well as pragmatic quality but also a form of denial. Which brings us back to that inability – or refusal – to look back, that need to be like a shark, to surge ever onward. It is also attributable to the fact that he was never really allowed to bask.

What do you give the English cricketer who has everything? The opportunity to lead a tour of the Caribbean. With that in mind, David Miller had voiced one grave fear:

> Gower is establishing within the England team a coterie of supporters and some of them, such as his admirable vice-captain, Gatting, would be happy to see a team ethic more vigorously imposed on the egocentric Botham. Can Gower, or indeed anyone, achieve that?

The esteemed editor of *Wisden* took the opposite tack:

> It became a source of great joy watching England come together as a team. Much of the credit for this belonged to Gower and his vice-captain, Gatting. Once Gower had started to make runs . . . he grew visibly in authority in the field.

Illingworth offered the highest praise of all: 'He's no longer the easygoing boy wonder. He is a man.'

All was right with the world on Monday 2 September 1985. Yet, if Gower had taken longer than Botham to reach the pot at the end of his rainbow, he had still got there too soon. Why couldn't all this have happened when he was *thirty*-eight? Why didn't he give it all up there and then, right there on that Oval balcony, clutching the fake urn and the bubbly, more beautiful than damned?

9   Orphan in the Underworld

'That with this little arm, and this good sword,
I have made my way through more impediments
Than twenty times your stop; but O vain boast,
Who can control his fate?
Othello, Act V, Scene II

Postcards From The Ledge: England's 1986 Caribbean tour. Here, without doubt, was the expedition to end all expeditions, on the Bounty to end all Bounties. An imaginative cineaste might have cast David as an enlightened Bligh (more Trevor Howard than Charles Laughton), Botham as Burkitt (more Richard Harris than Donald Crisp), Gooch as a grumpy Fletcher Christian (more Gable than Brando), and cricket, naturally, as the breadfruit.

'It was impossible to keep track of everything,' David recalls with the exasperation of a man rewinding a nightmare for the umpteenth time. 'It was hard to be exactly focused on the cricket. As an individual you think, right, I'm going to do something about this, I'm going to bat. You're not in the best frame of mind but you pull something out. The disappointment was that more people didn't pull something out as individuals, because they were all whingeing about what I was doing with Both, the South Africa situation, always something. The failing was to stop them whingeing.' Whingeing Poms? Perish the thought.

Was the euphoria of The Oval counter-balanced in any way by the knowledge that the Aussies had been more plonk than vintage wine? 'They were weakened but not that much,' David replies, naturally anxious not to demean either the individual or collective achievement.

Not as badly as '78–79, although in that series we did play against players who were on their way to becoming good players: Hogg and Border, Yallop and Hughes. In '85 there were plenty of good players in their side, and they played plenty of good cricket. It was held against me by three people who have no sense of irony, that when I spoke on the balcony at The Oval I said, 'I'm sure the Windies are quaking in their boots.' It was nothing more than a throwaway line. We all knew

170

it was going to be a very different ball game. But *so* many wheels came off out there. It wasn't a wagon; it was a whole effing train derailed.

David could have been forgiven for some bleakness of outlook. He and Allan Lamb were wending their way home from Italy having survived a dart at the Cresta Run, when Sylvia Gower died after a lengthy illness. David had only a week to make the arrangements and tidy up all the family affairs before embarking on the most daunting assignment of his life. Allan Lamb was mortified at the manner in which the news of his mother's death was communicated to David. 'Holmes phoned him at Geneva Airport: that was the worst thing he could have done. He handled it very badly. He should have waited for David to get home.'

But Holmes claims, with good reason, that he had little option:

There was the risk that the media would have got him at Heathrow, so I got him at Geneva Airport. I couldn't have made it to Heathrow in time. 'Um,' I said, 'there's no easy way to say this but I'm afraid your mother died this morning.' He was OK; he didn't break down. I knew there were others there who could talk to him. I don't believe in concealing things from people. He wasn't that close to her but it's inevitably a big blow. It was the last link. I don't think his frame of mind was that good because he was rowing with Vicki. He'd gone off without her, to do the Cresta Run, which I said was an effing stupid thing to do. If you're going to do that, I told him, you're going to get stick in the papers, which he did. But Lamby, with the best will in the world, is an act-first-think-later sort. There were a lot of things that were not quite right at that point, but mainly that the relationship with Vicki was going seriously wrong. It may sound callous, but his mum's death didn't turn sunshine to rain: there was a fair amount of rain around at that point. The horizon just got blacker.

The Cresta Run business had been merely the first of the winter's abundant controversies. When the *News of the World* got wind that David and Lamb intended to hurtle down the Cervinia track in January, Holmes issued a statement of denial, insisting they had gone purely and simply to support the British bobsleigh team in the World Cup. David was initially refused permission by the track authorities to sit in a bob steered by Britain's gold medallist, Nick Phipps, but eventually got his wish. Some bright spark even suggested to Peter May that the foolish boys should be ordered home. 'There are no risks in doing the Cresta Run,' insists Simon Strong, secretary of the British Bobsleigh Association:

It's very dangerous as regards broken bones but they weren't going fast enough for that to be an issue. Nobody gets hurt, especially if you're fit. Holmes was completely wrong to object. David did the bob at the hardest tracks: Cortina, St Moritz, Trevinnier. And tobogganing on the Zermatt Express. He loved it.

Lamb had introduced David to the boisterous Simon Strong a couple of years earlier. Strong, in turn, had met Lamb via the South African's brother-in-law, Tony Bucknall, the former England rugby union back-rower. 'Lamby really appealed to me. He's a ferocious hooligan, and I loved the way he played:

> He was very conscious of being South African, and exceptionally lucky. A hard man, much loved by everyone, and quite a good user of people. I arranged sponsorship for him at £10 a run in the Tests during his first summer playing for England: he'd earned an extra £5500 come the end of August, and so I persuaded him, much against his will, to donate £500 to cystic fibrosis; his son had it. He introduced me to Gower, who struck me as a civilized intelligence with a huge streak of hooligan in him. He was my favourite cricketer. I was delighted to meet him, even if I knew he wouldn't want to talk cricket. He'd clearly downgraded his accent. It soon became apparent that winter sports interested him: he and Lamby didn't want to fester in the winter: they wanted to *do* something. You could hardly imagine two more different blokes. David respected Lamby as a cricketer, and despite his independence of mind he is very willing to be led. Lamby saw in Gower someone he'd like to do hooligan things with. He does like civilized people.

Strong also divined another facet of the Gower character:

> I remember once in Verbier, a bloke swung at him while he was talking to this girl. He grabbed him by the throat and said something like, 'You bastard! Trying to take my girlfriend off me or something?' The next instant he found himself pinned to the floor by Gower. Next thing you know, the girl's gone off with Gower. These types thought they could get away with it. Gower would have been more careful in this country, though. He wasn't so much protective of his image as natural: he wouldn't find it an effort to behave. I like to think that's an attribute of someone who can do both, someone who's vaguely civilized and not an outright hooligan or a loud-mouthed yob.
>
> We had a wonderful time skiing in Verbier the week his mother died. We cocked up the flights coming back, forgot about the hour's time difference, had a hell of a run to the airport. Big lunch, drinks on the train. Got to the check-in desk and the girl said, 'Mr Gower, there's a message waiting for you at the BA inquiry desk.' So we said

we'd take care of everything and meet him in the bar. He came through looking slightly ashen. Didn't say a word. But we didn't think anything of it. When we got on the plane he called the stewardess over and ordered six bottles of champagne. Then he told us. He said that it mustn't detract from this great holiday we'd had. Then he came back to stay with me. It was the first time I'd ever heard him mention either of his parents, but there was a lot of emotion. 'My mother is the last thing I've got,' he said. He was extremely upset. The suddenness with which it happened possibly gave him something else to concentrate on. She'd not been well but there was no question of him having gone away with her on her death-bed. Vicki and Holmes had left messages at Geneva Airport: however you analyse that, we nearly missed the flight, so we would have had to have found a hotel, and Gower would have had the whole night to think about it. Why didn't they wait until he got back? Would a couple of hours have made such a difference? If he was worried about the press, Holmes should have been at Heathrow. David would certainly have believed Holmes did it in his best interests. He's that sort of chap: once a thing's done, it's done. Vicki had to leave a message because she wasn't on the trip. She didn't like skiing.

That, though, was not the only reason for Vicki's absence. Prior to the first Test, a reporter knocked on the door, compelling her to deny rumours that the engagement was over. While the liaison would linger a while yet, its sell-by date was fast approaching. David remembers this as an especially turbulent phase, one that his mother's passing smoothed all too briefly. Not that he expected Vicki to face the music all alone. To allay her fears of further harassment, David recommended she fly to Trinidad, scene of the second Test.

Trying to put up a decent fight against the most powerful and confident cricket team of this or any other era was hardly the stuff of light relief. Nor was the reception that greeted the South African rebels, Gooch first and foremost. 'There was always a feeling that when the first brick flew through the window we'd be sent home,' reflects Lamb. 'There was always that anti-feeling among the West Indian public, even before the tour started. It was a nightmare for a captain, though David batted well under the circumstances. He was just getting a side together, although we probably got a bit carried away after beating Australia. They weren't a good side. And we did go out with a bit of a popgun attack.'

Here was the tour where, or so we were led to believe, England's cricketing representatives swanned off to the sun, got stuck into the sex and drugs and rock 'n' roll then decided not to bother working. God forbid we should take defeat like men. Trouble is, being beaten by these dusky chaps still carried a venomous sting. It was all very well losing to the convicts, the Kiwis and the curry merchants; every tanning by the erstwhile calypso kings was a pike thrust into the breast of English *amour propre*. With media response reaching new heights in volume and self-righteous hypocrisy, every misdemeanour was seized upon as proof of obscenely wealthy young men behaving badly and stripping away a nation's self-esteem. Strange that 90 per cent of the newspapers responsible should have kidded themselves that the Tories needed any help.

The perennial quest for bad news had intensified during the previous summer when Rupert Murdoch shelled out the best part of US $500m for Twentieth-Century Fox. Wapping had to do its bit to foot the bill. The *Sun*'s thirst for the kiss 'n' tell and the envious snipe was positively unslakeable; shortly before the first Test, 'Freddie Starr Ate My Hamster' graced four million breakfast tables. And where News International led, Express and Associated surely followed. In a circulation war, there are no rules or prisoners. Which is why the cricket reporters were soon joined in the Caribbean by the Street of Shame's hardest. To David, 'every non-native face was a potential booby-trap', but he was mistaken: even some of the natives were landmines. The News of the Screws' Deep Throat was one Lindy Field, an ex-Miss Barbados in apparent need of a bob or three. No rock 'n' roll – unless one counts the way the beds were alleged to have boogied – but pots of sex and drugs. Yet, in a society where newspapers stump up small fortunes to encourage imaginations to run riot, it seems more reasonable to blame the paymasters. It is a vicious circle which only the press have the power to break.

After David had been bounced out by Courtney Walsh for 11 on the eve of the first one-day international, having been struck in the face in the process, he anticipated, not unnaturally, a veritable Spanish Inquisition from the Savonarolas of the press. But of greater import to them, apparently, was whether his 'affair' with Mrs Paul Downton had been the reason for his looking 'a trifle drained'. The genesis of this particular titillating titbit was a photo taken at the Middlesex stumper's wedding: 'England Captain In Peck On Chum's Bride's Cheek Shock Horror'. The *Sun* offered all the diligence and propriety one might expect of a paper which had made a daily call to Grace Road throughout the previous summer to discover the name of David's hairdresser (he was thinning on top, apparently). The *News of the World* insulted both readers and profession with an even more flagrant example of cynical condescension, commissioning an 'in-depth' appraisal of the first Test from that most respected of cricket voices, Henry Cooper.

By the same token, there were many PR balls-ups. Had his father been alive, might David have thought twice about imposing those infamous 'optional' nets in Barbados, let alone not turning up for them? As he says now, 'I don't think that applies because he wouldn't have been in the hotel room. He wouldn't have been phoning. It's more a question of management. A good tour manager might have said, "nice idea, but don't you think you ought to be with us?". And I should have been.' Having performed the same function in India to general approval, Tony Brown, who had captained Gloucestershire as recently as 1976, had been an unchallenged choice as manager for the Caribbean, but he may have lacked the requisite detachment only age and distance permits. Some viewed the drift away from the Colonels and Dukes with dismay. Willis, for one, feels this to have been a counter-productive trend, dictated as it was by the breathless nature of the modern tour: 'They were struggling to find managers then because the old boys wanted to go to Australia but not the West Indies or India.'

Yet Willis himself was cited as one of the ointment's larger flies. Regarded, alongside David, Botham and Lamb, as a member of the so-called 'Gang of Four', he nevertheless complained of 'cliques'. Gatting thought Willis 'should have given David a bit more support instead of being one of the lads. I couldn't help thinking he should have been out there doing some overtime and trying to find us some decent wickets to practise on.' Les Taylor was dumbstruck: 'Bob Willis as assistant manager! He wasn't the type of bloke who would sit you down quietly and tell you what you were doing right or wrong. He had some good ideas about the game, but . . . the thing was, David couldn't talk about his own feelings, so while he could talk to the batsmen, perhaps, he couldn't talk to the younger players.'

'You don't know how much he might have been helped by a good manager,' ponders Mike Brearley. 'Maybe Illy.' Holmes is in agreement: 'There should have been people around David to help. He needs managing, needs working with and talking to, because he's not a natural communicator. What was happening at that point was that Botham, and Gower to a lesser degree, were larger-than-life characters and the whole thing got out of control. The management didn't realize. The voluntary nets thing was simply a matter of presentation.' The following winter, long after the horse had bolted, a full-time manager was in place. One problem: that man was Micky Stewart. One way or another, David didn't have much luck with the Stewart clan.

Taylor refuses to class the Optional Nets Affair as a clanger:

Gower trusted individuals. He wasn't going to be the one to tell people they needed a net. They never did him any good, so how could he recommend them to anyone else? But who were we trying to make up to here? I'm a firm believer in putting on a bit of a show for the press but there's a limit. The press had their knives in anyway. They were absolutely diabolical. I saw people change on that tour. The number of tricks they pulled. You could see they were looking for trouble. It got to everybody. One day while we were staying at the Rockley Resort in Barbados, I got up to go for a jog before playing golf: there was a guy out there taking pictures – at six-thirty in the morning! You'd see a bloke in the supermarket and then he'd be around the poolside the next evening. You knew he was a reporter, looking for us to make a mistake. We were a bit cliquey – the southern lads fell together, the northern lads fell together, Gooch and Emburey went everywhere together – but we couldn't even go to the bar in small groups. People were scared of being seen talking to a girl so we drank in our rooms. Peter Smith of the *Daily Mail* was the press representative, if you like, a lovely bloke, but he should have got his boys together and suggested they wrote about what they saw, give the guys bit of support. It was wicked at times.

Chins rarely rose above a droop from the moment Botham and Gower (whom his fellow sailor perceived as 'mentally exhausted') sailed off into the Carib while their colleagues were getting their bottoms spanked by the Windward Islands in the opening game, bringing the wrath of the tabloids down on their heads.

Unlike most, Les Taylor set off believing England were capable of drawing the series ('There's no way there was a five-nil difference between the sides – we got demoralized more quickly than we should have') but then his job, as a bowler, was to attack the bodies of others, not defend his own. 'The attitude before we even started was, "shit, we can't beat them",' recollects Lamb. 'I remember some of the comments. "Garner, Holding, Marshall: how are we going to score runs here?"'

Willis is with Lamb every step of the way.

The spirit wasn't very good. Facilities were terrible. We did most of our preparation in Antigua, where they were really dreadful, and nobody got into any sort of rhythm to play. We lost the first match on a slow turner at St Vincent, and David wasn't on the ground. It was an irrelevance; the tour wasn't going to be decided by a couple of off-spinners playing for the Windward Islands. There was a feeling within the side that we were going to be annihilated, that it was just a damage limitation exercise.

The loss of momentum between September and February also played its part. David urged the powers-that-be to implement some form of pre-Christmas squad sessions, but the penny, lamentably, declined to drop until the next Caribbean tour. Willis was of a similar mind, and outlines one objection:

I went through this with Ian [Botham] in '81. I couldn't believe this, I said: here we were, finishing the season in September and we're not going to get together again before Boxing Day. But at that stage Ian was playing [football] for Scunthorpe and that, of course, was more important than getting the team together. The side should have got together beforehand, and I don't mean in a Micky Stewart-Lilleshall way, but money was the problem then.

Manpower more so. 'We had a good side,' asserts Lamb, 'for English conditions.' Willis concurs: 'We didn't pick a very good side. There was no way Tim Robinson was going to make runs. Les Taylor? Greg Thomas?' Not that Taylor was granted much opportunity to prove his detractors right. He admits he was a good three years past his peak – South Africa saw the best of him – and he duly sat out the Tests, thumbs a-twiddle, 'frustrated' at his county captain's apparent negligence. 'David told me I'd been brought in to tie the West Indies batsmen down and, as with the Aussies, I never dared hit top gear. All the same, he hadn't brought out a thirty-four-year-old pace bowler to carry out the orange juice. And I did take thirteen wickets at less than 20 apiece against the islanders: there's nowt easy there.'

In the first four Tests, Botham and Thomas, a profligate new-ball pairing, went for four runs an over. Says Taylor, 'The West Indies batsmen went after Greg as they always do with a new guy, but he bowled crap. I felt sorry for David because guys were letting him down by bowling badly and batting badly. The days of Botham changing a game single-handed were gone. It would have taken a hell of a man to get us back up once we were 3–0 down. I don't think God could have lifted us.'

As a first act, Jamaica was a politically correct take on Webster's White Devil. Taylor blanches at the memory:

It was demoralizing. I saw people frightened, batsmen being sick. I've never experienced an atmosphere like it. Everything went their way. It was a great move by Viv to give Patterson the new ball on his debut, in front of his home crowd, but the pitch was a disgrace. One bit green, one bit brown: if it hit a green bit it went straight up your nose, if it hit a brown bit it went even higher! World-class batsmen got hit – Gooch, Willey, and whatever I say about him as a bloke or captain,

Will could bat. Holding was pushing off from the other side of the road. The crowd were banging this sheet metal – deafening.

David tried to prepare his side. During net practice he set a bowling machine to nostril-peppering level. Some were unsure that this was the wisest move, reasoning that batsmen are better off going into a match girded by the feel of ball against sweet spot. But there was nothing sweet about the spot an animate bowler, Foster, hit on the captain's hands just before the first Test. 'He just threw his bat down and walked off,' remembers Taylor. 'I don't think that was the sort of example he should have been setting.' Maybe not, but then bowlers seldom have to put up with such hardships.

So what can a poor captain do? In the humble estimation of Michael Holding, not a lot: 'There wasn't much he could have done to change things, same as Botham in '81.' David was further frustrated by the bleating within the team, dismayed that nobody came to him 'face-to-face'. He felt as though 'they had let me down with a schoolboyish snigger-and-whinge attitude'. He also felt Botham ('a balancing act that went wrong') caused tension by taking advantage of his calculated latitude. And, as frustration mounted, so the People's Champion lost his cool. When Edmonds missed a simple catch off him during the one-day international in Trinidad, whereupon the crime was compounded next ball by a misfield that cost a boundary, Botham refused point-blank to pick up the ball. At the drinks interval, David sought out Edmonds and patted him on the shoulder, 'as much as to say,' interpreted the latter's eloquent wife, Frances, ' "come off it, old man, it happens to everybody".'

Frances Edmonds was accompanying the tour with a brief to write a diary with a difference, untainted by the insider's fear of compromise. The book's eventual title was all one needed to know: *Another Bloody Tour*. Adopting a more objective stance than most reporters could enabled her to see David for what he was. One suspects that, if he had proposed there and then, she would have whisked her hubbie off to Las Vegas for a swift annulment. 'He is a man of such affable kindness, and genuine humanity, the captain. His indefatigable good temper and cheerfulness is the obverse of a coin that a lot of the bandwagon critics are billing as vapid leadership, and lack of authority.' The Divine Mrs E saw the tour degenerate into 'an amalgam of petty politics and spurious sensationalism'. And nothing came more spurious than the Botham pot saga. 'Of course Both takes drugs – doesn't everyone?' asserted Tim Hudson, the hippie DJ-turned-agent who had persuaded his client to tog up as 'Rambotham' in a wholly potty attempt to seduce Hollywood. When the news filtered through to the Coffee Shop at the Trinidad Hilton, the

Divine Mrs E spotted Matthew Engel 'staring lugubriously into his luncheon gazpacho' and wincing, 'Oh God, now they're stabbing Botham in the front.'

Botham complained to David that colleagues were blaming him for the over-zealousness of the press, which was actually quite near the mark; the pettiness could hardly have reached such heights had he not been there. Besides, he was off-form and thus even more of a sitting duck than usual. Fortunately, the People's Champion found his friend 'very supportive throughout'. On a purely cricketing level, David believes, 'it all comes down to individual characters. In July you can be giving the best team talks someone has ever heard; by February you've lost the plot.' On the eve of the Barbados Test, one local paper reported that no fewer than thirteen members of the touring party had thus far consulted the physio. Among the various maladies listed was: 'David Gower, broken heart'.

West Indian reaction to the return of the South African 'rebels' was arguably the most disconcerting element of the trip. There had been no such clemency for Alvin Kallicharran and the other West Indian 'rebels'. West Indians, believes Desmond Haynes, 'felt it was wrong to ban our own kind and let the other rebels in'. Knowing the likely reaction to the erstwhile leader of the English rebels, Willis believes Gooch ought never to have returned to the Caribbean. Indeed, he might not have done had the TCCB not wheeled out the begging bowl. 'I thought that once I had served my sentence everything would be equal,' Gooch later confessed. 'That was one of the biggest mistakes I ever made.' But not *the* biggest.

While a tincture of sympathy is due, Gooch's stubbornness served him ill. The previous spring, a radio interviewer had asked him whether he would revisit South Africa. He implied that he would, that he thought it was his right as an individual to do so; this echoed, by and large, what he had said in his recently published book, *Out of the Wilderness*. Nevertheless, this triggered calls from the Caribbean for him to reaffirm his opposition to apartheid. When this did not come, Lester Bird, the Antiguan foreign minister, made it abundantly clear that he would not be welcome in his country. The TCCB, as Gooch's biographer Ivo Tennant saw it, 'at first maintained a diplomatic silence before issuing a statement on Gooch's behalf in a more apologetic tone than he would have liked'. Gooch took umbrage at Bird's attack, so much so that, even when the politician penned a two-thousand-word open letter to the *Times* with conciliatory undertones, Gooch kept the selectors on tenterhooks before belatedly accepting his tour invitation. 'Sticking to your guns is all very well,' thought David, 'until you start regarding minor pin-pricks as open wounds.'

Not that Gooch was the sole target for the anti-apartheid lobby. Les Taylor had also signed up for the 1981–82 tour, albeit for rather different reasons. Alec Bedser, the then chairman of selectors, had dropped a substantial hint to him:

There I was, standing in the showers at Grace Road after a three- or four-fer, and Bedser comes in and tells me, 'Keep yourself trim, you're going to India.' When the chairman of selectors tells you something like that and then they don't pick you . . . that upset me a lot. From that day to this there has been no call, no explanation. It's the lowest form of manners, but that's the way they work.

It was difficult for us in the Caribbean but Goochie reacted badly. He got no more flak than I did. I still got the death letters, I also had a wife and kids back home. It wasn't nice to walk out of the hotel thinking you were going to get a knife between your ears. It wasn't nice to have to be accompanied everywhere by an armed guard. The West Indians don't get that in Leeds. But I chose to put it behind me. Goochie was getting fed up with touring? I'd love to have been in a position to be fed up with touring. Was it an excuse? If he'd made a thousand runs out there, would he still have said he didn't want to tour any more? There were a lot of experienced people in South Africa: Woolmer, Amiss, Knott, Old. Yet, when it was decided no one wanted Boycs as captain, Goochie got the job. You'd always see him and Peter Cooke, the organizer, together: I always had my doubts about Goochie after that. The selectors bent over backwards to keep him touring because he was always going on about wanting to be with his wife and kids. He lost a lot of credibility when he split up with his wife.

Up to a point, it must be said, Gooch's reservations proved well-founded. Jamaica's cricket-loving ex-PM, Michael Manley, wrote of his 'lingering indignation' for the prototype Essex Man. In his *History of West Indies Cricket*, Manley stressed that Gooch, along with Willey, Emburey and Taylor, 'had chosen to be suspended from Test cricket before taking their place in the ranks of those who were prepared to make a statement against apartheid even when it cost them money'. Clive Lloyd, or so it was rumoured, had turned down $1m to play in Botha's garden of evil, Viv Richards had refused a similarly thick wad. When Marshall bowled Gooch for a duck on the third morning of the opening Test, mused Manley, some would have interpreted that he had 'rammed Gooch's arrogance about that South African tour down his throat'. It was that very perception of arrogance that sent the bile rising to black throats. As if to amplify their point, Lamb, the bonafide South African, went through the tour unmolested. Gooch's response, however, did not endear him to his teammates. 'To be honest,' charged Botham, 'Goochie's non-stop moaning was a right pain in the neck.'

Unnerved and out of form, Gooch sent a letter to Lord's after the third Test, expressing his desire to return to England before the party reached Antigua. 'A minuscule and now long-forgotten member of the Antiguan parliament,' as David saw it, had written some anti-Goochiness for 'some minor free-sheet rag'. The obstinacy that enabled Gooch to defy and tame the world's nastiest bowlers, David correctly surmised, proved in this case a mighty flaw. He did not use that precise word in his autobiography, but then perhaps that was his way of acknowledging that the same could at times be said of him.

The TCCB chairman, Donald Carr, flew to Trinidad, where he, manager, captain and player spent the best part of a day behind closed blinds. But it was David whose imprecations swayed Gooch, who said he stayed out of 'loyalty' to his friend . . . In the short term, the gambit worked, Gooch making 51 in each innings at St John's before Richards trumped everyone with a century at 78rpm. The long-term implications, conversely, were rather less satisfactory. 'I wonder what he [David] was thinking when Gooch took over from him after that disastrous Ashes series of 1989,' wondered Botham, 'and promptly left out both him and myself for the 1990 West Indies tour and whether, during those years when Gooch treated him as persona non grata, Gower didn't allow himself a wry smile over the affair. In hindsight, he probably regretted not packing for him and giving him a lift to the airport.' Had David not tried to help his pal, Gooch's England career would almost certainly have ended at 52 Tests, 3201 runs, five centuries, average 36.38. David, we may be equally certain, would have returned to the Caribbean in 1994 as player rather than commentator.

Through all the unceasing fire and endless brimstone, David somehow held his head high at the crease. In the Tests he was responsible for the most runs, the highest average and the top score. In fact, he made three of the top four individual scores. But these relevant figures – 370, 37, 90, 66 and 66 – cast the disparity between the sides in an even more terrifying light, though no more so than the two-toned minefield that prompted all that *weltschmerz* in Jamaica. 'Nothing,' asserted Michael Holding, 'was as significant as the jolt they got from their first encounter with our fast bowling on that devil of a pitch.' Indeed, so unwilling had David been to believe his own eyes, he paid a visit to Frances Edmonds's optician brother at the end of the first Test; his vision, he was duly reassured, was impeccable. In the last Test at St John's, with another 'blackwash' beckoning and a wrist injury sustained against Marshall in the fourth

Test leaving him in doubt until the morning of the match, he dispelled the threat of the follow-on with an innings whose tone resembled that of Peter Finch in *Network*: 'I'm as mad as hell and I'm not going to take it any more'. It 'looked to executioners both "awkward" and "fragile"', observed the Divine Mrs E. 'Better, it would seem, to look bullish for one than fragile for a ton.'

David nonetheless accepts that there was a grain or two of truth in Clive Lloyd's allegations of self-centredness.

I can answer that, not exonerate myself. If he'd said self-centred as in selfish I'd be upset. The whole tour was a horrendous problem, starting with my mother dying the week before we left. Going into the tour, trying to get over that; trying to concentrate on cricket, failing. Yes, I was self-centred. I allowed myself to be more worried, to hide away. It was my problem. To be a better captain ... what am I going to do? I would have tried to relax, keep the boys happy. He's right in the sense that a better captain would have risen above that better, would have hung on to the basics better, would have found things to do more easily, somehow kept it going. Which is the nub of it. Then you look at the other circumstances surrounding the tour, particularly the South Africa sub-plot. One way I did rise above it was, rightly or wrongly, trying to talk Graham into staying. Talk about being self-centred, he was the one who wanted to go home.

So why bother? 'Basically, he was an important figure. I spent more time than I wanted looking after him, making sure he was in a better state of mind.'

Come Antigua, the only reason anybody was in a better state of mind was the impending reunion with Blighty. 'It was a very bleak three months,' reiterates David. 'My failing would have been not realizing or being able to cope, not knowing how to lift the side. You acknowledge you are up against one of the best sides ever to play the game. You make all the right noises, as people will always do, then it comes down to how much you believe you can do to cope. And it was ...' The voice trails off, unable, for once, to summon up the apposite adjective. 'Then there was the Botham sub-plot. That tour had everything apart from England winning a game of cricket.'

Simon Strong recollects that David was in a far from sunny mood at the end, albeit not entirely for the obvious reasons. This had stemmed partly from an exchange of views with his opposite number Viv Richards. While giving the pitch a bit of unnecessary prodding, Richards made it quite clear that he regarded these delaying tactics as a bit off. David admitted fairly forcefully that he was not about to go missing the odd trick with his side facing another five-niller, and that the more Richards huffed and puffed, the more he would bide his time. Getting out to Harper shortly afterwards scarcely sunnied David's mood. 'He was very very low,' remembers Strong. 'Viv had been swearing at him, really sledging him, because he thought England might scrape a draw. David said that when he was out and it sank in he got seriously depressed. "If this is what cricket is about," he said to me, "if this is what captaincy is about, it's totally unjustifiable. The fact that Richards had to resort to that."' The one time the hosts were beaten all tour, in the second one-dayer at Port of Spain, a disgruntled Richards declined to attend the press conference. But Frank Keating had his cockles warmed by David's 'ambassadorial approach to the world'. The Divine Mrs E stood by her man to the bitter end: 'Whatever the critics may say about David Gower, he is every inch the perfect English gent in success and failure alike.'

David flew home before making a swift return to Antigua for a spot of richly earned R and R. There was no time for any meaningful reflection. When he returned to Leicester, a new season was days away, his phone had been cut off, and a Snowdonia of mail obscured the doormat. Relations with Vicki had been better. Unsurprisingly, it took him a fair while to put cricket back into the forefront of his thoughts, or even on the second row of the grid. The Leicestershire chairman was more than a little peeved when his captain rolled up to the pre-season cocktail party an hour late, the whole shebang having completely slipped his mind. 'When David came back from Antigua,' recalls Holmes, 'he was as low as I have ever seen him. Not a lot of bounce there.'

The fact of the matter, David would subsequently accept, 'is that we got stuffed by a bloody good side. But someone has to be the fall guy.' On 14 May, he was handed the rope: sufficiently long for him to hang himself, short enough to get the deed done quickly – two one-day internationals and the first Test against India. Allan Lamb deems this 'ridiculous', the pressure 'totally wrong'. Tony Lewis delved deeper: 'Giving him one Test does not help Gower or the team. It wreaks [sic] of posturing – selectors delivering a stricture in public to satisfy Gower's critics.' A captain with no tenure, argued the one-time England skipper, will find that his authority diminishes. 'How would you like to be Gower, twenty-one times a Test captain, winner of two Test series, having to parade in front of the cricket world with "L" plates on again – back and front?'

Yet, for all the barbs hurled by the national press, it was a reporter from the *Leicester Mercury*, Jon Culley, who provoked the strongest response. One of Culley's first pieces for his new employers was an overview of the Caribbean misadventures filtered through – and coloured by

– the reports of those who were actually there. It was not one-sided by any means: 'Even at their very best, even if everybody was tucked into bed every night before ten, even if Gower ordered a practice session every morning and every evening and never went windsurfing, England would still have been hard placed to draw a Test in this series, let alone win one. This is an awesomely powerful West Indies team.'

But what upset David was partly that Culley should have been passing judgement from his armchair, and partly the author's allegations of low morale and advocacy of the need for a full-time manager, 'a cricketing regimental sergeant-major to bring back some old-fashioned respect and pride'.

Stung into action, David paid an immediate visit to the editor. 'That was the first time I met him,' reflects Culley:

> I was in the office at the time. It was a very informal situation. He simply wanted the right of reply. He was probably concerned that it was his own patch and he deserved better treatment, or the local readers deserved an explanation. He felt a certain loyalty towards the Leicestershire public. He was very popular with them. He was angry but it was very much controlled anger. He didn't beat around the bush. He was quite happy to make his point and depart on amicable terms. He wasn't insulting to me, but he made his feelings quite clear about me commenting from an office in Leicester. Maybe I did go a bit overboard.

In order to head off any prospect of legal action, not to mention acting in the interests of fairness, Culley's editor acceded to David's request for a reply: 'The single root cause was that a very very good side played very very well against us,' he proceeded to write:

> All the players wondered whether the journalists were on the same tour ... morale is never sky-high when you're taking a beating, and some people did not play to their best by a long way, but morale was always OK ... If I'm guilty, then I'm guilty more of not pandering to the press than not thinking of the team.

David's most grievous crime in the Caribbean was to offend the sensibilities of the fourth estate, and hence the equally paranoid chairman of selectors. Vivid is the memory of Peter May trotting up to the Lord's press box to seek out and quietly remonstrate with the reporter whose paper's back page that morning had led off with the immortal 'Nuts to May'. A less acutely sensitive man would have brushed it off. Capable on occasion of making A. C. Smith sound like Danny Baker, May's dealings with the media had never been more than clipped since the wildly unsuccessful Ashes tour of 1958–59. On that occasion he, too, had been upbraided in public for spending less time in the nets than it was deemed a captain ought to; in his case, the distraction was his fiancée. Never again, swore his friend, Doug Insole, did May tackle the game with the same zest.

Hypocrisy ruled, OK. The Optional Nets Affair had cropped up just a couple of days after May had had a word or two in David's ear, stating the pressing need for rots to be stopped and, while he was about it, a touch more demonstration in the body-language department. David shrugged off the warning as merely a regurgitation of what May had been reading over his bacon and eggs. At the press conference to announce his 'provisional' captaincy, David found it difficult to contain his disenchantment: 'I've been asked to keep a higher profile. The chairman of selectors wants me to be more publicly demonstrative when it comes to showing authority . . . if they want cosmetics they should go to Boots. Maybe I should go out dressed in bright orange and wave my arms around a bit.' The assembled throng learned that he had been 'informed that they [the selectors] are determined to improve standards both on and off the field and have made it clear that they expect their players once again to show a real pride in playing for England.' John Woodcock listed some of the more treacherous acts:

Those standards have not least to do with appearances, which means shaving more than every third day (those, that is, without beards) and not looking like tramps or stretching out on players' balconies in front of thousands of spectators in only the briefest of shorts or being without blazers when meeting the Governor-General or taking the field in dribs and drabs. Such slovenliness was not to be seen last winter in the West Indian camp.

Don Mosey had never really forgiven the current generation of England cricketers since discovering that one 'relative newcomer' to the dressing room in 1984, upon being asked what the tactics were for the following day, told him, 'abruptly', that the priority lay in getting to the pub. The 'old guard', according to this thoroughly embittered observer, were 'not merely demoralized but seemingly disinterested'. It would have been 'entirely possible', he averred, 'to sympathize with Gower and his men in this goldfish-bowl existence had not the captain adopted, it seemed, a cavalier attitude . . . the adjective most generally applied to Gower's style of leadership is "laid-back", which can be interpreted in a number of ways from quietly controlled to sloppy, slipshod and slap happy.'

In a typically whimsical response to May's demand that he be more openly assertive, David had thirteen t-shirts run off before the Texacos: one 'I'm in Charge', the rest 'I'm Not'. The first one-dayer saw the Indians scoot home by nine wickets and captain out first ball. But he rebounded forcefully, winning the Man of the Match award for his decisive 81 off 94 balls in the second game: the series was lost on run-rate. Surely May and Co wouldn't hold that against him? Cue scores of 18 and 8 (lbw Kapil Dev) in the opening Test at Lord's, exacerbated by a five-wicket loss. Even then, he might have survived had May not spotted him popping his head around the sponsor's tent flap during lunch on the fourth day, to check on Vicki. On the double standards meter, May's anger struck David as a 9.8, maybe a 9.9. There he was, apparently supposed to be giving the impression that the *Enola Gay* had landed in the Long Room, while May and his fellow mandarins were guzzling and gulping every drop and dram the sponsor's caterers could muster.

If it was ever in doubt, May's mind was now fixed: Gower out, Gatting in. 'In many ways, it is because of his nature that he has lost the job,' wrote Martin Johnson. 'If May needs an arm-waver, he's got the right man this time.' Numbed as David was, both by the manner of rejection (Gatting got the nod before Gower got the sack) and the painkillers he had taken after injuring his right shoulder in a collision with a Lord's boundary wall, the post-gallows humour was well above-par. While the incoming emperor was being interviewed and snapped, the outgoing one was encouraged to throw over his 'I'm in Charge' t-shirt. 'I didn't think that was particularly tasteful,' said Gatting, whom Frank Keating espied 'fingering his beard like a nervous Henry VIII at a divorce trial in Rome'. The chairman of the Cricket Writers' Club thanked David for his 'charm, frankness and help'.

'I didn't know how the rest of the team would take it – though I knew everybody had been solidly behind David,' recalled his hastily appointed if not undeserving successor. 'Lubo had, after all, done a lot for England and I hoped the selectors would thank him accordingly. Perhaps he knew something was in the wind. When Peter May told him, he didn't seem particularly surprised: he came up and said, "Well, best of luck, mate, we'll give you a hundred per cent."' Mike Turner accused the selectors of insensitivity, insisting they should either have sacked him after the Caribbean or given him the captaincy for the whole of the India series. To him, David's reaction had been 'philosophical and gracious'.

'A professional amateur.' Such was the verdict of the estimable ex-*Observer* correspondent, Alan Ross, following the death of Peter Barker Howard May (Charterhouse, Pembroke College, Cambridge, Willis, Faber and Dumas Insurance Brokers). In the majority of reputable eyes, here, indubitably, was the finest English batsman to emerge since the war. As a captain he was solid and unadventurous, a stickler for decorum and, noted Doug Insole, 'quick to punish lack of effort'. As chairman of selectors, Insole noticed, May did not find it easy 'to communicate his views to the younger generation of cricketers'. It annoyed him that David had the gall to look as if a bad day in the office – OK, a bad three months in the office – wasn't worth at least one ulcer. But whatever the arguments in favour of Gatting as captain does that mean he was justified in informing the new captain of his promotion – and hence the rest of the dressing room – without first informing the incumbent that he could collect his P45? What, pray, is more important than common decency?

Resisting any impulse to resort to that habitual defensive flipness, David had never once tried to disguise his desire to carry on. A few days later, once reality had cast its deadening shadow, he said he felt 'as though the hypodermic has been pulled out of my arm and the adrenalin has stopped flowing'. By then he had happily obliged Gatting's request for a few pointers.

Life was about to change in all sorts of ways, albeit not pocket-wise: Wiggins Teape, the stationery company which had paid David in excess of £30,000 for a summer's worth of promotion the previous year, mulled over the viability of having an *ex*-England captain promoting products under the slogan 'Leader in the Field' – then increased the fee. Letters of support, meanwhile, poured in from sympathetic admirers appalled by his treatment: David was suitably touched. The shoulder injury, fortunately, ruled him out of the next Test, allowing time to 'reflect on the fact that the end of the world was not yet nigh, and that I'd be far better off getting stuck into my cricket and enjoying it once again.' Doubtless feeling the need to dissuade the sceptics, as well as convince himself, he publicly offered Gatting his unstinting support: 'Just because I am no longer in charge does not mean that I am not 100 per cent involved.' For the pair's first Test in reversed roles, at Edgbaston, Gatting would repeatedly refer to him as 'Skip'.

If Gatting felt he was any more in charge than his predecessor he was kidding himself, of course. The men in charge were men like May and Bedser, men who knew cricket but not cricketers.

10 *Nothing Rhymed*

Nothing old, nothing new, nothing ventured
Nothing gained, nothing still-born or lost
Nothing further than proof, nothing wilder than youth
Nothing older than time, nothing sweeter than wine
Nothing physically, recklessly, hopelessly blind
Nothing I couldn't say, nothing why coz today
Nothing rhymed
Nothing Rhymed, Gilbert O'Sullivan

On the first Saturday in August, Martin Johnson had a close encounter of an unnerving kind. Over the course of the twenty years he has chronicled his peaks and pratfalls, our unblinkered Boswell can remember innumerable off-the-record conversations with his Dr Johnson; only once has more than passing reference been made to the source of their relationship. On 2 August 1986, shortly after close of play on the opening day of Leicestershire's championship fixture at Canterbury, the pair discussed cricket.

In fact, it was something of a one-sided discussion, since Johnson did most of the listening: 'Gower sat down in the Wool Pack in Chilham with Chris Cowdrey, and I got involved, somehow. It lasted four hours, the most extraordinary conversation.' Any passers-by, David quipped with a modicum of seriousness, would probably have imagined Messrs Cowdrey and Johnson had come hotfoot from the Samaritans.

For Cowdrey, the experience was no less unusual:

I've often tried to advise David, but he doesn't like it, and I eventually worked out that it was best to leave him. If he needed help he'd very rarely ask. I don't know if it was his pride or what. Very occasionally I would say, 'You're not getting runs for Hampshire but you want to play for England: doesn't this suggest something to you? Or do you think you have a divine right to play, which we all agree you have?' Under the Gooch-Stewart regime, I told him, you're not going to get picked unless there's a way whereby you can improve your chances of selection. He didn't want to talk about it. He'd change the subject to windsurfing, or say something like, 'bat right-handed'. I think he always knew he was on a different level. He's on a different level to Gooch, to anyone. Gooch is no genius, but I'd put my life on him to get more runs in any one game anywhere in the world. David is the genius. He was always so far ahead of everyone else. But when it came to saying, well, why are you doing this or doing that, it was, 'hang on a minute, don't question me'.

Hard as David tried to play on through a fog of injured pride and extreme fatigue, mental more than physical, he was having trouble lying back and not thinking of England. Returning respectably to the fold for the third Test against India at Edgbaston, he made 49 and 26 to help secure the draw that ended England's ignominious run of seven consecutive defeats.

On the morning before the opening Texaco Trophy game against New Zealand the *Daily Mirror* revealed to the world that seven England players had been spotted in Manchester the previous evening drinking until the wee hours, David among them. Gatting deplored this as 'unprofessional and silly' (the revelry, not the *Mirror*). On that Saturday night at Chilham, he pondered pulling out of the first Test against New Zealand at Lord's but soon found his enthusiasm returning in dribs and drabs as an enthralling final day saw Kent win by five runs.

The Lord's Test was drawn, David contributing 62 to England's 307, followed by 3 in the second innings; in the second Test at Trent Bridge he made 71 and 26, the highest home aggregate in an eight-wicket defeat. On each occasion he had prospered fitfully without ever looking entirely at ease. Whether he made 0 or 100 was of no real concern, or so he would subsequently reflect.

Yet even on remote control he could still cut it. Unlike his specialist colleagues, for instance, he steadfastly refused to bow the knee to the rampant Richard Hadlee. Thus far, Hadlee had plucked eight of his scalps from the top five in the order, yet not once had he obtained a lock of those fair curls, limp as they seemed to have grown under rejection. Hadlee would later cite David as the only contemporary English batsman worthy of a place among his Ten Most Reluctant Victims. Those scorebook entries against his name at Lord's and Trent Bridge may well have been immaterial to D. I. Gower, but such resistance, surely, was indisputable proof of pride.

Such minor triumphs, however, could not obscure David's feelings of foreboding, hence the session at the Wool Pack. If years could be measured on a scale of crappiness, 1986 would have been his 10 (though not his only 10). In ascending order of pain, he had established a new benchmark for the worst captaincy record in Test history, been sacked for offending the very establishment he was supposed to symbolize, and become an orphan. And we'd only just waved goodbye to July. What delightful surprises could the next five months of 1986 possibly hold? For the first time in twelve summers, the concept of the flannelled fool rang true. What was David Gower doing earning his daily bread standing in a field? For the first time in his life, the rough outweighed the smooth: 'Someone clearly decided it was time to make life a little harder for me. My appetite for getting up in the morning and going to play cricket was vanishing.'

Fred Rumsey recommended taking a break. As a consequence of a more protracted one-to-one with Mike Turner, it was agreed that David could miss the last month of the county season. As he left Turner's office, relief swept through his mind like an overdose of Settlers. 'I don't want anyone to feel I'm letting the club down,' ran a prepared statement, a formal explanation as conscious of the players' initial prickly reaction as it was of the inevitable mutterings of the Leicestershire public whose support had never once wavered. 'I've spoken to the players and outlined the details,' the statement continued, 'and they seem to understand my reasons. I hope that Leicestershire members will understand the situation also.' Turner emphasized that the decision had been reached by mutual agreement: 'Both David and the club feel it is in his best interest and England's that he takes a complete break. It is fair to say that, after all the pressures he has been under, the problems of the West Indies tour and so on, he is suffering from physical exhaustion.'

Knowing that the final Test at The Oval represented his last opportunity of the summer to score a first-class century, David made it count, underlining yet again his facility for getting it right at the last. If he could do it then, then why couldn't he produce those same qualities to order? That was the gist of the argument of those who felt he had cheated his teammates by not doing it more often. But David needed that deadline, needed the extra adrenalin surge that comes from knowing you are on the brink.

The gasholders bore witness to no end of memorabilia that August week. John Wright, a good friend of David's, acquired New Zealand's first century in their presence, a fitting honour for a model professional; Gatting clubbed 121, his sixth century for his country in the space of seventeen Tests. And then there was Botham. On his return from a two-month ban, the Somerset Dope Fiend equalled Lillee's world record of 355 Test wickets with his very first ball, then passed it with his twelfth. Anxious to outdo himself, he then went out and equalled another Test landmark by battering poor young Derek Stirling for 24 in a single over.

190

Bottom of the bill, in headline if hardly aesthetic terms, came David's 131, his first Test hundred in nineteen stabs. Jon Holmes was not in the least bit surprised at his client's timing, literally or figuratively: 'I wasn't at all surprised that he went out and made that hundred. He's a lot tougher than people realize.'

Bordered as it was by intricate and dazzling embroidery, that toughness shone through the most authoritative English partnership of the summer. After Hadlee and trusty Ewan Chatfield had reduced England to 62 for three, it was David, batting at No. 3 for the first time since the opening Test against India, who accounted for the lion's share of a fourth-wicket stand with his captain worth 223. 'There is poetry in the man's batting,' David Lemmon would exult in that winter's *Benson & Hedges Cricket Year*. 'It is measured. It scans. There is liquidity of movement.'

Entering at 285 for four, just two runs behind New Zealand's first innings total, Botham could relax in the knowledge that this was his most promising launch-pad for a year. Not that this salvaged anything more tangible than self-respect: with rain rationing Kennington to sixteen overs on the last two days, New Zealand clung on to their first series victory in the Motherland. And England had lost two rubbers at home in one summer – a first.

By now, another log was hovering near the fire. David's benefit was now just four months away. And it was with that distraction uppermost in mind that Leicestershire decreed he should take a sabbatical from the helm. More relief. Since David's attention was seldom fully focused on his county obligations as it was, reasoned Turner, the dinners and the speeches and the fundraisers and the All-Star clown-arounds were not about to concentrate the mind any better: 'I thought I would have a real job to get his mind focused on anything. I can't remember it as a bee in my bonnet that I felt compelled to put to him. Had he said he wanted to remain captain, I'm quite sure he would have done so.'

Martin Johnson offers a somewhat different perspective.

The change was advertised as being temporary, but I thought Turner was being clever. Having spotted that Gower was congenitally useless at the job, he was going to let him down lightly and then they could come to this mutual arrangement whereby Peter Willey would take over. But, in fact, the opposite turned out to be true. Gower was reappointed for 1988. I remain convinced that that was a purely cosmetic job, (a), to keep him at the club – or what Turner perceived as necessary to keep him at the club – and, (b), to elevate Leicestershire's status with this glamorous captain, in terms of sponsorship attraction and all the rest of it. I don't think there was any sound cricketing reason.

Johnson has no hesitation in relating the incident that convinced him David would never make an acceptable county captain. It was 3 June 1980, shortly before the first Test against the West Indies. Leicestershire, chasing 199 in 135 minutes, required five off the last two overs with five wickets intact. David was still there, having apparently helped cut and dry the outcome by thrashing 63 in nine overs with Chris Balderstone.

'He was playing beautifully but suddenly he nodded off,' recalls Johnson:

They should have knocked off the runs a fair bit earlier but Gower didn't seem too worried. Turner popped his head round the press box door and said he was off, convinced as we all were that the points were in the bag. Gower proceeds to block the next five balls, then has a great waft at the last and it goes off the outside edge for four. A real panic shot. Kim Barnett came on with his leg-breaks to finish the match. All the fielders were round the bat and Tim Boon, who was making his second championship appearance at Grace Road, had an over to score a single. He drove the first ball to mid-off and there was a misfield; they could have got a run, but they didn't. Boon set off nervously but Gower, who had by this time taken his gloves off, was sat on his bat handle. Barnett kept landing it on the spot; five balls went by and they still wanted this bloody single.

'By now, Boon is in a complete lather. At no stage did Gower, as the senior player, try to speak to this young lad who was obviously in a terrible state. Boon clipped the last ball hard and straight to short-midwicket, where the fielder, to his great misfortune, was Peter Kirsten, who was pretty well one of the best fielders in that position at the time. As Kirsten ran in to pick up, the phone went: it was Turner. 'What was the margin?' he wanted to know. 'I should pour yourself a large Scotch,' I said. 'We've got six extra points for tying the scores, but the game was drawn.' Boon went home in tears; his parents had been watching.

'I went off to the pub with Mike Carey and Gerald Mortimer, and Gower was the first player in the door. He was always either very quick in the shower or very slow, ten minutes or an hour. Typical Lubo: he comes in with a big smile on his face and says, 'Hi boys, have a drink?' So we all chorused: 'Have a bloody drink!' We asked him what the hell had been going on out there. 'I don't know,' he answered, 'he (meaning Boon) should have got off the bloody road, shouldn't he.' What were *you* doing, we wanted to know. 'What do

At the end of a year that saw him lose the England captaincy, David gets back to where he once belonged with one of his most violent centuries. Perth, 1986.

David marks his 100th Test in distinctly inglorious fashion, caught Dujon in both innings *(left)* off Winston Benjamin for 13 and *(below)* down the legside off Malcolm Marshall for 2. Headingley, 1988.

Having fielded all manner of
flak for storming out of a press
conference 48 hours earlier,
David progresses towards
his century in the second Test
of his comeback summer as
captain. Lord's, 1989.

Deprived of the South African
defectors, David ponders the
slings and arrows after
England had sustained their
record home loss to Australia.
Trent Bridge, 1989.
(Mark Ray)

David secures a fifth
Australian tour by
reaching 100 in the
final Test against India.
"You don't fit in with
this team," Dilip
Vengsarkar whispered
as he walked off after
saving the match. The
Oval, 1990.

David drills Carl
Rackemann square
during his eighteenth
and last Test century, a
knock acclaimed by Sir
Donald Bradman as
one of the finest he had
ever witnessed. Sydney,
1991.

A rueful David departs after being dismissed glancing Merv Hughes down the legside. Adelaide, 1991.

Aquib Javed is eased through the offside for the boundary that took David past Geoff Boycott's national Test run record. It mattered more than it looked. Old Trafford, 1992.

Waqar Younis tries in vain to keep his emotions under control after persuading David to end his Test career without a stroke. The ecstasy and the irony. The Oval, 1992.

The emotional shield is present and erect as David leaves the Test arena for the last time. The Oval, 1992.

Charles Colvile cues his svelte co-commentator before the first Test against India, a match which the whole of England believed David should have attended with bat rather than mike. Calcutta, 1993.

David, Thorunn and daughter Alexandra pose at home for *Hello!*
magazine. Braishfield, 1994. *(Scope Features)*

you mean,' he replied. 'I was non-striker.' Yes, we said, but why didn't you make an attempt to become the striker, or at least have a word with him? 'Well, he's a professional cricketer, isn't he? What's it to do with me?' That was his attitude: very instructive, I thought. As far as he was concerned, it was up to the bloke down the other end to get the run. Nothing to do with Gower. He couldn't see that he had any part to play in proceedings.

There was, however, one sound reason for David's eventual reinstatement as Leicestershire captain: for all his failings as a rabble-rouser, the players far preferred him to his stand-in. Peter Willey claimed that the responsibility affected his batting, and the figures certainly indicated as much: in 1986 he averaged nearly 45 in the championship; the year he led, that plummeted to 32. But the fact is that he would never again achieve a first-class average of 30. After twenty years in the game, the parallel decline of body and form cannot have been easy to handle.

In his prime, Willey was as formidable a competitor as English cricket can ever have possessed. Those forearms would make Popeye choke on his spinach; he was the only man in recorded history to beat Botham in an arm wrestle. He is also the only man in recorded history to make Botham cower. Here was a bloke with enough grit to cover the M6. He had come up the hard way. No public school or family money for him. The commitment to calling was utter. A Northamptonshire debutant at sixteen, he joined the umpires' list after retiring a couple of months shy of forty-two. His technique was essentially rudimentary. The stance would have done Chaplin proud, provoking all manner of cracks about him expecting bouncers from widish mid-on. But that didn't stop the Sedgefield Sledgehammer from being quite possibly the most bloody-minded batsman ever. Of his twenty-six caps, fifteen were earned against the West Indies. Maybe he took the rand out of pique? How come I'm good enough to play against the best, he must have wondered, and yet I always miss out on the easy pickings?

Yet fire and devotion doth not necessarily make a leader. Willey found David's apparent casualness 'a bit irritating', but then it would have been unnatural for him to respond any other way. He was also never quite sure 'whether his mind was completely on the game'. For all that, he respected him for being 'one of the best players I've ever seen'. David, in turn, respected Willey for his courage, his assiduousness and his honesty, but recognized that he found the intricacies of man-management elusive. He was not alone in regarding Willey as a bit of a mixer, a stirrer. More, much more than this, Willey did it his way, always. Even more than David did.

David's county wages, of course, were a bonus, the smallest brick in an ever-expanding wall. There were the international and celebrity fees, the growing portfolio of commercial interests, and, underpinning all that, his parents' legacy (reportedly in the region of £250,000). Which is why he could afford to accept less from Leicestershire than he might have done. He was certainly much better paid when he moved to Hampshire. A combination of agent and financial nous served him well, although he did once lose money on a property deal. It would have been an unusual failure; his investments were invariably sensible if not shrewd. James Whitaker has mixed memories of a rainy afternoon in Swansea:

> Rain had prevented play so three of us went out for lunch, David included. The bill came to two hundred quid, sixty-five-odd quid each, which was just about bearable. Then he proposes that we play this game and the loser picks up the tab. I lost. But you didn't mind because it had been a fun afternoon.

David sustained his next kick with the announcement of the Ashes squad (after the previous winter's horrors, Gooch elected to stay home with Brenda and the girls, to share a more important load). Emburey, a veteran of one previous Ashes tour, was appointed as Gatting's vice-captain; his Middlesex chum lacked even that depth of experience. 'These have been the worst twelve months of my life,' David told the *News of the World*, needlessly. 'Not being vice-captain hurts the most. Especially when nobody has told me what I am supposed to have done wrong.' He was even denied a voice on the tour selection committee, although he did have a slight suspicion that this constituted a rapped knuckle or two for coming off much the worse for a twilight rum session with Botham. In the space of twelve months he had gone from king to commoner.

Before the party left Heathrow, Seagrams presented David with a dozen bottles of their finest and a cheque for £200, in recognition of the 'extra-ordinary good grace' with which he had accepted his sacking as England captain. Four months on and still no formal explanation. By inference, 'failure to wave arms' came closest. He set off Down Under feeling somewhat sorrier for himself than was either healthy or, by his own admission, necessary.

Distancing himself from the pack as usual, Scyld Berry of the *Observer* wanted to do a piece about The Future of David Gower: a two-day train ride across the Nullarbor Plain seemed to represent as good an opportunity as any. While David insisted he still had goals, that he was still motivated, he freely confessed that he had begun to think seriously about life after the ball, that from here, as a professional cricketer, the only way was down. Berry offered reassurances, maintaining that thousands, millions even, still delighted in his every move. He wasn't even thirty, for chrissakes. David got a bit annoyed: '"You can't retire, Lubo, please," he said. I thought that was a bit off.'

Berry obtained a handy story, his subject even more: a free session on the couch plus a reminder that life after the ball held few attractions. He hadn't planned on a confession, but nature held sway, as ever. David had never been a particularly efficient liar. As the train clickety-clicked so the words came tumbling out, kicking the mind into gear. There wasn't anything else he could picture himself doing to earn a crust. In any case, why make a decision when it wasn't absolutely necessary? Unwittingly, Berry had blown out the pilot light, then reignited it. Perhaps it was the mesmeric nature of the Nullarbor Plain itself.

The selectors had broken ground by appointing a team manager, and David's exclusion from the tour selection committee may not have been unconnected to the antipathy of the appointee. Micky Stewart had even had the tactlessness to voice his disapproval to Chris Kilbee, an old schoolfriend of David's. The criticism duly filtered back, putting the subject on his guard. To Stewart's soccerspeak way of thinking, David was a George Best, a waster. Had Illingworth compromised on his demands for absolute power he would almost certainly have landed the job ahead of Stewart. And how might things have turned out then? 'If I'd got the job, say, five years ago,' maintains the current El Supremo, 'David would still be playing for England.'

Stewart was quick to make his presence felt when the party landed in Brisbane, doing his level best to impose a ten p.m. curfew. Whereupon a fusillade of how-dare-yous from Botham and Lamb were supplemented by the captain's own objections and the idea was peremptorily shelved (Stewart eventually got his way the following summer in the wake of the Rothley Court Affair). What managing director insists his top salesmen be tucked in before News at Ten?

David needed to do a bit of candle-burning in order to generate the requisite sparks. 'He needed to go to a casino or a disco because he needed that space,' echoes Nigel Briers, a man of contrasting temperament who teaches Prince Charles's sons at Ludgrove School during the off-season and would no more foist his creed on them than on an admired colleague.

He needed to get some excitement elsewhere in order to keep it exciting on the field. Some of the best innings I ever saw him play came after he'd had quite a bit to drink on a Saturday night. One Sunday, we were going out to open the innings against Somerset when suddenly, halfway to the middle, he said, 'Look mate, I don't feel so good', turned round and went back to the pavilion to throw up. Then he came out and played it with a stick of rhubarb. He made 70 or 80 in no time. Why would you want to change him? What gives anyone the right to even think they could try and change him? The arrogance.

'I've got home at 6 a.m. and still got a hundred for England the next day,' boasts Allan Lamb, a man not averse to grabbing life by the short and curlies. 'Under Micky, when you weren't playing, you had to be *seen* to be practising.' This is confirmed by James Whitaker, a spiritual bedfellow of David's who had been chosen for his first and so far only full England tour: 'I'd never played under a manager before, so it was very strange being told specifically what to do all the time. It ostracized the individual. Micky used us younger guys as a way of getting his message across. Those who weren't playing in the Tests had to net at certain times, every day.' Lamb construed it as the start of a misguided attempt to appease the press; fortunately for Stewart, England did almost all their losing when it didn't matter. Prior to the first Test, which marked his debut as correspondent for the newly founded *Independent*, Martin Johnson outlined England's maladies: they couldn't bat or bowl, let alone catch. Yet Gatting's men wound up with the lot: the Ashes, the Perth Challenge and the World Series. While Elton John was gurgling champers with the boys at the MCG, nobody gave a damn what was being scribbled or said. The seeds, however, had been sown; four years hence, they would reach full bloom.

Little as he cared for Stewart's martinet tendencies – the manager's pre-match tonic for the troops was apparently four parts Henry V to six parts Bertie Mee – David cared even less for the manager's training regime, and resented his insistence on hovering over him during net practice. It was never quite clear what a man with eight caps and a career average of 32.90 could profitably tell a living legend. Four years later, David had a net session with Anguilla's finest, Cardigan Connor, then went out and tonked a sublime century at the SCG that wrung all manner of superlatives from Don Bradman himself. When Stewart cited this as evidence of the benefits of diligence and preparation, David 'didn't have the heart to tell him' he benefited a good deal more 'from not having him hovering over me'. Neither did he deign to inform the manager that, upon his arrival in Brisbane, a bottle of Bollinger had been deposited in his room by the company's Australian agent, or that, for the remainder of the tour, supplies of same were fruitful (and, better still, 'reasonably priced'). And David's love of Bordeaux earned him the nickname 'Fender', after the Surrey captain who used to travel the length and breadth of England with cases of claret in tow.

Stewart, however, had barely cranked up the starter motor. At that stage, there was no obvious schism between him and David, who admired his zest and wholeheartedness. David probably didn't take him all that seriously. After all, the position Stewart occupied was not only new, but the parameters were unclear. Was he there to chuck a few balls down in the nets? To act as a buffer between the captain and those dastardly hacks? To make sure all the coffins were suitably labelled? To glad-hand with the natives? What did disturb David were the hints of rigidity, a crime for which his own unbending genes had often made him culpable. Yet there is one fundamental difference between him and Stewart: David never once tried to change anyone else.

That winter, Lamb nonetheless insists, Stewart did not burrow under independent-minded skins with anything like his subsequent vigour. 'Micky was great then because he was finding his feet and was quite relaxed. It was only after that tour that it really became "this is how it should be done, this is how it's going to be done".' Has anyone ever *enjoyed* an England tour since? True, no team actively enjoys being taken to the cleaners two Tests out of every three, but the fact that England have not won an overseas series against major opposition in the past eight years certainly suggests something of a chicken-and-egg situation. Enjoyment breeds relaxation; a relaxed mind, by and large, breeds a more amenable man.

The son of a London suburban bookie, Stewart had shed the amateur trappings of Alleyn's and Corinthian Casuals to become a dedicated pro during his three decades at The Oval as player, captain and coach. Writing in *The Cricketer*, Phil Pilley contended that the paternal influence had been strong: 'Here, perhaps, is a hint of why Stewart has blended so easily into *professional* cricket. He had become, so to speak, the amateur-type son of professional-type forebears.' He represented his country as a sturdy, no-frills opener and a short leg with a taste for bodily risk. As one of the last cricketer-footballers of any note, he played football for Charlton Athletic and won caps for England as an amateur. He played cricket alongside Laker and Lock, under May and Surridge, at the head of Edrich and Pocock. No influential fixture in contemporary English cricket can match the success he enjoyed as a member of five successive championship-winning sides. As Surrey captain, he led the club to their most recent pennant (1971) and it was the commercial nous he garnered at Slazenger that secured Nescafé's backing for the youth scheme that produced so many splendidly forthright graduates, among them his son.

Over the past twenty-five years, on the other hand, Surrey have been the most turbulent, and frequently the unhappiest of counties. Time and again, world-class players have fallen way short of their reputations, distracted and undermined by personnel clashes and, more recently, an all-consuming desire by the club's management for Kennington to compete with its more glamorous rival north of the Thames. Stewart displayed a different sort of commitment. While his county were pursuing the championship in 1971, the *Daily Express* quoted him as follows: 'I find I am playing every ball, bowling every ball and fielding every ball. The captaincy has cost me over six hundred runs a season. I am snapping at my wife and children and sleeping no more than four hours a night.' When I used that confession twenty years later as the intro to a piece about him for the *Independent*, he called me from his carphone ten minutes before deadline to request that I remove it (I had faxed him a copy of the article, not a common practice by any means, at least two hours earlier). He was adamant: it was all poppycock. The quote was entirely fictitious. Strange, then, that David Hopps, co-author of the indispensable Book of Cricket Quotations, should subsequently inform me that, as far as he could remember, he had received no such complaint when he duplicated the *Express* passage. What does this illustrate? If Stewart did indeed utter those words, or those sentiments, did this denial imply a desire for a change of image? Was he ashamed that he could have taken it all so seriously?

Bob Willis has few fond memories of his formative years at Surrey, coinciding as they did with the dying days of Stewart's captaincy.

> Only three guys in that side ever socialized: Jackman, Mike Edwards and me. None of the rest drank pints of ale or swapped stories. There was terrible jealousy, and no sort of team spirit or cameraderie. All the second XI players wanted the first-team players to fail. When Micky went out to Australia in '86–87, I don't think he believed how Lamb, Botham and Gower behaved on a daily basis. He was probably poorly paid at Surrey and here were these guys who had a lot of money and spent a lot of money, who'd go out and order Bollinger and the best wine. Micky was used to Berni Inns; if he had one glass of Liebfraumilch that would have been about it. I think Micky had a problem with all that.

Given all these extraneous influences, it was only to be expected that, going into the opening match of the rubber, the words 'Gower' and 'form' only occupied the same sentence when accompanied by 'out of' and 'hopelessly'. 'Fender' had metamorphosed into 'Run-Glut'. If his brain had been measured for concentration level, the reading would have been zero. His first eight innings had brought 132 runs off 136 balls. In the second innings against Western Australia four days before hostilities commenced, he completed a pair. 'He looked as bad that day as any batsman I have ever seen,' avows Martin Johnson:

Even before he got out he was dropped at slip off Ken MacLeay, an absolute knob-ender too. MacLeay had bowled him six balls that he never got anywhere near. The harder he tried to make contact, the worse he got. By the end of the over, he was talking to MacLeay in mid-pitch with that stupid look on his face. The conversation ran something along the lines of: 'You'd better start ringing a bell. I don't know, I can't see it. I might have a chance if I could hear it.' MacLeay just stood there and laughed.

At Kalgoorlie airport a few days earlier, the twin pollutants of failure and alcohol had momentarily deprived David of his rag. That was the worst blow-up I ever saw from him,' asserts Johnson:

The plane was delayed and the Leicestershire connection were having a few drinks – me, DeFreitas, Whitaker and Gower. Then Botham wanders in. By then Gower had had a few too many and he was directed to take his baggage to another channel by this very pedantic check-in controller. Gower told him he couldn't see the point since there was a nearer one, so the bloke said, fairly politely, 'Look, I know you're England cricketers but a rule is a rule.' Gower got into such a temper I thought they might have kicked him off the plane. He threw bags around, effed and blinded, really verbally violent, probably the worst I've seen him in public. He was very good nearly all the time, but he could get very intolerant if people bothered him.

Gatting felt David needed a fillip, and duly restored some of his colleague's self-esteem by inviting him to sit on the tour selection panel. During those early weeks, David had struck his captain as 'a man slightly on the outside, almost detached even though he was with friends and admirers'. Gatting sympathized:

It must have been strange just being a player again. During the summer I'd turned many times to him for advice on and off the field and I wanted his help now, so Peter Lush got the all-clear from Lord's for him to join myself, Dusty Miller and Embers as a selector. Above all we felt it only right David should have some position of responsibility after all that he had done for English cricket.

Gatting also offered to go in at three if David felt happier at five, which he did, in itself a sign of low spirits. 'David is such an essential part of the side,' the captain noted on his log, 'we needed to make sure he was in the happiest frame of mind he could be to concentrate on the job in hand.'

And concentrate he did, though his rediscovery of the run tap at first brought scant relief. The results looked good on paper: 51 in the first innings, a stand of 127 with Botham, then 15 not out when victory was secured. Beneath the figures lay a hesitancy that amply encapsulated his state of mind. Indeed, had he not been dropped in the slips by a demure new baggy green cap by the name of Mervyn G. Hughes, he would have suffered three successive ducks. But at the same time, a renewed sense of responsibility was apparent. When Botham narrowly evaded being caught behind in mid-wahoo, David walked down the pitch for a discreet bit of ear-bending. The next ball was met by an immaculate forward defensive; a couple of hours later the People's Champion had chalked up one of his most critical Test centuries. Regrettably, there were to be no more. If only he'd spared his back and given up bowling.

On the second morning of the second Test in Perth, England, thanks to a double-century send-off from Broad and Athey, were sitting mighty pretty. The loss of Broad, Gatting and Botham for the addition of only 64 more soon clouded the horizon. 'Bob Hawke came into our dressing room before the start of play,' remembers Jack Richards, the Surrey stumper who had embarked on his Test career at Brisbane with a duck and was next in. 'He told us he would stay until Botham got out. Bruce Reid got him for a duck.' One local paper reported the PM's gleefully patriotic response as 'You bewdy!'

That morning, David had had a brief net, no more than twenty minutes. For the first time on tour, ball met middle with something approaching regularity. The rest was soon history. Shuffling to the off, a dismissive pull through midwicket off the lumbering left-hander, Chris Matthews, was duplicated with equal relish against Geoff Lawson. When the spindly Bruce Reid dropped one short outside off, it was force as much as timing that sent the ball whistling through extra cover. Shoulders were opened, blade swung with unaccustomed vigour, the crack echoing around the WACA with exuberant finality. The hundred scooted by: 125 balls. It was as if, as Peter Roebuck so elegantly put it, 'he were driving a Porsche through the countryside, a blonde in the passenger seat and champagne on ice in the back'. And Gatting never saw him in finer fettle: 'If there's one Gower innings I'd love to see again, it was that one. He was magnificent. Twice he put Reid through extra cover like that in the same over – whumph.'

There were not that many times in his career when David felt driven to prove a point to the world; this, assuredly, was one of them. He certainly can't remember hitting the ball harder, or getting much more 'face' on the ball. Was there a touch of anger?

A bit. As with Sabina Park in '81 and the Lord's one-dayer in '85, I was down on confidence and I had that extra need to prove something, to myself or others, to get yourself going and get the pressure off. On other occasions when you walk in with the same feeling I had that day in Perth, it goes wrong very quickly. I'd had a dreadful net two days earlier and that morning I'd had a half-pace net where I felt OK. So I walked out feeling better. But the great thing was that I had freed the mind. We don't pay enough attention to the mental side. Towards the end of the 1994 South Africa tour here, I had a brief chat with Hansie Cronje. It was by chance because Gordon Parsons, his brother-in-law, had been at a hotel in Birmingham for a one-dayer when I gave a half-hour lecture there on psychology, on freeing the mind to allow yourself to do things. Gordon asked me to talk to Hansie, so I said the same to him. If you run into problems, you're not happy and doubt emerges, so confidence goes down. Then people clutter your mind with technique. You can't handle it all at the same time.

If one's art comes as second nature, as a reflection and extension of self, technical analysis is of minimal consequence. For the first time all tour, David went in to bat *feeling* right. He felt wanted again; now it was down to him, and him alone.

In all, he and Richards put on 207, a record for England in Australia. The tenderfoot, mind, had the temerity to dominate the scoring. 'Perhaps he thought he had someone to better,' surmises Richards. 'He must have got pissed off with me nicking the strike all the time. When I got to 13, my bad-luck number, I walked down the wicket and said to him, "For Chrissakes, get me through." So he talked about wine. It was his way of calming me down. When I got into the nineties, I told him to skip the wine and talk me through. And he did.' Less than two years later, at the age of 30, the second Cornishman to represent England (after the immortal Jack Crapp) ended Gordon Greenidge's final Test knock on English soil, packed his bags, and took a job with a shipping company in Rotterdam. Richards, who recalls Surrey as 'the most miserable club in the country', was angry that his temperament – outward volatility and aggression masking inner panic – should have been judged more important than his performances. He seldom felt wanted. 'After that innings at Perth, I thought I was safe as houses, but by the start of the following summer I was out. I had a pregnant wife, a pregnant Dutch wife; I'd had enough of the insecurity . . .' Another maverick bites the dust.

Not that Perth prefaced a run orgy of 1985 proportions. David's only other innings of note in the series did not come until the final Test in his beloved Sydney, heading England's first-innings contributors with 72 in the most invigorating match of the rubber. But he still managed to finish second to Broad in the Test averages, with a mean in excess of 50, and it was his 45 off 47 balls that settled the first of the World Series Cup finals. 'He has the ability to turn it on when it matters,' theorized Gatting, who professed surprise at his colleague's capacity to disappoint the doubters. 'He probably has to reserve his big efforts for the important occasions now after non-stop cricket for the last ten years.' Botham and Small secured the urn for another two and a half years by cutting down the home team on the opening day at the MCG, and England would have won the series 3–0 instead of 2–1 but for Dr Who's cousin, Peter. David's careful effort during England's brave chase in Sydney ended at 37 when Border had him taken at short leg – the Australian captain's first Test scalp for four years. After the traumas of '85, how this must have pleased Captain Grumpy.

In March, soon after he returned to Stoneygate, David went to hospital for an exploratory operation on his right shoulder. The condition had flared up in the final year of Illingworth's tenure at Grace Road. 'I might have slept badly,' he surmises: 'I don't really know how it started. I can remember feeling the odd twinge and it was just a question of a gradual diminution of power. It took five years to develop into something that niggled. In 1989, they operated on the bone at the top of the shoulder where the tendons were rubbing, to relieve the pressure. It was largely successful, but I'm never going to be 100 per cent without taking a lot out. I could hardly throw at first.' Shortly before the op, he had begun to realize he was compensating in batting terms: 'When your shoulder opens out, the bottom hand comes through, so the top hand is not being used so much. It's more important now for tennis. It's the same action as serving.' In fact, what brought the whole matter to a head in 1989 was all that serving and volleying he had been putting in at the Leicestershire Tennis Club the previous winter. All of which explained his increasing deployment of the underarm lob.

On top of that came a row over his benefit year schedule. According to the list of events circulated among the first-class counties, there were to be fifty-eight functions in all, sixteen in March alone, and nineteen in Lancashire and Cheshire. Concerned lest this adversely affect their own beneficiary, Lancashire (the club) planned to make a submission to the TCCB. More than a third of the dates were part of a theatre tour in which he was due to regale appreciative throngs with his thoughts on cricket. 'Many of the functions,' he explained, 'are not ours as such but events staged by other organizations to which I have been invited. Myself and my organizing committee accept that we may have caused confusion by printing them in the calendar as benefit events.' By the same token, he added, quoting the TCCB guidelines on benefits, 'the principle is to represent a gesture of the public esteem in which a player is held . . . I cannot stop people inviting me to attend functions or making spontaneous donations.'

On 1 April 1987, David turned thirty. If Fred Rumsey had got his years right, the celebration did not turn out quite as he had planned.

A few weeks earlier, David had made one of his flip remarks: 'You cannot fool an April Fool baby.' Ridiculous. I told Vicki I was gonna get him for that. He'd arranged to see his cronies for his birthday, but, three weeks beforehand, I said I wanted to have dinner with him that night. There were certain loyalties there, so he accepted. He still tried to set up a party in Leicester with his mates but I told them to turn him down, to come in on the joke. I even told Cow he shouldn't go, that he should say he was going to London. And, true as a trooper, David was prepared to go ahead with our dinner. When the day finally came, his friend Tim Ayling kept him out of the way while Cow put his car in David's garage and Vicki put hers in the drive. Then, at the appointed time, Cow rang David on his carphone. 'I'm on the M2 but I must talk to Fred,' he said. No happy returns, nothing. David's face was quizzical. By now, Cow had put the phone down and was walking through the back door. David's face was something else. You've never seen a face like it. He was well and truly done. Perfect. 'Never say you can't fool an April Fool baby again,' I said to him. Then all his mates came in.

One of the joys of a being a professional sportsman, David would joke, meant delaying a decision on what he might do in the 'real world'. Originally, he now reflects, he had intended to avoid doing so until he was thirty-five: 'When I started at Leicestershire, I remember looking at some of the guys who were in their mid-thirties, and thinking: "They've done their best; they've been through their best periods."' Whether he would make it to thirty-five was another matter. When it came to committing thoughts to paper for his projected tour diary, Gatting expressed concern for David's health: 'I wonder just how much longer he can keep going at this pace. This is one reason why I wouldn't be surprised to see him take this next winter off, so that he can have a well-deserved break.' Others were less understanding. In early June, David announced that he would indeed be taking the following winter off, and thus miss both the

World Cup and the tours to Pakistan and New Zealand. John Sadler's acidic response in the *Sun* was predictable:

> David Gower won't be making runs for England during the coming autumn. He will be making money for David Gower. Lots of it. Thousands of pounds. More than £100,000, quite likely, in what promises to be a bumper benefit. We are led to believe Gower's benefit season was nothing to do with his withdrawal from England's World Cup campaign in October. Maybe . . . but the batsman whose impeccable sense of timing is acknowledged worldwide has badly mistimed his 'hookey'. Indeed, the shock of his decision is matched only by the eagerness of cricket's hierarchy to understand and sympathize.

Some rather more intriguing insights came to light on the morning of the fifth instalment of a series against Pakistan memorable for both bad weather and a superlative spell from Imran Khan at Leeds (gaining his countrymen an innings win in the only conclusive Test of the summer, and thus their first series win in England). 'Gower astride the crossroads' was the headline in the *Times* above an interview with a soggy golden wonder. The fact that David had mustered 174 runs in six innings against Imran's men up to then, it seemed, was simply a manifestation of inner unease. By mid-June, he had yet to make a first-class fifty; not until the end of July did he make his first fifty for Leicestershire. In the second Test he was dismissed for eight; he then casually explained, and not a little perversely, that he had felt 'too confident'. Perversely, not because the rationale made no sense (it did), but because it was hard to conceive of anyone else daring to admit to such a thing without fearing being dumped on from a great height for outrageous conceit.

By announcing his sabbatical well in advance, David had reached 'a cut-off point'. The worries, he claimed, had consequently eased. He had wanted 'to do the job properly right up to the break'. His 105 at Cheltenham the previous week had been his first century for his county in two years, but while the spirit was demonstrably willing, the concentration was palpably weak. He was aware that his international career had 'sometimes promised more than has been delivered' even if he did find it a little 'exasperating' to have represented his country in ninety-five Tests 'and still be considered on a knife-edge'. But did not that bring out the beast in him?

There were two possible upshots once the sabbatical was over, David reasoned as plainly as he could: 'I will either come back refreshed and ready to fight for my England place by making runs at county level early next season, or I will discover that I really am as lazy as people think and that I should do something else for a living. I am finding out something about myself.' Fortunately, for those who would surely have mourned such a premature exit, if not for his own peace of mind, this particular voyage of self-discovery brought him back to the port of embarkation. The one thing he was sure of was that he wanted to play Test cricket 'for another five years or so'.

David made the most of his furlough, tending initially to his benefit, another 'therapeutic' experience. Ample as they were, mind, the final returns were surprisingly low. His committee had been hoping to beat Gooch's £153,000; despite a guest date in the West End hit, *Run for your Wife*, the final tally, somewhat surprisingly, fell £31,000 short of this. Still, reckoned the *Leicester Mercury*, he did make £100,000 'in a good year'. This being the European Year of the Environment, he also donated a thumbprint and signature to the Leicester City Wildlife Project's Think Green Festival. 'It's not just the glamorous big cats that we should be interested in,' he urged, 'but things closer to home in our own city.'

Realizing that a change of scenery and a fresh challenge might do his friend the world of good, and knowing that his current three-year contract with Leicestershire had one year to run, Chris Cowdrey proposed bringing David back to his native county, on a handsome four-year deal. When it became plain that David was in no state to make a commitment of that magnitude, the talks ceased. But, by hook or crook, a change was gonna come.

11   *The Second Sitting of the Last Supper*

Cliff: Yes, but can he ever go back?
Judah: People carry sins around with them. I mean, maybe once in a while he
has a bad moment, but it passes.
And, with time, all fades.
Cliff: Yeah, but, so then his worst beliefs are realized.
Judah: I said it was a chilling story, didn't I?
Crimes and Misdemeanours, Woody Allen

While Gatting was going tum-to-tum with Shakoor Rana (and, far worse,
allowing his side to respond to extreme provocation by degenerating into
a gaggle of Minnie the Moochers), his predecessor returned to Africa, spent
a couple of weeks skiing, then popped over to Calgary for the Winter
Olympics. In the interim, Peter Willey resigned the Leicestershire captaincy. At the end of the previous summer he had complained that the dressing-room unrest at Grace Road had prevented him from enjoying his
cricket: 'I'm not the sort who can just go home and forget about things'.
Willey advocated David's return to the captaincy, and the latter expressed
his readiness: 'I experienced in three years what some captains don't experience in ten. The break I have had has been refreshing.'

The Gatting-Rana affair informed the new, improved, Gower regime:
'One can sympathize when there is provocation, but to stand and argue
the case is not the way to go about it. If there is a problem it needs to
be sorted out privately. It is not part of the entertainment.' The thrust,
clearly, was not discipline but behaviour. He conceded that the frequency
of his absences had made communication a bugbear during his previous
tenancy. 'I will make a bigger effort to keep in touch,' he asserted, then
added, somewhat pointedly, that the club were 'entitled to phone me
too'. He said he saw a captain's role as not unlike that of an amateur
psychologist, and predicted that the players' pre-season training with a
clinical psychologist, Dr Martin Landau-North, would be of value. On
a personal level, the overriding aim was to 'put the record straight'.

Having greeted England's narrow defeat in the World Cup final by
backing Gatting's reverse sweep, the stroke that arguably cost his side
victory, David grew increasingly concerned that he might not be afforded

206

the opportunity to achieve his aim. The fretting worsened when he was excluded from the Texaco squad to play the West Indies, all the more so when three home wins gave rise to all manner of optimism in advance of the Wisden Trophy series. By then, happily, David had been restored to the fold. Then the first Test at Trent Bridge was drawn, riches indeed after ten successive goings-over in the Caribbean mincer. David himself had quite a bit to do with this, adding 161 in three hours for the third wicket with Gooch after England, trailing by 203, had begun the last day on 67 for one. When the final hour arrived, he was 12 short of a century; it was thoroughly in keeping with the man's disdain for meaningless competition and cheap runs that the chance to bat on was declined.

All cricketing considerations, however, now paled beside the really big news: the Rothley Court incident. 'I would treat this story with immense contempt,' David advised one group of reporters, 'and have a good laugh about it like the rest of the country.' During that first Test, Gatting was alleged to have shared a birthday drink in his room with a barmaid. The TCCB opened itself up to all manner of abuse by claiming that it had accepted his denial without reservation, then still gave him the sack. David reportedly said that he suspected he would only be in the line of succession in the event of Peter May popping his clogs.

Clive Lloyd ventured the opinion that it would be a 'mistake' for England to reinstate him because he 'lacks authority when senior players question his tactics' and because he could not, in his view, inspire 'renewed effort when spirits are flagging'. Neither had David done his cause much good at Nottingham by saving his country from defeat in a pair of 'patriotic' blue socks. Micky Stewart volunteered the opinion that this sartorial crime sullied the image of the national team, and insisted that, if David really did have to bat in such non-regulation apparel, he should at least field in grey. The symbolism could scarcely have been more profound. The relationship between manager and star had entered an inexorable decline.

Chaos reigned thereafter. Emburey, Cowdrey and Gooch played pass-the-parcel with the toxic chalice as Marshall and his deputies ran amok. The tourists won the remaining four Tests by whopping margins, along the way rendering David's hundredth Test the palest shadow of his first. In one innings or other, he had top-scored in both his 98th and 99th, though returns of 46 and 34 said a good deal more about the balance of power than it did about the maker's form. Prior to No. 100, he left himself out of the Leicestershire XI when the tourists visited Grace Road. 'I didn't want to give the West Indies another dart at me,' he explained, 'another chance to undermine my confidence.' Had it not been for his new captain, he would have been dropped for No. 100. 'I picked him,' reveals Cowdrey. 'He was out of nick. They wanted a few changes and they wanted Gower and Downton out. That wasn't really fair on Paul because he'd got a few runs and kept all right. "Look," I told them, "these are my two biggest mates in the game." I got one of them: Gower. "It's his 100th Test," I argued. "Gives you a bit of a lift."' Trouble was, the lift was descending.

In many ways, much as David should have had the stage to himself at Headingley, it was apt that Cowdrey should have been the man jostling for spotlight room. The elevation of the Kent skipper to the national bridge was accompanied by more than a few arched eyebrows and knowing nudges. He was the chairman of selectors' godson, after all. And a Cowdrey. What next? Mark Thatcher? Yet for all the snide jibes about nepotism, not to mention his lack of obvious qualifications to play at Test level, the personable Cowdrey had motivated Kent with distinction and verve. As desperate measures go, it looked quite inspired.

Courtesy of that archangel of England's economic decline, shoddy workmanship, David's parade was soon being rained on. A sodden night had delayed the start of proceedings for 50 minutes, whereupon Gooch and his third opening partner of the series, the studious newcomer, Tim Curtis, faced one over from Marshall and one from Curtly Ambrose, then went off again. Nearly two hours were lost, not to another deluge, but a faulty drain. David was probably reflecting on the perversity of it all later that afternoon while he was getting out for 13. He had been applauded all the way to the middle, and responded with a microcosm of how some saw his entire career. Caught at short leg off a Courtney Walsh no-ball, the third he received, he proceeded to top-edge the Jamaican pipe cleaner behind square with a loose pull, then took two rapturously acclaimed fours off Winston Benjamin, including a spellbinding square cut that sped him past Bradman's 6996 runs. He had reached 6998 when Benjamin, in no mood to kow-tow even if David was his county captain, procured an edge with one that left the batsman off the pitch. On the Saturday morning, Brian Johnston asked David which two words he would most like to expunge from his career; the interviewee eschewed the obvious, as ever, and plumped for 'caught Dujon'. Then, in the second innings, David acquired runs No. 6999 and 7000 and fell immediately – caught Dujon. He was the fifth cricketer to win one hundred caps, the youngest by four years – and the first to be ditched for the next Test.

Cowdrey never made it to The Oval, either. Struck on the foot by a delivery from Somerset's Adrian Jones, he told the selectors that the injury might prevent his participation. Allan Lamb was also in doubt, but whereas the latter was given until the morning of the match to prove his fitness, the captain had to inform the selectors 48 hours beforehand. All of which rather implied that Messrs May and Stewart now harboured severe doubts about the suitability of the man whom, just a fortnight earlier, they had announced as the latest Lancelot. If these men were so sorely bereft of confidence in their own judgement, how could they be entrusted with such responsibility?

Cowdrey's summer congealed as Kent proceeded to lose the championship by a point. David then enjoyed a renaissance of sorts. Mind you, his first championship match after the Headingley Test did see him upstaged by a dog. The Worksop rain, admittedly, had made a positive result highly unlikely, and although David's unbeaten 72 was needed to stave off the lingering possibility of a Leicestershire defeat in a tedious contest, the canine trotted on to the square to request his money back, holding up play for several minutes.

A string of failures then persuaded David to promote himself to opener ('partly because we were struggling in that area, and partly to give myself an extra challenge') whereupon his next visit to the crease, against Nottinghamshire, brought his first championship ton of the summer. James Whitaker knew this was no mere coincidence:

> That morning he came into the dressing room steaming. 'Bugger it,' he said, 'I'm opening.' He needed to vent some frustration. He always played a lot better when he was angry. It was like Perth in '86–87, and Old Trafford in 1986, which is my most vivid memory of batting with him. We put on 180 and dug the side out of the shit. He'd just come back from that awful tour of the Windies, Patrick Patterson was bowling really fast and I joined him inside the first hour; my first task was to prevent a hat-trick. Gower had had a few champagnes the night before and was forever playing and missing, so at one point I gave him a bollocking. Look, I said, don't you think, as a captain, that you should stop batting as if you've only got one arm? He didn't like it, but he took it. Then he took 24 or 26 off Patterson's next over and came down the wicket. 'That any better?' he said. Sometimes you had to wind him up.

The anger may have been self-directed that day at Grace Road, but the Notts boys bore the brunt of it. They probably felt as if they were playing two opponents: a herd of plebs and a monarch in full regalia. Numbers 2, 3 and 4 in the home order, Briers, Willey and Whitaker, aggregated 10 runs as Cooper and Evans took due toll of conditions conducive to their accomplished seamwork; by the time the third wicket fell at 71, David had already swept past 50. When Boon fell at 112, his captain had accounted for all but 25 runs off the bat. His final score: 146

off 219 balls with twenty-one fours, plus a six off Franklyn Stephenson, the most dreaded fast bowler on the circuit. *Wisden* cited it as 'incomparable majesty'. The selectors took the hint and named David in the tour party bound for India.

Next stop Chelmsford, and more of the same. In reply to Essex's monumental 592 for eight declared (Gooch 23), Leicestershire made 268, David 172. Setting off with 50 off 40 balls, he racked up twenty-two fours and a six in four and a quarter hours, facing just 240 balls; when John Childs finally got him leg-before, he was on pace to match Graveney's world record for sheer greed (200 out of 298 at Newport in 1956). It took him past 1000 runs for the season, leaving him at the top of the Leicestershire averages for the fourth time in his career, and the fourth time in eight seasons.

'The *Leicester Mercury* didn't get half as many letters about him as you might imagine,' says Jon Culley.

> The readers understood him as a player. I never once saw him refuse an autograph, although I knew he might have done that if someone was rude or obnoxious. He was quite happy to chat with members in front of the pavilion, or walk round the ground and talk to people. If someone was angry with him I can't recall any confrontations. Part of it was his aloof air. There was always the fear that he might cut you dead if you challenged him. The members had a respect for him. They knew the way he played. He once told me that he always played the same strokes, the same way, from the start of an innings, whether he was playing for Leicestershire or England. But he wouldn't be lying on a bench ten minutes before the start of play in a Test match, trying to recover from a heavy night. The members felt it was worth putting up with the lazy flicks outside off-stump in exchange for all the times he did something wonderful.

David's delight at being recalled to tour India was offset less by Leicestershire's moderate season (eighth in the championship, equal fourteenth in the Refuge, knocked out in the second round of the NatWest and at the group stage of the B&H) than by the keen sense of injustice he felt at the treatment meted out to Cowdrey. Now passed over altogether, Cowdrey had every right to feel hard done-by, all the more so when he was fined for complaining to the press about 'shabby treatment'. David smelt a rat. Gooch's appointment as captain, he suspected, was a Stewart-inspired move. Stewart would have seen the two friends as peas from, if not the same, then certainly an adjacent pod. Like David, Cowdrey had a nasty habit of treating players as individuals as opposed to members of a regiment. Like David, Cowdrey saw the manager's status in an inferior light to that of the captain. Like David, Cowdrey was part of the cricketing aristocracy. Being on the manager's wavelength, Gooch would be more malleable. He, too, had come to the view that sweat was more important than inspiration. He, too, identified the press as the enemy, preferring to ignore or patronize than to rely on humour, the very humour that had originally brought him and David together as friends.

Now, however, the past was about to plonk the new England captain on his backside. Of all the reasons for appointing Gooch, none was more overtly persuasive than the fact that this was the only carrot that would entice him to renounce his decision never to tour again. The fly in the ointment was that he had intended to spend the winter playing for, and being amply rewarded by, Western Province. With half an eye on political demos and, worse still, potential withdrawals from the impending Commonwealth Games in Delhi, India objected to his presence. The tour was cancelled a few weeks before it was due to set sail. A month or so later, the chairman of selectors deselected himself.

Of all the many ironies and contradictions that permeated David's cricket career, nothing, surely, is more ironic and contradictory than the fact that Peter May should have been replaced by Ted Dexter. In terms of both professional and philosophical outlook, May and Dexter had about as much in common as Pol Pot and Mother Theresa. The former had no more time for the languorous flicks than he did for the laxity; the latter had no time for discourtesy or repressiveness. In only one respect were they not antithetical: they were both the finest English batsman of their respective eras. The inaugural chairman of the England Cricket Committee was also top of his class, and appeared to be the answer to David's prayers. They were both public schoolboys, both symbols of amateurism, both monuments to attacking batsmanship, both bon viveurs, both amiable yet elusive. Each was regarded with fondness, envy and scant comprehension. When he was tipped to be the so-called 'supremo' in February, Dexter delivered a manifesto that must have had David purring: 'I want England to be the most watchable and likeable team in the world. You don't achieve that by being surly, aggressive or difficult on the field, but we have some admirable examples of what I expect. David Gower has always been immaculate on the field in his behaviour.' It was, apparently, a marriage conceived, born and bred in heaven.

In April, David was confirmed as captain for the Texaco Trophy and all six Ashes Tests. Approving smiles were conspicuous. At the press conference, Robin Marlar noticed 'a tiny example of a common style'. David's tie was 'a treasured trophy from the Cresta Run; it's an odds-on bet that he'll have Dexter the aviator and biker on the ice runners as soon as he can'. Try and guess whom John Arlott was referring to when he expressed the following sentiments:

> Perhaps, indeed, [he] was a man born out of his period, but he came to terms with every development of his career through to aviation and television. He has been an original and an entertaining man; he preferred to debate a point rather than to quarrel. His immense relish has added zest to everything he has done, and often for those who watched him. It is tempting to say that we shall not look upon his like again: those who have enjoyed him will hope that there will be such another, but they will appreciate, above all, that he was – and that successor will be – an absolute rarity.

Arlott was actually referring to the inaugural chairman of the England Cricket Committee. He could so easily have been describing the committee's inaugural appointee.

The early omens on the field, it should be said, were almost extravagantly propitious. The Texaco Trophy was won against an Australian squad containing just four players with previous experience of an Ashes tour. When Gooch rumbled to a century in the one-dayer at Lord's, David said he could never remember the opener 'looking so assured in his strokeplay'. At the same time, David wisely chose perspective in his *Leicester Mercury* column before the first Test:

> I have been gratified to read that I now appear more positive as captain on the field. Certainly Ted Dexter has taken every opportunity to reinforce that impression. To be honest, though, I don't feel I am captaining any different than in my previous outings . . . you still won't see me running around and waving my arms to create an impression of galvanic energy. Thanks for the comments, though, chaps. Let's hope you are as kind at the end of the Test series.

'I don't think I realized how much I wanted another chance in the captaincy until I got it,' David would reflect. By way of celebration, he had begun the county championship campaign with a crescendo and a half. Having signed a one-year contract in November, mind you, there was a fair deal of pressure on him to do precisely that: 'I had been worried that it would take a while for me to get going; a slow start was not what I was looking for this season, of all seasons.' Leg-before for 4 on the opening morning was not quite what he or the congregation had in mind. Against Glamorgan, he went in again at 43 for one on the second afternoon and, for seven minutes short of six hours, bedded down on a cloud somewhere in downtown Olympus: the second-highest home score in Leicestershire's second innings of 415 for nine declared was 37; David made 228, a career-best. Facing 317 balls, he struck 24 fours and two sixes, passing the 20,000-run mark in the process. 'We struggled but he absolutely creamed it,' attests Nigel Briers. 'A great innings, brilliant, but then I'd seen him make equally brilliant 20s.' *Wisden* was no less enamoured, declaring it to have 'ridiculed' all the previous efforts in the match to put bat to ball. David saw it as an accurate reflection of his state of mind. It also 'assuaged the pangs of conscience' he periodically experienced over his county output.

Whereupon the Australians proceeded to ridicule English cricket. 'When defeat began to sour his life,' wrote Graeme Wright in *Wisden*, 'Gower was not able to dig deep into his own character to make his players respond to the crisis. Instead, they were carried along by the air of despondency which enveloped him.' If only it were that simple. There seems little point in dwelling overmuch on the Ashes series of 1989 from a purely cricketing perspective. No one bothered much at the time, so why bother now? The memory, more importantly, is too painful, even for one who claims to regard patriotism as the sole province of the scoundrel. Losing 5–0 to the West Indies on home turf felt like retribution for imperialism and racism, ditto the India–New Zealand double whammy of 1986. Getting blackwashed in the Caribbean wasn't so dreadful either, given the manifest superiority of the opposition and the prevailing circumstances. Besides, it all happened a mighty long way from West Hampstead. The summer of 1989, however, served up a slice of humble pie that would have choked Uriah Heep.

That February I had wagered £50 with a Melbournian acquaintance, not only that England would retain the Ashes, but that they would win the series 3–1. I had just seen the West Indies win the first three Tests of the Worrell Trophy series; I felt secure.

Not that I was alone in my misjudgement. Ted Corbett, who had also covered that Australia-West Indies series but was unfortunate enough to be employed at the time by the *Daily Star*, also discovered a 3–1 home win among his tea-leaves, and duly informed his readers. Before the year was out he had been sacked; high on the list of misdemeanours was inadequate tipmanship. How were we supposed to know that TCCB cricket chairman Ossie Wheatley had stuck his oar in (Gatting, surely, had done his penance)? How were we to know that our bonny boys had gone into battle with a second-rate captain who also turned out to be a second-choice captain? A second-choice captain, moreover, who was not only never apprised of the fact but kept largely in the dark, so to speak, when it came to the reappearance of the rand. How were we to know that team spirit would be rent asunder by the intention of a good many of those bonny boys to spend the winter helping white South Africa pull a teensy bit more wool over a few more pairs of eyes?

Although the South African subtext did not enter the public domain until the Ashes had all but vanished down the plug hole, the negotiations were hardly a closely guarded secret. David said he might feel impelled to consider an offer if it was obscene, but only then. Botham was humming and hawing. Before the series had even started, 99 per cent of the requisite signatures were in Ali Bacher's bag. Graham Dilley, for one, believed that more could have been done to discover the truth, even though he himself was among those who did their utmost to hide it; letters asking players to state their availability for that winter's Caribbean tour were not dispatched until the end of June.

While David suspected more than he knew, he did suggest to Dexter that some of the more valued players be put on contract, a proposition duly rejected by the TCCB on the grounds that there was insufficient time for full consideration. By the time the signatories had been unveiled, 'lbw b Alderman' was being inscribed on the headstone of Graham Gooch's Test career. Even then, the Gatting scenario, much as it had been lurking on the grapevine, was not fleshed out until November, when Dexter's report to the TCCB revealed how Ossie Wheatley had exercised his veto. England, the latter proclaimed, had 'a moral right to lead', though not, it seems, to forgive. Dexter had originally endorsed Stewart's advocacy of Gatting, stirred as he was by the manager's reminder of the glories of 1986–87. The ire fired by the more downmarket sector of the media was thus aimed in ignorance of the full facts, though whether prior knowledge would have changed the tone is debatable. David, moreover, found himself at a complete loss to shrug it all off.

David's only enduring regret as a cricketer, as mentioned earlier, was his decision, on the first morning of the rubber, to take heed of Dexter's weather forecast rather than the groundsman's prediction. You can never trust Headingley, of course. Keith Boyce, furthermore, had never been in the Justin Toper league of stargazers. Both sides, however, had scored heavily there four years earlier, and the Yorkshire pitch doctor reckoned that year's strip would behave much the same. By bowing to the consensus, by not asserting himself, David handed Australia the opportunity to compile a match winning total on a wicket whose beneficence bestowed the not inconsiderable total of 1452 runs. Leaving out the only spinner was also a bit of a clanger: more compromise. According to the tabloids in particular, getting out on the final afternoon was worth a beheading at the very least. A precis of the tirades would run roughly as follows: 'With 83 overs to survive and a Test match to be saved, what in heaven's name was the captain doing getting himself caught while attempting something fancy down the legside? Couldn't he see the trap? Is he blind, or just stupid?'

All the more ironic, then, that when Jon Holmes went through the following morning's outpourings over the phone, David's spleen should have been aimed at Martin Johnson. The best cure for the captain, the *Independent*'s master pith-taker had diagnosed, would be a frontal lobotomy. 'In fairness, I was a bit over the top,' Johnson now reflects.

> I was so angry I wrote the piece in about twenty minutes. And, just occasionally, it works in your favour. If I say it myself, it was a pretty good piece, but it was written in real hot blood. It was a little bit unfair, but that didn't occur to me at the time.

David was as incensed as he had ever allowed himself to be in public, declining even to mention Johnson's name: 'I could happily have slit the reporter's throat.'

The next day, the *Independent*'s sports editor, Charlie Burgess, informed Johnson that Holmes had been on the phone and that legal action was brewing. Johnson made a bee-line for David when he saw him at the Lord's nets prior to the next Test.

> We had a twenty-minute chat. I went up to him and said, 'What's all this crap about suing me?' He looked quite serious. 'Well,' he said, 'I did get very offended by it.' So I asked him why he hadn't phoned me up about it. 'Well,' he said, 'I was a bit upset. I didn't expect *you* to write something like that.' So I said something like, 'it's a bit silly to go on like this, how's about I square up with a magnum of champagne'. He said, "You're on," and we knocked off this champagne. And we had this jokey agreement that I would do it more often. Like most of his crises, it didn't affect him for very long.

The archers, though, were lining up, like the longbowmen at Agincourt, ready to launch their arrows into the sun and see them drop on the target from an Olympian height.

As usual, the Saturday of the Lord's Test was an occasion utterly bereft of native hope and glory. The hosts closed on 58 for three in their second innings, still 184 in arrears: not so much up a creek without a paddle as going down for the second time. At the press conference, David lost his patience when repeated reference was made to his alleged error in bowling Neil Foster from the supposedly wrong end. Abruptly announcing that he was off to see his chum Tim Rice's latest West End smasheroonie, *Anything Goes* (the punsters had a field day), he dashed off. Both teams had received invitations from the author, and Geoff Lawson noted in his diary his surprise at David's excessive punctuality: 'Sunday 25 June: Slept in this morning and lashed out with croissants for breakfast. When I looked at the papers I realized why David Gower was so early to the show last night. It's amazing how former players, including his recent teammate, Phil Edmonds, can get stuck right in.' Edmonds, together with another Lord's expert, Brearley, as well as Illingworth, had all been convinced David had bowled Foster from the wrong end. The choice, though, had been the bowler's, a fact David never managed to impart. He had been 'terribly tense' when he entered the marquee at the back of the pavilion to face the scribes, and threw in a characteristic one-liner along the lines of, 'why not refer to the notes you took at Leeds'. He knew he was sunk from that very moment. The tabloid editors considered their response with customary efficacy. 'Gower Must Go', roared one headline. Another spread the blame more evenly: 'Gower's Goons'.

Yet this was not simply an example of the petulant superstar avoiding his obligations because his ego cannot cope with contradiction. Nor was it purely a case of David lacking empathy for a bunch of journalists and ex-pros who had the scent of a scapegoat's blood in their nostrils. What really unsettled him was the scarcity of reason, the aggression, the venom: 'I sensed a hostile, unforgiving atmosphere . . . I felt, rightly or wrongly, that it no longer mattered what I said because it would be misinterpreted anyway.' Much to his almost immediate regret, he had succumbed to the pressure. A new fuse, typically, was in place by the time he hailed a cab in St John's Wood Road, resigned as he was to the inevitable fall-out: he couldn't help but smile. He knew he had made a crass misjudgment, yet it had all been strangely satisfying. He had stood his ground. In Australia's second innings Foster bowled 18 overs at the Pavilion End, the 'wrong' end, taking three for 39. 'That seemed to prove the point that Gower did not mess up the ends on Saturday,' reasoned Lawson, 'but I didn't see any apologies.'

There was, of course, another factor in England's collapse. Having spent the winter watching the West Indies take a few bite-sized chunks out of the Aussie ego, it was all too easy to underestimate Allan Border's desire to avenge the humiliations of 1981 and 1985. When Australia went into battle in the summer of 1989, they went as warriors, declining the niceties of playful banter and after-hour chin-chins. Sledging was in, socializing out. This time it was strictly personal. Their opponents, as luck would have it, were divided and distracted. A sliver of over-confidence also came into it, but then so did a shortage, not merely of ability but, more crucially, heart. For all Terry Alderman's relentless probing of 'the corridor of uncertainty' (a phrase Stewart borrowed from Dilley, who had himself borrowed it from Alderman), for all that the England batsmen were intent on playing across the line to straight balls, Lawson inflicted as much damage on England as anyone, dismissing David no fewer than six times during the course of the series (and eight times in thirteen innings all told that summer) – and more than once caught down the legside. Lawson's diary of the tour was enlightening. 'They just cannot believe they have been beaten,' observed our budding Pepys after the first Test, 'but you can already see the self-doubt.' When Australia won the second by nine wickets, he was astonished by the reaction: 'They are blaming bad luck and missing out on a few close umpiring decisions. Yet we won by *nine* wickets. If their attitude doesn't change, their performance won't improve because they'll blame circumstances and won't realize they have to lift their game.'

After Australia had won the fifth Test by an innings and 180 runs, the widest margin the baggy green-cappers had ever achieved in the old country, Lawson offered an objective view of David's predicament:

He certainly doesn't lead with any conviction, but you do wonder about the quality of the personnel under him. Despite his gallant attempts to remain dignified and philosophical in defeat, he has made a forlorn picture at times. I still remember that image of him at Headingley, on his knees at cover point as another Waugh square drive raced past him to the rope. It was certainly a portent of things to come.

One South African defector was adamant that there had been 'no game plan, and while the Australians deserve every credit for the skilful and professional way they have approached the series, England are in no danger of emulating them in that department'. Willis defended the ostensible game-planner with all the vehemence one might expect of the man who had sat him down in a Hale wine bar on the Monday evening of the Old Trafford Test, and helped persuade his companion that he should not resign purely to satisfy the tabloids:

Gower made only one tangible mistake in the series as captain after winning the first toss. He soldiered on manfully with his collection of disillusioned oldies and hopeful rookies, never giving the media the satisfaction of throwing in the towel. Occasionally his flippancy betrayed his more serious intention to do a good job. But he never had the tools for the task, and the detractors are kidding themselves in thinking a combination of Jardine and Brearley would have found anything more in England's empty cupboard.

That may have been a trifle harsh. For all the sense he talks, Willis is nothing if not a man of black and white. And the team manager did do his best to give Alan Igglesden a lift before his debut by hailing him as the seventeenth best fast bowler in the land. Yet there was not so much as a semblance of continuity. Instead, panic set in early and festered: only four players survived the first two Tests. Lawson was no more able to fathom the selectors than the rest of us:

> After the early statements about giving young players a chance, the players were dropped after one failure. DeFreitas is a good example. He had a bad game at Leeds, but that can happen to anyone. We regard him as one of their best bowlers and he continued to perform well in county cricket. No wonder he originally took up the South African offer. Bringing Eddie Hemmings back at the age of forty with the series three-nil our way and the Ashes lost was difficult to work out. That was a perfect time to put a young spinner in and give him some experience.

Paul Jarvis signed up for Ali Bacher's low-flying circus then admitted that the atmosphere in the England dressing room contributed to his decision to risk what became a five-year international ban (subsequently commuted to three by the sudden shift towards sanity that began with the release of Nelson Mandela). 'The whole atmosphere is one of "us" and "them",' began another rebel interviewed by the *Sunday Times*. 'Some players seem to know that however they perform they'll be turning up next time to collect the cheque. I am not sorry that I'm not playing for England, and I never thought the day would come when I said that.' Peeved at being dropped after one Test, Paul Jarvis, then a highly promising young fast bowler who had played for England under Gatting and had earned something of a reputation in his native Yorkshire for being a trifle precious, pointed the finger at his born-again skipper: 'If you bowl a bad ball and it goes for four and the crowd start getting at you, you need to be told what to do next and given encouragement. That does not happen under Gower, who leaves you to do your own thing and you get the feeling you are just there to make up the numbers.' Botham, who returned to the side after injury for the third Test, was more understanding: 'No one was really sure who was running things – Gower, Stewart or Dexter, least of all the captain himself!'

Another strain of criticism contrived to hit the nail on the head while simultaneously mashing the hammerer's thumb. Men of a certain age and mentality have a tendency to charge the modern English cricketer with forgetting about the honour of representing one's country, with treating a Test match as work. Leaving aside the suspicion that that honour is more professional than patriotic (and with good reason), such holier-than-thouism was surely unfair. In addition to the normal hang-ups – fear of failure, fear of making an idiot of oneself on telly – the England cricketer of 1989 also had to cope with an impatient jury, no small matter when the chasm between the rewards for county regular and international star is so vast. Then there's all that attendant neurosis about letting the nation down: who wants to be a goat in a land of declining self-esteem?

Jon Holmes has always recommended that his clients confront what is said and written about them, if only because newspapers and TV sets are so fiendishly difficult to avoid. 'Unlike most people in show-business, sportsmen do not set out to exploit their personal life and use it as a promotional tool. They expect the two to be kept apart.' Another of Holmes's high-profile clients, Will Carling, maintains that there is an intrinsic tension between critic and performer in all walks of entertainment. The two also share a symbiotic relationship: you scratch my back, I'll scratch yours. 'I tried always to be honest with the media, which doesn't necessarily mean that you tell them everything they want to know,' Mike Brearley once admitted. 'I felt also it was important to be yourself. Bob Willis came over as so wooden when I knew he wasn't. But he'd put the shutters down on his spontaneity as a defence. It's so hard not to take criticism personally but you have to reply with your intellect, not your ego.'

David suffered for not putting the shutters down on his spontaneity. The inanity of much of the media's questioning beggared belief, but he preferred the leg glance to the straight bat. His flipness had never gone down that well with certain pockets of the press. To many, it was piss-taking pure and simple, however polite. By walking out of that Lord's press conference that Saturday night, David replied with his ego.

As he did on the Monday, by making a century, his first since that opening championship match at Grace Road, and his first in a Test for thirty-one months. If contrition was a major ingredient, there was also a teaspoonful of fury. Never had his stomach been invaded by so many butterflies: 'It is one thing to want to do well when you go out to bat; it is quite another to need success as I did that morning. I scored the century I was after, and if it was far from being my most fluent, the relief was every bit as sweet.' Writing in *Wisden*, David Norrie reflected that David 'had hit the ball more sweetly but never with such determination and purpose'. The crowd stood to a man and cheered until Old Father Time looked set to topple from his perch.

There were a great many wisdoms spouted after the event – most commentators, lest it be forgotten, had originally backed England to win – yet the odd one struck a chord. 'Ted Dexter, looking like a boy caught with mud on his boots in the drawing room, disclaimed all partiality to error,' wrote David Frith after the final press conference at The Oval:

Later he was to tell a dinner gathering of Cricket Writers' Club members and guests that he was, of course, guilty of failing to save the

219

Royal marriage, and the seals in the North Sea. One saw his point. He is too shrewd a student of the game not to have recognized England's widespread poverty of technique, and too much the gentleman to have condemned his men in public. Nor is he any stronger than the next man in bowing to the temptation to keep on tapping further resources when things go wrong and there are probably 50 players as good – or as mediocre – as each other awaiting international selection.

By the sixth Test, the selectors were immersed in a simmering cauldron of indecision and mistrust. When Stewart, Dexter and David convened around the last-named's kitchen table to pick the twelve for The Oval, the relationship between manager and captain was low on pleasantries and high on grudging mutual tolerance. David had felt his input diminish from the moment between the third and fourth Tests that Dexter advised him to give the manager more of a say at the press conferences. Again, he stood his ground, but the message was clear. Although he had made it abundantly clear that he disapproved of David letting the press in on the plans for him to open in the Texacos, believing such ruses were much better sprung on the opposition, Dexter had been as staunch a supporter as all the Gladyses and Geralds who had spent the summer bombarding David with 'gratifyingly supportive' letters (which he invariably replied to). When David went into hospital between the first and second Tests, Dexter offered to lend him his Porsche to drive himself to and fro. During the Old Trafford Test, he invited David for Sunday lunch as compensation for scolding him in public for throwing a V-sign at some barrackers, a flash of temper expertly picked up by ITN News. Then Dexter really began to curse Wheatley's intervention. The nice touches evaporated; captain and chairman grew apart. Wheatley would say he was sorry that the truth had to come out at all. By concealing it from David, and refusing to let him be privy to his file on the South African rebels, Dexter destroyed the very essence of a good relationship.

David ended the summer with his usual melange of sublime and ridiculous: a fragrant 79 in the first innings at The Oval, then a legside dismissal. The rare luxury of a draw still meant that David's England ended the eighties in much the same shape as Maggie's: battered by recession and beset with self-doubt. 'It had been a relentless series, impossible to enjoy because we never once got into a position to compete on equal terms,' David lamented in his aptly titled account of the events of 1989, *On the Rack – A Testing Year*. The cover shot remains a source of regret: there he is below the Warner Stand, beaming away, arm resting on the shoulder of a laughing Stewart, Dexter to their left, gazing off somewhere in the vicinity of Venus.

220

If David could rewind one sequence from his career, and reshoot it, it would have been this series.

I'd like to start the summer of '89 again. There was a great chance to do good things. I'll probably change my mind tomorrow, but any changes would probably include batting first at Headingley. In the West Indies we were beaten horrendously by a very good side; in '89 we were beaten horrendously by a very confident side, one that grew in confidence as the series wore on, and became a very good side by the end of it. And their confidence sapped ours. That was a fiasco at Headingley. I regret being drawn into some inept thinking, not standing up. I'd done it at Old Trafford in the Texacos. Everyone was saying it was a bit green and we had to stick them in. I knew it wouldn't do anything because I'd been up there recently and seen it do nothing, realizing it was a soft pitch that was going to get worse. We batted, got enough, and beat them comfortably. At the end, people came up and said, 'good decision skip'. But when it came to the important game, I allowed myself to be a part of a committee, to be influenced by it. If you've done your best and lost, well, there's not much you can do about it. OK, you've lost. But if you've betrayed your own thinking, or allowed yourself to be talked into things like that, you can look at yourself with disappointment.

Worst betrayals, however, were still to come. For one thing, Leicestershire finished the summer even worse off than they had been the previous year: knocked out in the second round of the NatWest again, knocked out at the group stage of the B&H again, fourteenth in the Refuge again, and five places lower in the championship. After a heavy NatWest defeat at Hove, their captain observed: 'Like England, Leicestershire have players whose reputations currently exceed their performances.'

On the eve of the NatWest final, David attended a meeting with Dexter and Stewart at the chairman's residence, and was informed that the England committee felt a 'change of direction' was needed. Stewart obligingly offered a few plausible excuses for public consumption, principally the impending surgery on David's shoulder that would prevent his participation in the Nehru Trophy one-day bash in October. Yet not only did David refuse to be party to such an alibi, he also resisted the urge to save face by resigning. The messages and missives of support encouraged a change of heart. He went off to Portugal for a few days, but he was soon disabused of any fond imaginings that this might render him media-proof when the man from the *Mirror* called to ask whether he could confirm a story in the *News of the World* about him handing in his notice. Far from quitting, he replied, he had in fact, so far as he knew, been sacked.

Dexter and Stewart quickly issued denials. Their decision, theoretically, had not yet been ratified.

At 1 p.m. on 7 September 1989, Gooch, the man whose last visit to the Caribbean had almost curtailed his Test career, the man who had not played a Test overseas for the past three winters, the man whose opinions on captaincy made Dexter feel as if he had 'been hit in the face with a wet fish', was announced as captain for the West Indies tour. David had his suspicions confirmed by Teletext. He had left Stoneygate at 9.15 that morning, somewhat earlier than his wont, and driven his white Audi Quattro to Grace Road. He had arrived at 9.30 and had gone up to Mike Turner's office to discuss the next day's game. After a ten-minute team talk in the dressing room and a forty-five-minute prac-tice session, he returned home. He had planned to hold his own press conference at 2 p.m., the same time as the captaincy announcement was *scheduled* to have been made, so he could 'get out of the firing line for the rest of the day'. At 1.45, Dexter phoned to dot the i's. At 2.30 David was back at Grace Road for the delayed press conference. He said he felt aggrieved that Dexter hadn't contacted him first instead of forcing him to rely on 'rumour and speculation'.

Inwardly, David was bruised, his sense of fair play offended. This was not a proper way to behave. *He* wouldn't behave like that. Jon Culley's report in the *Leicester Mercury* described David as 'confused and angry'. The ex-captain summed up the prevailing state of affairs as 'crazy' and confessed he would 'be delighted if someone else can cop the flak'. The dignity, nevertheless, was as refreshing as ever. It goes without saying, of course, that he also offered Gooch his unhesitating support: 'I've played a lot of cricket with Graham over the years and have grown to know, like him and respect him enormously. He's a very professional man in his approach to the game and is dedicated. I wish him well.'

As fate would have it, Gooch's Essex were due at Grace Road the following day. While David was addressing the press, Gooch had been attending a meeting to pick the parties for the Nehru Cup and the Carib-bean. David was not among them. The next morning, Gooch took David aside for a quiet word, and, according to the latter, 'implied' that he had been presented with a fait accompli. Dexter had got in first, mind, phon-ing David while he was in Turner's office. David was flabbergasted. And hurt. At the time, he blamed Dexter. That said, he was not convinced that Gooch had been an entirely unwilling accomplice. It is, indeed, difficult to countenance a scenario whereby Gooch could not have got David aboard had he truly wanted him. Or Botham. He didn't: 'Ted and Micky had clearly decided that new blood was needed and that both these great players might find it difficult to fit into the new style that I was going to introduce. I didn't disagree with that point.' Gooch had no intention of wasting his time trying to sell either Gower or Botham the concept of rigorous fitness training. Not only had both got by without it, they had prospered without it. Just because Gooch had changed his spots didn't necessarily mean such a transformation was within everybody else's compass, and he knew it. If Botham's decline at least made his exclusion excusable, the same could scarcely be said of David. He was still averaging six and a half runs per innings more than Gooch, just as he had done for the past dozen years. The latter, however, was concerned lest David's tendency to 'go his own way' spawned 'splinter groups'. For all his fondness towards David, he felt, in short, that 'we' would be 'better off without him'.

Despite his manifold dealings with David down the years, Turner pronounced himself 'amazed' at this: 'When the call from Dexter came through, David left my office to take it on another extension and came back a few minutes later to resume our meeting as if nothing had happened. He gave no indication that he had been dropped and it was only later that he confirmed it was true.' So 'staggered' was Turner that he had to pester the member of staff who had taken down the list of names during the radio announcement. Was he positive he hadn't misheard? Dexter's public rationale concentrated on two fronts. He said that David's shoulder troubles had been a source of considerable discomfort and aggravation: 'It was felt a winter off was needed to get the shoulder working properly again. I'm sure a fully-fit Gower will have a lot more to offer as a batsman.' When Dexter had rung Turner's office a couple of hours earlier, according to David, he made no mention of the shoulder. While David had contributed 'more than somewhat', Dexter added, his overall form had been 'extremely sketchy'. Gooch, for instance, had stumped up 183 runs at 20.33 to his captain's 383 at 34.81, a mark bettered only by Robin Smith among the specialists: did that make Gooch useless in addition to being a wet fish?

When rain prevented a prompt start to play, David went across to the members' enclosure to keep the press happy. The topic of South Africa came up, of course; the question was swatted away with characteristic deftness: 'I am not sure if Ali Bacher would want to spend half a million pounds to sign up a guy with one shoulder.' The demotion had come as 'a big surprise, obviously'. He insisted, however, that he was 'not devastated'. Words of that ilk were 'too strong'. All the same, it was 'a bit of a blow'. Has cricket ever known a more masterly exponent of wry understatement? Throughout the interrogation it was all he could do to prevent the lump in his throat from slithering into a Kim Hughes-style farewell.

Gary Lineker sent a message of condolence via Holmes, describing the selectors' decision as 'unbelievable'. Graham Dilley expressed his incredulity in the direly named diary he wrote with Graeme Hick, *Hick 'n' Dilley Circus*: 'Gower is still our best player and he had to go to the West Indies. There shouldn't be any other reason for his selection and I just wonder what other forces have been at work. On balance I would have stayed with Gower as captain.' The *Leicester Mercury* was swamped with letters of support. 'It is rather awful the way he has been treated,' wrote Rodney Powell, an office manager from Market Harborough. 'Quite disgusting,' chimed in Terence Shelley, a shoe-stainer from Aylestone Park. 'I wrote to David Gower saying how sure we are the England selectors have made another mistake. We told him to keep smiling and things will work out.'

The bleeding, as ever, was mostly internal. David spent a 'miserable' night at Stoneygate. The next was no better. Leg-before for a duck had not exactly been the required riposte. 'Bloody game,' he pondered as he wallowed in the bath. 'Bloody game.' It was a game all right. The next day he went out and scored a self-affirming 109, ensuring his thousand for the season and rediscovering 'some lost youth'. Rather more, sadly, had gone for good. Not so much Anything Goes as Nothing Rhymed. Alone again, naturally.

12 Remake/Remodel

Hello it's me,
I've thought about us for a long long time
Maybe I think too much but something's wrong
There's something here that doesn't last too long
Sometimes I can't help seeing all the way through.
Seeing you, or seeing anything as much as I do you
I take for granted that you're always there
I take for granted that you just don't care
Maybe I shouldn't think of you as mine.
Hello It's Me, Todd Rundgren

If, in a previous life, David Gower had been Prime Minister, he might have been Pitt the Younger. If he had been a football team he would definitely have been the 1970 Brazilians. A singer? Bryan Ferry, who else? An actor? I'll cheat: Michael Caine with Leslie Howard's larynx and looks. A movie? David himself might argue a case for *The Sting*; it is, after all, his favourite movie. You can tell a lot about people from their favourite movie. Here was the world's greatest Rogue Movie. Which, in David's case, was precisely the nub of the appeal.

Now, if Graham Gooch had been a politician, he would have been Norman Tebbitt with Gladstone's whiskers. An actor? Broderick Crawford. A football team? He would say his beloved 'Ammers, but might I humbly suggest Don Revie's Leeds United: both were capable of the dazzling and the deadening, the sublime and the ludicrous; both were pros down to their jockstraps, riven with insecurity, driven by pocket and cynicism. David once regarded Gooch as the life and soul of the party, the England colleague he felt most comfortable with, a constant fund of light relief. A man can change when he is justifiably pilloried for commercial opportunism.

'Gower the batsman should not be rejected simply because Gower the captain was a failure. His only crime was to accept a job he was manifestly unsuited for. A job nobody in cricket would turn down.' Thus spake the *Sunday Times* after the 1989–90 Caribbean tour squad was confirmed.

Encouraged as David may have been by such a cogent appraisal of the matter in so prominent an organ, this was a time for action, not reflection. The most hurtful rejection of David's career (to date) forced him to do something even more painful: live for tomorrow. Or, if not live, then certainly plan. Over the next four years, reality would become increasingly more intrusive, runs correspondingly less significant. He would be the winner, cricket the loser. In hindsight, it proved to be the making of the man.

But behind the making of this particular man lay the undoing of a woman. For those of his admirers who regard fidelity as a moral imperative, David's complexion in the 1980s could have done with a dab of Clearasil. That said, he did become increasingly discreet about his extra-curricular dalliances as the years went on, unlike some ex-England captains one could mention. Once, while Leicestershire were playing in Swansea, players and captain spent the evening in a disco, whereupon three local lasses decided it might be fun to inform the *Sun* of spicy deeds of derring-do, *à quatre*. One veteran camp follower knew there was not a milligram of truth in this: 'I'd been with him most of the evening and I saw him go to his room alone. He was much more careful than that. The girls he saw were hand-picked girls, trustworthy girls.' Simon Strong remembers David being 'quite reticent' with women: 'While Lamby would charm the pants off a girl, make it very plain that this was what he was after, Gower was the complete opposite. He would let them do all the running. Then he'd pick 'em off at the end. He was unthreateningly charming.'

Prince Charming, however, now had a moral obligation. Worse – in some eyes – than following such a traditional and occasionally understandable approach to life on the road, was the suspicion that David had been stringing Vicki along. That he was merely using Stoneygate, and hence her, as the base every on-the-roadster needs. While there may have been some truth in that, this was, in essence, simply another decision put off by that Hamlet-like aptitude for procrastination. 'A couple of times I went to him and asked him what he was going to do about marriage,' recollects Chris Cowdrey. 'It was preying on his mind too much. That's all anyone talked about for years. You could see them growing further and further apart. He knew something had to happen, and I think he nearly married her just to keep the peace.' Not an uncommon temptation. David got the prod when he was dropped by England, when his profession rejected him. Anger, as so often before, gave him the strength to act, to do the needful, for himself *and* Vicki. Thereafter, the walls of hesitancy came tumbling down.

Breaking up with Vicki was eased by the presence of Miss Right.

Thorunn Nash met David at a charity ball in the late summer of 1985. She had a longstanding boyfriend on her arm that evening, not that that stopped her from asking David to dance: 'It was all so terribly boring. I knew nothing about cricket, except Botham. When I first saw David across the table I couldn't put a name to the face. My first impressions were that he was very nice, very charming. He danced very well.' Originally from Lancaster, Thorunn certainly came from mixed stock. Her recently deceased father had been an army major; her mother had settled in England after leaving Iceland. Having spent a number of her formative years in Berlin, she had attended a secretarial college in York and followed her sister to London, where she landed a job in Knightsbridge as secretary to David's dentist. The two had much in common besides blondeness. Shortly before their initial meeting, Thorunn had lost her father; shortly after, David's mother died. Both were enmeshed in relationships that were taking a long time to die. Both had a hankering for the outdoor life. Both, first and foremost, were only too willing to consign the past to another continent.

'At the time we met, David was still embroiled with Vicki and I only saw him when he was playing in London,' recalls Thorunn:

> I found him very gentle, very intelligent, very good company. And he told good stories. There was no aggression there, although he did surprise me a couple of times. We slowly got to know each other and enjoy each other's company but it was five years before we decided to spend more time together. I'd been with my ex for ten years. David split up first and said, 'How about it?' I was all for it and split up with my boyfriend. David was very low at the time. He'd had a hard time, but he's not the sort of character who mopes. He doesn't dwell on things. He gets on with life. I'm not nearly as good as him at that, but I've learnt.

Although David and Vicki had more or less decided to call it quits in November 1989, it was not until New Year's Day that they went public, pressured into doing so by the daily phalanx of snappers and hardnoses at the bottom of the drive. If nothing else, it was done in style, via a small ad in the *Times*: 'David Gower and Vicki Stewart would like to put themselves and their friends out of their misery and confirm that sadly they have decided to separate as amicably as possible and go their own ways. As the matter has already been the subject of speculation by some members of the press, they hope that this brief announcement will obviate the need for further comment. (Fat . . . chance.)' Vicki, to her credit, chose not to seek compensation through the courts. The fact that she had, to all intents and purposes, served as David's secretary, housewife, lover and surrogate mother for ten years (and fiancée for half that time) must surely have entitled her to a palimony claim of some description. On the other hand, she was doubtless aware of the likely legal costs of such an action and duly accepted a settlement some way short of what she might have been awarded. Then again, perhaps she simply wanted to put it all behind her. 'She used to call Colleen and me mum and dad,' recalls Fred Rumsey. 'She still stays with us. They'd grown apart, though more from David's point of view. She suffered the most. She had to piece her life back together.'

So too, for all that his foundations were more secure, did David. BBC Radio and the *Times* had signed him up to cover the Caribbean tour but that wouldn't start until mid-January 1990. There was time enough to adjust the set. Which, essentially, meant divesting himself of all reminders of the past. Top of the hit-list was the shoulder. After a quick jaunt to Hong Kong as a guest of the Lord's Taverners, he went to hospital in mid-October for an operation with two objectives: to relieve the compression and slow the build-up of scar tissue, a condition known as Dupytren's contractures. Friends had thoughtfully dispatched some Bolly to his bedside; at the end of the operation, there was an excuse to toast at length. Convalescence lasted five days, long enough for David to resolve to address his future on both romantic and professional fronts.

Having decided, in his own mind at least, that he and Vicki had reached the end of the road, the next step was to clear his head, as he put it, i.e. renounce the Leicestershire captaincy. Mind you, he had already received a push in that direction from the new chairman, Don Tebbutt. Back in August, Tebbutt had reportedly admitted that the club had been 'wrong in backing David', but later submitted that the sentiment had been taken out of context. On the same day these opinions were published, ironically enough, David had used his column in the *Leicester Mercury* to express his appreciation of the support he had received throughout the summer, explaining that it was that which had stopped him from throwing in the national towel. Mike Turner's message to his chairman was terse: 'County committees should support their own captain.'

While David was in his hospital bed, news came through that the club had agreed terms with a full-time team manager, Bobby Simpson. He described it as 'a good appointment'. Jon Agnew expressed the view that Simpson and David 'could be a good combination'. Illingworth, it transpired, had turned the job down, apparently because the salary would not compensate for the loss of his media earnings. David's Leicestershire contract expired on the last day of the month. When asked whether he might be seeking fresh fields, he admitted only that this was an option in the event of him losing the captaincy, itself not an eventuality he had seriously considered. He resigned nine days later, denying that the signing of Simpson had been a contributory factor. 'In the circumstances I can do without the extra burden of responsibility,' he told the press. 'I made the decision for two reasons. First, there is my own, selfish priority of working my way back into the England side. To that end I felt that being able to concentrate wholly on batting and scoring runs was the best course.'

Martin Johnson marked the occasion with a cautionary tale in the *Independent*: 'Easily bored, there was one occasion when Sussex found themselves short of a twelfth man and were startled when Gower, wearing one of the visitors' sweaters, bounced on to the field and plonked himself in the slips. Some saw this as a telling example of Gower not taking county cricket as seriously as he might.' Eighteen days later, David learned of the full circumstances surrounding his brief return to the national helm. He was beyond caring. 'I have reached the point where it hardly matters. But in a sense it would have been nice to have been told officially where I stood.'

The next step was to tell Leicestershire where they stood. Somerset, Kent and Hampshire had made formal approaches, and the last had the strongest allure. They had Malcolm Marshall and Robin Smith. As the likeliest of the trio to be sniffing silverware, moreover, they were commensurately more high-profile. For all that it was lower than Kent's, David resolved to accept Hampshire's offer during a week of fitness, physiotherapy and general chilling out at Champneys health farm. This had been his recompense for an ad placed in the *Daily Telegraph* on the first morning of the final Test, wherein a haggard-looking England captain had been depicted alongside a rather ruddier one, accompanied by the tag-line, 'I'd rather be at Champneys'.

So far as the press were concerned, David's destination had been a toss-up between Kent and Hampshire. He wanted to move nearer London, the centre of his social life. Both clubs were captained by long-standing acquaintances, Mark Nicholas in Hampshire's case. David's relationship with Nicholas's Kentish counterpart was felt certain to sway the balance, but even though his employers were holding out the more sizeable carrot, Cowdrey was convinced it would not be in David's best interests to go to Canterbury. 'I never wanted him to come,' he demurs:

And we never actually sat down and talked about it. The press made a big thing of the Kent v. Hampshire situation but for his benefit, it would have been wrong to go to Canterbury. We had a very slow wicket, which wouldn't have suited the way he played. OK, that's only half the games, I grant you, but we had a lot of batting at that time and not much bowling. He probably would have done all right, and I'm sure I could have got him to do a lot for the county, but . . .

When the Kent committee were discussing what offer to table, Cowdrey stated his view quite clearly: ' "I don't want you guys using him," I told them. "He's not coming here as a marketing gimmick. You can't send him round all the boxes, or expect him to stand by the tents every day and sign autographs, or get his picture taken by the local paper every day. You've got a superstar here: let him play." '

Nicholas had no such reservations. Aside from regularly bumping into each other on the field, he and David shared a number of mutual friends in London. Nicholas regarded David as 'a mate', and still does. Nearly two decades earlier, he had been in the year below David on the public schools' circuit and, for all his protestations, possesses much of the latter's super-ficial insouciance, particularly at the crease. Not unnaturally, for someone whose mother spent a good deal of her life on the stage, the Hampshire captain has always conveyed an air of theatricality, wittingly or otherwise. Better a man larger than life than a man who shrinks himself to fit. Cricket, furthermore, has provided a platform for both these men to rise above their insecurities. The essential difference is one of approach. Nicholas doesn't merely see cricket as self-expression or enjoyment: he absolutely adores the game. In his writing and commentary, he contrives to combine the heartfelt keenness of a fourth-former with the perceptiveness of a tribal elder. Forget all that twaddle about whether ex-players should deny jobs to 'proper' jour-nalists: what more could you ask of a cricket correspondent than that he should be able to blend expertise and enthusiasm? The greensward is his lifeblood. For David, it is merely an artery.

'I thought I could change him,' reflects Nicholas:

> although in hindsight, of course, I had no chance. I thought I was the clear and obvious mentor for the new Gower. I wasn't besotted with him – I'd grown up watching Barry Richards, so I could never hold any cricketer in awe after that – but I found him interesting, fair-minded, funny, different. He was the brightest cricketer I'd ever met, miles brighter than me. Hampshire needed either an injection of star quality or an exceptional player: with him I would get both.

Robin Smith had told Nicholas about a revealing incident when the former made his Test debut, which coincided with David's hundredth Test. David had just been dismissed for not very many, related Smith, when he returned to the dressing room on the first afternoon:

> He knew he was going to be crucified in the press the next day. Ambrose was steaming in from the sightscreen, and I was getting more

and more nervous waiting for my turn to bat. Barely had David taken off his pads when he tapped me on the shoulder and said: 'Do you like chatting before you go out to bat?' I couldn't believe that someone I had always looked up to could be so thoughtful towards me; I nodded, and he sat down. We passed the time in idle conversation, and we've been good friends ever since.

Smith also benefited in the short term. 'By the time Robin was on his way to the middle,' recounts Nicholas, 'he said he was beginning to relax.'

Hampshire were about to announce record profits of £64,000 when Nicholas phoned David, 'as a mate', and suggested, as Cowdrey had done a year earlier, that the answer to his depression was 'a complete change in life'. Which, roughly translated, meant shifting his main base to South-ampton. 'He said he was very flattered and that he might have a think about it. I rang him a week later and he said he was leaving Leicestershire, so I told him to come to Hampshire, that he would fit in.'

On 23 January 1990, David tendered his notice to the Running Foxes. 'A lot of people in Leicestershire were very unhappy about him going so soon after an enormous benefit,' recalls Mike Turner:

but they didn't know the background and the circumstances. I truly hoped that we might find a way to keep him, but, in my heart of hearts, I knew he had to go. My great difficulty was that he couldn't make up his mind and we needed to appoint a new captain. It just dragged on and on until Christmas, so I invited him over to my home on Christmas Eve. We had a bottle of Bollinger and a chat, to try and bring matters to a close. I even gave him a Christmas present. Even then he didn't make his decision until Boxing Day, or certainly prior to the New Year. Unfortunately, I got quite a bit of criticism from the club because I had allowed the matter to drag on for so long. But David was in a sort of inner turmoil and, in order, (a) I sympathized, (b) I wanted to do what was right for him, and (c) I wanted to keep him at Leicestershire if I possibly could.

Had Ray Illingworth been around to voice his opinion, the intense and dedicated Briers might have been appointed Leicestershire captain in 1984. Anointed as David's successor, Briers urged him to stay, publicly avowing that his departure would be 'an unbelievable blow'. With the infallible benefit of hindsight, some have suggested that David's decision to leave Grace Road was the least enlightened he ever made. Briers is not among them:

In some ways, I wish he could have stayed, because his heart has always been with Leicestershire, but he needed to go somewhere fresh.

Having said that, I still think it would have helped if he had only had to come back between Tests and bat. I know people say he needed the captaincy to give him a challenge at county level, but I got the impression he could have done without it. A county team needs a bit more stick and carrot. He expected people to look out for themselves, but while that approach is probably fine at Test level because the players under you have more ability and self-confidence, you need to be more forthright as a county captain. He did blow up on the odd occasion. One time at The Oval, he'd put Surrey in, we'd dropped a couple of catches and they'd made 80 or 90 in the first hour. When we finally took a wicket, he gathered us around in a huddle and really let rip. We were all dumbfounded. I know I enjoyed it. Being brought up under Illy, that worked for me. But that wasn't the Gower we knew and loved. Nobody wanted to drive with him because there would be these ruddy great oceans of silence. You never felt totally relaxed in his company because he could be quiet for long periods, all the more so once he started playing for England. Occasionally, very occasionally, you did get the 'don't fucking tell me how to play this game' attitude, and why not?

Briers knew his county were losing a total one-off:

To his credit, he hardly changed from the moment I first saw him playing for Leicestershire Young Amateurs in 1974, which is quite something when you consider how quickly success came to him. He was a class act, on and off the field. On Sundays, I'd push singles so I could watch him from the other end. But he was a purist, which was why he stopped playing on Sundays, even though his name would have been the first I'd have had on any Sunday teamsheet. We were playing Gloucestershire once, chasing 190-odd, and he and I had taken the score to 180 for nought. We were going to win by ten wickets, which is quite something in a 40-overs game. At which point he comes down the wicket and says, 'Right, next ball I'm going to hit over long-on.' He lined himself up for it, let go, but got caught just short. It was too easy for him. I'd come in with him at the start of an innings and be aiming to push one here, maybe block it, but he'd flippin' flick his first ball behind square for four!

James Whitaker was no less saddened by David's exit; he had made quite an impression on the young Whitaker:

He was a *huge* influence on me in terms of knowing how to relax. I liked his style, which is why I hate it when people talk about him being a bad influence. It was a privilege to play in the same side as him when

232

I was starting out. He encouraged you to enjoy your cricket, never rammed theories down your throat. His attitude to playing was closer to mine than anyone I've ever played with. He was competitive but he knew how to relax. It was a tremendous experience playing with him. He played the decent way. He was the first to put his arm around a bowler to calm him down. He didn't like controversy. In fact, I can't recall him being involved in a single controversial incident. If he'd been more aggressive maybe Leicestershire would have won more games, but it was never a cut-throat business to him. And if you're doing your best to enjoy something, you're more likely to be good at it.

Whitaker is only too happy to supply edited highlights of the legendary Cheltenham Piss-Up:

It had rained all day Saturday, and by the time we got to the ground on the Sunday the place was under water, so some sponsor invited us into their tent, and we duly got stuck into the beverages, so to speak. The rain stopped around four but the ground was still under water. It was one of those occasions when you were 100 per cent certain there wasn't going to be any play. Then, just before five o'clock, a ten-over game suddenly began to become a possibility. We were in the running for the Sunday League at that stage so it was quite important we won, which, somehow, we did, but we were in no state. David tried to reverse sweep his first ball.

'He happens to have a gift. It's easier to see in music – like Erroll Garner, who never learns to read but just sits down at the piano and has a huge, a *huge* amount to say with it – but it's true in writing and acting and any other art form.' Woody Allen's homage was directed at Chazz Palminteri's gangster-playwright, hero of *Bullets Over Broadway*. Hampshire should have sent Woody a membership form.

13 The Indian Rope Trick

Cancel my subscription to the resurrection.
When The Music's Over, The Doors

When David was invited to be a castaway on Desert Island Discs his choices, unsurprisingly, were appreciably closer to the middle of the road than the edge. Alongside a couple of undeniable classics (the 'Emperor' Concerto and 'The Arrival of the Queen of Sheba') and some pop chestnuts (Supertramp's 'Breakfast in America', Genesis's 'I Know What I Like In Your Wardrobe' and Elton John's 'Goodbye Yellow Brick Road'), the luxury was a VHS. The one permissible video? *Rumpole of the Bailey*. How David must have wished, a decade later, that he had had John Mortimer representing him on the England selection committee.

In fact, as he struggled through the final winter of the eighties, legal aid looked at one point as if it would be sorely needed. At the height of the to-ing and fro-ing, David took off for St Moritz with Simon Strong and another friend, Mark Horne; Allan Lamb was on hand as well, along with Lyn Wilson, the Northamptonshire chairman. Strong picks up the threads of an escapade that almost went beyond the confines of the drunken wheeze.

> We'd hired an Opel in Zurich, done the Cresta and on the Saturday gone skiing. This chap Digby Willoughby holds a party in St Moritz every year, real boys' stuff, drinking neat iced vodka in a certain way and getting fined if you transgress, so we went there after lunch: very silly, great fun. Lamb and Gower left the party before Mark and me to go to one Lyn Wilson was holding at his hotel. I was carried out by two Swiss, and Gower put me to bed around 9 p.m. Earlier in the evening we'd been talking about how, before the Swiss got their pollution controls, they used to drive around on the lakes. Gower and Lamby decided this would be a real statement, so David drove around the lake doing wheelies. Later, he did a few more wheelies with Lyn Wilson's two sons in the back, and ended up on the wrong side of the lake, sinking. I heard afterwards that the Wilson boys panicked: there

234

were no lights, David was seriously pissed and they were worried. David at least had the presence of mind to open the door and let the lads get out, but then he tried to reverse the car, and that only pushed him further into the ice. Then he rescued my ski boots from the boot and they started walking away, whereupon David realizes he's left the lights on. 'So what?' they said. He explained that the battery would go flat and they wouldn't be able to start it in the morning. So he got back into the car and sent it in a bit further. Unbelievable.

The Wilson boys would have been eighteen and nineteen, twenty and twenty-one, something like that. We had to keep that out of the press because of the Swiss law about endangering lives. On the Wednesday, Urs Nater rang me to say that the Swiss had done a big investigation, they knew someone else was in the car, and that if we persisted in saying David was alone they'd send down a diver. So I said, look, stall them until Saturday and we should be all right. We struck a bargain with the police. Jon Holmes said that endangering people's lives is not the public perception of David Gower, so I suggested we did a deal on the lifting up of the car from the lake. It would have been great for Budget, too. Sadly, Holmes knocked it on the head.

David happily went along with the press's inference that the other footprints alongside the vehicle belonged to some woman or other, until, that is, Vicki confronted him upon his return, and was duly apprised of the truth.

Life rejigged rather than reconstructed, David set off for the Caribbean breathing a little easier. After Gooch had checked to make sure there were no hard feelings – there weren't – a spate of injuries led to him being called up to play against Barbados shortly before his thirty-third birthday, though not before Gooch and Lamb, the vice-captain, had talked Stewart round. Pity he made so few. Hampshire, by chance, were bound for Barbados for their pre-season workout, so David hung around once the Test was over. He even came within a hair's breadth of playing in the final Test, a prospect that prompted all manner of tingles; unfortunately, Lamb's imprecations fell on stony ground as Gooch and Stewart decided to stick with the original tour party and risk Nasser Hussain's fractured wrist instead. Hussain, who batted with enormous courage, missed the first six weeks of the next season and didn't win another cap for three years. Nice one.

The start of David's first summer with Hampshire was no less of an anticlimax. After spending three weeks in his new skipper's cramped home (a fact of which he seldom failed to remind the landlord), David moved into rented accommodation with Thorunn as they set off in quest of 'somewhere suitable to put down the new roots'. His bat, forgivably, was feeling decidedly dicky during the first couple of weeks. Nerves, perchance? More likely it was the sense of disorientation. For the first time in fourteen years, he was starting a summer without Vicki and without Leicestershire. 'He was so keen to make the right impression,' remembers Nicholas. 'But why do people need to do that? Because they might not be that nice?' Or maybe, rightly or wrongly, because they feel deprived of affection, or a sense of belonging.

Not that David did much to endear himself during those early forays at the crease for Hampshire. His senior debut brought 32 runs in the Refuge League fixture at Canterbury; his home debut, against Gloucestershire in the same competition, brought a duck and an abandonment. On his championship debut on Mead's old patch, it is true, he did score 145, adding 256 in 48 overs with Robin Smith to set up victory over Sussex by about an innings and a half. Expectations decreased, however, as the summer wore on. That 145 proved to be his first and last three-figure score of the 1990 championship. The return to Grace Road was happier for new county than old boy: 28 in a low-scoring NatWest second-round tie to help Hampshire squeeze home by one run. In the semi-final against Northants at Southampton, his disciplined 86 was the highest score of a match that this time saw the hosts finish on the wrong end of a one-run margin. In general, then, same old song, same old dance. 'Occasionally he batted with almost ethereal skill,' Mike Neasom summed up in *Wisden*, 'but at other times he fell to shots of seemingly careless disdain.'

Buried beneath all the damning statistics, as ever, lay some gems. Against Derbyshire at Portsmouth, came a 48 worth another man's 300. 'He played out of his skin,' Nicholas marvels.

And we won that match by exactly 48 runs. Bishop and Malcolm were creating havoc when he came in at 11 for one, on a typically quick Portsmouth wicket. When he took strike they had four slips and a couple of gullies; within a couple of overs the field was littered with deep extras, deep gullies, deep backward squares. They had nowhere to bowl. We'd got past 80 after an hour or so and he was so pumped up he wanted the strike every ball. Then, after he'd made 48 off 45 balls, he plays this delicate cut to third man, who has to run round, so David pushed him for a second and got run out. Everything left the pram when he got back to the dressing room, and I mean everything. He screamed at people, yelled at the twelfth man, bounced his bat off a few walls.

At this stage of his career, one of David's prime sources of motivation was the status of his direct assailant. He relished the one-on-one, the duel-within-a-duel, and frequently stepped up a gear when the adversary demanded it. Nicholas recalls one such occasion in the six-run B&H zonal win over Northamptonshire in 1992, a critical victory in Hampshire's eventual march to triumph at Lord's. Against a hostile Curtly Ambrose, David made a match winning 118 not out off 95 balls, a competition-best. 'That was his best innings for Hampshire,' Nicholas swears. 'He was just standing there, flicking Ambrose off his hips, for God's sake. Robin Smith said he'd never felt more inadequate in his life. Awesome. David was always thrilling to watch, one of the top three or four I've ever seen. And he was always a better scorer off good bowling.'

There was, however, one area of David's crease method with which Nicholas had a major quibble:

> He had no need to go out and bat like an entertainer – he was an entertainer by nature. Tommy Cooper didn't have to try and be funny; he just had to walk on to a stage. But by trying to be an entertainer, David increased the risk of getting out. Brian Lara once told me that when he went in, he aimed to stay there for an hour: after that, he knew that the only person who could get him out was himself. Once, I can't remember where, while he was trying to regain his England place, David was creaming it all over the place, and I was at the other end telling him to take it easy, to just stay there. If he could have focused like Lara he would have made even more runs.

Perhaps he felt it was expected. Outside teammates and opposition, it usually was.

Once again, David saved his most sustained performances for the international arena. County form and humdrum efforts in the Texaco Trophy had given the selectors a convenient excuse to omit him from the Tests against New Zealand, even though two berths had been vacated by injuries to Larkins and Hussain.

The first nudge came against the Indians: set 305 in sixty-two overs, Hampshire swanned home with three overs and seven wickets to spare, spearheaded by David's unbeaten 126. Recalled to the Texaco squad, he made 50 in the first episode at Leeds and 25 in the second at Trent Bridge before being run out by the wicketkeeper's throw to the non-striker's end. Snoozing on the job again, Gower!

Though they were a damned sight more pleasant from the collective viewpoint (India won both Texaco games), the first two Tests were similarly so-so. At Lord's David made 32 not out in the second innings to expedite a declaration. First time round he had been sawn off by a stinker of a decision over a catch at silly point, having made 40 to Gooch's eventual 333. At Old Trafford he made 38 and 16, Kapil Dev unhinging him for the very last time. Come the final Test at The Oval, however, his contribution was looking a bit like a polyester woolly in a cashmere factory. Two-thirds of the England top six had made at least one century in the series: Gooch (3), Smith (2), Lamb (2) and Atherton. Azharuddin (2), Tendulkar and Shastri had done likewise for the visitors. This, it will doubtless be recalled, was the summer when runs did not so much flow from a tap as gush from a geyser.

One thing David most definitely didn't have to look hard for was incentive. The Ashes tour jigsaw was being pieced together: this was the last chance to change minds. He knew all too well how easy it would be for the selectors to ditch him unless he produced at least one innings of substance. In private, Gooch questioned Gower's desire to win and his ability to set an example. Gooch was sceptical about 'the way he maintained his standards', and frowned upon what he saw as an undue thirst for the spotlight. Tolerable as these flaws were in the context of a series at home, the claustrophobic nature of a tour, the England captain reasoned, would turn them into tiresome liabilities. Gooch also thought David no longer had the urge to enjoy his profession. Even if we accept that David had been emitting such vibes, it was surely because he was still feeling, if not hard done by, then certainly uneasy. Besides, it had been people like Gooch, after all, who, just eleven months earlier, had tried, and succeeded, in denying him the opportunity to do precisely what he enjoyed most about his profession.

A century, almost certainly, would be the bare minimum. The believers prayed, all the harder when he blew the first chance, leg-before for eight to Wassan's unassuming seam. To general incredulity, the hosts followed on 266 behind; Gooch and Atherton had cleared two-thirds of the deficit when David entered after tea on the fourth day, but there was still a man-sized job to do. Ex-king and country were still entrenched 24 hours later, England 477 for four, D. I. Gower not out 157. It was his highest score in a home Test since making an identical score at the same venue five years previously. In all, he faced 271 balls, striking twenty-two boundaries, vindicating the faithful.

Even though their representatives did their level best to demonstrate that they really couldn't bat, bowl or field, Englishmen tend to remember two things above all else about the 1990–91 Ashes tour: David's shot at Biggles and David's shot at Adelaide. One survivor of Gooch's first overseas mission as captain had likened the previous winter's Caribbean trip to an exercise in laboratory cloning. Emboldened by near-victory over the world's best followed closely by a prosperous summer, skipper and manager were adamant that the medicine was working. Instead, an oppressive regime bred disillusion and defeat. Predictably, the management's response to David's attempt to relieve that oppression, to sweep away the clouds of calumny, made Judge Jeffreys seem about as reasonable as Solomon. In Adelaide, Gooch would be looking on from the non-striker's end, eyebrows erect, moustache bristling, when David fell for the sucker punch in the final over of the morning, steering McDermott unerringly to Hughes at backward square as if by prior arrangement. If Hughes hadn't got him, there had been two more takers lurking nearby. David never could resist a gauntlet. So enraged was his partner, he took ten minutes to find his way back to the dressing room through the fumes. 'When Graham eventually came in and sat down,' recalls Nicholas, 'he just said, "What's he on?".' But make no mistake about it: the Tiger Moth Affair was the breaking of David's Test career.

Australia had already retained the Ashes when England flew from Albury to Carrara to take on Queensland between the third and fourth Tests. No England side on a full Australian tour had ever reached the third week of January without a first-class win; now, at last, signs of hunger. Shortly before lunch on the third day, with the hosts' 286 long since overtaken, John Morris overheard Lamb and David discussing a putative flight with a local instructor. Lamb himself was a non-starter since he was due to resume his innings, so, fresh from a rousing century and feeling 'pretty pleased' with himself, Morris baggsied David took him as co-pilot. When Robin Smith reached his century, it was all Morris could do to dissuade David from dropping water bombs on the middle in celebration.

'I'm not blaming anyone, because you're responsible for your own actions,' concedes Morris,

> but I honestly thought that with David being the senior player on tour and Lambie being the vice-captain, there wouldn't be much of a problem. There obviously was. It was never meant to be a prank with any malice involved. We just thought a bit of light-hearted fun would help lift spirits. It was my first tour, my eyes were wide and starry, but when I read the papers now and see the England team swimming with dolphins and cuddling koalas, it all seems so alien. I don't think I ever *saw* the ocean on that tour.

Not until the evening press conference did Morris discover that any damage had been done.

One of the journalists had turned round and asked about the two boys in the airplane, and the tour manager, Peter Lush, I believe, said, 'what boys in the airplane?'. At this point David and I had gone to pose for Graham Morris in our helmets and gear, for the Biggles shot or whatever, which I didn't see as a problem, but I think that turned out to be the biggest problem of all. David went out for dinner with David Frith, but when I got back to the hotel I received a message to report to the manager's room, so I was left carrying the can a little bit. David had given me the telephone number where he was dining and I rang to ask him what to say. He told me to be honest and that we'd sort it out tomorrow. The next morning I got a call to my room just before I was due to go into another meeting with the management, and was told not to bother coming. David had been there longer than expected and he was giving them a piece of his mind.

It was not so much *Biggles Flies Undone* as *Biggles Boggled*. Shirty as they were about Graham Morris's snapshots above all, three-quarters of the jury – Stewart, Gooch and Lush – voted to send the aviators packing forthwith. Only Lamb kept a grip on sanity, pointing out, among other things, that this might leave the batting a trifle undermanned. Even then, the upshot was a $1000 (about £450) fine apiece. 'David would have been sent home if I hadn't pointed out how ridiculous it was,' emphasizes Lamb. 'Graham and David were both frustrated with each other; and the more the tour went on, the worse the situation got. There was no time to relax. And on the rare occasions we tried, such as when Kerry Packer invited us to his casino on the Gold Coast, it ended in tears because everyone was so paranoid about the press. That was the tour David's career ended.' For the moment, John Morris's too.

Mike Turner, who sat on the TCCB Executive Committee, gave Jon Holmes the distinct impression that an appeal would find favour, so David inquired of Lush whether this was practicable. As it transpired, the terms of the tour contract precluded him from taking such an action unless he was sent home. Between times, David couldn't help but notice, Lush could scarcely do enough for him.

There is no man alive, David forever relishes telling people, with such a capacity for fun and games as Allan Lamb. The latter, nonetheless, had a certain sympathy for Gooch when the captain skulked off in Adelaide. 'What frustrated Graham was the fact that David never worked in the nets on the shots that were getting him out: Graham would. David was lucky: he had a feel for batting, but Graham couldn't see that. He didn't understand him. He thought his attitude was wrong. I'm afraid, though, that you just have to let David do his own thing.' If doing his own thing meant pausing during fielding practice to chat to the world's other David Gower, or pose for the snappers, Gooch was unimpressed. By his own subsequent admission, he knew David no better then than he had done in 1978. As Nicholas recalls: 'Graham used to say: "All I ask is that, between 9.30 and 6 at night, he *looks* as if he's trying to do what I ask of him."'

John Morris's earliest memory of his co-pilot remains indelible.

I was there with Neil Fairbrother that day at Edgbaston when he [David] made 200 against India, sat in the stands watching this man perform. I remember walking out of the gates at the end and there was this brown sports car, a coupe or something, with David Gower's name on it and the Leicestershire fox, and thinking, 'Crikey, this lad's really important.' Anybody who plays the game can only admire the way he struck the ball. Fantastic. The eyes and the hands worked perfectly together. There was always the feeling of, 'get Gower out early and we'll be all right'. I remember him getting 120 or something against Derby in a NatWest tie: wherever we set a field to him he pierced the gap. It was embarrassing in many respects, because the bowlers weren't bowling badly. If we moved the man squarer he'd hit it finer; if we moved him finer he'd hit it squarer. It was something to witness. The biggest loss to English cricket in my career was the way David Gower was got rid of after that 1990–91 tour.

While David was compiling his face-saver at The Oval six months earlier, Morris had spent a session bearing awed witness from the non-striker's end.

Just before lunch, Ravi Shastri came on and bowled me the biggest long hop you've ever seen in your life, which I patted gently back down the wicket. At which point David came down the wicket and told me what a fool I was for not hitting it for six. 'Relax and play,' he said. That's easy to say if you're David Gower, but at that stage I felt very conscious of having to stay at the crease. After that, however, I thought to myself, 'yeah, he's right'. In two and a half Tests, no one had ever said anything to me like that.

What, then, of Gooch's contention that David set an undesirable example?

Far from it. David was the only senior player I had contact with on the whole of that Australian tour, and that includes Gooch. I think I was able to relate to David more than Gooch because, although I'm nowhere near as good a player, I'm more of a David Gower than a

Graham Gooch, so we just got on better. So, when it got difficult for me, David was the person I went to. He's a nice fellow and we've talked about Carrara many times since; in fact, we laugh about it mostly, to be truthful. I came home disappointed, personally and as regards the team, but I'd averaged 39 in the first-class games and 30 in the one-day internationals, so I didn't think I had that bad a tour, but there was always this cloud hanging over me from then on. I paid my fine and took the can but I would have hoped the incident was forgotten the day I paid the fine.

The salient point was clear. While David had merely gone in for a bit of remodelling, Gooch had remade himself. Where was Zap, the wayward, overweight smiter who'd clobbered Lillee and Thomson the length and breadth of Lord's a decade and a half ago? Where was the joker who used to keep teammates in stitches with his impressions of Daniel and Procter? Where was the friend who had accompanied David to game parks and bistros, the friend whose career David had saved, yet who now cursed him at every turn? Banished, it seemed, by experience and responsibility. As a husband, father, and ex-rebel, all the things David was not, Gooch had renounced bank robbing in favour of a steady gig in charge of standing orders. Neither did it help that his marriage was in the red. Yet as a captain he had been reborn, as master batsman and major drudge. Sweat and uniformity were the key ingredients in Dr Gooch's remedy, and everyone had to take his spoonful. No exceptions.

Gooch's one attempt at compromise, if sense can be seen as such, had been to co-select the only batsman in the country who did not regard him as a superior. David feels he made a better stab at meeting halfway.

There was no time in my career when I consciously compromised, but maybe there was a little of that before the tour. Not so much compromise, maybe, as an effort to at least show willing. You need to do a bit of training, a bit of practice, to maintain your own levels if nothing else. No argument about that. And I did try and show a bit of willing before we left. But my contention is, you can do all that, fine, but it comes down to state of mind. The key is when it comes to the crunch, a wicket falls and you walk in to bat. Whatever you've done, however you achieve your ends through practice, it can be negated by a negative state of mind when you're walking out. You can practise for three months and be nervous as a kitten, so those three months are wasted.

To Gooch, conversely, this lack of interest in preparation reduced David's value: 'I felt that all he gave me was his great talent.' The heart bled.

Thorunn recalls all too vividly how the strain told:

One night, eight of us went out for a meal, including the Lambs. As we got up to leave, a couple of middle-aged spinsters, Gower fans, summoned David over. He was tired. They prodded and pulled him, and he can't stand that. They'd had a glass or two and were being painfully annoying. They wouldn't let him go. That was it. He gave them an earful. Everyone heard. I nearly died.

When England dropped over to New Zealand for a clutch of one-dayers in February, David sought the counsel of his good friend, John Wright. To the outsider, the solid, unspectacular opener's technique and approach seemed entirely at odds with David's, but that didn't mean his mind was narrow. 'Carry on regardless' was the basic gist of Wright's advice. But Gooch's message was less encouraging. The mutual respect between the two was still intact, for each other's skill most of all, but a gap had opened up which was in danger of becoming a chasm. David remembers 'various moans' from Gooch during the course of that New Zealand leg, the culmination of which was a heated exchange in Christchurch after captain had remonstrated with ex-captain during catching practice for chatting to a man whom he had discovered to be his name-sake. When the pair faced each other across a Wellington restaurant table, Gooch submitted this as 'an example of my irritation'. He also expressed his fear that David's 'lethargic attitude can rub off'. David, in turn, reassured him that he still wanted to play for England. The 'smooth words', Gooch asserted, were 'no longer enough'. The only way David would play against the West Indies was to prove himself all over again, for Hampshire. Which was a bit like telling Sinatra he could only play Caesar's Palace in future if he auditioned at the Southampton Top Rank.

Before the final Test in Perth, Gooch poured his heart out to Jon Agnew, then working for *Today*.

Gower needed 67 runs to beat Boycott's record, so I went to Gooch's room and we started talking. Suddenly it all started coming out about Gower, all his frustrations. And not only did he have a go at David, but the whole team. It was the worst team he'd ever played with, astonishing stuff. So, while we were on the plane to New Zealand I told David I thought it best if we had a chat, for his own good. He came to my room in Christchurch and I said, 'Look, you're struggling.' So he gave me his point of view, which was that he really had tried but he didn't like the whole philosophy. There was a team talk in Sydney which really got to him. Graham said: 'Well, you know, we're up against it here, lads, blah, blah, blah. What do you think, Micky?'

And David's fuse went. He had a go at them for being negative and crass, 'don't be ridiculous', that sort of thing. He felt he was being got at.

The management were so stupid in Carrara. It was a pretty miserable tour. A number of the players weren't happy with Graham and this relentless schedule of practice, practice, practice. It was almost as if you weren't *allowed* to enjoy it. When the players left Carrara and flew to Adelaide the atmosphere on the flight was probably the best it had been all tour. The players treated the Biggles stuff as a bit of a laugh. Then everything blows up the next day and you could feel the spirit go 'pfft'.

Yet, instructive as they are, these chapters are not what should be remembered most about the 1990–91 Ashes tour, a tour, lest we forget, in which David totted up 407 runs in the Tests at 45.22, second only to Gooch. What we *should* remember most is the Sydney Test, and David's final masterpiece. In all, he amassed 608 runs in six Tests there, more than on any other foreign field. Yet, for all his affinity for ground, city and inhabitants, he had never made a century there. Atonement, naturally, came only at the very last. Not for the first time, the circumstances were forbidding. He went in during the final session of the third day of the third Test, his side 2–0 down in the series and, with three wickets gone in their first innings, still 362 runs behind.

In terms of personal productivity, as it happens, David had been pootling along rather nicely. Despite a duck in Melbourne, he had top-scored in all three of the other England innings so far, including a century in the first at the MCG. Gooch's insistence that nothing David did in the middle would be enough was hardly inspiring. Then again, the mood in the England camp was about as bubbly as a slow day at Mr Shadrack's funeral parlour. The previous two Tests (the first of which Gooch had missed with a hand infection) had seen the England batting attain unscaled heights of hamfistedness: twice they had led on first innings; twice they had limped home a distant second. The previous two days of this Test had squared the circle. Gooch had lumbered about the field, putting the lug into lugubrious, a pissed-off panda surrounded by a bunch of chimps. John Thicknesse's tour summary for *Wisden* was spot-on: 'On and off the field, bad thinking was an ever-present feature. If the team weren't running between the wickets like headless chickens, they were behaving like lemmings searching for a cliff.'

The spreading cancer of soccerspeak was at least partly responsible. Laurie Brown, the physio, had tended to groins and hamstrings at Manchester United; Gooch loved West Ham almost as much as life itself; Stewart swapped notes and tactics with that extremely minor soccer genius, Graham Taylor. No England cricket team, certainly, had ever displayed a fuller grasp of the concept of sick parrots.

On that third afternoon in Sydney, David started as he meant to go on, setting off with a four threaded immaculately through the precise spot where third slip would have been. Steve Waugh was soon square driven. 'People always talk about the timing, but I was always struck by the power of his shots,' said Mark Nicholas. 'That feeling of "whoof".'

By the close, David had contributed 33 to an unbroken stand of 71 with Mike Atherton, whose leech-like persistence had brought him 94, six short of what, at seven hours and six minutes, would be the slowest century in Ashes history. In the opening over of the fourth day, David sent three fours skating across the outfield, disguising the unease he had felt overnight. In Alderman's following over he drove another boundary, then a two to pass 50. Then, off Rackemann, a flip through midwicket played with the studied nonchalance of a pools winner pulling a one-armed bandit. Not until 49 had been added that morning did Atherton finally reach three figures. In all, the pair put on 139, Atherton donating 11 of the last 68. David's century was his ninth against Australia, leaving only Hobbs ahead of him. 'The most marvellous knock,' exclaimed Richie Benaud after Geoff Marsh's staggering interception in the gully had ended the spell. Sir Donald Bradman declared it to be up there with Sobers's 254 at the MCG in 1972 as one of the most awe-inspiring expositions of batsmanship he had ever witnessed.

Not that the fun stopped there. Thanks in the main to David's enterprise, Gooch's astute declaration and a mature stint of flighty left-arm spin from another hardened maverick, Phil Tufnell, England briefly entertained thoughts of victory. When Rackemann's obdurate resistance was finally terminated by Devon Malcolm (who had been unaccountably ignored for the previous hour), the task of saving the Ashes bordered on the impossible: 255 in 28 overs. Undeterred, Gooch took David in with him, whereupon England's two most upstanding batsmen flayed anything in their path. The first four overs yielded 28 as David acquired his 8000th run in Tests; the next three reaped a further 21. Nine flowed from the next. David discarded his helmet, Gooch dispensed his reverse sweep: 81 off eleven. Captain Grumpy was getting steadily grumpier. It couldn't last. At 84, David swung Matthews to long-off and picked out Mark Taylor just inside the boundary, then exchanged smiles with Border as he headed for the wings. Rackemann conveyed his appreciation for a worthy foe. 'He seemed to be batting as gracefully and relaxedly as humanly feasible,' wrote David Frith. Gooch at least had the good grace to call David's first innings 'breathtaking'. What Gooch and Stewart did next stole the breath and locked it away for good.

Not that David was alone in suffering for his non-conformity. At Lord's in May, Gooch advised Allan Lamb that his services were no longer required as vice-captain, even though it was the latter who had led England to their stirring win in Jamaica barely fifteen months earlier, with bat as well as brain; one can only assume that the South African's connections with David made him unworthy of responsibility. When Lamb asked Stewart for confirmation, manager contradicted captain. Press paranoia, no doubt. The end-product was an unseemly public squabble between Gooch and Lamb.

By the time the wagons trundled away from Carrara, David had reached the farthermost tip of his tether. Mark Nicholas remembers receiving precisely two calls from him during their four years as teammates, and one came then: 'He said he was thinking of packing it in. He was clearly very low. "You can't do that," I said. "We're only just getting started." He'd been a breath of fresh air at Hampshire. He'd put bums on seats, the membership had gone up and the sponsors loved him. After that we had a couple more heavy phone conversations and I tried to talk him out of it.'

David escaped to Switzerland to tackle the Lauberhorn, the downhill skier's greatest challenge. At the top of the piste, he confessed to the man from the *Daily Express* that he was 'as tense now in playing terms as I've ever been'. One additional reason for this was that Boycott's national Test record now stood just 33 runs away, a fact that could hardly have eluded even those dismissive of statistical landmarks, let alone one whose time to set them was clearly running out.

Stoked avidly by the media, this desire, however, was more than counter-balanced by anxiety. Then there was the sheer fatigue, mental more than physical. When David missed a Sunday League game after wining none too wisely with the Lambs, the words 'tired' and 'emotional' figured heavily in the prognosis. 'He was quite low,' recalls Thorunn. 'And the harder he tried, the worse it got. "Life isn't about this," he kept saying. We were renting in Southampton: it was a gruesome year.'

David and Mark Nicholas had had a revealing dinner upon the former's return home:

David was obviously very tired so I told him not to bother with pre-season training. But when he came back, he had a nightmare. I tried everything to get him going, particularly on Sundays: shunt him around the order, move him around in the field, give him targets, give him roles. Nada. The way things were going, one of us had to be dropped, and the club wanted me, as captain, to play. So, at breakfast one morning when we were playing at Trent Bridge I told him that if he didn't get any runs I couldn't pick him. He took it amazingly well. 'I understand,' he said, 'what can I do?' So I told him to get into the nets and work his nuts off. I said the players needed to see that he cared, that people were genuinely concerned. To his credit, he never once said anything like, 'well, you were the one who talked me out of retiring'. That wasn't his style at all. He went into the nets with Chris Smith's bowling machine and Tim Tremlett chucking balls down. He really knuckled down.

Taunton provided some tangible evidence of this apparent assiduousness. David had failed to record so much as a half-century in his first seven championship outings of the 1991 season, but now he grafted for 69 off 158 balls on the most turgid of surfaces: he needed pace in a pitch in much the same way as a hinge needs oil. Seven times in the next fifteen championship games he reached 50, including a match winning 80 against Emburey and Tufnell on a Lord's Bunsen burner, yet not once did he progress. Centuries were what Gooch demanded. But that early stutter, and the captain's own match winning heroics in the first Test, had rendered a place against the West Indies about as likely as a recall for WG.

The NatWest Trophy proved more fulfilling. In the second round against Lancashire at Southampton, Hampshire resumed at 151 for two on the second morning with Robin Smith on 20 and David on 10, the target 111 off twenty-two overs: the pair scorched home in fewer than sixteen, sapphire and steel in irresistible tandem. He never even took guard in the semi-final at Edgbaston, but it was those lean, tapering fingers that held the pot aloft at Lord's. 'Little did I think when we had that chat at Trent Bridge,' reminisces Nicholas, 'that I'd be knocking on his hotel room door on the day before the final to tell him I couldn't play and ask him to take over as captain. The press made a big deal about it being a tricky choice between David and Paul Terry, but it wasn't. David had captained in so many big games: it turned him on.' Waqar Younis had David's measure for the fourth time that season, booming in one of those outlandish inswingers to trap him for 9, but by then Hampshire were well on their way to a four-wicket win. In reality, it didn't really matter what David did or didn't do for Hampshire that summer. Without him knowing it, the goalposts were being uprooted.

Gooch had received the OBE, Gower the brush-off. Lance Gibbs, the West Indies manager, was astonished: 'Dropping him is like us axing Viv Richards. I would have thought that with his Test record Gower should have been there. We certainly tend to stick with our tried and proven players. But the England selectors must know what they're doing.' A 2–2 scoreline implies that they might very well have done, although some suicidal batting against Tufnell, it should be said, lay at the heart of the tourists' defeat at The Oval. When Pakistan arrived in England the following spring, Wasim Akram lost no time in endorsing Gibbs's amazement: 'The last man we want to see back in the England side is David Gower. He's a great player and he's in superb form. How can England not play him? It seems incredible that Gower is not in their side, just because he has done a few things to upset Graham Gooch.'

Between February 1991 and July 1992 David remained 33 runs adrift of Boycott's record, not to mention one cap shy of outstripping Cowdrey's. He also missed another World Cup. During that span, England won five and lost three of their eleven Tests in addition to losing the World Cup final by a nose. Success, yes, but at what price? A dozen players had occupied the top six batting places during that period. Were we seriously supposed to believe David Gower was the thirteenth best batsman in England? Even Botham had been forgiven. If this wasn't personal, nothing was.

Opting for diplomacy over favouritism, a charge frequently made against him when the saviour of his career is under discussion, Mike Gatting prefers to submit David's continued omission as conclusive evidence of the foot-shooting expertise that has cost English cricket so dear.

We've cut our own throats with all the juggling over the years, especially with different captains. It hasn't exactly had a stabilizing effect. There were a fair amount of injuries, so the selectors weren't always to blame, but we haven't backed our judgement. We've listened to the media. The two most important factors to me are a settled side and a settled captain. When we won the Ashes in '86–87 we used thirteen players, and eleven played in at least four Tests. And we had a nucleus of players that could have seen us through for a chunk of the decade. We had Goochie, David, Lamby, Both and myself as batters, so we only had to find another opener: Broad, Robinson or Moxon. Fozzie [Foster], Both, Emburey and Edmonds as bowlers, but then we always had a problem with seamers getting injured. Dill [Dilley] was a case in point. He was a fine bowler, Gladstone [Small] too. And we picked people like Neal Radford. Look at all those one-cap players.

And perhaps consistent selection would have reduced the defections? Of all those incongruities, the discarding of David Gower, whose last dozen Tests had brought 1020 runs at 48.62, including four centuries (as many as Robin Smith and Gooch), was the hardest to fathom.

That said, Gatting was wrong in one respect: Gooch, Stewart and Dexter did ignore the media when it came to David's reinstatement. Or, at least, they did until the second Test against Pakistan was lost in June 1992. Until then, they had been sailing along quite merrily. They could afford to ignore the critics. Mushtaq Ahmed's cunning wrist spin, however, had punched a hole in the middle order at Lord's. On the Pakistan tour of 1983–84, hadn't Lamb hailed David as the best English batsman by far when it came to unravelling Abdul Qadir? For his part, David had actually been a good boy: with Hampshire enjoying the hottest streak Nicholas can recall, he totted up 583 championship runs at nearly 65, including 155 off 247 balls against Yorkshire on a Basingstoke pudding that defied any other batsman to reach 60. There was even more spring in the step when he was awarded an OBE in the Queen's Birthday Honours List (further testimony to HRH's good sense came with the simultaneous anointing of Botham). So, finally, back came the cavalier to reinforce Gooch's New Model Army. There was no intention, however, that this should have been seen as a trial run for the winter tour of India. So long as David persisted in being himself, in being different, Gooch would never trust him in such an environment. So long as Gooch was captain there was no earthly way David would raise the standard again on a foreign field.

Earlier in the summer, the man whose on-field demeanour was beginning to bear a close resemblance to a walrus with toothache explained that David's protracted absence from his team was attributable to 'a lethargic attitude'. This revelation followed the publication of extracts from Gooch's book on captaincy, a tome liberally sprinkled with references to his 'greatest failure in man-management'. Offered the right of reply, the failure could convey only dismay: 'It saddens me that Graham Gooch believes I do not care enough about my cricket. It worries me, too, that the mistaken impression that I no longer enjoy the game should threaten my chances of ever playing for England again. Gooch, of all people, knows that outward appearances can be misleading. I know nobody keener than him to play yet that is not always obvious when you watch him during matches.' Expert cheek-turner as he had become, this was as near as David had come to sniping at Gooch in public. Gooch admired that, as well he might. Besides, David knew where the Great British Public stood.

Which is at least partly why, on 2 July, the *Times* printed an interview with 'the prodigal'. Alan Lee was almost beside himself: 'No cricketer in England, and possibly the world, commands such unshakeable affection as the thirty-five-year-old bachelor who today returns from hibernation to resume his natural habitat on a Test match stage. The sporting public, with precious few exceptions, has loudly and bitterly bemoaned his absence. Today they rejoice.' David was suitably upbeat yet reluctant, typically, to sound any fanfares: 'I think most people would be happy with what I have achieved. But yes, there is scope for thinking I should have done better.' Lee signed off in positive fashion: 'He mused: "It is conceivable there are some good years still to come." Coming from Gower, that was as good as a declaration that we have not seen anything yet.'

At 12.17 p.m. four days later, David descended the pavilion steps at Old Trafford to a tumultuous reception. To join Gooch. 'The first over he faced encapsulated all that Gower has ever stood for,' observed David Frith: a snick through slips, a peerless cover-drive, a play-and-miss, two runs delightfully flicked off the pads. A no-ball from Wasim was top-edged; on 15, he was dropped high at slip. Perhaps his partner was unnerving him. The air was thick with I'll show yous. At 12.50, the scent came to fruition, the moment distilled by essence of Gower: a velveteen cover-drive that purred to the ropes in front of Wilson's Stand. One small step for England's No.5, one giant leap for cricketkind.

The national treasure eventually departed for 73, off 85 balls, attempting something lavish outside off. He then went up to the BBC gantry for some playful badinage with Boycott, who, unconfirmed rumour had it, had had his back to the action at the historic moment, and had had to be forcibly dragged up to face his conqueror. The praise was generous, the undertone grudging. That record had been the very vindication of Boycott's being. He had also spent the past couple of years backing Gooch to the hilt. Boycott vehemently denied the charges of sour grapes. Had the roles been reversed, had he, Geoffrey Boycott, been the pursuer, it seems more than probable that he would have seconded that emotion. But by going into print with his carefully worded objections to David resuming his Test career, he had rather led with his chin.

David needed no reminding of the symbolism. 'Of course I was aware of it. But then Geoffrey will look at it in his own way and say, well, I missed three or four years so I could have had 11,000. Ironically, the reasons I missed a couple of years are not entirely dissimilar but from the other end of the corridor. Geoffrey lost his three years because he had a conflict with the powers that be; mine was a conflict with the powers that be and they pushed me out instead of me pulling myself out.' In those heady moments after that cover drive had crossed the boundary, did he ever think, even for a millisecond, 'I'm better than Boycott, better than Hammond, better than Hutton'? 'It's a brief thought. Obviously I was aware of the target, but there was nothing personal about it. It's not a comparison. It doesn't mean anything. But beating Geoffrey, in a sense . . .' The voice trails away, trying to find the most equitable means of expression. As it searches, it is hard to resist the thought that its owner is also suppressing a spasm of self-vindication.

Yet he is certainly not vindictive.

If somebody else had been at the top there would still have been satisfaction getting there, being No.1. It's a target, a little target. When I walked out that morning needing 30-odd to get there I'd been waiting a year and a half to have that chance. That was nothing to do with Geoffrey, or anyone. All it means is that you have to cross a figure out on your CV. Which is why losing it is not a major factor. It would be nice to still have it. I'd like to have held it longer, to have had the chance to add to it and make it harder to overtake. That's the only gripe. But it's not as important as working out what to do next with your life, or working out how to get better at what you do next. If I want to sit at my desk and ponder about that for half an hour, that's half an hour that could have been spent a lot better.

At Headingley, it was noses to the grindstone. On the fourth afternoon, David entered at 27 for two: 72 more and the series would be squared. In the context of the whole match, however, England had lost their last nine wickets for 55, Gooch had survived a run-out call that wasn't even close, and Mushtaq's trio of googly variations were all beginning to hum. When the target was finally achieved after three hours of cricket at its most hypnotic, David was still there. Few had seen a display of such cool mastery against high-quality spin. Even fewer could remember why he had ever been left out.

While Waqar and Wasim were wreaking a horrible revenge inside ten sessions in the Oval Test, David satisfied his detractors with a couple of major aberrations. On the opening day, he was on 27 when he cut at the sprightly Aquib Javed and played on. In the second innings, he had made a single when Waqar darted one back a mile off the seam. The Gower bat was pointing in the general vicinity of the North Star when the bails were ungrooved. Had we but known that was to be our lot, we would surely have demanded a stewards' inquiry. As it was, David Gower's exit from the Test arena could scarcely have been more undignified.

What ensued was a combination of high farce and nationwide wrath. Having topped the England averages with 150 runs at exactly 50, against arguably the best attack in the game, David was excluded from the sub-continental tour. The wounds still itch:

Graham eventually came on the phone, having known about it for three days, forty minutes before the squad was due to be announced on national radio, on his way to playing at Derby, which I never forgave him for. To leave me hanging there . . . I was infinitely more angry with being dropped then than for the Caribbean the following year. Having played a major part in winning the Headingley Test, and helping save the one at Old Trafford, having got back in and done a job satisfactorily, not to be picked for India was an insult. When Graham rang me I gave him as much stick as he deserved. I respect him for what he's done for himself, what he's achieved as a player. I used to like him very much before he got serious about it. What I won't forgive him for is trying to pass that seriousness on to others. There's a limit.

'David was devastated,' affirms Thorunn.

What made it worse was that Goochie had been on the phone a few days earlier and the implication then was that David would be in. It was very hard to console him. We had a brief chat and then he went into his study to ponder. He didn't get over it as quickly as he might because of the media. On the other hand, it was quite good for him to get all those calls of support. The number of letters he received was overwhelming. I used to get annoyed with the way he was so laid-back about Gooch and Stewart. It was an appalling way to behave.

On 18 September, David and Thorunn were married at Winchester Cathedral. Gooch was not on the guest list. Chris Cowdrey performed the honours as best man, dutifully confirming, upon reading out the telegrams, that none had arrived from anyone with a name beginning in 'G'. The legacy of the past two weeks, however, had left its mark. The stag night at Alderney, as Simon Strong recalls, had stretched into breakfast when David had a contretemps with the man from the *Sunday Express*:

David stayed at Both's place after we'd had a party in the First and Last restaurant. He was clearly hung over the morning after; Both, me and Lamby were the only ones who weren't. We were still going very heavily when this reporter asked David if he could have a few words. I suppose he felt entitled because David and he worked for the same paper. 'No thanks,' said David, but the guy pressed him. So David tore into him. The reporter's only retort was, 'Well, don't you like working for the *Express*?' For which he got another verbal tirade.

Blame, for once, could not be attached to Stewart, even though it was his influence that had helped start the wretched business in the first place.

The team manager had resigned, with effect from the end of the summer. The final verdict: devoted but blinkered. 'No number of dossiers on the opposition, fielding charts, training routines and fitness assessments can be a replacement for talent,' averred Bob Willis. 'The "champagne boys" [Botham, Lamb and Gower] were simply the best players, and Stewart's reign will be remembered for not producing one player who seriously and genuinely challenged this trio.'

Stewart's replacement was Gooch's Essex mucker, Keith Fletcher, a keen admirer of David's. Fletcher had a tricky first assignment: fob off the media. It was, he explained, a simple matter: three middle-order batsmen of a certain age – Gatting, Gooch and Gower – was one too many. And naturally, now that he had done his stir for defying the Gleneagles Agreement, Gatting simply had to tour because he was such an accomplished player of spin. Even more accomplished than the man who had defied all that Mushtaq could conjure up? Surely Ted Dexter could have been a tad more inventive. Keeping lips sealed, the first and last chairman of the England Cricket Committee fled to Sunningdale to practise his chips, instead of cashing them in as the country hoped. A county captain, who wishes to remain anonymous and whom Dexter had been with not 48 hours earlier, walked over for a chinwag. Not for 45 minutes did Dexter realize that he was engaged in conversation with someone totally unrelated to the man he thought was standing next to him.

Riled all the more by the absence of any official explanation, the great and the good took umbrage. Two MCC members, a Kent businessman, Dennis Oliver, and Donald Trelford, the former editor of the *Observer*, joined forces and marshalled resistance. Politicians and countless other troubadours answered the call, from Lord Bonham-Carter and Lord Gilmour to Harold Pinter and David's good chum, Tim Rice. The 'rebels' cited the omissions of David and two other dodos, Jack Russell (A Proper Wicketkeeper) and Ian Salisbury (A Proper Leg-Spinner), as proof of selectorial incompetence. Admirable sentiments indeed. A motion was proposed, to wit: 'The Marylebone Cricket Club has no confidence in England's cricket selectors.' What this was really all about, of course, was the future of the bacon-and-egg tie. The MCC no longer had an obvious role to play in the running of cricket. It had a voice, but one vote out of twenty on the TCCB was scarcely the average ex-major's idea of The Way Things Should Be. The club did retain influence in a masonic sort of way, filtered through the likes of Doug Insole, but for some that was not enough.

It would nevertheless be unfair, not to say wrong, to infer that this was the sole motivation. The whole country was up in arms and this was merely the most public manifestation of that anger. From a purely cricketing perspective, Barry Dudleston encapsulates it as well as any:

No matter how much corporate hospitality there is, no matter how many ways you package the game, if people like David don't get the credit for it then we're all in trouble. To do it the way he did had almost become a dirty word. If you bored people to death, that was fine: you were giving 100 per cent. I've never known a nicer person, who has given more value, who has been treated so badly.

Harold Pinter was in favour of the rebels' motion, but also anxious to raise a philosophical point. 'Cricket is still a game of joy and self-expression really,' avows the man whose plays persistently highlight the role played by the greensward as a mirror of his nation.

All this training is a pain in the arse. It doesn't make you a better player. Look at that Yorkshire side of the thirties. Look at Emmott Robinson with that barrel of a belly. Gower was quite unique. Gave me more pleasure than anyone, until I saw Lara. I met him in a restaurant once and sent him over a bottle. Until he got up to shake hands, I'd never realized how tall he was. It was a very nice encounter. I thought the world of him. But he was disgracefully treated. I never quite understood the politics, but I know it had nothing to do with cricket.

Pinter said his piece during a heated meeting in the Long Room: 'The MCC were trying to glide away from it all but they didn't stand a chance of just brushing us off. I said that the club had to realize that this wasn't a light, irresponsible issue. It was an issue at the very heart of people who loved the game.'

'Shortly after the squads were announced,' remembers Jon Holmes,

Trelford, or someone from the *Observer*, rang me and said they were going to have a go in the paper that Sunday. I didn't think we should be seen to be openly encouraging, so I said, 'marvellous, do what you can but we can't get involved'. It was the wedding weekend. David thought it was funny when I told him. He wasn't even a member of the MCC. They'd written a letter to him saying he could be a member but that he had to show his commitment to the game in some way! So he wrote back and told them that, due to pressure of work, he couldn't show that commitment. Typical. I don't think the Colonel took it too well. But the MCC thing was good publicity, and it kept David going at a point when he could have been sinking. He told me he found it a bit embarrassing but he said it with a giggle. It was people acting independently. Even if it had got seriously embarrassing, it would have been a bit arrogant to ask them to stop.

Dennis Oliver, the decent egg who played Captain Mainwaring to Donald Trelford's Mr Hodges, was not prepared for the glare of media attention, and put his foot in it more than once. David *was* embarrassed, primarily by the way the campaign was portrayed as being about him rather than the broader issue, and distanced himself from it as best he could without wanting to appear unappreciative.

I spoke to Oliver briefly and wrote to him, and vice-versa, but I never got around to meeting him. He was in Barbados for the Test in 1994 and I invited him for dinner on one of the yachts, but then time became a problem. If you analyse it properly, my name was at the top of the list because it is the sort of name that goes to the top of a list. The principle they tried to raise was slightly different. It was centred around me but it was an overall principle, not specifics. It was interesting to watch but it was their debate, not something for me to get worried about or get involved with. The MCC should have a debate every winter.

On 27 January 1993, the no-confidence motion was debated at the Methodist Central Hall, Westminster. The proposers were the ex-MCC president, Lord Bramall, Lord Griffiths and Hubert Doggart: a field marshal, a judge and a headmaster. The ayes had it by 715 to 412. 'It would have been clear to a neutral, fair-minded observer, if one was present,' noted Matthew Engel, 'that the proponents won the debate as well.' As expected, however, the postal vote went against Pinter and his fellow zealots, 6135 to 4600. More than 7000 votes were left uncast. 'I don't approve of these rebellions,' one peer informed Trelford when the two got chatting at the Beefsteak Club. 'But I've read what you've had to say. Thought it was better than the other side. So I'm abstaining.'

For the likes of Pinter and Rice, a rather different battle had been lost. Back in the real world, England were about to start a Test match in Calcutta and David was preparing to cover it for Sky TV. Bishen Bedi summed up the local response: 'The man who should be out in the middle batting for England is instead sitting in the press box. Personal pride should not hold England back as far as picking Gower goes. A country's cricketing pride must come before personal feelings.'

In his maiden Editor's Notes for *Wisden*, Matthew Engel railed against the perversity of it all with his customary eye for justice:

This party for India was chosen at a moment when reconciliation was being offered all round, to John Emburey for instance. Now Emburey is a fine cricketer and a nice man. But he is the only person in the whole shabby history of these enterprises who actually signed up for rebel tours to South Africa on two separate occasions. Short of standing on the square at Lord's on the Saturday of a Test match and giving a V-sign to the Long Room, it is hard to imagine how anyone can have shown greater unconcern about whether he plays for England or not. For him, forgiveness was instant.

Emburey is more than a fine cricketer. He is a credit to his profession, and an excellent bloke. He is also Graham Gooch's best friend.

Long after the dirty deed had been done, *Cover Point*, the cricket video 'magazine', invited Gower and Gooch to nominate and analyse the other's best innings. David never saw Gooch bat better than at Leeds in 1991: Gooch plays Horatio, courage and cussedness paving the way for England's first home win over the West Indies in twenty-two years. In analysing the innings, David sprayed compliments like confetti. Gooch, in turn, nominated David's glorious sign-off at The Oval in 1985, peppering some low-key flattery with a few digs about technique and sloppiness. Now that's what I call mean-spirited.

There was, of course, one blindingly obvious explanation. Now Gooch had reached the summit himself, he grudged sharing it with a man who regarded perspiration as the enemy. Jon Agnew concurs: 'Graham seems to be of the opinion that unless you work hard you don't deserve success. You know, natural talent is one thing, but unless you are seen to be giving buckets of sweat, then you don't deserve to be the greatest. Which doesn't make a lot of sense.' There were times during the Dexter-Gooch-Stewart regime when deciphering the thought processes of the Gang of Three was a job best left to Stanley Unwin's interpreter. All the same, this was an open-and-shut case for Machiavelli himself.

14   The Long Goodbye

The rules are changed
It's not the same
It's all new players in a whole new ball game . . .
I know what happens
I read the book
I believe I just got the goodbye look
'The Goodbye Look', Donald Fagen

Why on earth did David Gower bother carrying on? 'You can draw a parallel with me,' suggests Mike Gatting. 'I wasn't prepared to give up the game when things began to go sour. I wanted to try and prove a point on the field, yes, but I also wanted, in my own bloody-minded way, to prove another point: why should people be treated like this? David went about it the other way. Eventually, he took himself out of the game, in defiance of Lord's, the media, take your pick.' David had a similar point to prove. He also felt slighted. He, too, resolutely refused to accept that he had had his chips. In this instance, however, naivety did its worst.

Throughout the winter, David had felt confident that, with a bit of tinkering here and there, he could still cut the mustard. Come summer, he would only just have turned thirty-six. More crucially, he remained unsure how to fill the void. Where would the next challenge come from? There was one obvious avenue, of course: 'Because I'd sooner win the pools or the lottery than set up a company, it had to be something I had half a clue about. Playing another sport is half a clue, talking about the same sport is more than half a clue, and writing about the same sport is about a third of a clue. I decided to be pragmatic.'

Jon Holmes insists, nonetheless, that at no stage in the aftermath of his omission from the Indian tour party did his client even threaten to throw in the towel. 'He said he'd give it another go. He felt he had a bit more left in him. He also felt he was right.' Thorunn identifies another motive: 'He would have carried on if he could have played Test cricket and nothing else. He adored it.'

To bounce back from the ropes the way David set about doing certainly suggests as much.

At the start of the 1993 season I knew there needed to be one last effort. The disappointment was, having made a slowish start then got into form with 150-odd against Notts, I fell on the ball trying to take a catch at slip, cracked a rib and missed three weeks. That was the moment that mattered most of all. About a week later they were going to be picking the side for the third Test and they were going to make a change. If I'd have made a decent score the following week I would have been the perfect man for that change. Instead, I was doing bugger all, apart from cleaning the pool – which I could do, gently – and the opportunity slipped by. As the summer slipped on, and the rules changed slightly, it was too late. If I hadn't cracked that rib, if I'd gone on and made a big score in the next match, that would have been the resurrection. I'm convinced of that.

But was this not self-delusion? The goalposts did indeed shift once more: Ashes lost yet again, Atherton succeeded Gooch as captain. A new generation was moving in. Atherton, understandably, wanted to banish the past as far as he could. Conveniently enough, certain fixtures and fittings had been considerate enough to dismantle themselves. Botham had goosed his last bump; Gooch had said his touring days were over; Lamb's broadsword was sounding a bit tinny. The only members of the Famous Five in the frame for the Caribbean were Gatting and Gower. Atherton and his fellow selectors felt there was room for one wrinkly and one wrinkly only (and ultimately did without one altogether). Not the least of the new skipper's virtues was his citation of David as his boyhood idol. Fletcher and Dexter, on the other hand, regarded Gatting as the likelier to exert a beneficial influence, a contentious opinion if not entirely without merit. Furthermore, while Gatting had been mesmerized by Shane Warne and (wrongly) ditched, doubts about his vision and reactions, and hence his capacity to blunt Ambrose and Co., were less pronounced than they were in David's case.

Mark Nicholas is not in complete disagreement:

[David] was visibly determined at the start of the season, didn't need pumping up at all, but I'm not sure whether he quite had the speed of eye any more. When we played against really quick bowlers he got a bit haphazard. He'd go for it, take it on, almost as a native response to a personal attack. He never coped with Waqar. He played Ambrose well, but Walsh always used to get him out. I may be being harsh, but I think his reactions were slower. I know Gooch didn't think his eye was as quick as it was, and that he might therefore not be a particularly good bet against top-class pace.

After David's century at Melbourne in 1990–91, Gatting volunteered the opinion that he had begun to become more circumspect. In Brisbane, he had greeted his first two deliveries with a glide and a glance; at the MCG, noted Gatting, he had been considerably more restrained, as if trying to prove that he could control himself. He had subsequently proved that on more than one occasion, for Hampshire and England, notably against Waqar, Wasim and Mushtaq at Headingley in 1992. Since that final England tour, moreover, David had addressed his batting problems with unprecedented industry and rigour, netting regularly with Tim Tremlett, and consulting Tom Graveney and Bob Woolmer about his technique. But it was the mental aspect that concerned him. Provided he could get his mind in the right shape, he felt, everything else would follow. Which is why he enlisted the services of Brian Mason, a personal counsellor and motivator. This arose from a phone call made in June 1991 by the late Michael 'Barrel' May, then a member of the Hampshire general committee. May had urged him to write to David, recalls Mason, 'because he feared that otherwise David might be lost to English cricket, so disillusioned and disheartened was he at the time'. David, Mason insists, answered the ensuing missive with unexpected enthusiasm. 'Come at once,' he wrote, 'the sooner the better.'

Being a supporter of both Warwickshire and Hampshire, Mason arranged an initial discussion when the two counties met at Portsmouth. He remembers: 'David agreed to see me after the game and in the meantime I spoke to Woolmer, who had been speaking to David at great length about his technique. Woolmer said he thought that he and others could help David on that level if I could devote my attentions to getting him into the right frame of mind off the field.' David and Mason met a couple more times before the end of August, the latter concentrating his efforts on goal-setting and motivation. 'He was a demanding listener. Quite often he said he had done this sort of thing before and was there anything I could add to it. Of all the people I have worked with, I have rarely had a more difficult task than with David. Not because he was unwilling to co-operate but partly because of his reserved nature and partly because, to be honest, I was a little bit in awe of him.' Mason advocated that David bat at three, in order to satisfy his need to be constantly 'tested and stretched'. The following March, the pair met up again: 'He seemed more assured, more determined,' remembers Mason, 'more resolute.'

For all that rejection and confusion had dented confidence and ego, David was resolution personified prior to sustaining that rib injury the following July. Indeed, the century at Trent Bridge that preceded the mishap could hardly have been more pointed, coinciding as it did with the onset of hostilities in the Ashes series. Fashioned on a pitch that had the home spinners queuing up for a bite, it was an innings which reinforced his captain's belief that David was the Englishman best equipped to ward off Warne. 'Different class,' Nicholas insists. 'He made 153 and we won by 169 runs: he was literally the difference between the sides.' Not that such conviction was uncommon. The reality, as ever, was somewhat at odds with the dream. Grounded as they were in balanced cricketing logic, such fond hopes were doomed when confronted by one-eyed prejudice.

The selectors were deliberating over their personnel for the sixth Test while David was collecting a century at Old Trafford. Not unnaturally, he assumed he was in with a decent shout. Not a whisper. Half an hour before the start Thorpe gets hit on the hand by a net bowler, breaks a thumb, faints, and pulls out. Had David been playing at Lord's as opposed to Swansea, he might well have got the call instead of Mark Ramprakash. The latter's more than useful contribution to England's sole victory of a woebegone series served as superficial vindication; reality, in any case, has no respect for 'if only'. If David had scored a century at The Oval it would have changed precisely nothing. The century he subsequently registered against Sussex at Portsmouth certainly did.

Shortly before that final Test, Atherton had confided to one county captain that he and his fellow selectors were scared to pick David. Yes, scared. It was not hard to fathom the reasoning, crass as it was: to have restored David at that juncture would have made it virtually impossible to leave him out for the winter, a decision that had, to all intents and purposes, already been arrived at. Another cock-up on the PR front? Another public outcry? Another savaging from the media? These are a few of a new captain's least favourite things. Why would Atherton want his new regime tarred with the same brush as the old? Credible to a degree, but still, in essence, absolute tosh. There was only one consideration that should have occupied the minds of Atherton, Dexter and Fletcher: was David Gower one of the best six batsmen available? But then side issues of that nature had long since been struck off the agenda. An England XI picked purely on the basis of ability? An England XI selected with no heed paid to personality? Dream on.

Wearing one of his multiple other hats, Homes had a briefing session with Atherton a month or so before the end of the season.

Mike had just become captain and he asked me whether I thought David would 'do it' for him. And I said yes, yes I do. Then he asked me whether he needed to give him a target. Say, three hundreds by the end of the season. I said, 'Well, I think he's demonstrated enough, you should know that.' So he went back to David and said: 'Score three hundreds before the end of the season and you should be in there.' And David did exactly that, including one against Lancashire when he survived being 80-odd not out overnight, which was a death score for him. I think he thought, 'Well, if that's not enough, that's it.'

For someone who had spent the vast majority of his life actively not seeking advice, David certainly made up for lost time during that summer and early autumn. 'He sort of asked my feelings,' recalls Chris Cowdrey. 'His way of asking was to say, "Well, I could retire I suppose." I think as soon as they started to ease him out cricket became very hard for him. He wasn't top dog any more and he didn't know why he wasn't playing. I think the thing that really ate at him was playing county cricket for county cricket's sake.'

Among those close to David, none was more insistent than Fred Rumsey that he should quit while he was ahead:

When England failed to pick him for the Caribbean there was no point in carrying on. I went to stay with him in Braishfield and we discussed his future. It had always been one of my bugbears with him. I was always a big heavy, insisting he pave the way, take an interest in commerce, think about the future. I argued that he might get another year if he was lucky, that here was an opportunity to create a new career, and that neither the *Sunday Express* job nor the BBC job might be available in a year's time. I felt the time was right. If he had stayed on there might have been problems getting into TV, but Sky had taken off and positions created. The competition was quite hot, too. The decision to retire was not an emotional one.

Mike Turner had recently ended his association with Leicestershire, in circumstances, regrettably, that reflected little credit on either the club or the man who had done more than anyone to keep it viable. His home, however, remained at the end of the alleyway adjoining Grace Road, and he cherishes the memory of an unexpected visit from the man he had nurtured as a boy:

Right out of the blue. There was a knock on my front door and he's standing there. 'Just come in to discuss with you the question of retirement,' he said. Which, to me, summed him up. He happened to be speaking at some function in Leicester. We had a cup of tea and talked for a couple of hours, though not about retirement. I wasn't too thrilled with life either at the time. He had to make a decision, and I think he was disappointed not to have been picked for the West Indies, but that didn't seem to be uppermost in his mind. I think he'd already had the offer to cover the tour for Sky, so it just seemed a natural sequence of events. Retiring was the logical step.

Nicholas felt likewise: 'He couldn't fulfil himself any more. He wasn't besotted by the game. It was a vehicle to show his talent on a stage and make money. People couldn't have it more wrong about Botham craving attention and Gower being remarkably discreet: Beefy would like to live in peace and quiet, go fishing, play with the kids, whereas David can't live without the limelight.'

When David initially spelled out his dilemma to Nicholas, the latter offered to have a new contract drawn up avoiding the need to play on Sundays. He found such contests a 'crushing struggle', the contempt never more amply illustrated than by the day he turned up ten minutes before the start, when he was due to be opening. 'He told me he enjoyed his cricket during the week but he thought the Sunday game was an abomination,' remembers Nicholas. 'He hated the fact that you could hit a glorious cover-drive off the middle of the bat that has the crowd on its feet, and only get a single.'

In terms of Hampshire CCC, there was another factor for Nicholas to consider.

The selectors were always ringing me and asking me how he was behaving. For the first two years, I couldn't see what everyone was making such a fuss about. That first year he was marvellous in team meetings, great with the young players. He was brilliant. He's a good bloke, a very nice man, a man who has this extraordinary charm that enables him to get away with murder. One of the problems in his last year was the fact that he walked from slip to slip as if he didn't give a hoot. He didn't chase. That wasn't a problem in itself but it carries over. People started to murmur. Midway through the summer, two young players who were absolutely besotted by him, go a long way for him, came to me and asked me what was going on. They didn't feel he was pulling his weight. Right then, for the first time, I could see why Gooch made what seemed to be indefensible decisions.

Kevan James, the experienced former Middlesex all-rounder, was unconcerned:

I couldn't care less what he did when he wasn't batting. He fitted in well because he doesn't take himself too seriously, although I do think he found it difficult to cope with the fact that Hampshire are the only county I know where the players go out together at the end of a day's play. He did like to get away from it all. Mark would always ask him to say his bit in team meetings: he was a calming influence. 'Take it easy, guys,' he'd say, 'don't forget it's only a game.' And no one else could do the things he could. From the day he arrived we thought we had a matchwinner, someone who'd win us four or five games a season we wouldn't otherwise win. And he did it, by and large. The effect on the opposition was amazing. It's not so much the runs you miss as the effect he had on them. Since he's been gone, they've started to declare again.

Adrian Aymes, Hampshire's effervescent wicketkeeper, can't resist a dig at the selectors: 'We always used to joke that the best ball to bowl to him was a half-volley. He averaged 35 for Leicestershire and 40 for us. He'd improved. To blame his Hampshire form for not picking him was ridiculous.'

Much as he is fond of him, and much as he would hate such a sentiment to be misinterpreted as damning criticism, Nicholas does feel David might have 'given' a little more, to him as much as Hampshire. In terms of runs and, latterly, of setting an example, there is some justification for such a gripe. But not much. 'The very fact that a superstar signs a contract for you is giving,' counters Cowdrey. 'David gave to Hampshire. People came to see him in the big one-day games. But he irritated Mark, who didn't know if he was trying, didn't know if he had any interest in Hampshire. Malcolm Marshall felt he had to prove something there, so they say, but David didn't.'

Yet any misgivings Nicholas may have had over David's input were overshadowed by his concern for a friend. 'I felt desperately sorry for him. Over the past couple of summers he'd been talking increasingly about the psychological side, not the game or technique. I told him that if there was any danger of him undermining the way he wanted to be remembered, or playing below his capabilities, he should get out.'

'I'm quite surprised he hung on as long as he did,' admits Paul Downton.

He carried on initially because that England run record meant more to him than many realized, but he got very introverted and bitter. Since 1989, we'd had a piecemeal David Gower, not one we want to remember. I'd retired in 1991 because of my eye injury and we'd talked a lot about him following suit. The irony now is that, compared with Gooch and Gatting, he looks a million dollars. He could have gone on for another five years.

'David didn't want to make the decision quickly,' recalls Jon Holmes.

He left it and left it, let people speculate. I had to fiddle about with the offers that were coming in – BBC, who'd offered him the radio job before Agnew got it, *Sunday Express*, Sky – so eventually we decided to meet at his house. When I get there he's wearing a dhobi. I didn't say a thing. He said he was 85 per cent there, so I said that that, as far as I was concerned, was as sure as he was ever going to be. After we agreed that that was indeed the case, I asked him if he had a camera handy. 'Why?' he asked. So I told him that when, in future, I tell people he's a bit eccentric, I want to show them this. 'You're taking a mind-boggling decision,' I said, 'and you're wearing a silly rug wrapped around your head.'

For a cricketer who spent his entire career trying not to think too much, it seems only apt that David should have ended it unwittingly. The final curtain rang down on the morning of 20 September 1993: D. I. Gower b. Such 25. The wheel had spun full circle: his final first-class innings had been terminated by a spinner, the very breed who had made life so uncomfortable for him at the outset of his career. That said, he had made a century in the first innings, 134 off 194 balls, his fifty-third in first-class cricket, taking him past 1000 runs in a season for the thirteenth time. Unlucky, indeed, for some. The opposition opener trumped him, mind, belting a hundred in each innings to speed past 2000. The name was Gooch, Graham Gooch.

On 14 November, 1993 completed a hat-trick as evil as the game has ever witnessed. Finally, the procrastinator had relented. Having seen Laertes (Botham) and Fortinbras (Viv Richards) take the bull by the horns, David put the grapevine at ease by announcing that he, too, had had his fill. Writing in *Wisden Cricket Monthly*, he fired a dart at his erstwhile friend: 'That word "commitment" has been very much ringing in my ears ever since the last-but-one England captain made it a key issue in Australia on the tour of 1990–91. Although it was abominably misused in that particular situation, it is certainly relevant to this one . . .' Neither was he able to completely resist the odd quip: 'I pay little heed to comments such as Keith Fletcher's, made after my announcement, supposedly suggesting that I was still in their thoughts. There had only been six or seven weeks of speculation in which to pick up the phone and quietly broach the same topic if the thought were that important.'

Chris Cowdrey had raised that selfsame subject during the summer:

I said he should seek a meeting with Dexter, Fletcher and Atherton, that he was in a big enough position to do that. No one else was. 'Go and talk to them,' I said, 'and say you want to play for England. Ask them whether they would recommend you kept playing, or whether you should retire? Totally off the record.' The answer would have been that he was not in their plans: they couldn't say that publicly, of course. And then they bring back Gatting. Now I'm a Gatting man, but I found that unbelievable.

David never did request that meeting. His reaction, according to those who know him well, would have run roughly along the lines of, 'After all I've done, why should *I* make the move?' Cowdrey underscores the point: 'No one ever said to him, "You've got a chance of getting back." He needed someone to say that.'

In his own way, David also needed to see the subsequent odes to joy and lost innocence. 'Let us call him a genius,' proposed Simon Barnes in the *Times*. 'I don't want to confuse Gower with Leonardo da Vinci: only with Best, McEnroe and Campese.' Michael Parkinson had got his elegy in early with an interview in the *Daily Telegraph* midway through July, headlined 'The man with time to spare nears end of run': 'When I tell my grandchildren about David Gower I will say that apart from the obvious glories of his batting, what I was most grateful for was that he never gave me cause to be concerned about or ashamed of the game of cricket.' Mike Turner went directly to the heart of the matter: 'A free spirit has been frozen out and the game is the loser.' Comments of that ilk at least made up for the occasional shard of fatuousness. 'He should have applied himself more,' grumbled Alec Bedser in an impromptu aud-ition for the lead role in *Pontius: The Movie*.

What, then, of the great British public? While conducting my research for this book, I asked readers of *Wisden Cricket Monthly* to write to me with their thoughts on the following poser: David Gower – Wasted or Waster? Every respondent, without exception, arrived at the conclusion I had hoped for. Terry Power wrote from New Zealand, recalling the time, an hour or so after the end of the 1983 Headingley Test against his countrymen, when he spied David in a crowded village bar:

You wouldn't have credited that there were so many Kiwis in Yorkshire till you saw how packed it was. In the middle of this big, swirling, noisy throng was Gower, the only England player in sight. His willingness to mix, talk and stick around among the opposition was commented upon favourably by all and sundry for weeks after. He was warmly thought of here. The Queensland plane episode produced repeated reactions: (a) harmless fun, and why not; (b) rather him than Lamb, Gatting or Botham, especially Botham, who had a loud yob reputation earned during his visits; (c) fancy thinking they can succeed while not using talent like that.

Joyce Pooley from Thorpe Bay in Essex steadfastly refused to beat about the bush: 'The man I hold responsible for the waste and premature retirement of David Gower is Graham Gooch. A player like David Gower only comes along once in a lifetime and the waste of his talent reflects badly on those responsible.' Mrs Polley signed off thus: 'If you write anything I disagree with, I will write and say so, just as I told Essex County Cricket Club the reason for my resignation.'

David Frith swears that the WCM mailbag that November tipped the scales at three times its normal weight. Two letters were published. 'So David Gower has been forced into retirement,' wrote Bob Bee from Canterbury, 'by a combination of inverted snobbery, illogical thinking, and a blatant disregard of the wishes of the cricket-loving public of this country. Certainly ability, Test record, and willingness to participate did not enter into the equation! Perhaps that religious sect that predicted that the world would come to an end recently were not so far wrong after all – mine certainly has!' Eddie Hewitt from Enfield invoked the Bard:

> Gower can scarcely be likened to King Lear, but he was, similarly, more sinned against than sinning; and the wonder is not that he endured but that he endured so long. Coriolanus might seem a more suitable comparison, as a champion who was then rejected by his former employers: revenge, however, is not in Gower's make-up. Perhaps we should simply remember him as one who played the game not wisely but too well.

Braishfield, Hants, October 1994. The boys with the black stuff are busy resurfacing the tennis court at Chez Gower. For David, Thorunn and baby Alexandra (just turned one), summer is about to start all over again. The girls will spend most of the Ashes tour in Sydney while the bread-winner jets hither and thither. David says he could quite happily spend every winter Down Under.

Lurking discreetly on a sideboard is an invitation from the Winchester Conservative Association. The CD racks are symptomatic of a trim and tidy home: arranged in strict alphabetical order, they run the gamut from Amadeus to Zappa. The bookcase in the lounge reveals Best of Punch, autobiographies by Dickie Bird, Peter Shilton and Brian Clough, the odd Jeffrey Archer, and stacks of Wilbur Smiths. The appeal of the last-named is unsurprising. The son of a Rhodesian cattle farmer who told him he would starve as a writer, Smith blends consummate skill as a weaver of ripping yarns to a strong African consciousness. He supported Helen Suzman's Progressive Party, believes fervently in an Africa for Africans, and insists that only Chief Buthelezi can unite the South. Many of his major characters boast handicaps: *The River God* is narrated by a eunuch; *The Sunbird* features a pair of hunchbacks. 'I do it often to make a more memorable character,' he recently explained. 'If you put an unsurmountable object in the hero's way, it makes it a little more powerful.' As an English cricketer who overcame being born on the wrong side of the tracks, an absence of sibling comradeship, and the early loss of his parents, battled against an overdose of integrity, suffered occasional lapses into diffidence, exhibited a worrying tendency to keep his job in clear perspective, and struggled with a painfully low boredom threshold, David Gower knows all about surmounting tricky hurdles.

My attention was drawn to the OBE. Surprisingly, he demurred when asked whether this was his most cherished item of fan mail. That honour, he revealed, belongs to the inscription on a plaque awarded to him by a national newspaper: 'For Fun, Style and Excellence'. He liked 'the gist of the citation' and would be more than delighted to have the same words engraved on his headstone. I stated my preference for the framed poem by Richard Digance in the hall, just beyond Craig Campbell's evocative portrait of *The Shot That Beat Boycott*:

> I wish I'd played for England like you did
> I wish I'd been a quarter as good as you . . .
> . . . I wish for just an hour I'd been David Gower
> But I never was and never ever will.

Did he feel as if Gooch had cheated him? The initial groan is worth a thousand words, none of them complimentary.

The rift had become slightly greater. The arguments we had in 1990–91 have never been resolved. We've agreed to differ. It's not a problem when I see him. We take the piss out of each other. Mind you, I wasn't impressed when he wrote that stuff in the *Mail on Sunday* just after I retired, admitting he might've been wrong. Great, thanks Graham. I'll go to the Caribbean for you. I was angry at that. Had he kept going blindly down the same route, I could have put it down to inflexibility, stubbornness, but going back on it . . . Having said that, I could apologize for the selections I've made, a list of twenty people I've dropped. No, I don't bear a grudge. I won't let him get away with it either. I'll make the odd gag, but I don't believe in prolonging these things.

The first public confrontation was aired on David's Radio Five show the following summer: 'Graham had spent most of the winter doing dinners, Q&A evenings, and being asked why he didn't pick me, and he always went into this stock answer. So we set him up. We knew the first call would be along those lines. "Er, Graham . . ." Mischievous? Yes.

Deserved? Yes. Slightly rude? Yes. He dealt with it. "Maybe I was wrong," he said. "We all make mistakes."'

The frustration is that over the past three years or so I could have played Test cricket. Had I done that, and had it gone well, I might have played even more. It is a mystery to the public, and to me a little bit, in the sense that we don't know for sure what would have happened if I had been picked during that period. That's why it's slightly frustrating and slightly disappointing to all sorts of people. They bear a grudge on my behalf. I use it as a tool for speeches, to amuse people over dinner. The possibility remains that it could have gone wrong and we'd be no better off than we are now. Either way, I made a choice. We're moving ahead.

One step in that direction was being appointed cricket correspondent for the *Sunday Express*. As baptisms go, the summer of 1994 came somewhere between hot and incendiary. First there was the outright hostility of the man David was replacing, Pat Gibson, one of the most respected correspondents on the circuit. This was understandable, up to a point. After all, Gibson was more than a decade away from his pension, he had been doing a perfectly decent job at the paper for twenty years (*Daily* then *Sunday Express*), and now he had been elbowed aside, not by an experienced practitioner, but by a name. For all that, it was Gibson's employers who were surely the ones who deserved his ire. 'I had a chat with him at Lord's,' David recalls.

'This is not a quarrel between you and me,' I said. 'I understand perfectly that you have a sense of resentment, but I didn't fire you. I didn't appoint myself.' He said he was sorry he'd been this way, 'but here am I finished at 52' or whatever. So I said, well, I'm sorry too. If he wants to bear a grudge it's his problem. Fortunately for me, market value means something. I can't afford to feel guilty about that.

Then came Pocketgate. When the Atherton dirt-in-flannels affair erupted midway through the Saturday evening of the Lord's Test against South Africa, I knew of at least one correspondent who had long since gone west. Make that two. The story spread like wildfire: 'Psst. Gower switched off his mobile and refused to cover the story. Didn't want to dirty his hands.' The truth, however, was rather less dramatic:

I'd written my piece, including a reference to what Atherton had been doing. We'd seen it on TV. Switching off my mobile wasn't a Machiavellian move. I'd asked the desk whether everything was fine. 'Right,' I said, 'I'm off.' I knew Ian Cole was covering the press conference.

The truth is, yes, I should have left that mobile phone on for Laurie Hacker to ask me for a comment piece for the final edition. It would have buggered up a perfectly good Saturday night. I would have left a Thai restaurant at ten o'clock with a mission to hack out three or four hundred words quickly. In a way, I'm much happier I didn't. Having the benefit of a week to watch and learn was invaluable. I could have written the wrong thing in a hurry. It's wrong to say I switched the phone off deliberately.

Like Richie Benaud, David is not a natural reporter. Reporting requires speedy conception and even swifter execution, which can work against quality and inventiveness, particularly in a tabloid. He is much better suited to the spoken word. His voice adds resonance to his observations; without it, a dimension is lost. That does not mean he cannot do a highly serviceable job as a journalist. A broadsheet Sunday might provide more stimulation, but one suspects that writing will always remain a second string, as it does with Benaud.

Besides, moving ahead really means ascending the ladder marked Great TV Sports Commentators. This particular Magnificent Seven reel off the tongue with ease: Harry Carpenter, Richie Benaud, Dan Maskell, Bill McLaren, Peter O'Sullevan, Henry Longhurst and Cliff Morgan (John Arlott is disqualified on the grounds that he was best appreciated when his brush had to range across an entire canvas rather than being confined to sky and horizon). If you were looking for a Top Ten, you might want to draft in James Hunt and David Coleman. And perhaps David Gower. He is already Benaud's heir apparent. In five years' time he will have the grey hair and the necessary gravitas. In ten years' time, if he is still getting enough of a buzz, he will probably be the Sheik of the Mike. You only to have seen that Jameson ad campaign – 'The old smoothie (and . . .)' – to know that Rory Bremner will be living off him for a good many moons to come.

The reason I say all this with such conviction is quite simple. Admission to the exclusive Great TV Sports Commentators Club requires five qualities: a distinctive voice, knowledge, appreciation, the ability to add something to the pictures without resorting to puerile trivia or rampant ego, and, above all, fairness. David is long on all:

I try and be honest, to look for the best, which is perfectly natural for me because I've heard a lot of crap over the years. And suffered a little myself, as others have, by being harshly treated for minor matters. So it's also natural for me to work out why things have gone wrong. It's very easy to say, 'He's out', 'That's a bad shot'. But it's harder to analyse why, what leads to that shot. I'd sooner take Benaud as a role model. He'll make a top-spinner out of something that hasn't turned. But I'd sooner follow that than try and find fault. I understand fallibility only too well.

That niceness was tested to the full during the Brisbane Test in November 1994. With English backs to the wall, Gooch was dismissed aiming a wild smear against Warne in the second innings. David was on-air at the time:

> In a way it was quite funny. We'd had this running saga. Whenever an interview with Gooch was needed, it was always 'Send Lubo'. Did I want to interview him? Like hell I did. In Brisbane it was like a penny dropping. Should I or shouldn't I? I was aware that if you rip in for the sake of it it's pretty transparent. 'That was a wipe,' I said. 'Dreadful.' Fair comment. It was nice to be there at the right time.

More characteristic was the following interchange between Bob Willis (BW) and David (DG) during the evening session of the third day's play in Sydney. Graeme Hick, on 8, has just spooned a shot to second slip as if giving catching practice to a group of five-year-olds. Mark Waugh drops the chance:

> *BW*: Awful shot by Hick. Virtually off the face of the bat to second slip. Waugh, the best slip in the world, has dropped two catches in the match. Should've had it.

> *DG*: I don't know if Waugh didn't have trouble picking the ball out against the stands. When you see a slip move backwards it means he hasn't seen it properly.

> *BW*: It didn't go that quickly.

> *DG*: All pace is relative.

> *BW*: But David, what was Hick trying to do. He couldn't guide the ball over slips from there. Extraordinary effort.

> *DG*: It wasn't a good shot. Got too close. Best off leaving balls like that. He has to forget it. He's had his life. He and Mike Atherton have to keep ploughing on. (Hick strokes Fleming through the covers) . . . Oh, that's a fine shot.

> (*NB*. Hick went on to make 98 not out before his captain decided to declare and make a point.)

Montcalm Hotel, Marble Arch: March 1995. Perched on a wall in the far corner of David's suite is a portrait of the man himself. You can tell he's quite proud of this, even though he does his sheepish best to shrug it off. No, in answer to the first question, he didn't miss it at all. He'd played in three benefit games Down Under – for Bradman, Dean Jones and Rupertswood.

A lot of people said, 'Why did you give up?' Thank you, I'd say, very kind of you. But I just couldn't contemplate a comeback. Every now and then the heart sees a flat pitch, like the one at the MCG for Deano's tribute match. It was a day-nighter and I quite enjoy batting under lights because I'd rarely done that before, and I made 70-odd. I *refused* to give it away. Lillee was still trying, so it was fun to smack the ball and play well against him. You start to get conned by that. You think to yourself, 'right, perhaps a few nets and a few runs and I could get back into this'. But you must let the head rule.

No twinges at all? Not even when Gooch broke your caps record in Perth?

I suppose there were a few there. It was quite funny in the commentary box when it was being discussed. And, of course, I was on-air at the start, so I had to announce the teams: 'Graham Gooch, playing in his 119th Test . . .' I played up to the audience. To have finished level would have been nice. When people ask me about a comeback, I say, 'Well, if you can guarantee me one Test match. Just one . . .'

At the turn of 1995, Brian Mason had still been adamant that his former client could, and should, return to the England XI, and duly distributed an article detailing all his reasons, to *every* national newspaper. 'I start this campaign,' he wrote, 'because above all else, he has a God-given natural talent which was cut short, through no will or fault of his own, very prematurely . . . this awful waste of what is, after all, a Divine natural gift . . . a crying shame and a blow to natural justice . . .' Mason gave Ray Illingworth much the same spiel. While appreciative of such evident concern and eloquent advocacy, David had begun to react in a similar fashion to the way he had responded, latterly, to the MCC rebels. All the more so when Mason pitched up in Perth: 'That annoyed the shit out of me. He'd gone off his trolley. He even wrote to Thorunn. I must admit, I lost it a bit. I told him it was nothing more than romance. "No," he said, "I've spoken to Illy. There's a place for you if you score some runs." So I said: "How can I put it? I don't *want* to make a comeback."' What could he do? His hands, after all, had not so much been tied as cut off.

At Chez Gower five months earlier, father and daughter had appeared to be hitting it off a treat. Had impending parenthood, and its responsibilities, been a factor in that decision to slope off into the sunset? 'Not really. You can't separate it, it's all part of the same story, but the truth is, regardless of whether I was playing Test cricket or not, I was becoming less enchanted with playing every day, and if you don't play every day, you don't get a chance to do anything more.'

This sounded suspiciously like a plea for the return of the amateur. And why not?

Because in English cricket, you don't have a choice to be picky. Try and it rebounds on you. If you had nothing else to do, no other avenues to explore, no alternatives, then you carry on being a professional. But having played so much international cricket, the thought of only playing county cricket wasn't enough because you need something to drive you. You need to drive yourself to produce the high points, or make up for the low ones. Without that extra incentive, whatever it might be, and in my case it was the thought that I could be back on that stage, you lose some of your motivating force. And if you lose some of that you lose your performance. It's just a spiral after that.

Thorunn firmly believes that fatherhood has changed the man: 'Being parents has made both of us less selfish. He has become a family man. He does put his family before himself. He's asked Holmes to turn offers down.'

Had she detected any other changes since hubbie hung up his bat?

He's put on some weight, mainly on the trunk, maybe half an inch round the waist. He isn't quite as fit as he once was, but there is a Nordic ski machine upstairs. A couple of weeks ago he was feeling guilty about not using it, so for the past fortnight he's been on it every day. He *is* a lot more relaxed. He's still getting the buzz you get from a new career you enjoy and although he does get bored easily there's enough variation in his work at present to keep him on his toes. His idea of getting away from it all is sitting on his tractor mower and doing the lawn. I wasn't happy about the Cresta Runs but he still loves them. He *needs* to be able to let off steam, to go off and do something silly. He spends far too long in his study – doing articles for the paper, writing pieces for benefit brochures, replying to letters. He's *always* replying to letters. What he'd really like to be is a game warden. He's very much into saving elephants and rhinos. He is involved with SAVE and he's a trustee of the David Shepherd Conservation Foundation. He's even led sixty-eight people on safari. He doesn't miss playing at all. I thought he would, but he has absolutely no desire.

Is he satisfied with what he produced as a cricketer?

I'm quite relaxed with what I've accomplished but aware that if I did want to look at it properly, then it could have been better. How can I put it? I suppose I'm aware of times when I wasn't as determined as I was, say, at Perth in 1986. But I found it hard to maintain that sort of peak, that sort of attitude, because that's not me. What I have done is come to terms with the fact that you can't change your innate nature. You can work on it but you can't change it. There are times when you forget to apply everything to the game. Compare me to Graham. Graham's got to the stage where he can overcome that sort of failing.

But what about the joy that numbers condense, the way he did the things he did, the very qualities that lifted him above the merely competent and into a class of, if not one, then certainly very few? Does being the embodiment of an ideal not compensate for an imposed sense of underachievement?

Yes, it does. That's actually quite important to me. I find it quite flattering. You feel as though there's something extra you've achieved because it's so easy to hide behind figures. But I'm very happy to take it on to a different level. If for some extraordinary reason it has made a difference to the quality of life in terms of going to Lord's and watching a game, then fine. And in a way that's the way I prefer it.

In the case of David Gower, cricketer, means always were more important than ends.

15　Grace and Flavour

Eddie: Who's better, Sinatra or Mathis?
Boogie: Presley.
Scene from *Diner*

'We'd had a cracking game of tennis and too many beers,' recollects Tim Ayling, a Leicester squash coach and David's racket partner for a decade or more.

> When we got back to David's house in Stoneygate we were slurring our words, swaying all over the place. Vicki was in a rage. She'd just got back from visiting her parents and it was the first time they'd seen each other in a few days. 'I thought I told you to feed the cat,' she was shouting. 'Call that feeding the cat?' He'd fed the cat all right, but he'd never picked up the dirty saucers.

To some, that story is David Gower all over: a ratepayer on Cloud Nine. Yet there are too many contradictions in our subject's life to permit any definitive conclusions. Stubborn yet open-minded; loyal yet periodically unfaithful; an erratic, wilful talent who played like a zillionaire yet compiled one of the most even of all Test CVs; an apparent stranger to nerves whose most memorable performances came with back to wall or belly aflame; a supreme practitioner of the competitive arts who neither gloated nor whinged; a country boy with Africa in his blood and the city in his head; a lover of the limelight who holidayed in St Moritz and Verbier, worlds where no one knew him from Adam. No friend claims to truly know the man behind the front, yet in so many ways he has been an open book. Did the Thatcher Era throw up a more honest, modest, genuine hero? Has cricket ever thrown up a more complex, more elusive, more infuriating one?

'Cricket can only flourish if it is played by civilized people with the highest standards of sportsmanship and good humour.' When he espoused that theory shortly on the eve of the 1995 season, it was hard not to believe that Prince Philip had David foremost in mind. He might have added self-effacement. Orson Welles once listed his own manifold achievements to an audience, then leaned forward and declaimed: 'Isn't it a pity there are so many of you and so few of me?' It is hard to imagine anyone less likely than David to make a claim of such heightened arrogance, amply justified as he would be in doing so. The key word is civilized.

But is this unassuming manner simply another brick in the facade? Mark Nicholas recounts a couple of examples that refute such an inference:

> While David was having a bad time of things in 1992 and 1993, a lot of people rang me up and spoke to me about him on his behalf, such as Gary Lineker and Colin Cowdrey. 'He's a bit low,' they would say, 'what can we do?' I've never met a man who had more people caring about him. And he never knew. Absolute lack of ego. Very disarming and, consequently, it misleads people. Before the start of the 1993 season, we had a practice match at Southampton, capped versus uncapped, Shaggers versus Non-Shaggers or whatever. It was a cold April day, he played crap and his team got peed off. At one point, the ball went for four while he was at long-on, back to the middle, chatting to a mate. The next morning, Tim Tremlett and I took him aside for a few words. We had to tell him about the esteem guys like Shaun Udal held him in. He was everything they aspired to be.

Having been at her husband's side for the most turbulent five years of his life, Thorunn feels qualified to shed some light on the impact of the loss of his parents. 'I'm sure it had an effect. There is a tendency to get self-centred when you have no parents or brothers and sisters. I know there's a great sorrow there that his father never saw his success. There is no immediate family but he gets encouragement from mine. Initially he found that hard to handle because he wasn't used to it.'

Should we wonder at his clutching his cards so close to his chest? In circumstances such as these, it is often more instructive to cast beyond the conventional parameters and canvass the views of an outsider. Granted, Rory Bremner is far from wholly unbiased. In 'the nutty years', as he puts it, he served as David's court jester, 'to help him unwind'. David has always enjoyed the company of high-flyers in other spheres. Indeed, he was more inclined to while away his leisure time with the likes of Bremner or Tim Rice, Dennis Waterman or Robin Askwith, than with members of his own profession (proof both of that lust for escape and the cerebral gap between him and his peers). 'There is a recognition among actors and comedians,' says Bremner,

> that we have something in common with sportsmen because we all work under such pressure, but being a sportsman is much more

difficult. The trouble with cricket is that the margin for error is so small. True, doing stand-up in front of a live audience can be nerve-racking: I don't *know* whether they're going to laugh. But at least I can stand there and say what I want. David once described how, when he was facing a delivery, *three* shots went through his mind. He had time to consider two shots and play a third! Most of us have a problem thinking of one. Sometimes, when I'm frazzled, I think about his qualities, most of all his grace under pressure, the way he kept his dignity. It was because he realized he was on the side of the angels.

Bremner recalls how his wife, Suzy, once penetrated that thick outer layer:

The pair of them went out for a drink and he was in a spiky mood, a bit grumpy. 'Well,' said Suzy, 'if you're going to be all snarly and bity, let's forget it.' All of a sudden this extraordinary change came over him. He opened a bottle of champagne and said: 'I wish more people would talk to me like that.' He had a problem with the hero-worship. He once said that if he got out to a bad shot, he wanted to come back to the dressing room and hear someone say, 'That's a stupid shot, you're a complete idiot, go and have a shower.' He found it hard to handle the silence, the reverence.

David, of course, has long been a staple of Bremner's act. As the latter makes these observations, in fact, he cannot help but lapse into mimicry.

He has a very interesting pattern of speech. He also enjoys language, which is very much to his credit. Stephen Fry and I used to joke about the way he describes things. One time when we were in the Caribbean we decided to describe the weather in Gower-ese: 'Well, I think the chance of rain is fairly remote, the sky is not exactly green, obviously one would say this is not too unpleasant a spot, and there's a fair chance that something cold and bubbly might appear at some stage before the sun disappears over the yardarm.' The way he speaks reflects a number of his qualities: understatement, wry humour, modesty. He has that nervous laugh. My first impression of him was that smile, that crooked, hangdog grin, the one Champneys used for that advert. There is a shyness there. He is also a man without attitude, which is both rare and refreshing in a sportsman these days. Sport is very sentimental. When David wasn't playing for England during the nutty years, we felt deprived of a toy. We felt angry. When he retired, we paid tribute at the end of the show. We edited some clips and put the Blue Danube on the soundtrack: no commentary needed. All we were trying to say was, 'Here's a great player who retired two years too soon, here's some classical music, now just watch.' It's the tingle factor.

Wisden, sadly, has no room for the tingle factor. Instead, the one immutable law of cricketing achievement, the one that dictates that a man's place in posterity be determined by numbers in a scorebook, stipulates David to have been an underachiever. Given the risks he took to charm us, to brighten our summers and winters, it is hard to see what *more* he could have achieved. As usual, Oscar Wilde was spot-on: 'The greatest men fail, or seem to have failed.'

Not least in Wilde's homeland. Too many of those in a position to pass judgement wear their envy and inadequacy on their sleeves. The gallery, of course, can be equally unforgiving. 'The love from fans is the cruellest love,' argued film director Terence Davies, 'for it denies the star any human imperfection and will not allow the idolized to fade or age.' David got lucky. His fans accepted him for what he was, accepted the imperfections. Pity others could not.

But did he warrant such affection because he was a great cricketer, a good egg or a symbol? Let's kick off with some semantics. Terence Hawkes, Professor of English at the University of Wales, avers, quite rightly, that greatness is a man-made invention. He even refuses to use the G-word to describe Shakespeare, as flagrant a breach of the laws of academia as it is possible to imagine. 'Suppose Shakespeare had died at birth,' he has hypothesized.

> Would we be going around with a great hole in our culture? I don't think so . . . I don't want to say these texts are great because I want to allow historicism its full play. I believe in change of societies, and the idea that certain texts are the products of genius freezes change, because it appeals to a notion of transcendent values. I don't believe in that. Who knows, another writer might come along who changes our idea of greatness.

The word 'great' has been so abused its meaning has been diluted beyond recall. We hail 'great' shots and 'great' songs as if our critical faculties have gone into permanent hibernation. The boy done great. Colgate tastes great. Persil washes great. Vinnie Jones is a great competitor. Ronald Reagan is the great communicator. Creating pecking orders, moreover, serves little purpose other than to satisfy man's urge to hunt and collect, to pigeonhole and pontificate. Besides, debating the respective merits of sporting stars from different eras is something of a redundant exercise. It *is* fun to speculate whether Laver would have beaten McEnroe, or Matthews out-dribbled Giggs, or Louis outpointed Ali, but where is the common ground for meaningful comparison? Environments change, rules change, technology changes. Prizes rise; motives alter. Sport has never been better rewarded than it is now, and surely no more ruthless.

But what the hell, let's go for it. David Frith, editor of *Wisden Cricket Monthly* since its inception in 1979 and England's pre-eminent cricket historian, is keen to distinguish between 'Great' and 'great'. 'Had he been Australian, his reputation and status would have been godlike,' Frith emphasizes.

They tolerate a certain amount of failure there. But people won't forgive him for cheating them as spectators. We were angry with him if he didn't bat for an hour or two. To me he is Great with a capital G for aesthetic appeal, and a small g in terms of the practical, the effectiveness. Has anyone been worthy of capital Gs for both? Bradman, of course, was a capital G in terms of effectiveness but nobody remembers his style. Hammond would come close, and, over the last twenty years, maybe Greg Chappell.

What, then, of the opposition? Dennis Lillee, universally acclaimed as the most accomplished of fast bowlers, and seldom one for hair-splitting, is in no doubt that David qualifies for a neighbouring pew on Mount Olympus. 'David's greatness lay in time – he had so much of it – and consistency. His consistency was remarkable for a bloke who was always willing to attack, to whom defence was the last option. His innings were a work of art, a painting. I doubt he would ever have been dropped in Australia.' Desmond Haynes is convinced that the West Indies would never even have considered such masochism. 'One of the greatest-ever England players and a wonderful person too, which is important,' enthuses Andy Roberts. 'I always felt it was disgraceful how he was treated by Gooch and Co.' In 1987, Malcolm Marshall, the most complete and prolific of all Caribbean quicks, attested that David 'holds the key to the England performance and his is always the crucial wicket'. 'Only mediocrity is consistent,' opined the orchestrator of Tottenham's League and FA Cup 'Double', Danny Blanchflower. As the figures in the appendix to this book illustrate, and the tingle factor proves, David came closer than most to giving this the lie.

I embarked on this book with one aim uppermost in mind: to demonstrate that David Gower was, and remains, a man out of time. It isn't that simple, unfortunately. That uncontrollable need for Englishmen in authority to trim sails is hardly unique to the last third of the twentieth century. 'Our selection committees have always been notorious for having a stupid, in-built need to drop good players,' stresses Fred Rumsey.

Look at Trueman. He didn't endear himself either, did he? Just before I won my first cap at Old Trafford in 1964, Cowdrey had been dropped, Graveney and Statham weren't even in the picture, and I came in for Trueman, who in turn took my place for the final Test, and got his 300th wicket. Other countries play their best players until they drop. We dropped David after he'd scored three centuries in his last nine Tests!

Look at David Boon. Could a specialist batsman averaging 17.71 in his maiden series win 100 caps for England? And what of the way the West Indies have persisted with the mercurial genius of Carl Hooper? Having a winning side helps, naturally, but then the reason 'we' don't have a winning side is because 'our' pride in 'our' country is being sapped on an hourly basis by every man or woman who sleeps rough, every titbit of political sleaze, every pay dispute in health and education, and every line closure on a provincial railway. Perverse as it may seem, David Gower, the quintessential Englishman, the Old Smoothie, is probably less a man out of time than a man out of country.

And yet, and yet. My editor, a man who knows far more about cricket than I do about publishing, wanted to use the word 'enigma' in the title of this book. I resisted. With David Gower, what you see is what you get: a singular man of singular talent. Whether the venue is Braishfield or Brisbane, the song remains much the same as it was in Dar es Salam and Loughborough, Canterbury and Stoneygate: honest, decent and truthful. How many other legends can claim such a hat-trick?

Englishmen retain a deep affection for David Gower. So do Australians and Bajans, Africans and Indians too. While his mate was at the crease, Tim Rice invariably refused to watch: he thought it might jinx him. Rory Bremner was similarly superstitious: 'I used to think, if I turn on Ceefax now, he'll get out.' Few men can have commanded such public protectiveness. It exists partly because he was a Great (note capital G) cricketer, partly because he is a good egg, but mostly because he symbolizes virtues and values that are in danger of extinction. And the flaws that beset us all.

So, charge your glasses (with something vaguely cold and bubbly, of course) and raise a toast to David Ivon Gower. To grace and flavour.

David Gower – A Statistical Appreciation

by Paul E. Dyson

For a cricketer of David Gower's style and flair to be subjected to an analysis consisting purely of rows and columns of figures would be totally contrary to the way in which he should be remembered. Nevertheless, a selective statistical analysis of his career is appropriate, a) to refute a number of false claims; b) to form a meaningful basis for comparison; and c) to fill some important gaps. Two major topics are addressed: consistency and the ability to rise to the challenge. All figures are correct to April 30, 1995.

Batsmen with 8000 Test Runs

	Tests	Inns	NO	Runs	HS	Av	100	50
A. R. Border	156	265	44	11174	205	50.56	27	63
S. M. Gavaskar	125	214	16	10122	236*	51.12	34	45
G. A. Gooch	118	215	6	8900	333	42.58	20	46
Javed Miandad	124	189	21	8832	280*	52.57	23	43
I. V. A. Richards	121	182	12	8540	291	50.23	24	45
D. I. Gower	117	204	18	8231	215	44.25	18	39
G. Boycott	108	193	23	8114	246*	47.72	22	42
G. St A. Sobers	93	160	21	8032	365*	57.78	26	30

Highest Scores in Tests for England on Most Occasions

i) top innings score				ii) top match aggregate			
	Inns	Top score	%		Tests	Top aggregate	%
Hobbs	102	31	30.39	Hobbs	61	22	36.06
Sutcliffe	84	25	29.76	Hutton	79	28	35.44
Barrington	131	38	29.00	Barrington	82	23	28.05
Hutton	138	40	28.99	Gower	117	32	27.35
Hammond	140	40	28.58	May	66	18	27.27
P. B. H. May	106	28	26.42	Boycott	108	27	25.00
Boycott	193	46	23.83	Hammond	85	20	23.53
Gooch	215	51	23.72	Gooch	118	27	22.88
D. C. S Compton	131	30	22.90	Cowdrey	114	24	21.05
Gower	204	46	22.54	Compton	78	17	21.79
Cowdrey	188	37	19.68	J. H. Edrich	77	16	20.78
I. T. Botham	161	27	16.77	Lamb	79	15	18.98

Comparing Performances Between Tests Played at Home and Abroad

	Home		Away		Difference
	Runs	Avge	Runs	Avge	in average
Richards	3136	49.78	5404	50.50	0.72
Boycott	4356	48.40	3758	46.97	1.43
Gavaskar	5067	50.16	5055	52.11	1.95
Gower	4454	42.82	3777	46.06	3.24
Gooch	5917	46.23	2983	36.83	9.40
Border	5743	45.94	5431	56.57	10.63
Miandad	4481	61.38	4351	45.80	15.58
Sobers	4075	66.80	3957	50.73	16.07

Comparing Performances Between the First and Second Innings of Test Matches

	First Innings		Second Innings		Difference
	Runs	Avge	Runs	Avge	in average
Gooch	5002	42.39	3898	42.84	0.45
Gavaskar	6159	50.90	3963	51.47	0.57
Richards	6045	50.80	2495	48.92	1.88
Sobers	5109	59.41	2923	55.15	4.26
Boycott	4795	45.67	3319	51.06	5.39
Gower	5317	46.64	2914	40.47	6.17
Border	6803	48.25	4371	54.64	6.39
Miandad	6504	56.56	2328	43.92	12.64

A total of 18 batsmen have scored 18 or more Test centuries and Gower's proportion of his centuries which are scores of 150 or more places him fourth on this all-time list.

Highest percentage of centuries being scores of 150+

	100s	150s	%
D. G. Bradman	29	18	62.1
Hutton	19	9	47.4
Hammond	22	10	45.5
Gower	18	8	44.4
Miandad	23	10	43.5
R. N. Harvey	21	9	42.9
Sobers	26	11	42.3
Gooch	20	8	40.0

Comparing the Cumulative Test Career Records of the 'Three G's'

Year	Gatting			Gooch			Gower		
	Tests	Runs	Avge	Tests	Runs	Avge	Tests	Runs	Avge
1978	2	11	3.66	7	301	33.44	6	438	55.12
1979	2	11	3.66	17	754	30.16	16	1174	52.13
1980	7	246	22.36	26	1401	33.35	22	1416	44.25
1981	14	618	24.72	35	2000	33.33	31	2042	41.67
1982	22	797	22.77	42	2540	35.77	44	2897	42.60
1983	24	918	23.54	42	2540	35.77	53	3742	44.02
1984	30	1144	23.83	42	2540	35.77	65	4486	43.55
1985	41	2246	37.43	48	3027	37.83	76	5385	45.63
1986	48	2725	38.38	59	3746	37.08	86	6149	44.88
1987	58	3563	40.95	59	3746	37.08	96	6789	44.66
1988	67	3848	38.10	68	4541	38.15	100	7000	44.02
1989	68	3870	37.57	73	4724	36.90	106	7383	43.42
1990	68	3870	37.57	81	5910	41.61	109	7674	44.10
1991	68	3870	37.57	91	7028	43.92	114	8081	44.15
1992	68	3870	37.57	99	7573	43.77	117	8231	44.25
1993	74	4227	36.75	107	8293	43.87	117	8231	44.25
1994	74	4227	36.75	113	8655	43.49	117	8231	44.25
1995	79	4409	35.56	118	8900	42.58	117	8231	44.25

Both Gatting (1990–92) and Gooch (1982–84) were banned for touring South Africa with unofficial teams.

Bibliography

Bateman, Colin, *If the Cap Fits* (Tony Williams Publications, 1993)

Botham, Ian, with Peter Hayter and Chris Dighton, *My Autobiography (Don't Tell Kath . . .)* (HarperCollins, 1994)

Boycott, Geoffrey, *Boycott: The Autobiography* (Macmillan, 1987)

Boycott, Geoffrey, with Terry Brindle, *Put to the Test* (Arthur Barker Ltd, 1979)   *Opening Up* (Arthur Barker Ltd, 1985)

Brain, Brian, *Another Day, Another Match* (George Allen & Unwin, 1981)

Brearley, Mike, *The Art of Captaincy* (Coronet, 1987)

Brearley, Mike, and Dudley Doust, *The Ashes Retained* (Hodder & Stoughton, 1979)

Edmonds, Frances, *Another Bloody Tour* (Kingswood, 1986)   *Cricket XXXX Cricket* (Kingswood, 1987)

Engel, Matthew, *Ashes '85* (Pelham, 1985)

Frindall, Bill, *England Test Cricketers* (Collins Willow, 1989)

Gatting, Mike, *Triumph in Australia* (Queen Anne Press, 1987)

Gatting, Mike, with Angela Patmore, *Leading from the Front* (Queen Anne Press, 1988)

Gooch, Graham, *Testing Times* (Robson Books, 1991)

Gooch, Graham, with Alan Lee, *Out of the Wilderness* (Willow, 1985)

Gooch, Graham, with Patrick Murphy, *Captaincy* (Stanley Paul, 1992)

Goodyear, David W., and Robert Brooke, *The Genius of Gower* (B & G Publishing, 1993)

Gower, David, with Derek Hodgson, *A Right Ambition* (Collins 1986)

Gower, David, with Martin Johnson, *Gower: The Autobiography* (Fontana, 1993)

Gower, David, with Alan Lee, *With Time to Spare* (Ward Lock, 1980)   *On the Rack: A Testing Year* (Stanley Paul, 1990)

Hick, Graeme, and Graham Dilley with Patrick Murphy, *Hick 'n' Dilley Circus* (Macmillan, 1990)

Hopps, David, and Peter Ball, *The Book of Cricketing Quotations* (Stanley Paul, 1986)

Illingworth, Ray, with Don Mosey, *Yorkshire and Back* (Queen Anne Press, 1980)

Kapil Dev, *The Autobiography of Kapil Dev* (Sidgwick & Jackson, 1987)

Lawson, Geoff, with Mark Ray, *Diary of the Ashes* (Angus & Robertson, Sydney, 1990)

Marks, Vic, *Marks Out of XI* (George Allen & Unwin, 1985)

Marlar, Robin, *Decision Against England* (Methuen, 1983)

Marshall, Malcolm, with Pat Symes, *Marshall Arts* (Queen Anne Press, 1987)

Martin-Jenkins, Christopher, *Cricket Contest* (Queen Anne Press, 1980)

May, Peter, with Michael Melford, *A Game Enjoyed* (Stanley Paul, 1985)

Meredith, Anthony, *Summers in Winter* (Kingswood, 1990)

Ray, Mark, and Alan Lee, *The Ashes: England in Australia 1990–91* (William Heinemann, 1991)

Roebuck, Peter, *Ashes to Ashes* (Kingswood, 1987)

Scott, Neville, and Nick Cook, *England Test Cricket: the Years of Indecision* (Kingswood, 1992)

Taylor, Bob, and David Gower with Patrick Murphy, *Anyone For Cricket?* (Pelham, 1979)

Tennant, *Graham Gooch* (Witherby, 1992)

Willis, Bob, with Alan Lee, *The Captain's Diary* (Willow, 1983)

Wisden Book of Test Cricket Volume I, ed. Bill Frindall (Macdonald and Jane's, 1978)

Wisden Book of Test Cricket Volume II, ed. Bill Frindall (Queen Anne Press, 1990)

Wisden Cricketers' Almanack

Index of Names

286

288